Applied Mass Communication Theory

Now in its third edition, this dynamic textbook blends coverage of the major theories and research methods in mass communication to enable students to apply their knowledge in today's media and communication careers.

Maintaining a focus on modern professional application throughout, this text provides chronological coverage of the development and use of major theories, an overview of both quantitative and qualitative research methods, and a step-by-step guide to conducting a research project informed by this knowledge. It helps students bridge their academic coursework with professional contexts including public relations, advertising, and digital media contexts. It provides breakout boxes with definitions of key terms and theories, extended applied examples, and graphical models of key theories to offer a visualization of how the various concepts in the theory fit together.

Applied Mass Communication Theory's hybrid and flexible nature make it a useful textbook for both introductory and capstone courses on mass communication and media theory and research methods, as well as courses focused on media industries and professional skills. Instructors can access an online instructor's manual, including sample exercises, test questions, and a syllabus, at www.routledge.com/9780367630362

Jack Rosenberry is a Professor Emeritus of the Department of Media and Communication at St. John Fisher College in Rochester, New York, U.S.A. In addition to co-authoring this text, he is the co-editor of *Public Journalism 2.0: The Promise and Reality of a Citizen Engaged Press* (2010) and author of *Community Media and Identity in Ireland* (2018). His research agenda has focused extensively on community journalism, and he has directed several projects for the Kettering Foundation about the relationships of journalism education and practice with citizenship, communities and democracy in the digital age.

Lauren A. Vicker is Communications Professor Emeritus at St. John Fisher College in Rochester, New York, U.S.A. She is past chair of the Communication/Journalism Department, where she taught courses in public speaking, interviewing, group dynamics, mass communication theory and research, career seminar, and communication skills for health care professionals. She has also served as director of the internship program and hosted the department's podcast for four years. In addition to Applied Mass Communication Theory, she has published in the areas of interviewing and diversity hiring, group dynamics and team projects, communication skills in colleges of pharmacy, and business communication. Vicker is an active member of the Team-Based Learning Collaborative and offers professional development seminars on teamwork skills.

Applied Mass Communication Theory

A Guide for Media Practitioners

Third Edition

**Jack Rosenberry and
Lauren A. Vicker**

Routledge
Taylor & Francis Group

NEW YORK AND LONDON

Third edition published 2022
by Routledge
605 Third Avenue, New York, NY 10158

and by Routledge
2 Park Square, Milton Park, Abingdon, Oxon, OX14 4RN

Routledge is an imprint of the Taylor & Francis Group, an informa business

First edition published by Pearson 2009
Second edition published by Routledge 2017

Library of Congress Cataloging-in-Publication Data
Names: Rosenberry, Jack, author. | Vicker, Lauren A., 1953- author.
Title: Applied mass communication theory : a guide for media
practitioners / Jack Rosenberry and Lauren A. Vicker.
Description: Third Edition. | New York : Routledge, 2022. |
Revised edition of the authors' Applied mass communication theory, 2017. |
Includes bibliographical references and index.
Identifiers: LCCN 2021015909 (print) | LCCN 2021015910 (ebook) |
ISBN 9780367639914 (hardback) | ISBN 9780367630362 (paperback) |
ISBN 9781003121695 (ebook)
Subjects: LCSH: Mass media–Research. | Mass media–Philosophy.
Classification: LCC P91.3 .R67 2022 (print) | LCC P91.3 (ebook) |
DDC 302.23072/1–dc23
LC record available at https://lccn.loc.gov/2021015909
LC ebook record available at https://lccn.loc.gov/2021015910

ISBN: 978-0-367-63991-4 (hbk)
ISBN: 978-0-367-63036-2 (pbk)
ISBN: 978-1-003-12169-5 (ebk)

DOI: 10.4324/9781003121695

Typeset in Sabon
by MPS Limited, Dehradun

Access the Support Material: www.routledge.com/9780367630362

To my children, Sara Rosenberry, Sean Rosenberry and Erin Schwarm, who over the lifetime of this book's three editions have gone from mere youngsters to wonderful young adults putting their own theories of life into practice.

- Jack Rosenberry

To Matt, Melissa, Chrissie, and Guilherme, and their special gifts of Lizzy, Juliet, Kaio, and Enzo

- Lauren Vicker

Brief Contents

Contents

Introduction to the Third Edition

THE VALUE OF MASS COMMUNICATION THEORY

The reaction that many communications students have when they learn that a course is going to emphasize theory is something like the reaction toddlers have when faced with a serving of broccoli: "Ew-w-w-w! Do I have to eat this (learn this)? Can't I just have ice cream instead!?"

In this analogy, the ice cream is the skills material that most communication students enjoy spending their time with because they find the coursework interesting and even fun, such as learning how to craft a social media plan, design an advertisement, organize an event, edit a video, or write a news story. It is easy for students to see the relevance and practical value of such courses, and how they connect to "the real world." Those connections, and that relevance, are not as obvious for theory-based courses. That doesn't mean, however, that theory isn't relevant to the work of media practitioners.

A lot has changed since the previous edition of this text, published in 2016, and even more since the first edition, which dates to 2006. Newspapers have been transformed from print to online publications, streaming audio and video have supplanted broadcast content for many people, social media has assumed more prominence in all aspects of our lives, and students have learned that it's more important than ever to be familiar with more than one area of mass media in order to be successful. This makes the role of mass media theory more important as well, since theory is the way we draw all these different aspects of communication together.

To illustrate this, consider a theory that's on many people's minds because of attention from the media: The theory of global warming or global climate change. As discussed in more detail in Chapter 1, theories are statements that seek to describe how certain things relate to one another in ways that will predict or explain the relationship. The theory of global climate change says that changes in the composition of the Earth's atmosphere are causing the planet to retain more heat from the Sun, which raises the temperature of the atmosphere and oceans in ways that affect global weather patterns. The main culprits in atmospheric change, according to the theory, are greater amounts of so-called "greenhouse gases," such as carbon dioxide, that trap the Sun's heat. The theory offers the further explanation that human activity – notably burning fossil fuels such as gasoline in vehicles and coal in power plants – contributes to the situation.

When it was first proposed the theory of global climate change wasn't accepted universally and still is doubted by some people, despite the large volume of scientific

DOI: 10.4324/9781003121695-101

evidence developed over the past few years that supports the theory. Nonetheless, global climate change remains a *theory*: It is a *possible* explanation for how the observed phenomena are related, and a prediction of what will happen over future decades. Instead of proof, we have suggestions (more formally called hypotheses) and evidence about the effects of temperature changes over recent years, predictions about future impacts if temperature trends continue, and proposals for changes in human activity to alter the volume of greenhouse gases that are being produced. The key idea to take away from this discussion is that even though global climate change is "just a theory," it can improve our understanding of the world around us. This understanding becomes even more valuable as more research adds validity to the theory.

For example, environmentalists use the theory's predictions and explanations to encourage people to change their behavior to reduce greenhouse emissions. Government policy makers take the theory into account in deciding about matters such as fuel-efficiency standards for cars and pollution controls for factories and power plants. Insurance executives consider whether the predictions of increased coastal flooding and more hurricanes packing more destructive power should affect how they issue policies in places that could be affected by those events. Importantly, none of these people dismiss the relevance of the concepts or the potential impacts of global climate change because "it's just a theory." Indeed, all of these examples illustrate how global climate change theory and its growing scientific validation can be a valuable tool for understanding the real world a little better and guiding decisions made within it.

In similar fashion, knowledge about theories of mass communication can help students who plan on careers in the media to understand their work and its implications better. It's one thing to be able to craft an effective social media plan or design a clever advertisement. Comprehending the impact such communication is likely to have, however, and how it will make that impact, can be understood through theories of persuasion and attitude change. With respect to social media, the classic theory of information diffusion by Everett Rogers goes a long way toward explaining how material goes viral. Understanding what communication scholars call "political economy" and its implications are vital to understanding shifts in the business structure of the media and its implications for ideas the media present to their audiences.

To return to the original example, certainly most college students today are familiar with global climate change theory. Many of them may even use the theory to guide their own behaviors: Conserving energy where they can, recycling and composting, encouraging friends and family members to do the same, or looking at fuel-efficient or electric models when the time comes to buy a new car. In the same way, those students will find that knowledge about formal theories of mass communication can be beneficial in helping them understand the implications of their work when they become media practitioners. In fact, the theory of agenda setting (Chapter 4) helps explain why today's students know so much about global climate change in the first place: News coverage has given the theory greater awareness and prominence among the greater public.

Like the toddler who grows up and figures out somewhere along the way that not only is broccoli good for you, but can be a tasty side dish as well, the college student who learns about theory will find out that it can lead to a greater depth in understanding of media practices that will make him or her a more effective professional.

PLAN FOR THE BOOK

This third edition is divided into two main parts:

Unit 1: Mass Communication Theory

Many college mass media programs require students to obtain a general understanding of theory, usually in the second or third year of their program. The six chapters in this section will introduce readers to mass communication theory and then walk them through a chronological progression of the development of theory in mass communication. This chronology includes an historical overview, a look at how individuals interact with media (the psychological perspective on media effects), a review of how large groups, up to and including the whole society, interact with media (the sociological perspective on media effects), and a review of critical and cultural theories of media and society. Because increased globalization over the past decade has been met by an increase in the study of mass media beyond just the United States, a chapter on international communication is included. What will make this unit useful is the integration of the theories into a model that shows how they relate to each other. Real-life, practical examples are provided along the way, so students see the value of theory in practice.

Unit 2 and Appendix: Mass Media Research

Many mass media theory courses also include the requirement that students complete an original research project. This may be a research proposal or a complete project that includes data collection and analysis. In unit 2 readers are introduced to types of mass media research, quantitative and qualitative. A new appendix provides a general outline of how a student might conduct a research project, write the paper, and present the results.

Looking Ahead as a Conclusion

While this text focuses on mass communication theory, it is clear that most students are in college primarily to plan their careers as media practitioners. The final chapter in this book provides information that bridges theory and the real world of work informed by a discussion of current trends in the online environment.

Student and faculty readers of this book are welcome to submit comments and questions on this book and the material presented here. Please feel free to email the authors at any time for a prompt response to any concerns. Suggestions for improving this book for future editions are also encouraged.

Jack Rosenberry   Lauren Vicker

March 2021

CHAPTER 1

Theory and the Study of Communication

The starship *Enterprise*, answering a distress call from another vessel, finds itself in danger from a rogue energy field that has already destroyed one ship as the *Enterprise* crew watched, and is now coming perilously close to the *Enterprise* itself:

CHIEF ENGINEER SCOTT: There's just no way to disrupt a gravimetric field of this magnitude. ...
ENSIGN DEMORA SULU (INTERRUPTING): Hull integrity failing.
SCOTT: ... But I do have a theory.
CAPTAIN KIRK: I thought you might.

From the opening scene of *Star Trek: Generations*
(Berman, Moore, & Braga, 1994)

This chapter will:

- Describe how theory contributes to the development of knowledge
- Introduce different types of theory, both the social scientific approach and alternative ways of theorizing about communication
- Describe some of the common goals and functions for theory, as well as evaluation criteria that can be used to judge whether a theory is worthwhile.

As human beings, we all know a great many things, especially taking into account the flexible meanings of the words "to know." We commonly say we *know* someone who is a friend or acquaintance. We *know* what types of foods we prefer, and which ones we don't like. We know basic intellectual concepts (such as 2 + 2 = 4) and more complicated ones. We *know* personal data about ourselves and others, such as ages or birthdays, and we *know* general facts about the world around us, such as the names and activities of celebrities who interest us. We also know how to do things, from shooting a basketball to driving a car to solving mathematical equations to writing a paper for a class.

These examples should show that knowledge is a complicated and wide-ranging thing. In fact, there is a formal way of exploring and explaining the quest for knowledge, called epistemology. Varied definitions for epistemology can be found, but they all involve the nature and scope of knowledge and how people validate or justify

DOI: 10.4324/9781003121695-1

what they know or believe. A simpler definition would be that epistemology is how we come to know things, or how we acquire knowledge.

THEORY, RESEARCH, AND KNOWLEDGE

Such questions about acquiring knowledge lie at the heart of a book about theory and research. This is because knowledge, theory, and research are closely related; theory coupled with research can create new insights and extend knowledge in any field, including media and communication. The general process of developing theories and using research to explore and validate them is the same in any discipline, from medicine to physics to psychology to anthropology. The same is true in communication as an academic discipline; theory and research are fundamental to understanding details of how people communicate. The Introduction to this book gives an example of using global climate change theory as a tool for gaining greater knowledge about changes in the environment, quite literally. More generally, what is a theory, and how can theories be applied for a better understanding of the world around us?

Defining Theory

Theory is a common word, and most people have at some point in their lives learned about theories, especially in the natural sciences. For instance, most people have at least heard of the "Big Bang" theory in astronomy. Other common natural science theories are Darwin's theory of natural selection (or evolution) in biology and Einstein's theory of relativity in physics.

One thing all of these theories have in common is that they attempt to explain something about the world around us by answering a question:

- How did the universe come into being? The Big Bang supplies one possible explanation.
- How did various species of plants and animals arise? Darwin tries to offer an answer.
- How are energy (e) and matter (m) related to one another and what predictions can be made about what happens when one is converted to the other? Albert Einstein's famous equation of $e = mc^2$ seeks to explain these relationships.

In mass communication, some theories seek to explain what happens when, for example, some topics get more coverage in the news than others, or what happens when audiences are exposed to certain content such as graphic violence or sexuality on television, in movies, or in music recordings. Others examine general impacts of media on society overall. Several chapters of this book explore these theories individually and describe in detail what they are meant to predict and explain.

Trying to find a single, formal definition for theory is not easy because many such definitions exist. They range from very simple to very complex ones, depending on the source and the author. Whatever the approach, definitions of theory share some common themes:

- Theories seek to answer questions about how certain things are related to one another.
- Answers to these questions offer explanations or predictions about how some aspect of the world works.

As researchers Kerlinger and Lee put it, "The basic aim of science is to explain natural phenomena. Such explanations are called theories" (Kerlinger & Lee, 2000, p. 11).

So, does Scotty have a theory that will save the *Enterprise*? Not really. What he has is a hypothesis – an idea that he thinks might work, and wants to test. (His hypothesis, as it plays out in the movie, is that a release of antimatter can disrupt the dangerous energy field and save the *Enterprise*. It does work; the ship is damaged but survives – so his hypothesis was proven correct.) Defining a theory as something that predicts and explains how certain phenomena are related to one another means Scotty's idea can't be called a theory (Box 1.1). The distinctions between theories and hypotheses, and also how they are related to each other, are discussed in Chapter 7.

BOX 1.1

Definition of Theory

Theory: A statement that predicts or explains how certain phenomena are related to one another.

Types of Knowledge

Theory and research are associated with what is called scientific knowledge, which is a specific way of knowing things about the world around us. The important words in that description are *way of knowing*, which goes back to the question asked in the first paragraph of this chapter and the examples there (Box 1.2).

Those examples that open the chapter illustrate two important "ways of knowing," namely *experience* and *authority*. Experience is learning from something by directly participating in it, while authority is learning something by taking someone's word for it. People who attend a sporting event know firsthand who won the game and what the key plays or moments were (experience), but anyone who wasn't there can see a news report about it after to find out the same information (authority). Because we can be in only once place at a time, however, most of what we come to know about the outside world does rely on authority. People know who won the last presidential election, but not because they counted all the ballots personally. Instead, the knowledge comes from authoritative sources: Election officials who tallied the votes and news media that reported the results. Most of what students learn in school has the same basis, coming from resources (textbooks and other readings) and teachers that are, presumably, authorities on the topics.

Knowing that you prefer pizza to sushi (or vice versa), on the other hand, is purely experiential; so is riding a bike. Learning by doing is the only way to acquire that knowledge. Learning to drive a car or play a sport also comes mostly through experience (practice), although this knowledge also may come in part from the authority of a classroom teacher in a driver's education course or a coach who helps the athlete learn helpful techniques.

As useful and valuable as these ways of knowing are, a third way of gaining knowledge is the most important for our purposes here. This is *scientific knowledge*, which is defined as learning through systematic, accurate observation of evidence in such a way that it can be verified and validated. This type of knowledge is embodied in the *scientific method*: Defining a problem or question to be answered, investigating it by collecting evidence, and evaluating the evidence to determine the answer to the question. This approach is taught to most people in elementary school or high school, often accompanied by application of the principles with simple experiments in classes such as earth science, biology, or chemistry.

BOX 1.2

"Ways of Knowing"

Experience: Learning something by firsthand participation.
Authority: Learning something by taking someone else's word for it.
Research: Learning through systematic, accurate observation of evidence in such a way that it can be verified and validated.

Communication Theory Genres

One common way of studying communication practices has its roots in the scientific method, as described above. This style of developing knowledge draws heavily on observing parts of communicative processes that can be measured with some of the tools that are discussed in Chapter 8, using a technique called the positivist approach or "communication science" (Chaffee & Berger, 1987). Because communication processes and impacts happen in many ways that cannot be precisely measured, this is not the only way scholars seek to learn more about communication. Some of the other ways of researching communication topics are discussed in Chapter 9.

Communication Science

When most people hear the word "science," they think about the natural sciences, which are disciplines that seek to explain the physical world around us. "Science," however, is more than biology, chemistry, and physics. Communication theory belongs to a different set of disciplines called *social* sciences, or fields of study that explore how people behave within societies by using the scientific method to study social phenomena (Box 1.3). The social sciences include economics, political science, psychology, and sociology, to name just a few.

Studying communication as a human activity has been defined as a discipline that "seeks to understand the production, processing, and effects of symbol and signal systems by developing testable theories that explain phenomena associated with production, processing and effects" (Chaffee & Berger, 1987, p. 17). In other words, theory and research can be used to develop knowledge about the processes and effects of communication by observing and verifying measurable evidence. This is done at various levels including interpersonal, group/organizational, and mass mediated communication. Many of the original theories of mass communication as described in Chapter 2 are rooted in this style of research, as are most of the theories of the "effects tradition" described in Chapters 3 and 4. This style of investigating communication has its roots in other social sciences that use many of the same research techniques and tools, notably sociology and psychology. In fact, the first scholars in the emerging field of communication studies in the early 20th century were mostly sociologists and psychologists. Their contributions are described in Chapter 2.

BOX 1.3

Definition of Social Sciences

Social sciences: Fields of study that seek to explain how people operate within societies by using careful research to study social phenomena.

Interpretive Theory

The other major way of learning more about communication processes and effects focuses on interpretation of texts and human actions. Rather than gaining knowledge or developing meaning from measurable observations, this research tradition uses the words or other symbols themselves as well as the symbols' context and the scholar's own understandings of other texts and contexts to determine meaning. (It should be noted that in this context the word "text" does not necessarily mean words on paper or a screen; a "text" could be an ancient culture's picture drawings or a modern culture's films or advertisements.)

Scholars from this tradition tend to think empirical science-styled theory is too simplistic. In the view of interpretive theorists, use of quantitative data and scientific method to investigate how people communicate does not allow the researcher to do anything other than measure certain aspects of behavior. But interpretive scholars are interested in broader understandings, and they think that just measuring something narrowly cannot help in understanding why or how certain behavior occurred or what its implications are. This is because the measurements, no matter how precise they are, usually lack context. For the interpretive researcher, context is crucial to understanding. (Interpretive theory is discussed in more detail in Chapter 5, and the methods for conducting it are covered in Chapter 9.)

Critical and Normative Theory

Some other types of theory don't just investigate media phenomena, but also offer viewpoints about them. Theories of this type, which are closely allied with the interpretive tradition, are known as critical and normative theories.

Critical Theory. Critical theory rejects the idea that merely offering explanations or predictions is sufficient for studying communication effectively. Instead of documenting or evaluating social reality – as positivist and interpretive theory does – this body of theory seeks to *reform* social reality. To scholars in this tradition, theories are not academic exercises; rather, what theories propose should be meaningful for a society and should be focused on making society better for its members. The critical school emphasizes the social structures in which communication takes place and the issues of who controls the communication system and to what result.

Critical studies start from the viewpoint that media effects on society are not always helpful, or even benign. It is largely based on the ideas of Karl Marx, best known for his theories on economics and government. Marx was a "critical theorist" who sought reform through his criticism of the established powers in 19th century European society. He argued that a ruling class, whom he called by the French word *bourgeoisie*, dominated and oppressed the working class, or proletariat. Marx created a theory of politics and economics, called communism, which was designed to address these abuses.

Extending these ideas to critical studies of communication results in a perspective that mass media are part of the power establishment, and that by their nature they support the status quo by giving voice to and furthering the influence of a dominant class that keeps many members of society unfairly oppressed. Partly because of its European roots, this viewpoint-based form of theorizing is particularly popular outside of the United States. Many American scholars, however, work in this tradition as well, and this book explores these ideas in more depth in Chapters 5 and 6.

Normative theory. Finally, one body of theory does not seek to explain, interpret, or reform what it theorizes about. This is normative theory, which attempts to describe not how things are, but how they *should be* (Box 1.4). It has similarities to critical theory, because it does not accept the status quo as the best possible approach. Normative theories do, however, seek to establish ideal standards for the way society should operate. (The name comes from the term "social norms," which are values and guidelines for the operation of a social system.)

In addition, it is important to recognize that social norms differ from culture to culture. American norms, for example, emphasize personal liberty; extending these norms to mass media puts high value on freedom of expression, as embodied in the U.S. Constitution's First Amendment. Other societies may not have the same values, and may view the importance of free speech or a free press differently. This is why the well-known set of normative theories called the Four Theories of the Press identify not only the free-speech or libertarian ideal, but other models that involve more government control of the media. Chapters 5 and 6 are also where normative theory is discussed further.

Types of Communication Theory

Communication science: Testable theories that explain phenomena associated with production, processing and effects of symbols and symbol systems used to communicate (Chaffee & Berger, 1987).

Interpretative theory: Subjective interpretation of meaning from words/symbols themselves as well as their context, combined with the scholar's own understandings of other texts and contexts.

Critical theory: Analysis that seeks to reform media systems that are part of the power establishment, which they do by giving voice to and extending the influence of a dominant class in order to support the status quo.

Normative theory: An attempt to describe not how things are, but how they should be according to some ideal standard of social values.

Theory's Purposes

Theory has several purposes, and several accompanying ways of assessing whether it is productive. The main purpose or goal of theory is posing questions that provide explanations about phenomena. As specifically applied to mass communication, theory can be used to:

- Explain effects of mass communication on those who are exposed to it.
- Explain the ways people use mass media, and why they use it.
- Explain how people learn from mass media.
- Explain the role of media in shaping values of those exposed to it (Severin & Tankard, 2001, p. 12).

Pretty much anything that seeks to offer an explanation could be called a theory, and anyone can theorize about any topic whether or not they are qualified to do so. Not all theories are created equal; quite frankly some are better than others. Some criteria that are often used to evaluate the worth of a theory (Littlejohn, 1999) take into account a theory's:

- **Scope,** meaning how generally or widely the theory can be applied. For example, a theory that seeks to predict or explain how advertisements of *one* particular company communicate their message or the impacts of *one* specific television show would not be very valuable because of its narrow focus, compared to a theory that applied to a wide range of advertisements or programs.
- **Appropriateness,** or logical consistency of the theory to the assumptions behind it and what it is theorizing about. For example, both of this book's authors live in houses with even numbers in the street address; both also are college professors who hold doctorate degrees. So, they could theorize that people with advanced

college education tend to live in even-numbered houses. This theory would have little appropriateness since there is nothing that should logically connect a person's street address with their educational achievement.

- **Heuristic value,** or the ability to generate new ways of thinking and new research ideas about the subject of the theory. Some theories have been used as the basis for hundreds of pieces of research, and even inspired "spinoff" theories that developed more ways of thinking about the topic. Theories that can accomplish this are valuable tools for understanding how things work.
- **Validity,** or the degree to which a theory is able to predict and explain the events as the theorist proposes that it will. A theory that supposedly was able to provide such explanations, but in practice could not, would not be very valuable.
- **Parsimony,** or simplicity. In general, simpler theories are superior to more complicated ones.
- **Openness** or adaptability to new conditions and, especially in communication, to new technologies. Some "classic"' theories developed in connection with newspapers and broadcasting more than 50 years ago, such as reinforcement theory and agenda setting, have stood the test of time when applied to how people communicate with newer methods such as social media.

Other criteria cited by scholars to evaluate the worth of a theory include:

- **Practicality** or usefulness (Baran & Davis, 2006). Theories that fail to address real-world phenomena in a practical or useful way are not very valuable, according to these scholars.
- **Testability,** sometimes referred to as whether the theory can be "falsified." Sparks (2002) defines falsification as the ability to say, in advance, what sort of data could be observed that would demonstrate that the theory did not work as intended. For example, the theory of gravity says that large bodies such as stars and planets are attracted to each other and also explains why smaller objects are attracted to the surface of a planet rather than floating away from it. It is, however, possible to specify the conditions under which gravitational attraction and motion of a body cancel each other out, leading to the weightlessness that space travelers experience. Being able to falsify the theory in this way helps give it more credibility. The logic of falsification is that if something cannot be proved wrong, it cannot be proved right, either. Something that cannot be proved either true or false is either a statement of faith (such as belief in an afterlife) or an opinion ("I don't think green is a good color for a house"), but it is not a theory.

APPLIED MASS COMMUNICATION THEORY

Perhaps the best rationale for studying communication – and in particular symbolic communication, or the use of words and images to signify real-world objects and more abstract ideas – is because the act of communicating is the essential element of human society. Humans have engaged in symbolic communication for thousands of years. For most of that time, communication took place between individuals or in small groups in face-to-face interactions. It has only been in the modern era that mass communication technology such as printed materials, television broadcasts, and Internet connections have been a part of the equation. It is only in the past few decades that these types of communication have been formally studied (through theories and research) to help answer questions about the way human beings relate to one another in society.

Theory's Relevance

Chapters 2 through 6 of this book present details about many of the formal theories that scholars use to understand and interpret mass communication and its impacts on human society. Many students think these formal theories are irrelevant and impractical, so they resist the idea of spending time learning them, like the toddler faced with a plate of broccoli in the book's introduction.

This is not surprising. Many mass communication programs emphasize skills development, built around classes in which students learn to write news stories, craft public relations plans, create advertisements, produce podcasts, edit video presentations, and develop social media content. Most students enjoy the classes that teach these skills and feel as if learning them is the reason they are studying communication in the first place. They find it easy to see the relevance of such courses, especially if they work in campus media, do an internship, or have a summer job in a media organization where they can practice classroom learning in real-life settings. On the other hand, courses that dwell on theory do not seem as relevant. Such courses are so, well, theoretical – which many students take to mean the opposite of practical.

What students who have this attitude fail to consider is how closely theory relates to real life. It is important to remember that while the theory itself may be an abstraction, its principles are anchored in reality and often helpful in answering important questions. As noted previously, the Big Bang and other theories of astronomy seek to answer questions of how the universe began and how it has developed. In the introduction, a similar walk-through example applies the theory of global climate change to real-life situations. The theory may be an abstract idea, but the questions it helps people to answer are very real.

Although one of the best-known theorists of the social impact of television is George Gerbner, no newly graduated student interviewing for a job at a television station will be asked to identify Gerbner or engage in a discussion with the station manager about Gerbner's theory of cultivation. One of this book's authors worked for more than 20 years as a newspaper reporter and editor, and never once heard the words "agenda setting" mentioned in the newsroom.

Complaints that media organizations don't pay obvious attention to these theories miss the point. Journalists may not sit around in their newsrooms saying "we're going to set the agenda on this story," but when they talk about "the public's need to know," isn't that the same thing? A news organization that does an investigative report about a political scandal creates the report with the goal of bringing public attention to the situation – which is how agenda setting is defined. Just because journalists don't sit around talking about agenda setting in those exact words doesn't mean they aren't actively, and often deliberately, engaging in it.

For example, the newspaper in the city where the authors live published an article one January saying its editorial focus for that entire year would be on four key areas of community concern: Housing; health care; survival of small businesses; and racial injustice. The article described how the organization's editorials and guest columnists would be elaborating on those topics for the coming months as a way to set a deliberate agenda for coverage. It's a pretty safe assumption that the editorial board offices at the newspaper weren't decorated with photos of agenda setting's founding theorists Maxwell McCombs and Donald Shaw. Just the same, the ideas and research of these scholars were behind the paper's effort as the editors described it.

Research Relevance

The same sort of relevance can be attached to the research procedures covered in Chapters 7 through 9, because one fundamental rule about working in media is that communicators must know their audiences. *NCIS* (and its many spin-offs) and *Sesame Street* are both television shows, but have little in common. Similarly, an "edgy" drama produced for adults for Netflix differs dramatically from a children's film shown on the Disney Channel. Story selection, writing style and advertising are different in *Maxim* and *Men's Health* than they are in *Glamour* and *Cosmopolitan*, and different still for a magazine devoted to a particular activity, hobby, or demographic. Far and away the U.S. magazine with the largest circulation is one focused on a demographic, *AARP The Magazine* (for adults over 50). That publication is vastly different from *Highlights* or *J-14*, both geared toward younger readers. Likewise, people with different interests and from different demographics use Facebook, Twitter, Snapchat, and Instagram in different ways.

How do the writers, producers, and managers of all these different media outlets know who their audiences are and what appeals to them? They find out from research, including data coming from external bodies (e.g., A.C. Nielsen for television and Arbitron for radio) and increasingly from social media metrics that can be monitored internally using tools such as Chartbeat, Crowd Tangle, and Google Analytics. Such research shapes how practitioners go about their work as they get feedback from their audiences on the success of their message strategies. Public relations campaigns frequently end with research about how well the campaign worked in reaching the target audience, as well as whether the goals of the campaign were reached. News operations monitor attention to the content they publish online throughout the day with web analytics. Similar tools are used by social media platforms and video streaming services to evaluate their audiences.

Granted, research such as this, which is meant to guide professional decision-making, differs from the academic research described in this book, but it is not as different as some students think. The main difference, in fact, is in formatting, since professional research reports are organized somewhat differently from research papers prepared for academic presentation. And even those differences aren't as stark as some people imagine. A professional research report will start with an introduction and overview of the field from secondary sources, not very different from the introduction and review of the literature used in academic papers. Both types of reports document the methods by which their findings were derived and conclude with the significance of the findings for the audience as well as directions for future research.

Even more significantly than understanding the format of a report, the research skills described in this book relate directly to what many students will find as professionals in the field. Data collection and analysis incorporated into most professional reports use one or more of the research techniques described in Chapters 8 and 9. Quantitative analysis (Chapter 8) has become especially important to anyone whose work involves online analytics. In fact, so-called A/B testing of online content to check on the appeal of two different approaches is a simple experiment with two different treatments followed by a post-test to evaluate their relative effectiveness. Surveys, focus groups and occasionally even content analysis are prominent tasks among marketing, advertising, and public relations professionals. Observing the world around them and interviewing the people in it describes the research practice of ethnography (Chapter 9), but that also describes how journalists, documentary film producers, free-lance writers, and public relations writers spend their day. Developing a deeper understanding of these research techniques has huge benefits for aspiring media practitioners.

CONCLUSION

In short, much of our ability to understand life and the world around us depends on understanding how various things relate to one another. The principles people rely on to predict and explain these relationships can rightly be called theories, and the methods we use to examine these relationships constitute research. Students who think studying theory and research is pointless or impractical are dismissing two very important tools that they can use for better understanding of the world around them. This book will illustrate how many of the theories introduced in Chapters 3 through 6 apply to popular areas of media work.

In other words, students who think the time spent learning about theory and research practices will be time poorly spent might be surprised to find out just how valuable this knowledge is to many media professionals. Along the way, this book uses many current examples to illustrate the connections between theory and practice. When students can identify theory operating in the mass media, whether in their classes, co-curricular activities, internships, or even everyday life, they are on their way toward becoming truly educated and insightful media professionals.

QUESTIONS FOR DISCUSSION/APPLICATION EXERCISES

1. Take a theory you know something about, perhaps one in natural science or social science that you have learned about in another class, and apply the criteria from this chapter to evaluate whether it is a good one. As a reminder, those criteria are: Scope (breadth of application); appropriateness (logical consistency), heuristic

value; validity; parsimony (simplicity), openness (adaptability); practicality; and testability. The more "yes" answers you get (e.g., yes, it can be applied broadly; yes, it's simple; yes, it has practical value) the stronger a theory it is. Be sure to describe what characteristics of the theory make it generalizable, simple, practical, etc.

2. Visit the Pew Research Center on the Internet, Science and Technology at http://www.pewinternet.org/ and examine some of the research published there about media topics. What are some of the most common methods that are used?

REFERENCES

Baran, S., & Davis, D. (2006). *Mass communication theory: Foundations, ferment and future* (4th ed.). Belmont, CA: Wadsworth.

Berman, R., Moore, R. & Braga, B. Star Trek: Generations screenplay final draft (March 16, 1994). Retrieved from http://www.imsdb.com/scripts/Star-Trek-Generations.html.

Chaffee, S.H., & Berger, C.R. (1987). The study of communication as a science. In Berger, C.R., & Chaffee, S.H. (Eds.). *Handbook of communication science* (pp. 15–19). Newbury Park, CA: Sage Publications.

Kerlinger, F., & Lee, H. (2000). *Foundations of behavioral research* (5th ed.). Fort Worth, TX: Harcourt College Publishers.

Littlejohn, S. (1999). *Theories of human communication.* Belmont, CA: Wadsworth Publishing Co.

Severin, W., & Tankard, J. (2001). *Communication theories: Origins, methods and uses in the mass media* (5th ed.). New York: Addison Wesley Longman.

Sparks, G. (2002). *Media effects research: A basic overview.* Belmont, CA: Wadsworth Publishing Co.

CHAPTER 2

Historical Developments in Mass Communication Theory

This chapter will:

- Provide a definition and description of mass communication as a social practice.
- Describe how mass communication research is rooted in older social sciences, especially psychology and sociology.
- Describe some of the earliest research into mass communication processes by researchers in those fields, often considered the founders of communication research, and discuss how their work provided a basis for later research.
- Outline several specific early research themes of mass communication, including:
  - Bullet theory.
  - Propaganda and public opinion studies.
  - Information theory and cybernetics.
  - Lasswell's structure-and-function models.
  - Two-step-flow and reinforcement theories.
  - Limited effects paradigm.
- Discuss how theory evolves and changes over time, and relate these historical developments to the current era of research.

In our hyper-connected, hyper-paced culture, many people don't place much value in understanding the past. However, a scene from the popular Disney movie *The Lion King* illustrates how useful past events can be in understanding the present.

The wise old baboon, Rafiki, comes upon Simba as a young adult, still living in the wilderness. Rafiki reminds Simba that he is the legitimate heir to the throne of the lion king, and that once upon a time he aspired to take it. "That was a long time ago," Simba replies, stating that he has learned to live in the present ("hakuna matata") and that things from the past don't matter to him anymore. Rafiki responds to this statement by hitting Simba over the head with his walking stick. When Simba asks "Why did you do that?" Rafiki replies "It doesn't matter; it's in the past." He then swings the stick at Simba again. This time, the young lion knows what's coming and ducks to

DOI: 10.4324/9781003121695-2

avoid being hit. Simba, obviously a quick study, has learned Rafiki's lesson: Knowledge of the past is vital in understanding the present (and future).

That is why any study of the current state of communication as a discipline, and the active theories that comprise it, must start with a look at the historical theories that preceded these modern ideas. This includes a review of theories that, over time, have been updated by later research and, in many ways, made obsolete, but which still have continuing relevance as the origin of more current, relevant approaches.

Communication has a relatively short history as a formal field of study, beginning around 100 years ago in the 1920s. Some of the key developments, such as emergence of new effects theories in the 1970s, are within living memory of many communication scholars today. The field has come a long way in its short history, as the earliest theories have evolved into newer ones that seek to predict and explain mass communication more subtly and precisely. Nevertheless, it is worthwhile to study these older theoretical approaches because they provide the "genetic material" from which contemporary theories are drawn and because, as Simba learned the hard way, knowing about the past really does help in understanding the present.

THE EVOLUTION OF THEORY

As Chapter 1 discusses, theory is a way to explain or predict the relationship of certain phenomena. For example, Albert Einstein's famous theory of $e = mc^2$ seeks to explain the relationship of energy to matter and Charles Darwin's theory of natural selection seeks to explain how different species of plants and animals evolved.

These examples come from physics and biology, two of the disciplines known as *natural* sciences that seek to explain the physical world around us. (Others in this category include chemistry, astronomy, geology, etc.) Communication theory is generally thought of as belonging to a different set of disciplines called *social* sciences, or fields of study that seek to explain how society functions and how people function within it. "Social" and "society" have the same root, the Latin word "socius," which means "companion." The social sciences include, to name just a few, economics, anthropology, political science, psychology, sociology – and communication.

Social science is a more recent intellectual development than natural science, which has been around for thousands of years. Natural sciences, such as astronomy and chemistry, trace their roots to efforts of ancient civilizations to develop "scientific theories" to explain the natural world around them. For example, in the 2nd century, the astronomer Ptolemy theorized that the Sun, Moon and planets were bodies that revolve around the Earth, a scientific breakthrough that replaced mythological explanations such as the Sun being the chariot of one of the gods. A few hundred years before that, the Greek philosopher Empedocles developed an early theory of chemistry that said matter was composed of the four elements of earth, air, fire, and water. The social sciences, however, are far newer. The term "psychology" was first used in the 1500s; modern economics can be traced to the publication of Adam Smith's *The Wealth of Nations* in 1776; and the term "sociology" to describe the study of people and their associations is attributed to Auguste Comte in the 1830s. As mentioned earlier, communication as a distinct field of study has emerged only within the past 100 years.

All fields of scientific inquiry, whether natural science or social science, have a history of theoretical development. All of them have evolved over time with later discoveries built upon the foundations of earlier ones. For example, chemistry has progressed from Empedocles's four elements to a periodic table with more than 100. An important thing to note, however, is that the basic idea is the same. Empedocles theorized that matter was made up of certain elemental units; modern chemistry has the same basis. New discoveries bring more power, sophistication and subtlety to how people understand the concepts. This kind of evolutionary development has been going on in the natural sciences for thousands of years, and in many social sciences for a few hundred. The same dynamics can be applied to communication, and even though it is a much newer field of study, some dramatic developments can be identified.

A generally held belief that dominates thinking in a discipline is often called a *paradigm*. Various theories can operate within a given paradigm, which is an umbrella set of assumptions or ways of thinking about an aspect of the world. Ptolemy's Earth-centered universe is an example of a natural-science paradigm that held sway for hundreds of years. When a new way of thinking replaces an older one, such as the discoveries by Copernicus and Galileo that the Earth revolved around the Sun rather than vice versa, it is called a *paradigm shift*.

Even though communication theory is only a few decades old, it already has developed different paradigms, or undergone paradigm shifts. Eminent communication theorist Denis McQuail, for instance, describes the idea that information transmission has a measurable effect on recipients as the "dominant paradigm" of communication study and contrasts it with the "alternative paradigm" represented by cultural and critical studies (McQuail, 2005, p. 65). Stanley Baran and Dennis Davis discuss five "eras" of communication research, starting with the mass society perspective, followed by the social scientific/empirical perspective, the consolidation of studies done in the empirical era to create the limited effects paradigm, the emergence of the cultural and critical studies perspective, and finally, the current paradigm, often described as "moderate effects" (Baran & Davis, 2006).

This book follows a similar approach. This chapter traces the origins of mass communication theory in the direct effects/transmission model paradigm, then describes how the limited effects paradigm emerged from scholarly investigation that illustrated this original paradigm's shortcomings. This discussion is followed by a look at how limited effects gave way to the modern era, which encompasses both the critical theory/cultural studies approach as well as a variety of effects theories that describe significant effects of mass communication either upon individuals, large groups, or society as a whole. At the same time, these theories do not go so far as to suggest the broad-based, immediate, powerful, direct and uniform influence of the media that the first historical paradigm presumed. This history is meant to help students understand how mass communication theories evolved as context for understanding the current state of the field.

BOX 2.1

Definition of Paradigm

Paradigm: A dominant way of thinking about a situation. A theoretical paradigm can fit a number of specific theories under its umbrella.

HISTORICAL PERSPECTIVES

Before even thinking about mass communication as a discipline, and the paradigms and theories that help to explain how it works, it is first necessary to consider mass communication as a human activity. One of the reasons mass communication is such a new academic discipline is that mass-mediated communication among human beings is also a relatively recent development. People have been looking at the stars and wondering what the world around them was made from since before recorded human history, so it makes sense that sciences such as astronomy and chemistry should be our most ancient ones. Humans have not engaged in mass communication for nearly as long; in fact, for nearly all of human history communication has *not* been in "mass" form, which comes from the same root as "massive," meaning in large quantities.

Personal vs. Mass Media

Arguably, the thing that makes human beings unique is our ability to engage in *symbolic* communication. The mere fact of communicating is not uniquely human because other creatures also communicate with one another. For instance, bees do a "hive dance" to direct other members of the colony to food sources, birds and even whales "sing," and anyone who owns a dog or cat can tell a playful bark from a threatening growl, or a contented purr from an angry hiss. All of these are communication tools, but fundamentally different from the way humans communicate using symbols such as language and visual imagery.

The dominant way that people have engaged in this symbolic communication throughout human history, however, has *not* been in mass or mediated form, but on a much more personal level. The rhetorical tradition of "mass" communication as one message to many people (as opposed to interpersonal and small group communication) does go back a few thousand years. Aristotle's *Rhetoric* gave instruction to speakers on how to persuade an audience. Even then, the communicators were speaking in person to a crowd of people within earshot. Without the aid of microphones and amplifiers, "mass" communication was delivered by men with booming voices to audiences in specially designed amphitheaters that would help the sound to travel.

As we generally use the term today, mass communication refers to communication that is mediated or enhanced by technology to reach a large audience. It is generally one-way, communicator to audience, with little opportunity for immediate feedback from the audience, although new media technologies are changing that.

Technology and Mass Communication

Although writing was developed in Phoenicia, Egypt, and China many centuries ago, large-scale reproduction of any individual set of symbols was not even possible until the invention of movable type just a few hundred years ago (around 1450). Even then, the earliest printed materials had small "press runs" compared to, say, a contemporary newspaper, magazine, or best-selling book. While this technology for reproducing, preserving and transmitting written work in large quantities – the printing press – has been around for the several hundred years since then, the technologies for recording, preserving and transmitting sounds and moving images appeared much more recently, only within the past century and a half.

Thus, mass media are truly a modern development and, like many other modern devices, an invention of the Industrial Revolution. The first media to be produced and distributed on a large scale to a massive audience were the "penny press" newspapers that developed in American cities in the mid-19th century and in Europe around the same time. Before that, the vast majority of communication was personal and done without the aid of any sort of media. Community and family traditions took the form of oral histories or hand-written letters from one individual to another, and current events were passed along among individuals through discussions in the town square or at social gatherings. Even the colonial era and early 19th century "press" from which the penny papers evolved consisted primarily of business-oriented and political publications with narrow readerships.

The beginnings of the modern newspaper era, which can be seen as the dawn of American mass communication, are traced to the founding of the *New York Sun* by Benjamin Day in 1833. Day's success was imitated in other American cities that were growing rapidly because of immigration from Europe and migration within the United States of people from the countryside to the cities in search of factory jobs. The expanding city populations provided the audience. The inventions of the Industrial Revolution provided publishers with the means to serve those large audiences with up-to-date news. The most important of these were the telegraph, which allowed information to be sent instantly over great distances to aid in reporting, and steam engines, which drove ever-larger and more sophisticated printing presses (Emery, 1962). Within a few decades, newspapers had become big businesses, bringing great wealth and power to press barons such as E.W. Scripps, Joseph Pulitzer, and William Randolph Hearst. The history of newspapers in Europe followed roughly the same pattern, although about a decade or two behind the United States.

The important point here is that within a period of about 50 years, from the middle of the 1800s to the end of that century, people had gone from hearing about news and events from their friends and neighbors in the town square or at the church social to reading about it in the newspaper. As they consumed this information, so did thousands of other residents of their communities. Instead of an individualized version of an event told or written by someone the recipient knew, everyone read the same account provided by someone whom they did not know personally. The era of institutionalized communication to massive audiences using modern technology had begun.

This era accelerated as the 20th century got under way. Magazines, books, and printed advertising (such as the Sears-Roebuck and Montgomery-Ward catalog) joined newspapers in competing for audiences' attention. Edison's phonograph (1870s), motion picture cinemas (1890s), and radio (commercialized in the 1920s) represented the dawning of electronic media. Television was first demonstrated in the 1920s but took hold in American and European markets only after World War II ended in 1945. The technological pace and variety of mass communication methods has been growing and expanding since, introducing (among many other innovations) cable and satellite communications, digitization of audio, video and text files, and the Internet.

It took thousands of years for astronomy to evolve from the ancient Greeks' observation of the "wanderers" in the nighttime sky – the planets visible to the unaided eye – to current investigations of planets orbiting other stars that may be like our own. It has taken communication only a little more than 100 years to go from Marconi's original experiments with wireless radio-wave communication to digital broadcasting, cable and satellite content distribution, podcasts, and streaming audio and video.

DEFINING MASS COMMUNICATION

Characteristics of the Mass Communication Process

Clearly, newspapers, magazines, movies, radio and television broadcasts, and Internet streaming are methods of mass communication; in the context of communication scholarship, the messages sent through such media draw the most attention. At the same time in a more general sense, what constitutes mass communication, and what are its characteristics? For Aristotle, it was shouting in the amphitheater. In the contemporary era, however, is a teacher in front of a class "mass" communicating? Would the answer be different if it were a seminar of 15 students vs. a lecture with 500?

Although ours is a media-saturated society, and individuals absorb uncountable media messages every day, much of the communication that people engage in still is not massive and not mediated. This includes conversations with friends, family, and associates, in instrumental settings such as the workplace and classroom, and in social settings such as the home or dining hall. Personal-yet-anonymous conversations with, say, a store clerk or bank teller are still commonplace, and even many "mediated" communications are of the personal variety as well, such as e-mail, mobile-phone voice calls and texting, and social-media messaging.

Mass communication messages, however, are different from these interpersonal ones. Among the things that set mass communication messages apart are their scale, direction, impersonality, simultaneity, and transience. All of these characteristics influence the content and style of the messages and the impact on their audiences, and these characteristics relate to much theory-based media research.

Scale. The word "mass" indicates that the scale of a message's reach is large, much larger than one person talking to two, or four, or 14 others. Many newspapers and magazines distribute hundreds of thousands of copies; millions of people may see a popular television show or hear a popular song through broadcast or streaming services. Creating messages on such a large scale requires use of technologies that tend to be large-scale themselves, and correspondingly complicated and expensive, such as printing presses and broadcast facilities. Because this technology is used to *mediate* the message – literally, to come in the middle of the sender and the recipient to help transfer the message – mass-communicated messages are frequently called mass-mediated messages, and the tools for sending them are called mass media or simply "media."

Direction. Mass-mediated messages employ what is called a one-way flow. A conversation between two individuals generally contains much "back and forth" exchange; even a larger-group "conversation" such as a classroom lecture-discussion allows for a two-way flow of information. In mass communication, though, the message goes in one direction, from creator to recipient. Any feedback that is provided to the sender by the receiver is delayed and indirect, such as a comment on an online news story.

Impersonality/anonymity. Related to the one-way flow, the creator of the message doesn't know who might receive it. While she might know some of the recipients personally – a journalist who writes a story can count on her sources and colleagues reading it, for example – the message creator can't possibly know all of the audience members who might see or hear it. Unlike interpersonal or small-group messages that have a small set of designated recipients, mass-communicated messages are deliberately public, meant to be accessed by anyone who may be interested in seeing or hearing them.

Simultaneity. Not only is the message large-scale, anonymous and public, but it is sent to all the potential recipients at the same time. The messages may be received at slightly different times; people may watch a popular streamed show at different times, or read a news organization's web story sometime after it was posted. At least from the creator's standpoint, though, the message is released to all of the potential recipients at the same time, and most of the messages receive the audience's attention within a short frame of time.

Transience. A characteristic that is related to the simultaneous nature of mass-communicated messages is that they tend to be consumed and disappear within a short time. A television or radio program has to be consumed literally as it is produced (broadcast), unless it has been recorded (which is, of course, becoming more common with digital recording devices and on-demand services such as podcasts). Some media do have more "shelf life" than others; a popular movie will stay in theaters for a few weeks, and a weekly or monthly magazine may be kept around until the next issue arrives. In general, however, the nature of the message is transient, designed to be replaced by a new message from the same medium fairly soon.

Audience. Mass media audiences have attributes that mirror these qualities of the messages and senders. McQuail identifies characteristics of the mass audience as large in number, widely dispersed, heterogeneous and not organized to any degree, as well as non-interactive with the senders and anonymous to them (McQuail, 2005).

Implications of Mediation

The symbolic nature of communication combined with some of these characteristics of the mass process give a special importance to the study of mass media forms and practices. McQuail notes that mass media have a number of perceived purposes, which include providing a window on events, being a mirror of events, being a filter or gatekeeper for information reaching the audience, being a guide to or interpreter of events, being a forum for the presentation of ideas, and being a disseminator of information (McQuail, 2005). All of these purposes are slightly different in meaning for the audience, but what they have in common is that all of them provide a view of the world outside the audience's lived experience. In fact, most of the contact people have with the world outside of their immediate lives comes through mediated communication, which has powerful implications for the organization and functioning of human society. This is because the "reality" that people experience in this way is affected by the symbols they are exposed to and the media through which those symbols come to them. The media organizations that are responsible for creating and delivering symbolic messages are social institutions themselves, with different reasons for existence and different motives for engaging in communication. This means that "mediation is unlikely to be an entirely neutral process. The 'reality' will always be to some extent selected and constructed and there will be certain consistent biases" (McQuail, 2005, p. 85).

HISTORICAL PERSPECTIVES AND ONLINE COMMUNICATION

The characteristics described previously and McQuail's description of the purposes that media fulfill come from a classical view of the mass communication process. However, the development of the Internet has called into question many traditional distinctions attributed to mass communication, and in essence has blurred the lines between mass and interpersonal communication. For instance, it is no longer necessary to have access to a printing press or broadcast facility to reach thousands or even millions of people with a message; Internet apps allow anyone to post messages that can be seen literally around the world by anyone else with access to the network. Some celebrities from the worlds of entertainment, sports, and politics have social media followings in the tens or even hundreds of millions, dwarfing all but the largest legacy media outlets such as broadcast TV channels. The Super Bowl is generally the most-watched television broadcast of the year; in 2020 it had about 100 million viewers (Breech, 2020). By comparison, pop star Katy Perry's 107 million Instagram followers around the same time put her in 20th place on the platform. Soccer star Cristiano Ronaldo was the top individual on the list with 241 million worldwide followers; Instagram's corporate account topped the list at 375 million (Brandwatch, 2020).

The development of two-way, computer-mediated technology in the mid-1990s forced communications scholars to reconsider what was, at that time, the most traditional division in the field: the distinction between interpersonal and mass-mediated communication. Traditionally, research into the connection of mass and personal communication focused on how interpersonal communication reduced or altered impacts of mass mediated communication, such as the two-step flow theory (discussed later in this chapter). More recently, Rafaeli and Sudweeks (1997) studied two threaded-message groups similar to Reddit called Usenet and Bitnet and called them "(either) the largest form of conversation or the smallest form of mass communication." This meant rethinking the defining characteristics of each approach, especially the notion that mass media were strictly a one-way flow. Building on the idea, Reardon and Rogers discussed how distinctions such as number of recipients (traditionally high for mass media, low for interpersonal), and potential for feedback (low for mass media, high for interpersonal) were blurred by computerized two-way communication, noting that "The new interactive technologies have certain of the characteristics of interpersonal channels, and certain of the qualities of mass media channels" (Reardon & Rogers, 1988, p. 297).

The idea of treating the Internet as anything other than a mass medium now seems rather old-fashioned. When the Internet underwent booming growth in the late 1990s, the confusion between mass and interpersonal communication expanded along with it. The Internet "didn't fit researchers' ideas about mass media, locked, as they have been, into models of print and broadcast media," according to Morris and Ogan, who added: "Computer-mediated communication at first resembled interpersonal communication and was relegated to the domain of other fields" (Morris & Ogan, 1996, p. 40). Morris and Ogan were among the first to propose treating the Internet as a mass medium, albeit one that "contains many different configurations of communication" and one that "plays with the source-message-receiver features of the traditional mass communication model, sometimes putting them into entirely new configurations" (p. 42).

In both their traditional formats (such as broadcasting) and these "new configurations" of Internet communication, mass-mediated messages have important characteristics and effects that are worth studying. As the emerging social phenomenon of mass communication evolved in the early 20th century, it was natural for people to wonder about how it was going to affect the society in which it existed. Some of that curiosity turned into more serious, scholarly inquiry, which helped to create the first mass communication theories.

THE DISCIPLINE OF MASS COMMUNICATION

The earliest evaluations of how individuals and society might be affected by mass communication came from existing social science disciplines that, not coincidentally, investigate how people act and interact on the individual level and in social organizations, namely psychology, sociology, and political science. Many of the "founding fathers" (and they were all men) of communication as a field of study were either sociologists or psychologists, and applied their knowledge and skills in those areas to the then relatively new phenomenon of mass communication.

Social Science Roots

On the psychological side, the governing principle was behaviorism, a branch of the science often associated with Ivan Pavlov – famous for his experiments with the salivating dogs – and B.F. Skinner, who applied the principles of stimulus and response to human behavior. Behaviorists say that actions are essentially conditioned responses to external stimuli – including media messages. Sociology contributed the idea of functionalism, which says that social structures and widely adopted social values are the key determinants of a society's organization and operation. In this view, media institutions are part of the social structure and help to maintain or alter social knowledge and social norms.

BOX 2.2

Definition of Functionalism

Functionalism: A sociological theory that the structures of a society – its institutions and organizations, including mass media organizations – play a key role in defining the norms and values of the society and the way people behave and interact within it.

Because they were the tools at hand, these two perspectives were used to analyze the emerging social environment in which mass media could suddenly reach millions of people with the stimuli of identical, simultaneous messages, using the power of the popular press as well as emerging technology, such as radio broadcasts. This analysis led to the logical conclusion that the media must have the potential for effects that were powerful, direct, and uniform (affecting everybody the same). These effects were both on individuals and on the social order as a whole. The fear, of course, was that these could be negative effects. Baran and Davis (2006) call this the "mass society" perspective, and make it the first of five eras they identify. They describe this era as centered on fears that mass media would damage existing social orders, especially by undermining the power of elite individuals within the society and overwhelming older, traditional cultural values that contributed to keeping the social order intact.

Even as this transmission of effects paradigm was taking hold, however, an alternative way of looking at the impacts of the media was beginning to form as well, rooted in the concept described previously about how people interact with symbols to shape their view of the world around them.

Transmission of Direct Effects Paradigm

The widespread view that mass media could exercise a powerful and pervasive influence on those who were exposed to its messages was rooted in several characteristics of the social scene when this view took root in the middle part of the 20th century (Curran, Gurevitch, & Wiillacott, 1982). These factors were:

- Larger audiences than ever before were being exposed to simultaneous identical messages, through the then-new technology of radio broadcasts.
- A perception that other social changes – notably recent industrialization and urbanization that had caused confusion in social roles and changes in social structures – would leave this massive audience susceptible to outside influences.
- Anecdotal evidence that people had been powerfully affected by propaganda during World War I.

Bullet/Hypodermic Theory (1930s)

This process by which media would have these powerful and pervasive effects is often referred to as the bullet (sometimes "magic bullet") or hypodermic needle theory of media effects. The bullet term is attributed to Wilbur Schramm and the hypodermic expression to David Berlo, two icons in the development of communication theory (Severin & Tankard, 2001). Both names for this theory are metaphors for the type of impact a media message was thought to have on its recipients. In other words, the media could "inject" audiences with a message that would immediately, powerfully, directly, and uniformly cause them to adopt a new idea or attitude, like using a hypodermic needle and syringe to inject a substance into the body. The "bullet" image is that if the message hit the target it would have a substantial effect, akin to a shot from a weapon hitting its target.

Implicit in this theory is the assumption that the audience is passive and vulnerable to the actions, and the messages, of the mass media. An often-cited example is the *War of the Worlds* radio broadcast on the day before Halloween in October 1938. Actor/director Orson Welles and a theater troupe created a radio drama built around a supposed invasion of the Earth by people from Mars, based on a story from noted science fiction author H.G. Wells but modified to sound as if it were a news report about an actual event. Millions who heard the broadcast believed the attack was really happening, and the ensuing panic was seen as evidence of the power of radio to affect people's beliefs about a situation.

A group of social scientists from the Radio Research Project at Princeton University investigated the incident, ultimately publishing a book-length report on it. Among their findings were that at least 6 million people heard the broadcast and that more than a million of them were frightened or disturbed by it. The researchers interviewed people who had fled their homes, rescued family members, and took other drastic actions in their terror. In a summary of the project they wrote: "The fact that this panic was created as a result of a radio broadcast is today no mere coincidence ... By its very nature radio is the medium par excellence for informing all segments of a population of current happenings ... and for exciting them to *similar reactions directed toward a single objective*" (Cantril et al. [1947], in Schramm & Roberts, eds., [1971], emphasis added). The italicized portion of the quote illustrates how bullet theory was the operative one behind this research, assuming that a message would have powerful, immediate, direct, and universal effects on those exposed to it. It's worth noting, however, that later research challenged these findings, and that the image of mass panic may be a myth promulgated by newspaper coverage after the broadcast (Chilton, 2016).

It may be tempting to think that the Bullet Theory is still operating in society today. There are examples of powerful influences of the media; witnessing terrorist attacks and natural disasters does move people to action. However, scholars no longer believe that mass communication effects operate in a vacuum – that is, media effects are not thought to be so direct and so powerful that they can, all by themselves, move an individual or an entire society to action. Media effects are the result of a combination of forces, and the evolution of the theories, even at this early stage, shows how media scholars adapted to an understanding of the power of the message.

BOX 2.3

"War of the Worlds"-like Hoaxes in the Internet age

The fictional *War of the Worlds* broadcast in 1938 was likely the first example of a media-generated hoax, perpetrated with the power and reach of radio to help it spread more widely and more believably. A similar event would be unlikely today because the professionalism of broadcast outlets would prevent presentation of such a program, and because if one radio or TV station did try something similar it would be debunked quickly by competing stations.

Such safeguards, unfortunately, don't apply to the Internet, which has become home to some famous (and infamous) hoaxes over the years.

One of the most notable ones, from 2010, was a story about a young woman who supposedly quit her job by emailing a photo sequence to her boss, with all of her office colleagues copied in. The photo series has the woman – identified only as "Jenny" – holding a dry-erase board with a string of messages about why she was leaving. Most of them make critical, yet humorous, comments about her boss, Spencer. It was all a hoax, first published on a humor website. Like the *War of the Worlds* broadcast, it was believed by millions and took on a life of its own. It even drew responses from people offering jobs to Jenny – who was really an actress named Elyse Porterfield (ABC News, 2010).

A hoax that repeatedly crops up on Instagram claims that the platform is about to change its privacy policies in ways that could lead to deletion of a user's information – unless the user re-shares the post. Needless to say, many people do re-share. Other recent Internet fakes included the so-called "broom challenge" and reports about an upscale restaurant in London, England.

The "broom challenge" stemmed from a statement supposedly from NASA about the ability to stand a broom on its bristles – but only on one particular day (February 10, 2020), because of a quirk in the Earth's gravitational field. Viral sharing gave the message wide publicity and on that day people around the Internet, including celebrities and local news personalities, posted videos showing brooms indeed standing on end. The problem? NASA never made such a statement, and the standing brooms had nothing to do with any gravitational oddity. It turns out that, depending on the broom, some of them will stand any time, and others won't. A CBS News reporter proved that by standing up a broom on February 11 and reporting on it (Brito, 2020).

The restaurant hoax was perpetrated by a London resident who created a website for a non-existent restaurant called The Shed at Dulwich and posted fake reviews and photos about it on Trip Advisor in 2017. People from around the world sought reservations – which were always unavailable, thereby adding to the restaurant's mystique. Of course, the reservations were not available because the restaurant didn't exist (Rosenberg, 2017). In an article about the ruse, the creator later explained that he did it to show how easily online ratings such as Trip Advisor's could be gamed, and also how gullible people could be regarding online information (Butler, 2017).

The Internet does seem to be especially fertile ground for hoaxes of these types, which frequently spread through social media. A Syracuse University professor who does research about misinformation says this is because people are primed to believe information they come across that fits with their worldview because of the difficulty of evaluating it on its merits or against some external standard (Martineau, 2019). Where this turns serious, of course, is when this tendency leads people to believe online misinformation about topics such as COVID-19 treatments or the effectiveness of vaccinations. Throughout the COVID-19 pandemic, medical professionals reported difficulty getting some patients to believe accurate information on those topics (Yasmin & Spencer, 2020).

Public Opinion and Propaganda (1920s to 1940s)

Concern with mass media in the era between the world wars was strongly related to the fear that it could arouse emotions that might undermine a democratic society. This fear drove the earliest systematic studies of mass communication. These included the Payne studies at the University of Chicago, which in the 1920s investigated whether film violence could have an effect on children, as well as the propaganda studies conducted by Harold Lasswell and other scholars around the same time.

The study of propaganda is important to the history of the communication field both because it was among the first communication topics to be studied systematically and also because it deals with two issues of ongoing interest, namely attitude change and the effects of communication on individuals and society. Interestingly, many of the views that led to scholarly investigation of propaganda are still held by many people who are quick to "blame the media" for perceived social ills such as permissive sexual practices and violent behavior. The notion that media institutions fulfill a propaganda function lives on in the work of many critical theorists such as Herbert Schiller, Robert McChesney, and Noam Chomsky/Edward Herman, whose works are discussed in more detail in Chapter 5. Widespread misinformation and disinformation online used to shape political opinions has also become an important concern. Researcher Renee

DiResta calls this "computational propaganda," summed up in her phrase that "if you make it trend, you make it true" (DiResta, 2020, para. 9).

An influential 1920s treatise on the topic of media "sway" over public opinion and how it could threaten the social order came not from a scholar, however, but a journalist named Walter Lippmann. Communication scholar James Carey has called Lippmann's *Public Opinion*, published in 1922, the book that founded the field of communication study (Rogers, 1994). Lippmann's thesis was that the understanding people had of reality – what he called "the pictures in our heads" – was an incomplete and fallible one because any individual had a limited range of personal experience and because of the natural limitations of getting information from the media.

According to Lippmann, the volume and complexity of information that would be required to truly understand the outside world made it impossible for people to develop an adequate understanding of it. Lippmann wrote strictly about the influence of newspapers because at the time radio was in its infancy and had not at that point emerged as a news medium; television had not yet been invented. According to Lippmann, newspapers routinely published only a fraction of information that was available to them, and even this limited amount of information was too much for any one person to absorb. (Imagine trying to read every word of even one day's newspaper and remembering all of the important points covered in it.) As he put it: "The real environment is altogether too big, too complex and too fleeting for direct acquaintance. We are not equipped to deal with so much subtlety, so much variety, so many permutations and combinations. And although we have to act in that environment, we have to construct it on a simpler model before we can manage with it" (Lippmann, 1922, p. 16).

For Lippmann, this meant people relied on simplifications such as stereotypes and developed a world view based on exposure only to a limited amount of detail. Thus, he concluded, average people could not form intelligent opinions about public policies or public leadership. The notion that we could have a democracy guided by "public opinion" was a false one and the contemporary fears about the impact of propaganda were realistic ones, in his view. (Lippmann's ideas were a precursor to the agenda-setting theory discussed in Chapter 4.) An alternative view was voiced by pragmatist philosopher and educator John Dewey, who said newspapers needed to move beyond purely reporting events to become vehicles for public education and places for debates that would structure discussion of public issues. According to Dewey, the media's role should be "to interest the public in the public interest" (Baran & Davis, 2006, p. 86). The effectiveness of the media to truly inform and educate as compared to just reducing ideas to soundbites and stereotypes is a matter of debate to this day.

Heightening concerns in the 1920s and 1930s was the observation that mass media, especially radio, could be used as a tool to sway the minds of large segments of the population. The impact of Adolf Hitler's radio broadcasts in Germany were cited as evidence. Social science researchers concerned about the impact of the media on the social order and the prospects for the media to undermine a liberal-democratic society based on personal and political liberty focused their attention on these European propaganda efforts.

Political scientist Harold Lasswell actually took an interest in propaganda well in advance of the Nazi revolution in Germany. He studied propaganda from the *first* World War (1914–1918) from a behaviorist standpoint for his doctoral dissertation and extended the work beyond that, publishing a report in 1927 that defined propaganda as "the control of opinion by significant symbols, or, to speak more concretely and less accurately, by stories, rumors, reports, pictures and other forms of social communication" (Lasswell, 1927, p. 627). Lasswell's view wasn't so much an application of the bullet theory, however, as a psychological analysis based on the use of "master" symbols that have the ability to evoke emotions and actions. Partially echoing Lippmann, he further argued that social disorganization caused by technological advances was responsible for propaganda's taking such a prominent role in modern life. Overall, he took a critical view of the practice of propaganda and concluded that its strong effects posed a potential threat to democratic society.

Research into the practices and effects of propaganda remained popular in the inter-war period. In 1937, not long after Hitler consolidated his power in pre-war Germany, the Institute for Propaganda Analysis was founded. Its stated purpose was to help educate the public about propaganda in order to make people more resistant to its effects. A book published under the auspices of the institute, *The Fine Art of Propaganda*, listed seven devices or techniques used in propaganda expression (Lee & Lee, 1939, in Schramm, ed., 1966, pp. 417–418):

- **Name calling** – giving an idea a bad label to make people reject and condemn it without examining the evidence.
- **Glittering generality** – Associating something with a "virtue word" to make people accept and approve it without examining the evidence.
- **Transfer** – Carrying the authority or prestige of something respected over to something else in order to make it acceptable, or carrying over some sort of disapproval to make people reject and disapprove of it.
- **Testimonial** – Having a respected person say that a particular idea is good, or a hated person say it is bad.
- **Plain folks** – Attempting to convince the audience that the speaker's ideas are worthwhile because the speaker is a "person of the people/common man."
- **Card stacking** – Selecting and using facts and logical or illogical statements to give the best (or worst) possible case for an idea.
- **Bandwagon** – Attempting to convince people that everyone who is of a similar group as they are has accepted the idea.

Propaganda remained a popular topic for scholarly inquiry throughout the 1930s, and even into World War II, when Lasswell directed a project through the Library of Congress to do content analyses of news media of that time for evidence of propaganda (Rogers, 1994). As the war ended, however, scholarly interests turned to other pursuits.

BOX 2.4

Contemporary Use of Propaganda Devices: Donald Trump, Master Propagandist?

FIGURE 2.1 Nominee Donald Trump speaks at the 2016 Republican National Convention in Cleveland. Alex Wong/Getty Images.

Although the negative connotations of propaganda make many people think of totalitarian regimes, use of the "master symbols" identified by Harold Lasswell as the heart of propaganda are readily identified in U.S politics also. One clear example is how politicians use the propaganda devices identified by Lee and Lee in 1939. Donald Trump's 2016 and 2020 presidential campaigns and his presidency in between included clear illustrations of all of these devices (Figure 2.1).

Name calling: Trump made heavy use of insulting labels for political opponents, frequently delivered through his Twitter account. In 2016, candidate Hillary Clinton was labeled "Crooked Hillary," and his 2020 opponent was "Sleepy" Joe Biden. Journalists who wrote unflattering stories about Trump were accused of peddling "fake news" and of being "enemies of the people." Near the end of his term, *The New York Times* listed all of Trump's Twitter insults, categorized alphabetically by topic. Under just "A" they documented more than 150 tweets directed against about 25 people or organizations such as ABC News, CNN reporter Jim Acosta, and Georgia Democrat Stacey Abrams (Quealy, 2021).

Transfer: Trump was well known for his business success, as displayed for ten years on the reality TV show *The Apprentice;* he presented this ability as his main qualification for the presidency. During the 2016 campaign, he said he was such a good negotiator that he would persuade Mexico to build – and pay for – a wall to prevent illegal border crossings. (This didn't happen; U.S. taxpayers funded the portions of the wall that were built.) He made similar claims about negotiating with China, European allies, and other countries to protect U.S. interests.

Testimonial: Getting an endorsement from another respected politician is one of the most common ways candidates build their credibility. For his part, in 2016 Trump earned endorsements from many leading Republican officials, including even some of the candidates he defeated in the primaries. Throughout his presidency he also sought, and received, strong support from Republican allies in Congress and from conservative media outlets such as Fox News.

Glittering generality: Trump campaigned on a promise to "Make America Great Again" in 2016 and to "Keep America Great" in 2020. However, he never explained what qualities embodied greatness or how, specifically, he planned to implement them (in 2016) or sustain them (in 2020).

Card stacking: Trump had a well-deserved reputation for making statements that were inaccurate. The *Washington Post* documented approximately 30,000 mis-statements or outright lies during his four years in office, capped by his repeated claim at the end of his term that he had been defeated for re-election only because of fraud and cheating by the Democrats. (No evidence of that ever was documented.) Even short of complete fabrications, Trump engaged in the more classic version of "card stacking" by presenting favorable facts and ignoring inconvenient ones. For example, as the U.S. economy began to recover from severe job losses caused by the COVID-19 pandemic in early 2020, Trump took credit for improving job creation numbers. Even as this was happening, though, many of the jobs destroyed earlier had not yet been restored. Trump talked only about newly-created jobs without acknowledging that the country still had a net loss of jobs and millions of people were still out of work.

Plain folks: Trump's main appeal was to working-class, older, white voters who feared a decline in their status because of social and economic changes. Even though he was personally wealthy, Trump identified with this group through promises to protect them against anyone who threatened their security and status. This in fact was the heart of his personal and political appeal, something that was largely unrecognized before he was elected in 2016. After he became president, news stories done by reporters dispatched from Washington, D.C. and New York City to the rural Midwest to interview Trump supporters in small-town restaurants practically became a journalistic cliche.

Bandwagon: Early in the 2016 campaign, Trump was not seen as a serious candidate; however, after he won some early primaries, his popularity soared and he became the frontrunner, and eventual winner of the nomination, in true bandwagon fashion. In 2020, he then secured renomination with only token opposition. Even by the time he left office, under the cloud of being the only president ever impeached twice, political polls showed his support among Republican voters remained strong.

Lasswell's Structure and Function (1948)

After World War II ended, several powerful ideas that researchers had begun investigating during the war emerged, giving shape to the study of mass communication and starting to make it into a social science of its own.

Two of these ideas came from Lasswell, whose propaganda studies had a behavioral basis but also embodied sociology's functionalist approach; i.e., that social institutions such as the media had specific roles or functions that contributed to the overall operation of the society. Functional analysis often focuses on how individuals are affected by broader social forces, generally through a positivist approach that applies the scientific method to human behavior. (A discussion of positivism and communication research is found in Chapter 7.) Applied to media analysis, this became a search for factors such as message or source characteristics that could predict or explain the effects of a message on its audience (Rubin, 1986).

In an influential 1948 article, Lasswell identified the media's roles as:

- **Surveillance** of the environment, which discloses threats and opportunities affecting the community and its components.
- **Correlation** of various parts of society in responding to that environment.
- **Transmission** of cultural heritage from one generation to the next (Lasswell, 1948, in Schramm & Roberts, eds., 1971, p. 98).

Building on Lasswell's work, Charles Wright later added a fourth function of **entertainment** that is usually addressed along with the first three identified by Lasswell to create a four-function typology of the functions of media in modern society.

In the same 1948 article that laid out these functions of the media, Lasswell described also the basic form of "an act of communication" as having the following pattern:

- Who
- Says What
- In Which Channel
- To Whom
- With What Effects

This simple formulation was extremely influential because in it Lasswell managed to identify various parts of the structure of communication that could be used as points of entry for scholarly inquiry on a functionalist basis: the originator of the communication (who), the message itself (what), the medium of communication (channel), the audience (whom) and, perhaps most significantly of all, the impact that these four components could have (effects). Lasswell was not the only theorist in the post-war era seeking to describe the shape of the processes used for communication, however.

BOX 2.5

Media Functions and Sports Reporting

FIGURE 2.2 Photo by dennizn, via Shutterstock.

When people use television, radio, print or online publications, and mobile apps to follow their favorite sports teams, they employ all four functions of the media as identified by Lasswell and Wright:

Surveillance: This function refers to using the media to gather the basic facts about the team's performance. How did the team do last night? Did it win or lose? Were any key players injured, or did any return from injury? Did any of the fan's favorite players have a really good game?

Correlation: How does the surveillance information matter to the fan's (or, in this case, the team's) position in society? How did last night's results relate to the season's overall performance? Did the team solidify its place in the standings? Did it secure a playoff berth?

Transmission of cultural heritage: Following a team through the media teaches non-fans, casual fans, and even hard-core fans more about the sport itself, from terminology to rules to historical performances. When current performances break records set by great players in past seasons, the transmission function recalls the heritage of the game. Longtime fans also love to trade stories about team legends from the past, and many teams have multiple generations of fans from families in their communities.

Entertainment: This is perhaps the most obvious and extensive function of the media for sports fans, who watch their teams on TV, follow them in print and online publications, participate fan forums on the Internet, listen to and call in to sports-radio discussion programs, and maybe even take part in fantasy leagues.

Shannon and Weaver's Information Theory

Another idea that helped to shape the emerging paradigm as one of message transmission that affected recipients came in 1949 from two researchers at Bell Labs, Claude Shannon and Warren Weaver. Their model also can be analyzed from the functionalist perspective because, like Lasswell's inventory, it seeks to break down communication into a series of steps that each contribute to the overall process and can be analyzed individually with regard to audience implications and effects.

The Shannon-Weaver model, as it has come to be known, was really meant to apply to transmission of electronic signals, such as the electromagnetic waves that carry telephone conversations or radio and television broadcasts. It was extended to apply to the information process more generally because it was a simple yet powerful way of deconstructing communication into several recognizable parts:

- **Source**: Originator of the communication.
- **Message**: Content of the communication.
- **Channel**: Means of carrying the communication.
- **Receiver**: Recipient of the communication.

This was a major step forward in communication research because "more than any other theoretical conceptualization, [Shannon and Weaver's model] served as the paradigm for communication study, providing a single, easily understandable specification of the main components in a communication act" (Rogers, 1994, p. 438).

In the scientific paper that proposed this model, Shannon and Weaver introduced several other concepts that also were rapidly incorporated into the field of communication study, again extending beyond their intended purpose of describing electronic signal transmission. One was the concept of noise, which is anything that can corrupt the message along the way. In the original formulation, "noise" resulted from electromagnetic interference with the signal and a loss of signal strength over distances. Another concept Shannon and Weaver introduced is a definition of information as "reduction of uncertainty." A message with a high level of information was one that left nothing to chance – no uncertainty – on the part of the receiver. Shannon and Weaver actually sought to quantify the amount of additional "information" that the signal would need to carry in order to overcome a specific amount of interference with a mathematical formula based on statistical probability; this is why they called their idea the "mathematical theory of communication."

For a good modern example of both of these concepts, think of a poor cell phone connection – which of course actually does come from corruption of the electronic signal carrying the call. Anyone who has ever had a conversation when the call signal was breaking up has experienced "noise" in the channel and a corresponding reduction of information/increase in uncertainty: "What did you say? When do you want to meet?" The concept of noise is further extended in the rhetorical tradition to anything that interferes with the reception of a message, such as a speaker's PowerPoint slide with text that is too small to be read from the back of the room or a cell phone that rings during a lecture, distracting the audience and interrupting the speaker. Similarly, students who use their cellphones in class are voluntarily injecting a lot of noise into the communication stream by distracting themselves from the classroom activity, and therefore are certain to take less information away from the lesson.

Another concept Shannon and Weaver's model used was redundancy, which was a way to overcome noise and improve the overall reliability of the message reception. In the poor cellphone connection example, "redundancy" can be taken very literally. One or both parties in that situation will need to deliver redundant messages – that is to say, they repeat themselves – in order to make sure all of the information they are trying to convey makes it to the other caller.

Cybernetics

Another mathematically-based conception for understanding communication as a systematic process grew out of the work of Massachusetts Institute of Technology professor Norbert Weiner, who developed mathematical modeling of feedback within a system. Feedback can be defined as "control of the future conduct of a system by information about its past performance" (Rogers, 1994, p. 397). A home thermostat is a simple form of feedback system control, since it monitors the system's past performance (indicated by how warm or cool the house is) to direct future operation (turning the furnace on when the house cools and turning it off again when a certain temperature is reached). When a system is changing or in flux, feedback can either amplify the change or suppress it. Continuing the example, the goal of a thermostat is to keep the house at a fairly constant temperature, which is done by minimizing (or suppressing) the change in temperature. The science of developing systems that use feedback to regulate themselves became known as cybernetics. As applied to communications, cybernetics says that the communication process in a social system can lead to stability or instability of that system by amplifying or countering disruptive changes. Taken together, the ideas from Shannon and Weaver, Weiner, and Lasswell became a form of systems theory about how mass media could affect society. Recall that functionalism says that social structures are related to the stability and the orderly operation of a society, and that media organizations are one of the social structures that have an impact on this; information theory and cybernetics helped to define the way these impacts happened.

BOX 2.6

Shannon and Weaver Model

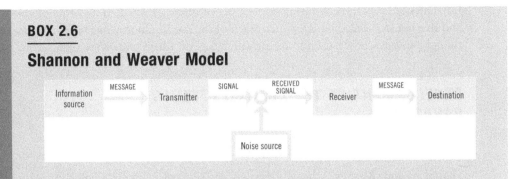

FIGURE 2.3 Source: From C. Shannon and W. Weaver, The Mathematical Theory of Communication (Urbana: University of Illinois Press 1999), p. 98. Copyright 1949 by the Board of Trustees of the University of Illinois. Reprinted with permission of University of Illinois Press.

Parts of the Process: Shannon and Weaver's Model

Shannon and Weaver's model helped solidify the "transmission" paradigm through the terminology it introduced that identified specific parts of the act of communication:

Source: Origin of the communication.

Message: The substance of the communication itself.

Channel: Means through which the communication is carried.

Receiver: Destination of the communication.

Noise: Anything interfering with proper receipt of the communication.

Redundancy: Characteristics that compensate for noise or add to information (see next definition).

Information: Perhaps the most difficult part of Shannon and Weaver's model to conceptualize because "information" has nothing to do with the content of the message. Rather, it is a characteristic of the message, defined as "reduction of uncertainty" with regard to the communication. A message with high information value is one with a low level of uncertainty and thus a greater likelihood of being understood. Low information, of course, is the reverse: A message with high uncertainty because of noise or other factors.

Summary of the Transmission of Direct Effect Model

The idea that messages are transmitted, received, and have an effect on people was the dominant paradigm in communication theory through the middle part of the 20th century. It started with the study of propaganda's supposed effects on people throughout both world wars and continued with Lasswell's formulation that separated the communication process into functions that the media served, also ending with the notion of effects. In similar fashion, Shannon and Weaver's model was based on information transmission. Thus, the transmission model of direct effects had all of its pieces in place, and this era stood as the high-water mark of the paradigm in which media messages were thought to have powerful and direct influences on those who were exposed to them.

DEVELOPMENT OF THE LIMITED EFFECTS PARADIGM

Empirical Studies in Social Psychology

Shannon, and Weaver, who were engineers trained in physics, brought a perspective from the natural sciences to the definitions of communication as an ongoing process and its constituent parts. Lasswell was a political scientist who employed the socio-logical theory of functionalism. Around the same time that they were contributing their ideas to the emerging communication paradigm, some social scientists also were making investigations that applied new techniques for social science research to the task, especially from the developing area of social psychology. For the most part, these investigators were setting out to determine whether the perceived effects of mass media exposure really were as powerful as the assumptions about propaganda effects and the bullet theory/transmission theory predicted they would be. Could news in the media have an impact on whom people would select as their leaders in a society? Were people truly as vulnerable to propaganda as the theories suggested? If so, did this mean the United States could succumb to totalitarian demagoguery as the German nation had?

Hovland and the Experimental Section (1940s)

Perhaps the first true "test" of the effectiveness of persuasive messages such as propaganda came from a series of psychological experiments done on U.S. Army soldiers during World War II. Carl Hovland, a psychologist from Yale University who worked in the research branch of the War Department (now known as the Department of Defense), was assigned to evaluate soldiers' reactions to motivational films called the *Why We Fight* series. These were documentaries produced by famous Hollywood director Frank Capra that were designed to help new recruits, especially draftees, understand the rationale for the war.

To measure effectiveness of the films, Hovland designed a classic experiment in which some soldiers were exposed to certain stimuli (certain films) while others were not; the attitudes of both groups were then measured by having them fill out questionnaires. In the end he reached a curious conclusion, considering the prevailing theories and what he and the Army officials thought he would find. After viewing the films, the experiment subjects knew more about the basis of the war, so there was an effect on their knowledge level. The films, however, didn't appear to have much impact on the men's motivation to serve as soldiers; in some experiments, the motivational levels of soldiers who had not seen the films were nearly identical to that of soldiers who had been exposed to them. This in turn led Hovland to conclude that facts don't change attitudes.

However, the experiments also controlled for other message characteristics, such as the credibility of the source and whether the film presented one or both sides of an argument of which it was trying to persuade the viewer. Some of these characteristics were found to affect the persuasiveness of the appeal. Hovland's wartime investigations thus helped to undermine the bullet theory and assumptions behind propaganda theory, but also provided an intellectual and theoretical basis for studies of persuasion that are still used, and are discussed in more detail in Chapter 3.

Lazarsfeld and the Bureau of Applied Social Research (1940s–1950s)

Like his contemporary Hovland, sociologist Paul Lazarsfeld set out to measure the effects of a medium on an audience, in this case radio. Lazarsfeld first came to communication research as head of the Radio Research Project of Princeton University (which also was behind Cantril's *War of the Worlds* project described previously). After World War II, Lazarsfeld became director of the Bureau of Applied Social Research at Columbia University, which became the pre-eminent sociological research organization of its time. From 1937 through 1960, scholars associated with the bureau produced 52 books as well as 350 scholarly articles, book chapters and other publications (Rogers, 1994). The bureau's work also contributed to the advancement of quantitative methods in social science research, especially the use of surveys.

Several of the bureau's projects were focused specifically on the impacts of mass communication, notably studies of media influences on voters in Erie County, Ohio, during the 1940 presidential race and in Elmira, New York, for the election in 1948. The results of this research were published as books in 1944 and 1952, respectively. Further insight was drawn from a study done in Decatur, Illinois, about what influenced homemakers' attitudes toward certain household products. That one was published in 1955. Each of these projects began as a test of the influence that mass media – newspapers and radio – would have on decisions made by members of the communities under study. All of the projects concluded that the direct effects of the media were less than the researchers had hypothesized, and far less than would be predicted by the prevailing theories of the day.

Lazarsfeld designed the 1940 voting study with an assumption that the media would be key influencers of people's decisions. It used a panel design, with the same people interviewed repeatedly throughout the project to evaluate their initial viewpoints and any changes they underwent. Ultimately, however, only 54 of 600 people who were interviewed switched their views of the candidates from the beginning to the end of the study. In his discussion of the study, Rogers says that "Lazarsfeld concluded the media had minimal effects on the 1940 presidential election campaign" (1994, p. 288). The Decatur study resulted in a book titled *Personal Influence: The Part Played by People in the Flow of Mass Communication*. In this book Lazarsfeld and co-author Elihu Katz concluded that "messages in the mass media provided information to many individuals, but it was when this information was transmitted from one individual to another as personal influence that individuals were motivated to make decisions and take action" (Rogers, 1994, p. 298).

Two-Step Flow and Reinforcement Theories (Late 1950s)

The term "two-step flow of information" was originally used in the book about the 1940 voting study (called *The People's Choice*, written by Lazarsfeld with two co-authors). But Elihu Katz, who was Lazarsfeld's collaborator on other studies including the Decatur one, popularized the concept later when he wrote a summary of several works done by the

Bureau of Applied Social Research. In an influential article titled "The Two-Step Flow of Communication," he reviewed the Ohio, Elmira, Decatur and some other studies and said all of them demonstrated that information is gathered and analyzed by opinion leaders who pass on the information and opinions from the media to others in their social circles. In the article, Katz concluded that opinion leaders and those they led through the two-step flow process of opinion formation usually were not that different from one another and that what opinion leaders tended to do was "focus the group's attention on some related part of the world outside the group, and it is the opinion leader's function to bring the group into touch with this relevant part of its environment through whatever media are appropriate" (Katz, 1957). It was thought that the opinion leader had greater access to mass communication, but much of the research centered on trying to discover the characteristics that distinguished these leaders from those who followed them.

Another summary was provided by Joseph Klapper, who said that the media tended to reinforce existing ideas and attitudes rather than create or shape them directly. Klapper started by describing the current state of media research at the time (the late 1950s), noting how researchers and the general public were confused by inconclusive and contradictory studies. He argued that communication research to that point in time suggested that the media were just one of many things that influenced people: "Mass communication does not ordinarily serve as a necessary and sufficient cause of audience effects, but rather functions through a nexus of mediating factors. These mediating factors are such that they typically render mass communications a contributory agent, but not the sole cause, in a process of reinforcing the existing conditions" (Klapper, 1960, p. 8).

Klapper called this the "phenomenistic" view of communication effects, because it was an "assessment of the role of that stimulus [of the media] in a total observed phenomenon" (Klapper, 1960, p. 5). It has become better known by the more recognizable term "reinforcement theory" because Klapper also concluded that research showed "mass communication is in general more likely to reinforce the existing opinions of its audience than it is to change such opinions" (1960, p. 49).

BOX 2.7

Updating the Two-Step Flow

The two-step flow theory of Lazarsfeld and Katz was more or less replaced by diffusion of innovations theory (discussed in Chapter 4), and made further obsolete by greater media access by the general public. The original formulation assumed not everyone would have extensive access to mass media, and that people therefore would pay the most attention to messages referred to them by an influential person rather than ones they heard directly. However, once everyone had a television set people no longer relied on "opinion leaders" to receive and then spread the news.

But two-step flow may have some renewed relevance in understanding sharing of news on social media platforms.

When President John F. Kennedy was assassinated in 1963, the vast majority of people found out about it from another person (Greenberg, 1964). However, the earliest information about the September 11, 2001 terror attacks on the World Trade Center and the Pentagon reached people directly from a news source. About 62 percent of the people who knew about the attacks within an hour of when they happened found out from TV, radio or the Internet. About 97 percent of the people surveyed had learned of the attacks within three hours, and about half of them got their information from the media (Kanhian & Gale, 2003).

Social media sharing of news is turning around this dynamic. According to a 2020 study by the Pew Research Center, about 53 percent of Americans reported they either "sometimes" or "often" receive news from referral on social media sites. The most sharing comes from the largest platform – Facebook – but others in the mix are YouTube, Twitter, Instagram, Reddit, Snapchat, LinkedIn, TikTok, and WhatsApp (Shearer & Mitchell, 2021).

According to an earlier piece of Pew research, social media sites are now more popular than newspapers for news access (Shearer, 2018). This survey showed that television (49 percent), news websites (33 percent), and radio (26 percent) were the three most popular ways Americans accessed news. Social media (20 percent) moved ahead of newspapers (16 percent) for the first time.

BOX 2.8

Reinforcement and Political Echo Chambers

Joseph Klapper's summary of a decade's worth of research concluded that the media are most successful at reinforcing attitudes people hold rather than creating new ones. It's sometimes called phenomenistic theory, since it describes a social impact that results from a shared life experience, called phenomenology. In this case, the shared phenomenon is exposure to a particular medium. (Phenomenology is discussed in more detail in Chapter 9.)

This reinforcement effect can be observed with special prominence among politically conservative media because of a tendency of those with conservative political views to consume media that reflect their existing outlook. This can be done on television (Fox News, Newsmax, One America News Network), radio (hosts such as Michael Savage and the late Rush Limbaugh), and the Internet (Breitbart, InfoWars, Gateway Pundit, and similar sites). These media create a reinforcing system – sometimes called the "echo chamber" effect – in which material reported in one place is presented in others, adding exposure and perceived credibility to particular facts and viewpoints. The conservative political views of the audience are, as Klapper theorized, reinforced by repeated exposure to the shared conservative ideas.

This was documented in some detail by Benkler, Faris, and Roberts (2018), who analyzed the online referral networks among these conservative outlets to demonstrate that their audiences relied heavily on them – and them alone, without getting information from non-conservative sources such as broadcast network television or national newspapers. The analysis found that "media producers and social media users on the right read, share, and quote almost only right-oriented media... the further right a site is the more attention it gets" (p. 56). Further, within this right-wing ecosystem, "false narratives that reinforce partisan identity not only flourish but crowd out true narratives" (Benkler et al., 2018, p. 39).

Partisan media can be found on the other end of the political spectrum also, including television (MSNBC) and online (Huffington Post and Talking Points Memo blogs). The liberal media network, though, is not as extensive and overlapping as the conservative one. Also, according to Benkler et al., these sites are integrated into a media ecosystem that is much more resistant to promoting false partisan narratives because it includes a wider range of perspectives and more outlets, such as national newspapers, that emphasize a fact-based approach.

INTERPRETIVE THEORIES AND NORMATIVE PERSPECTIVES

The early research into mass communication discussed so far in this chapter – whether touting the influence of media institutions and messages or reporting on their limitations – largely took the functionalist perspective of media organizations as social institutions that perform certain activities *within* society with resulting consequences *for* society. Another group of sociologists approached the question of mass media and society from a different perspective – one rooted in the idea that human communication involves symbolism and how people react to the symbols around them.

Symbolic Interactionism

This approach looks at social organization literally from an opposite perspective from functionalism. Rather than analyzing society "top down," from the viewpoint of social structures and their impact on people, the way functionalism does, this other approach, known as interactionism, considers the way that individual human beings react to their surroundings and others around them. It is rooted in the pragmatic philosophy espoused by John Dewey and George Herbert Mead. According to this theory, most of the information people receive about the world around them and most of the reactions that they have to that information involves communicating with symbols – mostly words and images. This has become known as symbolic interactionism, a term coined by Herbert Blumer, who studied with Mead at the University of Chicago and continued his work.

Lindlof defines symbolic interactionism as "the study of how the self and the social environment mutually define and shape each other through symbolic communication" (Lindlof, 1995, p 40). In other words, the way people react with and through symbolic communication is how society and culture are formed. "The symbolic interactionist emphasizes that all that humans are, can be traced to their symbolic nature. ... We see, we think, we hear, we share, we act symbolically ... It is through symbolic interaction with one another that we give the world meaning and develop the reality toward which we act" (Charon, 2001, p. 89). Sociologists Berger and Luckmann (1967) built upon this idea with a theory they called the social construction of reality that described how situations created by social interaction come to be seen as "objective" and "real" – in other words, come to be seen as if they were something other than human creations. This was the forerunner of a research approach known as media ecology, which is explored further in Chapter 5.

Normative Views of Media and Society

While social scientists were trying to ascertain how mass communication practices affected audiences and society at large, other ideas were emerging about what role and impacts mass media should have, ideally, on society. These ideas fall into the realm of normative theory, which seeks to define and identify what norms or values are optimal for social progress and development.

Marketplace of Ideas

The most influential normative theory of the media in the U.S. tradition is based on freedom of expression, as embodied in the First Amendment. In its purest form, this is a normative theory known as libertarianism, or absence of restraint on the media and imposition of as few restraints as possible on other parts of society as well. The philosophy that led the framers of the Constitution to address freedom of the press in a legal sense is rooted in the idea that personal liberty entails various related social and political freedoms, including:

- Social mobility (as opposed to an aristocratic system of nobility and peasantry).
- Self-determination (democratic representative government).
- Free and open economic systems (market capitalism).
- Free expression in which all voices could be heard, resulting in a marketplace of ideas among which people can choose what they wish to believe.

All of these are part of what Thomas Jefferson, in writing the Declaration of Independence, called "certain inalienable rights" and summarized as "life, liberty and the pursuit of happiness."

Fourth Estate Theory

Freedom of expression is inseparable from these other social and political freedoms because it is closely related to social development, which is supported by new ideas being introduced into society, and also to self-governance. Free expression is a requirement for self-governance because it facilitates how people know enough about actions and policies of elected officials when it's time to vote (Kostyu, 2006). Accordingly, the media in general and journalism in particular have a special role in helping democracy to succeed. The relationship is summed up in Thomas Jefferson's frequently cited quote that "The basis of our government being the opinion of the people, the very first object should be to keep that right; and were it left to me to decide whether we should have a government without newspapers or newspapers without a government, I should not hesitate a moment to prefer the latter" (Emery, 1962, p. 167).

The media are expected to fill the Fourth Estate's functions of serving as a "government watchdog" and providing accurate, credible, relevant and sufficient information that becomes the basis for public opinion. This has been summarized by one pair of analysts as, "Civilization has produced one idea more powerful than any other – the notion that people can govern themselves. And it has created a largely unarticulated theory of information to sustain that idea, called journalism" (Kovach & Rosenstiel, 2001, p. 193).

These normative theories are related to some of the ideas about epistemology explored in Chapter 1. In this case, however, what matters could be called public epistemology, or how people come to know what they need to know (individually and collectively) for society to function properly. Some of this knowledge comes from experience, but mostly it comes from authority. Any single individual can't experience everything everywhere and must rely on reports, such as those in the news media, to know certain public facts. For example, an investor needs to know what stock prices are. A student needs to know whether the rules for taking out or repaying student loans have changed.

Fourth Estate theory says public epistemology is most relevant with regard to political information, an idea that is closely related to the work of a mid-20th century political philosopher and legal scholar named Alexander Meiklejohn. In a book called *Free Speech and Its Relation to Self-Government* (Meiklejohn, 1948) and in other publications, he made the point that the First Amendment guarantees the political freedom of the people of the United States by ensuring that they are presented with open discussions of all issues, even from unpopular viewpoints. The value in free speech, therefore, is that it produces informed voters.

Building from this, Gans (2003) describes press and politics as following a four-part process in which: (a) journalists inform citizens; (b) citizens are assumed to be informed if they pay attention to the news; (c) better-informed citizens are more likely to participate in politics; and (d) more citizen participation will improve democracy. More succinctly, in a comment that echoes Jefferson's adage, Gans notes that "The democratic process can only be truly meaningful if citizens are informed. Journalism's job is to inform them" (Gans, 2003, p. 1).

Social Responsibility and Theories of the Press

With these historical roots, libertarian theory and the marketplace of ideas provide the dominant normative theory for how people think about the media in U.S. society. During the 1940s and '50s – at around the same time that social scientists such as

Lazardsfeld were investigating the impacts of emerging mass media on society – debate began to arise about just how well Fourth Estate theory was working, just how free the media ought to be, and whether there might be such a thing as too much freedom of the press. (Note that because this concerns the issue of what *should* happen or how things *could* be organized for the best results, it's considered normative theory.)

In the mid-1940s, a panel of distinguished media experts was convened to consider the role of the press in American society. This body's formal name was the Commission on the Freedom of the Press, but came to be known as the Hutchins Commission after its chairman, University of Chicago Chancellor Robert Hutchins. After nearly two years of meetings, it issued a book-length report in 1947 that in essence developed a new normative theory for the press that moved away from the libertarian ideal. While acknowledging that the First Amendment meant the press was supposed to be free of government controls, the commission also said the press had a responsibility "for making its contribution to the maintenance and development of a free society" (Blevins, 1997). Consequently, the commission said newspapers also should provide:

- A truthful, comprehensive account of the day's events in a context which gives them meaning.
- A forum for the exchange of comment and criticism.
- A means of projecting the opinions and attitudes of the groups in a society to one another.
- A way of reaching every member of the society by the currents of information, thought, and feeling which the press supplies.

These purposes for the media came to be known as "a social responsibility theory," one of four such theories of the press elaborated upon a few years later by another group of scholars. Fred Peterson, Theodore Siebert, and Wilbur Schramm's landmark *Four Theories of the Press,* published in 1956, described a continuum of normative theory on press freedom and social (government) control, ranging from:

- **Libertarian model,** which was an absence of government control in order to foster growth of a marketplace of ideas. This approach is often associated with the United States, because of the First Amendment. Even the U.S. system has formal and informal restraints, though, so a "pure" libertarian model really doesn't exist other than in theory.
- **Social responsibility model,** in which the media exercise self-restraint to promote a diversity of viewpoints and promote social norms, but allowing for government regulation, if necessary, to limit the most dangerous impulses of a totally libertarian approach. The United States is generally thought to fit the social responsibility model because the media are constrained to act more responsibly by a combination of voluntary practice and limited government regulation. For example, federal telecommunication laws require that broadcast licensees operate "in the public interest, convenience and necessity." As part of this, Federal Communications Commission (FCC) guidelines on indecent content limit what can be presented on the public airwaves and companies that violate them face

sanctions. A television station in Roanoke, Va. was fined $325,000 by the FCC when it aired a sexually explicit video clip of an adult film website during a news broadcast (Johnson, 2015). U.S. media also follow voluntary guidelines directed toward social responsibility, such as the Motion Picture Association of America movie-rating code, the Entertainment Software Rating Board (ESRB) labeling of video games, and television ratings that work in conjunction with a TV set V-chip to block certain types of content if programmed to do so. Taken together, these examples illustrate a set of practices, both voluntary and government mandated, that are designed to promote the socially responsible outcome of preventing inappropriate material from reaching young audiences. Another important constraint on media content that serves the public interest is that media outlets in the United States can be held legally accountable for their actions if they publish material that is defamatory to subjects or infringes on their privacy. While the US system is oriented toward social responsibility, European models of state-chartered broadcasters, such as the British Broadcasting Corporation and media regulation provided by the European Union, are often said to be even stronger examples of this normative theory. This is discussed further in Chapter 6.

- **Authoritarian model,** in which the government controls the press through censorship and licensing. Historically, this had been the most common model from the rise of monarchies and nation states until the emergence of more libertarian approaches in the late 1700s. Authoritarian control also existed in the modern era, such as in Nazi Germany. Even today, countries such as China, Syria, and Iran are known for the tight leash they keep on the media.

- **Totalitarian model,** which has some similarities with the authoritarian approach in that it has strong state control over the media. It goes beyond regulation to include state ownership and operation of media outlets to use them as propaganda tools. Siebert, Peterson and Schramm's book (in a chapter written by Schramm) referred to this as the Soviet model because it had its purest application in the Soviet Union from the 1950s through the 1980s (Siebert, Peterson, & Schramm, 1956). During this time, the leading news sources from that country were the Communist Party newspaper *Pravda* (Russian for "Truth") and the news agency TASS, which was run by the government. Both existed to support the state by promoting its point of view. Good current examples of a similar approach are North Korea and Myanmar.

(The Four Theories of the Press also serve as the basis for a popular set of comparative international media models, and are reviewed in that context in Chapter 6.)

Of the four, the one that is thought of as most significant (in some ways, normative) is social responsibility. This is so because of a general belief that if the media did not behave responsibly for themselves, the government should have the ability to get involved to encourage or force that behavior. "Social responsibility theory holds that the government must not merely allow freedom; it must actively promote it" (Siebert et al., 1956, p. 95). The goal should be to develop a media system that would serve the public interest. In many respects, the notion that broadcast regulation and licensing are designed to serve "the public interest, convenience and necessity" is an example of government involvement to help ensure the media operate in this manner.

BEYOND THE EARLY THEORIES

The field of communication study and the theories associated with it are relatively recent developments in the scholarly world, and they coincide with the emergence of the electronic mass media in just the past 100 years. The beginnings of communication study can be traced to influential work in related disciplines of psychology, political science, and sociology that sought to evaluate how mass media affected individuals and society at large.

Rogers traces the field's formal beginnings more specifically to the University of Iowa in 1943. He writes that "Inauguration of the first communication Ph.D. program in a school of journalism … directly led to the division of the communication field into two sub-disciplines: mass communication and interpersonal communication" (Rogers, 1994, p. 17). With its "genetic roots" in other social science fields, the new discipline took on a largely quantitative spirit focused on the effects of mass media and their messages on audiences. The emergence of a systems model, effects-based paradigm of inquiry in the late 1940s amplified the empirical research trend established earlier by such founders of the field as Lasswell (content analysis), Hovland (psychological experiments), and Lazarsfeld (survey research).

The field evolved in this direction for the next 40 years to the point that in 1987, two influential researchers could proclaim that an era of "communication science" had been established. They defined this new "science" as one that "seeks to understand the production, processing and effects of symbol and signal systems, by developing testable theories, containing lawful generalizations, that explain phenomena associated with production, processing and effects" (Berger & Chaffee, 1987, p. 17). Berger and Chaffee acknowledged other social science fields as providing the roots for communication as a discipline, but added that "in the past two decades … an increasing number of communication researchers have advanced their own theories for testing instead of relying on work in allied disciplines" (1987, p. 16). Many of those theories, which emerged in the 1960s and 1970s, are the basis of the next two chapters in this book.

However, in the generation of communication research that came before the one Berger and Chaffee were describing, conclusions about the nature and power of those effects underwent a pendulum swing, or possibly an actual paradigm shift. Spurred by the work of empirical researchers over a 30-year period from the 1920s to the 1950s, the early view that media have massive, powerful, immediate, universal, direct effects on audiences gradually shifted to the view that they have little to no direct effects, which is quite a contrast. Klapper (1960) concisely summarized the principles of the limited effects paradigm as being that (1) the media rarely have a direct influence on individuals; (2) rather, this influence follows a two-step flow; (3) most people's lives have other influences upon them that cause them to reject or modify what they think about most messages from the media; and (4) when media effects do occur, they will be modest and isolated.

Lazarsfeld perhaps deserves the most responsibility for the change. "Early propaganda theorists championed the powerful mass media, but later communication scholars did not find evidence of such strong effects when they investigated the impacts of the media in voting behaviors, consumer decisions and other types of behavior change. ... The voting study [by Lazarsfeld in 1940/44] launched the era of limited effects in mass communication research" (Rogers, 1994, p. 287).

Later research – in the era described by Berger and Chaffee – was successful in demonstrating that neither the direct effects posture nor the limited effects one was correct, and many modern scholars see both views as exaggerated with the truth lying somewhere in the middle (Perry, 2002). The early view *overestimated* media effects based on assumptions without much detailed research, while the empirical view *underestimated* them, partly because of limitations inherent in the research styles. Hovland's experiments involved before-and-after questionnaires of subjects viewing 50-minute films, while many of the Bureau of Applied Social Research studies were short-term projects, lasting just a few weeks or months. Later scholars said these research designs may not have allowed enough time or collected enough data to evaluate media impacts sufficiently. Media influences simply may take longer to make their effects known than can be measured in a short-term experiment or snapshot survey, or may have influences that are largely indirect and thus not captured by the survey instruments.

The new generation of media researchers described by Berger and Chaffee came on the scene just when it appeared that "limited effects" was taking hold as a paradigm; a famous 1959 article by Bernard Berelson said communication research was destined to become moribund and "wither away." Berelson reached this conclusion by arguing that the research programs of the early investigators such as Lasswell and Lazarsfeld had slowed down as evidence accumulated about a lack of direct media effects, and no new ideas were emerging to replace them. Starting in the early 1960s and picking up momentum in the 1970s, a new generation of researchers developed new theories and validated them using some of the empirical procedures pioneered by the World War II generation, as well as more sophisticated ones. Doing this, they demonstrated that within certain boundaries and under certain conditions, media could indeed have short-term and long-term influences on individuals and on society at large.

This is the modern era (or contemporary paradigm) of moderate effects, and consists of a large body of active and productive theories that mostly follow one of three major threads:

1. Theories associated with how people perceive, use and understand information as it comes to them through the media as just one of many behavioral stimuli. This is related more closely to the psychological component of communication science's roots as pioneered by the work of people such as Hovland and Klapper. It focuses on individual effects and on audiences as active users of media content and is discussed in more detail in Chapter 3.
2. Theories associated with the impact of media outlets and institutions on social realities based on what information is presented and how it is presented. These theories largely extend from the functionalist perspective that drove so much of the original research in the field to describe, predict, and explain media influence at an institutional level on large groups or toward the society as a whole, and are covered in Chapter 4.
3. Theories associated with audience constructions of social realities based on information they obtain from the media. This viewpoint incorporates ideas of

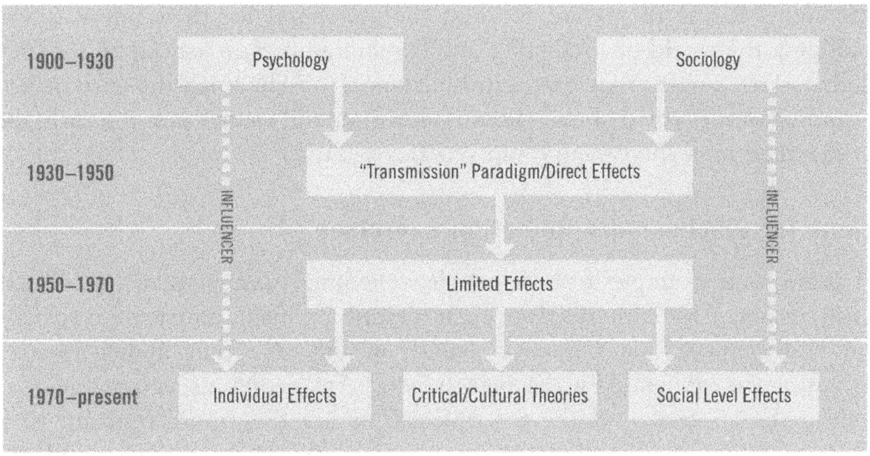

FIGURE 2.4 Chart showing theory evolution.

symbolic interactionism and perspectives known as the "ritual view" of communication (Carey, 1989) and the social construction of reality (Berger & Luckmann, 1967). Research in this tradition takes a more holistic view of media's effects on society and culture, using qualitative rather than quantitative inquiry, and the "critical" view that issues of power, ideology and social reform should be first and foremost in media study. It is covered in Chapter 5.

CONCLUSION

Research into mass communication and the development of communication as a scholarly discipline are relatively new. They have primarily developed in just the past few decades, compared with natural sciences that are thousands of years old and even most social sciences that are a few hundred years old.

It is noteworthy to recognize that all three of what are now the most active threads of mass communication research have their roots in the ideas developed in the mid-20th century. (See Figure 2.4). The direct effects/transmission paradigm was the first to emerge, and the limited effects paradigm replaced it as researchers sought to validate the original paradigm and found they couldn't. The limited effects tradition, in turn, was questioned by researchers who thought that saying the media have no influence on individuals or society was too doctrinaire or too simplistic. Through research, scholars explored these theories and tried to validate them but ended up with different theories that updated the field instead. At the same time, more interpretive approaches also were emerging to challenge the dominant paradigm of mass communication research's earliest decades.

From this perspective, the field's earliest ideas (such as the bullet theory) can be seen as analogous to the Ptolemic view of the Earth-centered universe. In other words, these theories are obsolete by current standards of knowledge, but still deserve respect and attention because they were the best tools at hand for their times as ways of understanding the world or predicting and explaining certain aspects of it. They also provided a starting point that has been built upon to help reach the current levels of understanding of the world of mass communication, and elements of the early theories can be identified in current theory and practice today.

Questions for Discussion/Application Exercises

1. What are some examples of how people sometimes presume that the bullet theory is still an operative and effective one in describing media impacts on society?
2. The bullet/hypodermic theory is based on the idea that audiences are very susceptible to influence by the mass media. Are people as vulnerable – and as likely to be affected – as the theory says, or are they more resistant to media influence? Cite at least three examples from the current media and cultural landscape that illustrate or support your point.
3. Lasswell and Wright defined the four functions of the mass media as surveillance, correlation of individuals' responses to the world around them, transfer of cultural values, and entertainment. Come up with three to five different examples of each of these functions "in action."
4. Think about your own news gathering and sharing habits. How much of it involves social-media referral as predicted by the two-step flow theory? Are you more of an information follower of what others share, or more of an opinion leader, finding and sharing things yourself?
5. Is it fair or unfair to label communication efforts of the government and other powerful institutions in U.S. society to support their positions as propaganda? Why or why not?

REFERENCES

ABC News. (2010). Whiteboard hoax. *ABC News*. Retrieved from http://abcnews.go.com/Technology/hoaxed-woman-quit-job-dry-erase-messages-fake/story?id=11374956

Baran, S., & Davis, D. (2006). *Mass communication theory: Foundations, ferment and future* (4th ed.). Belmont, CA: Wadsworth.

Benkler, Y., Faris, R., & Roberts, H. (2018). *Network p[ropaganda manipulation, disinformation, and radicalization in American politics*. New York: Oxford University Press.

Berger, C.R., & Chaffee, S.H. (1987). The study of communication as a science. In Berger, C.R. & Chaffee, S.H. (Eds.). *Handbook of communication science* (pp. 15–19). Newbury Park, CA: Sage Publications.

Berger, P., & Luckmann T. (1967). *The social construction of reality*. New York: Anchor Books.

Blevins, F. (1997). The Hutchins Commission turns 50: Recurring themes in today's public and civic journalism. Paper presented at the Third Annual Conference on Intellectual Freedom, April 1997, Montana State University-Northern. Retrieved from http://mtprof.msun.edu/Fall1997/Blevins.html

Brandwatch. (2020). The top 20 most followed Instagram accounts. Retrieved from https://www.brandwatch.com/blog/top-most-instagram-followers/

Breech, J. (2020, Febuary 5). 2020 Super bowl ratings revealed: Chiefs-49ers ranks as the 11th most-watched show in TV history. CBS Sports. Retrieved from https://www.cbssports.com/nfl/

news/2020-super-bowl-ratings-revealed-chiefs-49ers-ranks-as-the-11th-most-watched-show-in-tv-history/

Brito, C. (2020, Febuary 11). What is the broom challenge? Internet hoax sweeps social media. CBS News. Retrieved from https://www.cbsnews.com/news/broom-challenge-nasa-internet-hoax-02-11-2020/

Butler, O. (2017, December 6). I made my shed the top-rated restaurant on TripAdvisor. And then served customers frozen dinners on its opening night. Vice. Retrieved from https://www.vice.com/en/article/434gqw/i-made-my-shed-the-top-rated-restaurant-on-tripadvisor

Cantril, H. (1947). The invasion from Mars. In Schramm, W. & Roberts, D. (Eds.). (1971). *The processes and effects of mass communication* (revised edition) (pp. 579–595). Urbana, Ill: University of Illinois Press.

Carey, J. (1989). *Communications as culture*. New York: Routledge.

Charon, J. (2001). The importance of the symbol. In O'Brien, J. & Kollock, P. (Eds.). *The production of reality: Essays and readings on social interaction* (3rd ed.) (pp. 89–96). Thousand Oaks, CA: Pine Forge Press.

Chilton, M. (2016, May 6). The war of the worlds panic was a myth. *The Telegraph*. Retrieved from http://www.telegraph.co.uk/radio/what-to-listen-to/the-war-of-the-worlds-panic-was-a-myth/

Curran, J., Gurevitch, M., & Woollacott, J. (1982). The study of the media: Theoretical approaches. In Gurevitch, M., Bennett, T., Curran, J., & Woollacott, J. (Eds.). *Culture, society and the media* (pp. 11–29). London: Meuthen & Co. Ltd.

DiResta, R. (2020). Computational propaganda. Yale Review. Retrieved from https://yalereview.yale.edu/computational-propaganda.

Emery, E. (1962). *The Press and America: An interpretive history of journalism* (2nd ed.) Englewood Cliffs, NJ: Prentice Hall.

Gans, H. (2003). *Democracy and the news*. New York: Oxford University Press.

Greenberg, B.S. (1964). Diffusion of news of the Kennedy assassination. *Public Opinion Quarterly* 28 (2), 225–232.

Johnson, T. (2015). FCC Slaps Virginia TV Station With $325,000 Indecency Fine. Variety online. Retrieved from https://variety.com/2015/biz/news/fcc-slaps-virginia-tv-station-with-325000-indecency-fine-1201458034/.

Kanhian, S.F., & Gale, K.L. (2003). Within 3 hours, 97 percent learn about 9/11 attacks. *Newspaper Research Journal* 24 (1), 78–91.

Katz, E. (1957). The two-step flow of communication, republished. In Schramm, W. (Ed.) (1966). *Mass Communications* (2nd ed.) (pp. 346–365). Urbana, Ill: University of Illinois Press

Klapper, J.T. (1960). *The effects of mass communication*. New York: Freedom Press.

Kostyu, P. (2006). The First Amendment in theory and practice. In Hopkins, W.W. (Ed.). *Communication and the law 2006 edition* (pp. 23–41). Northport, AL: Vision Press.

Kovach, B., & Rosenstiel, T. (2001). *The elements of journalism: What newspeople should know and the public should expect*. New York: Crown Publishers.

Lasswell, H. (1927). The theory of political propaganda. *The American Political Science Review* 21 (3), 627–631.

Lasswell, H. (1948). The structure and function of communication, republished. In Schramm, W. & Roberts, D.F. (Eds.). (1971) *The processes and effects of mass communication* (revised edition) (pp. 579–595). Urbana, Ill: University of Illinois Press.

Lee, A.M., & Lee, E.B. (1939). The devices of propaganda. In Schramm, W. (Ed.) (1966). *Mass communications* (2nd ed.) (pp. 417–418). Urbana, Ill: University of Illinois Press.

Lindlof, T.R. (1995). *Qualitative communication research methods*. Thousand Oaks, CA: Sage Publications.

Lippmann, W. (1922). *Public opinion*. New York: Harcourt, Brace and Co.

Martineau, P. (2019, August 22). Why people keep falling for viral hoaxes. Wired online. Retrieved from https://www.wired.com/story/why-people-keep-falling-viral-hoaxes/

McQuail, D. (2005). *McQuail's mass communication theory* (5th ed.) London: Sage Publications Ltd.

Meiklejohn, A. (1948). Free speech and its relation to self-government. New York: Harper Brothers.

Morris, M., & Ogan, C. (1996). The Internet as mass medium. *Journal of Communication* 46 (1), 39–50.

Perry, D. (2002). *Theory and research in mass communication: Contexts and consequences.* Mahwah, N.J.: Lawrence Erlbaum Associates.

Quealy, K. (2021, January 19). The complete list of Trump's Twitter insults (2015–2021). New York Times online. Retrieved from https://www.nytimes.com/interactive/2021/01/19/upshot/trump-complete-insult-list.html#

Rafaeli, S., & Sudweeks, F. (1997) Networked interactivity. *Journal of Computer Mediated Communication* 2 (4). Retrieved from http://www.ascusc.org/jcmc/vol2/issue4/rafaeli.sudweeks.html

Reardon, K., & Rogers, E. (1988). Interpersonal vs. mass media communication: A false dichotomy. *Human Communication Research* 15 (2), 284–303.

Rogers, E.M. (1994). *A history of communication study: A biographical approach.* New York: The Free Press.

Rosenberg, E. (2017, December 8). 'The Shed at Dulwich' was London's top-rated restaurant. Just one problem: It didn't exist. Washington Post online. Retrieved from https://www.washingtonpost.com/news/food/wp/2017/12/08/it-was-londons-top-rated-restaurant-just-one-problem-it-didnt-exist/

Rubin, A.M. (1986). Uses, gratifications and media effects research. In Bryant, J., & Zillman, D. (Eds.). *Perspectives on media effects* (pp. 281–301). Hillside, NJ: Lawrence Erlbaum Associates.

Severin, W., & Tankard, J. (2001). *Communication theories: Origins, methods and uses in the mass media* (5th ed.). New York: Addison Wesley Longman.

Shearer, E. (2018, December 10). Social media outpaces print newspapers in the U.S. as a news source. Washington, DC: Pew Research Center. Retrieved from https://www.pewresearch.org/fact-tank/2018/12/10/social-media-outpaces-print-newspapers-in-the-u-s-as-a-news-source/.

Shearer, E. & Mitchell, A. (2021, January 12). News use across social media platforms in 2020. Washington, DC: Pew Research Center. Retrieved from https://www.journalism.org/2021/01/12/news-use-across-social-media-platforms-in-2020/.

Siebert, F.S., Peterson, T., & Schramm, W. (1956). *Four theories of the press: The authoritarian, libertarian, social responsibility, and Soviet communist concepts of what the press should be and do.* University of Illinois Press.

Yasmin, S., & Spencer, C. (2020, August 28). 'But I Saw It on Facebook': Hoaxes are making doctors' jobs harder. New York Times online. Retrieved from https://www.nytimes.com/2020/08/28/opinion/sunday/coronavirus-misinformation-faceboook.html

CHAPTER 3

The Individual Perspective on Mass Communication Theory

This chapter will:

- Introduce the theories that focus on the individual's relationship to the mass media.
- Define key terms associated with the psychological tradition and consider how these theories are impacted by mass media.
- Focus on key theories of the active audience including:
  - Uses and gratifications.
  - Media system dependency theory.
- Examine selective processes and media effects on attitudes and behavior including:
  - Social learning theory.
  - Schema and information processing theory.
  - Third person effect.
  - Hostile media effect.
- Examine models of attitude change with special relevance to mass media:
  - Social judgment theory and source credibility.
  - Maguire's information processing model.
  - Elaboration likelihood model.

Chapter 2 introduced the beginnings of research and theory in mass media, so that, by the end of the 1950s, the field was firmly established as a discipline. While the early theories laid the groundwork for the move from the powerful effects to the limited effects and then to the more moderate effects perspective (refer to Figure 2.4 in Chapter 2), several paradigms were evolving at the same time. While the discipline was establishing its own scholars and body of research, it continued to borrow from allied fields in the social sciences.

This chapter examines the theories that focus primarily on the impact that mass media has on individuals. Some of these theories actually began as psychological or interpersonal communication theories and are only by extension related to the mass

DOI: 10.4324/9781003121695-3

media. Others were specifically developed as a response to the impact the media was seen to have in society. While these theories look at media effects on individuals, the subtext is that these individuals will, in turn, impact the societies in which they live. Some overlap will inevitably be apparent between these theories and those in the next chapter, which specifically addresses the sociological perspective.

Communication theory can be traced back more than 2,000 years to Aristotle's *Rhetoric*, which formed the basis for many theories of public address and persuasion that have evolved over the centuries since his time. Aristotle is considered to be the father of public speaking. While his "mass" communication involved delivering speeches to large live audiences in amphitheaters (without the benefit of microphones and sound systems), significant elements of Aristotle's rhetoric can be seen in communication today. Most prominent among them is the concept of persuasive communication. Aristotle was basically concerned with persuasion, i.e., how can a speaker get an audience to agree with or buy into his message? According to Aristotle's theory, the concepts of *ethos* (credibility), *pathos* (emotion and passion), and *logos* (facts and evidence) must be present for a message to be successful. The same central focus on persuasion is true of most communication today, particularly communication in the mass media. Advertisers are trying to persuade consumers to buy their products or services using *ethos* (attractive people with white smiles to advertise a new toothpaste); public relations practitioners persuade various publics to support their organization or cause using *pathos* (images of families waiting in line for food to illustrate the need to increase funding for SNAP benefits); and social media sites strategically place messages specifically targeted to individual users using *logos* (data charts that show how the corona virus is spreading to different parts of the world). Executives at television networks and streaming services scramble to find the shows that will appeal to the largest audiences – they, in essence, persuade us that their programs are the best to watch (and then, in turn, persuade the advertisers to buy time on their networks or persuade the consumer to subscribe to their service). News organizations are persuasive in their editorial opinion content as well as news placement and features designed to attract readers. Persuasion is at the heart of the mass media.

Also in the tradition of Aristotle, the early theories of mass media were characterized by a focus on the messages that were sent out. Mass communication was generally viewed as one-way: Messages were sent out from a source to a "mass" audience, which was seen as a homogeneous group of message-receivers. Message reception was conceived of as affecting all audience members in essentially the same way. As was noted in Chapter 2, propaganda theory supposed that the media would be influential in changing audience members' attitudes, and the bullet theory predicted powerful and uniform reactions to messages as was seen with the *War of the Worlds* broadcast. However, when Carl Hovland researched the effectiveness of propaganda films to change World War II soldiers' motivation, he found little effect from one-sided messages. Hovland completed some groundbreaking research documenting some of the means by which messages had persuasive effects, for example, the impact of the credibility of the source of a message. Lazarsfeld's voting and consumer-research studies provided further evidence that perhaps media effects didn't happen in the dramatic ways that the early theories had originally proposed.

A turning point in communication research came in 1959 with Bernard Berelson's famous essay on "The State of Communication Research," in which he maintained that great ideas that had given the field vitality over the previous 20 years had "worn out" and no new ideas had emerged to take their place (Berelson, 1959, p. 6). While the concept of no new ideas in an academic field was, of course, unlikely, Berelson gave communication scholars license to take their research in another direction. Elihu Katz responded by proposing that the field move away from its media-as-persuasion focus and instead ask the question, what do people **do** with the media (Katz, 1959)? This was the first formal call to a shift in focus, an active audience-centered focus.

THE ACTIVE AUDIENCE

On May 25, 2020, George Floyd, a 46 year-old Black man, died in Minneapolis, Minnesota, after being handcuffed and held on the ground as a white police officer kept his knee on Floyd's neck. While bystanders recorded the scene, Floyd was repeatedly heard saying "I can't breathe" in the eight minute and 46 second video. Floyd had been accused of passing a counterfeit $20 bill, which led to the encounter with police. When an ambulance arrived on the scene, Floyd was unresponsive and later pronounced dead at the hospital.

The following evening, protests began in Minneapolis with some protesters vandalizing police cars with graffiti, and police used tear gas and rubber bullets to disperse the crowds. Some local businesses were set on fire. The National Guard was activated to quell the violence.

Over the following days, protests erupted in many U.S. cities, including New York City, Atlanta, Los Angeles, Memphis, Chicago, and Louisville, as well as Washington, D.C. In addition to protesting the killing of Mr. Floyd, protesters also marched against the killings of Breonna Taylor, a young EMT in Kentucky, killed while she slept with her boyfriend when police tried to serve a warrant at the wrong house, and Ahmaud Arbery in Georgia. Arbery was shot while jogging through a white neighborhood when two white men accused him of theft.

These incidents led to a resurgence of the Black Lives Matter protests reminiscent of the marches that had taken place years before when other Black men were killed at the hands of white police officers. While most of the protests were peaceful, there was sporadic violence, looting, injuries, and even deaths. The hashtag #BLM went viral, and not just across the United States. Marches broke out across the United Kingdom and all of Europe, as well as Africa, Asia, and all of North and South America. A group of workers at McMurdo Station in Antarctica took part, making the protests active on all seven continents.

During focus groups with students at the authors' institution, many described how they learned of and followed the movement on social media with the hashtags #BlackLivesMatter #BLM #SayHerNameBreonnaTaylor #breonnataylor #nojustice-nopeace #GeorgeFloyd #icantbreathe, and others. Most students were quite familiar with the marches and knew the details of what led to the protests. They found out through a combination of news sites and friends that they followed, mostly on Instagram. In addition, some who lived in cities where protests were taking place actually joined in the marches.

FIGURE 3.1 A Black Lives Matter protest in Cincinnati. Julian Wan/Unsplash.

The data supports the viral nature of social media around these issues. Twitter reported 390 million tweets about Black Lives Matter between May 25 and June 15, 2020 for the U.S. alone (Bianchi, 2020). Vox reported that Instagram had shifted its focus to social justice issues, leading to a change in the platform. Civil rights groups have intentionally been using the platform to mobilize their followers into action. In three weeks, the Black Lives Matter Los Angeles account went from 40,000 followers to 150,000 (Stewart & Ghaffary, 2020). TikTok was also featuring videos supporting the movement and even providing advice to protesters (Janfaza, 2020).

These hashtags on social channels help users tap into an online community of like-minded individuals with a focus on these issues. Even with social media, a medium geared toward passive involvement scrolling through posts, audience members can take an active posture in their consumption by deciding whom to follow. This concept of the active audience is addressed by a number of popular theories.

Uses and Gratifications

"It's a dialogue, not a monologue, and some people don't understand that. Social media is more like a telephone than a television." - Amy Jo Martin, CEO, Digital Royalty.

"For decades, media companies have largely controlled the tools through which consumers were told what to buy, wear, or think. Now consumers possess the same ability to produce, distribute and curate content and distribute it to their peers in real time across social media platforms." -Simon Mainwaring, CEO, We First, Inc.

The quotes above illustrate social media's impact on the audience in comparison to traditional media, and research over the past two decades has taken this into account. Although Katz's response to Berelson was seen as a defining moment in the development of new theories, as early as the 1940s some researchers had begun to consider the kinds of gratifications an audience received from exposure to mass media. Herta Herzog is often credited with the first such study, in which she interviewed 100 radio soap-opera fans to find out why so many housewives were attracted to soap operas. She was able to identify three primary reasons – emotional release, opportunities for wishful thinking, and obtaining advice. Herzog didn't try to measure the influence of soap operas on women, just gather their reasons for listening (Lazarsfeld & Stanton, 1944, pp. 23–25). While other researchers of her time followed similar research designs with other media choices, the examination of uses and gratifications failed to dislodge the limited effects paradigm in any meaningful way. The descriptive, qualitative nature of the research, which did not examine the psychological origins of the needs being gratified, failed to generate much support within the research community. (Differences between quantitative and qualitative research are addressed in detail in Chapters 7, 8, and 9.)

In order to provide more theoretical rigor to this line of research, Katz, Blumler, and Gurevitch described five elements of the uses and gratifications model:

1. The audience is conceived of as active...an important part of mass media use is assumed to be goal directed.
2. In the mass communication process, much of the initiative in linking need gratification with media choice lies with the audience member.
3. The media compete with other sources of need satisfaction.
4. Many goals of mass media use can be derived from data supplied by individuals themselves...they can report their interests and motives.
5. Value judgments about the cultural significance of mass communication should be suspended while audience orientations are explored (Katz, Blumler, & Gurevitch, 1974, pp. 21–22).

Considerable energy and controversy were directed at the first two points, the notion of the active audience and the assumption that people are very deliberate in their use of media most of the time. For example, do people consciously choose every television or streaming program they watch? Rather, do they sometimes use the computer or TV as background noise, or pay attention to only a fraction of what's on and ignore the rest, or let algorithms suggest what they should watch? Some research has described television viewing as ritualistic and habitual, a passive activity requiring little concentration (Severin & Tankard, 2001, p. 298). If some of these concepts are applied to present-day use of social media, it is clear that much of it comes from habit. Students will deliberately seek out YouTube videos on subjects that interest them, such as cooking shows or sports updates. After (and sometimes during) class, students habitually pull out their phones and check Twitter, Snapchat, or Instagram, skimming quickly through their feeds to see if anything of interest has popped up since the last time they checked.

Several different ways of thinking about media and audiences emerged from the research and writing on the uses and gratifications perspective. Katz, Gurevich, and Haas (1973) put the needs into five categories:

1. Needs related to strengthening information, knowledge, and understanding, called cognitive needs. For example, a student might check the weather on the local news station's website or a weather app to find out how to dress for tomorrow's football game.
2. Needs related to strengthening aesthetic, pleasurable, or emotional experience, or affective needs. For example, a fan of hip hop music might subscribe to the weekly feed of her favorite DJ on Spotify, so she can listen during her cardio workouts.
3. Needs related to strengthening credibility, confidence, stability, and status, which combine cognitive and affective needs into something known as personal integrative needs. Students are encouraged to read advice from sites such as *Inc., Forbes,* and LinkedIn prior to job interviews, so they increase their confidence going into a stressful interview situation.
4. Needs related to strengthening contacts with family, friends, and the world, which are called social integrative. At the author's campus (and, it is reported, at other schools) students gather in the TV lounges of residence halls to watch the reality show *The Bachelor* and its spinoff *The Bachelorette.* Men and women follow the show on social media and even place bets on who will and won't receive a red rose. Gatherings to watch the Super Bowl, the NCAA March Madness tournament, and the National Basketball Association playoffs are also examples of these social interactive need-based experiences.
5. Needs related to escape and tension release, which weaken contact with self and social roles. Students frequently report that they go to YouTube at the end of a stressful day and watch whatever might pop up in their feed to relax. This might include a music video by a favorite artist, a cooking or make-up tutorial, or clips from late-night comedy shows.

While research strategies are discussed in detail in Chapters 8 and 9, it is important to note here that the uses and gratifications research was controversial from the beginning for two reasons:

1. The classic research methodology was based in the behaviorist tradition, which meant researchers learned the answers to their questions by studying stimuli and responses. The new research model required that people respond to surveys, which seemed too subjective for the tastes of some scholars who thought it was impossible for people to accurately and objectively "self-report" their own behaviors. Moreover, the way people's uses and needs were categorized was also seen as too descriptive and too subjective, and not based on scientific procedures (since the questionnaires suggested the categories used).
2. Research on media *uses* was confused with Lasswell and Wright's depiction of media *functions* (which are discussed in Chapter 2). The four elements that Lasswell and Wright labeled – surveillance, correlation, transmission, and entertainment – were the *functions or goals* of the media industries. However, the media *uses* that emerged

were too similar to the functions and made it difficult to focus on the active audience, rather than the media purpose (Baran & Davis, 2006, pp. 264–265).

These concerns about uses and gratifications research have persisted over the years. However, as the limited effects paradigm waned, several developments made the audience-centered research more popular:

- New survey research methodologies became available that gave survey results more credibility.
- Researchers began to realize that media uses might have an impact on media effects.
- There was a growing concern that all the effects research focused only on the negative aspects of the media (Baran & Davis, 2006, pp. 268–269).

Furthermore, newer media technologies, especially social media, have only increased the control that audience members have over the media they consume, control that becomes more apparent with each passing technological development. Note that there was a time when there were only three major television networks playing on only one television set in a typical American household – with no remote control. Most college students' grandparents and even some of their parents can remember a time like that. Fast-forward 40 years to the explosion in media availability, choices, and delivery. Beyond television remotes and more channels, audience members can control what they see by skipping through commercials and watching their favorite programs whenever they want, not on a network's time schedule, and not necessarily on a television. Consumers can download podcasts and videos and take their favorite programs with them, or stream media directly from music-sharing and video sites, while sharing their own videos with the world on YouTube or TikTok. As a result, many students report that they rarely watch television, instead streaming programs on their phones or laptops. Media researchers have had to adjust to the changing media landscape, and to take notice of the active audience and the role it plays in determining what it consumes, when, and how. For example, new survey techniques make it easier to participate in research surveys about products, services, and even political candidates. Many websites include a pop-up box asking visitors to take a survey at the conclusion of their visits. Major League Baseball now allows fans to vote online for their favorite players to participate in the All-Star Game – a total of 35 times! On Twitter and Facebook survey participants can not only have their opinions registered, but they can instantly see how many others agree with their perspective.

While changing media technologies have increased the complexity of doing research on media choices and the active audience, they have also allowed for some new research venues. In one study, Ferguson and Perse studied college students' use of the web in comparison to their use of television. They found that, after using the web for school work, students used the web most often for entertainment, for playing games, and browsing sites for fun. This use of the web for diversion predicted accurately that it might compete with or even displace television (2000, pp. 168–169). The authors suggested that television networks expand their web presence, which has clearly happened in recent years. For example, entire series of television shows can be viewed online, and network-affiliated streaming services like CBS's Paramount Plus, , NBC's Peacock, and Disney Channel's Disney Plus are increasing in popularity. Students report that during the global pandemic when so much learning moved online, they used their computers a lot more for entertainment rather than switching to their phones after they completed class or their homework.

Carolyn Lin conducted research to examine how advertisers can use internet-based venues more effectively. In two separate studies, she found that the motivation of users to access online services must be considered in deciding whether to select television vs. online media for advertising dollars (Lin, 1999, 2001). In fact, Lin's subjects reported that online services were capable of satisfying a wide range of needs including surveillance, social interaction, entertainment, and escape (2001, p. 32). Lin concluded that advertisers needed to get more intentional about their research in order to better target their budgets to take advantage of online opportunities. This has clearly happened with the growth of advertising analytics and targeted ads on Facebook and Twitter, for example, but fails to explain how a senior college professor's Hulu stream continuously ran ads for baby formula during her shows.

Thomas Ruggiero predicted that while researchers will continue to ask the same questions – why do people use a particular medium and what do they get from it? – the uses and gratifications theory will need to be expanded to include new concepts related to the transforming technology of the internet. The theory must be modernized by considering factors such as the high level of interactivity, the interpersonal aspects of this mass medium, computer-mediated social networks, and 24-hour retrieval and exchange of information and ideas (Ruggiero, 2000, pp. 28–29). It appears that this research adaptation is already under way. For example, Whiting and Williams (2013) conducted in-depth interviews with users of social media and were able to identify ten uses and gratifications, many of which overlapped with those described previously but also included convenience and expression of opinion. While the subjects' ages ranged from 18–56, Facebook was the social media tool mentioned most often in this study. Sundar and Limperos (2013) reviewed uses and gratifications research conclusions mainly from the first decade of the 21st century, and noted that what was referred to as "the audience," is more likely now to be referred to as "users" (p. 505). They make the case that technology has had such a huge impact on the users that researchers must expand their views of usage categories (especially in new vs. traditional media) to be more dynamic and detailed. Some of these technology-related categories might include realism, community building, dynamic control, and filtering/tailoring, among others. They recommend that future researchers develop a survey instrument to include these new category refinements (p. 522).

Uses and Gratifications continues to be a popular theory underlying much of the research in this area, and not just in communications. In a study reported in the *International Journal of Information Management*, Ifinedo (2016) surveyed university students in the U.S., Canada, Mexico, and Argentina about their needs to adopt new social networking sites. His results confirmed that the uses and gratifications categories of self-discovery, entertainment value, social enhancement, and maintaining interpersonal connections were positively related to their adoption of social networks.

More recently, Perks and Turner (2018) analyzed focus groups of students who listened to podcasts on a regular basis to determine their reasons for listening and what they feel they gain from the experience. They found that students use podcasts to displace other media because it aids them in multitasking and also is more customizable than other media. As a result, podcasts help listeners feel more productive as they can exercise while listening and also learn something along the way. Students also felt that they forge connections with hosts and other listeners as part of the podcast experience.

At about the same time that uses and gratifications was emerging, another theory that supports the active audience framework was being developed – media systems dependency theory.

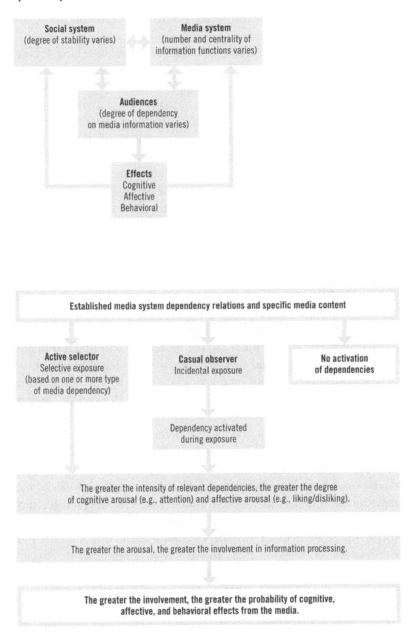

FIGURE 3.2 Media System Dependency.

Media System Dependency Theory

A farmer in Kansas hears of an approaching tornado and needs to know if he should move his livestock. A school principal in Florida knows that a hurricane is brewing in the Atlantic Ocean and has to decide whether to send the children home from her school early. A salesperson in Chicago sees traffic backed up on I-90 for miles and contemplates whether to alter his route. A college student in Buffalo wakes up to an ice storm and needs to find out if classes are cancelled. Each of these individuals, facing a potential, life-affecting crisis will most likely turn to the media as a source of information and advice.

In times of turmoil and uncertainty, the media become a valued source – at times the only source – of information. This is the basis of the Media Systems Dependency Theory, developed by Ball-Rokeach and DeFleur (1976). It is termed a *systems* theory because it examines the relationship among social systems, media systems, and audiences, and how each of those interact with and affect one another. At the same time, media systems dependency theory really focuses on individuals and how dependent they are on the media as a way to understand media effects (Ball-Rokeach & DeFleur, 1976, p. 5). In fact, Baran and Davis define the theory as: "the idea that the more a person depends on having needs gratified by media use, the more important the media's role will be in the person's life, and therefore, the more influence those media will have" (Baran & Davis, 2006, p. 324). College students whose smartphones are always within reach can identify with a certain level of media dependency. Similarly, most communications professors are dependent upon the media to deliver course content, via computer projection systems, interactive websites, course management systems (such as Blackboard or Canvas), or even podcasts. These are ways that faculty depend on the media to help them perform their jobs and stay in contact with their students. The key to understanding the theory, however, is realizing that the more people become dependent upon a medium, the more they will find it influential in their lives. Thus, media dependency and media effects are inextricably linked.

Perry has noted that as society increases in complexity, media perform a greater number of functions, and people tend to become more dependent upon them. This dependency increases even further in times of conflict and change (Perry 1996, p. 60). Many people's dependence on the media was demonstrated on and shortly after the terror attack on the World Trade Center in New York on September 11, 2001. When they first learned of the terrorist attacks on the World Trade Center and the Pentagon, most people responded by immediately turning to their televisions (social media was in its early stages at the time). Regular programming was pre-empted for days on most networks. Hindman (2004) studied public approval of both the media and the president following the September 11 attacks. He found at the time that the public tended to turn to the media in times of crisis to help resolve some of the uncertainty and ambiguity surrounding a catastrophic event. Further, the public appreciated the media's role in both providing information and communicating the human impact of the tragedy. At the same time, while President George W. Bush's approval ratings soared after September 11, partisan differences regarding the president also became more firmly entrenched. As Perry predicted, even when the country became temporarily united, disruptions in the social system actually intensified the media effects (Perry, 1996, p. 40).

Almost 20 years after the September 11 attacks, the U.S. was impacted by a group of radical extremists attacking and attempting to take over the U.S. Capitol as it was certifying the election of Joe Biden for president. The attackers were supporters of President Donald Trump who maintained, without evidence, that he had been the real winner of the election, and encouraged the attack. While research has not been done on the incident at the time of this writing, citizens found out about the violent incident through alerts on social media news sites, email blasts, interruption in regular programming, and, apparently more frequently, texts and Instagram posts from their friends and family. The authors of this book, actually working on the manuscript at the time of the event, found out through multiple alerts on their phone and smart watch, then turned to YouTube streaming and cable news for more information.

While studies using dependency theory have continued over the past decades, it is sometimes studied in conjunction with other theories to determine media effects – for example, Wang and Yang (2007) studied media dependency and certain obsessive personality traits in a study of online shopping behavior among Chinese students. At the same time, social media has opened new doors for research – for example, Lee (2011) conducted a content analysis of YouTube user comments following the death of pop star Michael Jackson. He found that YouTube actually facilitated the grieving process for Jackson's fans by allowing them to share their emotions with others and seek additional information (p. 472). Such a broadening of perspective has allowed media dependency wider applicability and broader explanatory power, which are, after all, key functions of a good theory (as described in Chapter 1).

In an examination of media dependency and the COVID-19 pandemic, Muñiz (2020) surveyed 630 citizens in Mexico about their media dependency and their perception of risk regarding the virus. He found that consumption of television and online news sites as well as Facebook seemed to generate an increase in risk perception of contracting the corona virus (p. 13). At the same time, interpersonal and social channels seem to encourage less of a risk perception and warrant further study.

Both uses and gratifications and media system dependency theory rely on the concept of the active audience to explain their influence. The next section will look at theories that evolved from psychology which, while still examining the impact on the individual, take a less audience-centered approach.

INDIVIDUAL INFLUENCES ON MEDIA EFFECTS

Perception and Selection

Karen Kelly came to St. John Fisher College from Ilion, New York, population 7,800. The total enrollment of Ilion's combined junior/senior high school at the time was slightly more than 730. To her, Fisher was a big school (3,000 students) in a big city (Rochester, 200,000 people). Sharif Farag came to Fisher from the borough of Queens in New York City, where he attended Forest Hills High School, with 3,800 students in the high school alone. To Sharif, Fisher was a small school in a small city. Karen and Sharif had totally different perceptions of the exact same place. Why? It's clear that their different backgrounds and different experiences gave them different views of the same place. That is the essence of the process of perception and the related concept of schemas.

Perception can be likened to a filtering process. While thousands of stimuli vie for our attention at any one time, humans have a finite capability for processing information from those stimuli. Thus, people employ filters that allow them to pay attention to some stimuli and not to others. Perception allows a student to focus on reading a textbook and block out other stimuli such as the hum of the overhead fluorescent lights, the feeling of his body pressing against the chair, the assignments in other courses waiting to be done, or the phone call from his mother that he needs to return. Obviously, some students are more successful at this filtering process than others. Some students can write a coherent paper while texting with friends, listening to music streaming from their laptops, keeping an ear out for a food delivery, and enjoying a double latte, while others need total freedom from distractions in order to concentrate (which is why most college libraries have "quiet" floors). Whatever the tolerance of individuals, the ability to focus on specific stimuli and tune out others is one characteristic that distinguishes all humans.

The process of perception works differently in different individuals. In addition to being from different high schools in different environments, Karen and Sharif come from different cultural backgrounds and are different genders. Some factors that account for these perceptual differences include:

- Biological differences.
- Cultural differences.
- Different socializing environments.
- Different education levels.
- Different religious backgrounds.

The above list can probably be collapsed down to a single factor: Experience. No two people perceive the world in exactly the same way because no two people (even identical twins) have had exactly the same experiences. These perceptual differences manifest themselves in a number of different ways. A student from New York City may find Rochester warm and welcoming, or may feel stifled by the "small town" environment. A student from a rural town may find Rochester big and exciting or overwhelming in its size and diversity. It all depends on the individual's perceptions. While perception comes from personal experiences, perceptual processes also affect the way individuals respond to messages in the mass media. James Potter describes three different perceptual channels that might be used:

- The **automatic** perceptual channel, in which message elements are perceived but processed automatically in an unconscious manner – for example, while scrolling through their Twitter feeds, most people noticed some posts include the words, "Download now." They know those tweets and links are there, but, as a rule, are not really paying attention to these paid ads.

- The **attentional** perceptual channel, in which message elements are processed consciously – for example, after making a purchase on eBay, a student might see an email confirmation pop up in his inbox and note that, but feels no needs to open the message and read it.
- The **self-reflexive** perceptual channel, in which people are consciously aware not only of the elements in the message, but also of their processing of those elements – for example, during a commercial break in the "bombshell" interview featuring Oprah Winfrey with Meagan Markle and Prince Harry, a teaser for the local news reports a huge accident that has closed down a local highway. A student who takes that road to get to her internship the following morning pays attention and reminds herself to check out social media for an update after the program (Potter 1999, pp. 236–237).

Potter's typology of perceptual channels is difficult to verify empirically through research. Psychologists have, however, described several selective processes that can have an impact on how individuals are affected by the media. Joseph Klapper, who is discussed in Chapter 2 for his work with the limited effects perspective, was among the first media scholars to describe these processes in terms of mass communication. In 1960, Klapper wrote:

> …People tend to expose themselves to those mass communications that are in accord with their existing attitudes and interests. Consciously or unconsciously, they avoid communications of opposite hue. In the event of their being nevertheless exposed to unsympathetic material, they often seem not to perceive it, or to recast and interpret it to fit their existing views, or to forget it more readily than they forget sympathetic material (Klapper, 1960, p. 19).

More than half a century later, it's still easy to identify with these sentiments. Klapper was describing selective exposure, selective retention, and selective perception. By and large, people choose media messages that are in agreement with their prevailing attitudes and interests – selective exposure. A politically conservative student might watch Fox News, while a politically liberal student might watch MSNBC. People also seem to remember media messages that agree with their attitudes and interests – selective retention. A student listening to a speech by the college president might recall the part of her message that focuses on tuition increases, while a student with a full athletic scholarship may focus more on the news of athletic center renovations. People also tend to perceive messages in ways that fit with their attitudes and interests – selective perception. A student from a rural area might perceive the new Wal-Mart as bringing more goods and lower prices to her area, while another student from a more urban area might see Wal-Mart as the exploitation of low-wage workers and a threat to mom-and-pop retailers.

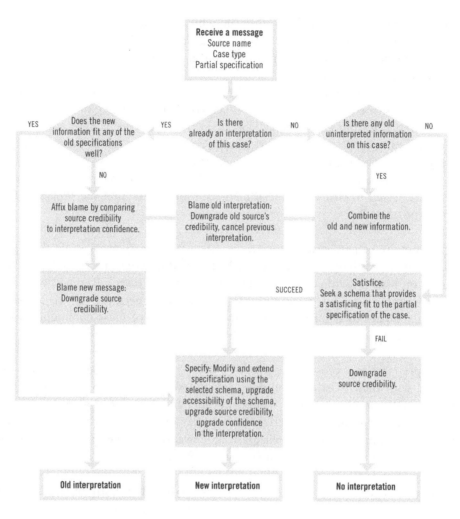

FIGURE 3.3 Schema/Info Processing.

Schema Theory

So far, the topic of perception has been discussed as a psychological construct, but there has not been a theory attached to it. One theory that relates to the process of perception and how we filter information is known as schema theory.

Robert Axelrod is a political scientist who used the concept of information processing to build schema theory. He borrowed Singer's definition of a schema as a "pre-existing assumption about the way the world is organized" (Axelrod, 1973, p. 1248). So, when new information becomes available, an individual tries to interpret it based on the way he has always interpreted information about the same situation. It explains how an individual tries to make sense out of a complex world (pp. 1248–1249). For example, consider the college student working on a current events assignment for his journalism class late one evening. He flips on the television and comes upon *Late Night with Seth Meyers* and one of his signature segments, "A Closer Look." Based on his past experience, the student knows that, even though he discusses politics, Seth Meyers is more of a comedian than a journalist. If the student were looking for a serious analysis of a news event for his journalism assignment, he would know based on his past experience, that his professor would not accept Seth Meyers as a source. While the student might appreciate the entertainment value of Meyers, he would have to turn to PBS, CNN, or another serious news site for information. This is an example of using a schema to process information – the schema is prior knowledge of Seth Meyers and the professor's expectations, which form the basis for the decision not to use him as a source for a journalism assignment.

Another scholar noted for her work on schema theory is Doris Graber. She describes schemas as "cognitive structures consisting of organized knowledge about situations and individuals that have been abstracted from prior experiences...used for processing new information and retrieving stored information" (Graber, 1984, p. 23). While the concept of a schema may seem confusing, another way to think about it might be as a pattern of existing knowledge, interests, and attitudes that an individual has, like a partially completed jigsaw puzzle. The schema is the backdrop, the outline. Information is received from the environment and filtered through the schema. If the new information is the right size, shape, and color, it fits into that jigsaw puzzle to help complete the picture. The more complete the puzzle, or schema, the more ability the person has to process that information.

Graber notes that schemas perform four major functions:

1. They determine what information will be noticed, processed, and stored, so it becomes available later for retrieval from memory.
2. They help individuals organize and evaluate new information so that it fits into their established perceptions.
3. They make it possible for people to go beyond the immediate information presented and fill in missing information.
4. They help people solve problems because they contain information about likely scenarios and ways to cope with them (p. 24).

For example, consider a task that college students must master at most schools – registering for classes through an online interface. For a first-year student, this registration process might seem complex and scary. The course registration schemas of freshmen are very limited, since most of them were scheduled into high school classes by their guidance counselors. The college student must make course selections, be sure the times don't conflict, schedule classes around work and other activities, be sure prerequisites are fulfilled, meet with their advisor to get their registration access code and then navigate the secure website where registration is done online at a specific time. The first time through can be pretty challenging. Fast-forward to registration for senior year. It's still anxiety producing, but not because seniors don't know the process. By now, their schemas are more complete and the registration process is easy to accomplish (provided the classes they want at the times they want with the most popular professors are not closed out). Those seniors who choose to go on to graduate school will undoubtedly be able to negotiate a new registration system more easily since their schemas have successfully accommodated a working knowledge of online registration at the undergraduate level.

While the above example may help to illustrate how schemas work, it may not be a pure "mass" communication example. However, individuals use schemas all the time to respond to messages in the mass media. Most students who receive an email informing them that they can make $10,000/month working from home a few hours a week if they only click on "this link," will recognize an e-mail scam and know to delete the message without responding. Students know that the *Wall Street Journal* is more difficult to read than *Cosmo* or *Maxim*. They know they will be more likely to find their high school friends on Instagram than on Facebook, and they can evaluate invitations from others in social networking spaces based on their past experience and decide whether or not to respond.

In a study reported in the *Journal of International Marketing*, Davvetas and Diamantopoulos (2016) investigated the role of schemas in how consumers perceive brand preference in global vs. local brands of products. Their results suggest that global brands are perceived as superior, because consumers are impacted by the perceived functionality of the global brand as well as perceived possible criticism by their reference group (p. 16). In other words, name brands seem to be viewed as better by consumers because of their wide geographic reach and use by others in the consumers' social groups. These schemas seem to come from the brand's reputation and cultural positioning. The study was limited to consumers in Austria, which, while a popular place to do research on brand preferences, might have limited applicability to other global cultures.

It is important to remember that schemas represent social learning (Graber, 1984, p. 147). People acquire schemas over time by learning from and observing others as well as by direct experience. The mass media play a role in schemas in the same way that they play a role in social learning theory: While some schemas develop from personal contact and face-to-face interaction, schemas can also evolve from exposure to mass media. Social learning theory is discussed later in this chapter.

Information Processing Theory

The work of Axelrod and Graber points up an inextricable link between the concept of schemas and another theory, information processing theory. Baran and Davis note that information processing theory is actually a large set of diverse and different ideas about how people interpret and process all the information they receive (Baran & Davis 2006, p. 286). It has been a complex field of study for cognitive psychologists. However, among mass media scholars, research on schemas and information processing in mass communication has generally focused on how individuals process news stories. Doris Graber, discussed earlier for her work in schema theory, maintained that people are overwhelmed by too much information, so they need processing mechanisms to help them pull out the information they want to get. Graber took Axelrod's model and related it to how individuals process a news story:

First comes the reception of a message. The integration process starts the series of questions to determine whether and how the new information related to stored concepts and whether it is worth processing. ... If the information is worthwhile and is reasonably well related to established schemas that can be brought to mind, it is integrated into them. If not, the new information or its source may be discredited or rejected or the new information may alter or replace the previous schema that has been called into question (1984, p. 125).

To illustrate this processing, consider a student receiving an email from the Student Activities Board notifying the campus that the administration is planning to cancel the annual spring festival, which in the past has featured a concert, picnic and other activities near the end of the school year. How would the Graber model be applied to this situation?

1. Does this cover a topic the student already knows about? Yes, Springfest has been an annual event the entire student body looks forward to each year.
2. Is the cancellation a familiar or predictable occurrence, based on previously stored knowledge? Maybe, because the administration has been trying to limit the incidence of underage drinking on campus, and drunken behavior at the festival was a problem the previous two years.
3. Does it make sense or contradict past experience for the administration to cancel Springfest? It could do either, since the funds are from the student government but the administration could veto plans if they don't approve.
4. How can the source of the email be evaluated? Credible, because the campus group that sent the e-mail (the Student Activities Board) is the planning committee for the festival.

Further, Graber's research revealed that people process news stories using a number of different strategies:

1. Straight matching of a news story to a schema: The administration always wants to spoil students' good times, so they are doing it again.
2. Processing through inferences: Deducing that this is like when they cancelled the drag show.
3. Multiple integration of a story with several schemas: It could be framed as taking control from students, as a safety issue, as pressure from the board of trustees, as distrusting students, or as treating students like they are still in high school (pp. 123–137).

Graber also maintains that news stories are processed with schemas as a result of media cueing. The pictures, headlines, and graphics that accompany a story will link it to a particular schema (p. 124). For example, a news story on a big snowfall might show children happily sledding in a park, angry motorists stuck in traffic, or the mayor at the city's emergency command center. Each image would evoke a different schema for the consumers of that medium and prompt different responses (Chapter 4 explains how this concept of media cueing is similar to the concept of framing).

The results of other research reveal three dimensions of news information-processing strategies that people consistently use:

1. Selective scanning, skimming, and tuning out items.
2. Active processing, going beyond or reading through a story to reinterpret it according to the person's needs.

3. Reflective integration, replaying the story in the person's mind and using it as a topic of discussion (McLeod, Kosicki, & McLeod, 1994, p. 148).

It should be noted that the strategies noted above were applied in relation to an individual reading a hard copy of the newspaper more than two decades ago. However, while the news is consumed very differently these days, information processing still happens in the same way. In a survey of 5,844 college students across the country, Head, DeFrain, Fister, and MacMillan (2019) found that over 99 percent of the respondents had engaged with the news in the past week. Students received their news from social media, discussions with peers, online newspaper sites, discussions with teachers, and news feeds. More than two-thirds received their news from five different sources. Consider the schema of a typical college student scanning her Twitter news feed. She skims over and tunes out information about farmers striking in India, wildfires in Australia, a shark attack on a beach off the Florida coast, and then she comes across a story about student loans. As a college student, she is likely to read the story all the way through and process it, to interpret it according to her needs. Her state representative is pushing to have student loans refinanced to a lower interest rate; that is news she can use. Part of her schema helps her determine how to find ways to graduate with less debt (her current interest rate is higher because she needed a second loan this year) and how she feels about her elected official (she might vote for him in the next election). Further on in the news feed, she comes across a story about a new federal law that will make it easier for college students to apply for financial aid. The FAFSA form is being simplified and the family income level for the Pell Grants has been raised (Kelchen, 2021). She reads this even more carefully and realizes that it won't go into effect until after she is done with her undergraduate studies. However, she brings it up with her parents, because she has a younger brother who will also be attending college in a few years. This is reflective integration of the news story into her schema, which will affect future evaluation of information about the same topic, especially if she also decides to go to graduate school.

In applying information processing theory to mass media, the research has focused primarily on how people process television news, and how the broadcast news media hinder rather than help people's understanding of news stories (Baran & Davis, 2006, pp. 290–292). This is done because the average newscast tries to cover too many stories in too short a time period, condensing complex information into short segments and human interest scenarios that confuse the viewer. Also, the extensive visual images are often overwhelming and actually detract from understanding of the content. At the same time, viewers don't give television news stories their full attention and rely on routine activation of schemas to process news stories, rarely engaging in reflective processing. (This may explain why banners often read, "BREAKING NEWS!" or the anchor frequently exclaims, "Look at this!" or "You've gotta see this video.") Given that television news is no longer the dominant medium, it is likely that further research on information processing will need to expand its focus. Some early research has been done in advertising and children's programming (Baran & Davis, 2006, p. 292), but there has not been a huge rush to conduct research in this area. However, the following section describes a theory that has generated more interest, as it looks at perception and information processing in a unique way.

Third-Person Effect

Another theory that is also closely linked to perceptual processes is the third-person effect. Davison identified the third-person effect as one in which an individual who is exposed to mass media messages believes the messages have a greater impact on others than on himself (Davison, 1983, p. 4). Davison did a number of small experiments in which he surveyed people about their perceptions of the effects of different mass media messages regarding presidential elections, newspaper strikes, children and television commercials, and media bias. In each instance, he found that people perceived that others would be more influenced by mass media messages than they themselves would be (Davison, 1983, pp. 1–15). One of the more interesting applications of this phenomenon came in the area of censorship – the censor rarely admits that he is affected by a mass media message but maintains that he must protect others from being affected by these messages (p. 14). This issue played out recently in upstate New York, when a county executive threatened to withhold funds from the public library if patrons were allowed to view pornography in the library. The concern expressed most often was that, even though it is legal for adults to view pornography, children in the library would walk by, see the pornographic material, and be affected by it, a clear application of third-person effect.

As might be expected, a lot of the strength of the third-person effect comes from messages that are seen as negative or socially undesirable. For example, McLeod, Eveland, and Nathanson found that college students perceived that the effects of antisocial language in rap music would be more likely to affect others than themselves. Those with the strongest third-person effect were also most likely to favor censorship of rap music (1997). David and Johnson (1998) investigated the impact that television programming and advertising had on perceived body image in a study of 144 female college students. They found that the third-person effect was stronger for those with high self-esteem (i.e., women who felt good about themselves thought that other women would be more affected by television's depictions of ideal body size than they would). Lo and Wei (2000) surveyed more than 2,600 Taiwanese high school and college students about their attitudes toward Internet pornography. They found that women perceived that pornography had a greater impact on men than on women, and that women were more likely to support restrictions on Internet pornography.

In a study of online gaming, Zhang (2013) examined gender differences and the third-person effect. Her survey of more than 5,000 gamers revealed that both men and women thought that the other gender would be more susceptible to the negative effects of online gaming, and women especially thought men would be more susceptible because men are perceived as spending more hours playing online games. Interestingly, Zhang found that the more time people of either gender spent actually playing games, the weaker was the third-person effect for both genders.

While it hasn't been a pivotal theory of mass media, some more current studies are tying in third-person effect as one of several theories that explain how people respond to mass communication. For example, Schweisberger, Billinson, and Chock (2014) examined framing of news stories, influence, and the third-person effect on students who examined news stories on Facebook. Among their conclusions were that people who evaluated stories that were not personally relevant to them nevertheless thought those stories would have a greater impact on other people (framing is discussed in more detail in Chapter 4).

How good a theory is the third-person effect? In an analysis of this question, Baek (2017) evaluated the third-person effect in light of the criteria for a good theory presented in Chapter 1. In evaluating early research on media effects through to the current status of the research, Baek concludes that the third-person effect fits the criteria for a good theory. In particular, it has significant heuristic value, having generated over 100 studies and led to the development of other "spin-off" theoretical models (p. 80). It is parsimonious, having started with one basic hypothesis, and has predictive power in terms of influencing opinion change (p. 79).

Additionally, in an era in which censorship, FCC regulations, and privacy are recurring concerns, the third-person effect may explain many phenomena around us. Baek (2017) suggests this and other areas as avenues for future research.

Hostile Media Phenomenon

In the mid-1980s, three researchers from Stanford University conducted a study of student perceptions of media coverage of the 1982 "Beirut massacre" and Israeli responsibility for civilian casualties.[1] The students viewed six network news segments that detailed the coverage of the event and had the most film footage (Vallone, Ross & Lepper, 1985, p. 580). Their findings led to a theory known as Hostile Media, in which partisans view media coverage of controversial events as unfairly biased and hostile to the positions they hold (p. 584). It appeared that basic cognitive and perceptual processes lead media consumers to see issues as black or white and perceive bias in the media against one side or the other.

Three decades later, Perloff examined issues around this concept of a hostile media and noted that it changes the perspective of media effects and their impact on individuals (Perloff 2015, p. 702). Rather, it examines the perceptions that ego-involved individuals bring to communication and the way their perception can influence their communication, not as an effect of media exposure but a response to the way that the media portrays certain events. In this way, it is an offshoot of uses and gratifications.

Perloff notes that news coverage is viewed as neutral by nonpartisans and the two groups with opposing attitudes see the same story as biased (p. 707). He comments that, "social identity theory suggests that media coverage of an ego-involving issue will activate group identity and increase the salience of the issue among members of a group that champions a particular political or social cause" (p. 710). Studies have investigated the cause of this hostile media bias and have linked it to perceptual processes described earlier in this chapter, as well as different standards and prior beliefs about media bias (p. 711). More research is needed to take into account the amount of news that individuals now consume through social media sources. However, it is clear that conservative news outlets are often viewed as biased by liberal consumers, and liberal news outlets viewed as biased by conservatives. This is seen most often in political news coverage, but also holds true in news coverage of social and health issues such as education and mandatory vaccination.

Thus far this chapter has considered the ways that people use and interpret the messages they receive from the media. The media, however, play another important role in the formation and change of individual attitudes. The next section examines several key theories that look at theories of attitude change or persuasion.

INFORMATION AND ATTITUDE CHANGE

Early Theories: Social Judgment and Source Credibility

As mentioned in Chapter 2, information on persuasion and attitude change has been part of interpersonal communication for centuries. In the 1930s, Sherif's research on social norms led to his social judgment theory, which examined the impact that other people have on developing norms of behavior (Sherif, 1963). Individuals are dependent upon their social groups to help formulate standards for how to behave in society – social norms. For example, students know that they must wear clothes to class, even in extremely warm weather. Social norms, and many laws, prohibit individuals from strolling through society naked. In fact, this norm is so ingrained that most people would not even consider going out without clothing in any weather. The clothing norm, and others like it that are learned through observing others, help society function smoothly – waiting in line at the grocery store, raising a hand to ask a question in class, stopping at a red light, returning books to the library. Sometimes people do violate these norms, but if they do, sanctions generally are imposed upon the person – for example, a driver who runs a red light could be fined if he is caught by the police or a "red light" camera.

However, this book is concerned about the impact of MASS communication, and it is true that many of our social norms, trends, customs, and even language come from the mass media. Fashion magazines dictate the styles worn by many college students, both male and female; political campaigns focus frequently on the appearance of a candidate and the 10-second sound-bite to make an impact; and social media movements have been responsible for forcing the government to address scandals and public officials to resign. New words such as "cyberbully," "frenemy," "selfie," "GOAT," and "nothingburger" have become part of our language through media influence. Thus, even though the early research on social norms exclusively examined the influence people and groups have on each other, that influence can also be traced to the mass media.

It was noted in Chapter 2 that Carl Hovland did some of the early research on persuasion when he examined the role that films played in soldiers' motivation to fight in World War II. In addition to this area, Hovland also collaborated with Sherif and others in a number of studies of social pressure and persuasion. Among them were his studies of **source credibility**. Hovland discovered that where a message comes from and who delivers it can be major factors in whether that message is perceived as credible and persuasive by the recipient (Hovland & Weiss, 1951). A clear illustration of this can be found in celebrity endorsements. Manufacturers are willing to pay millions of dollars for being able to market their products with the names of celebrities behind them. Basketball icon Michael Jordan, who retired almost 30 years ago, remains one of the most famous athletes of all time, turning his superstardom into contracts with Nike for his Air Jordan shoe, as well as sports drinks, cars, breakfast cereal, and others. The concept behind this is source credibility.

The three main components of source credibility are knowledge, trustworthiness, and charisma or dynamism. To be believable, a source must demonstrate all of these characteristics.

For example, Angelina Jolie, well-known for her award-winning career as an actor and filmmaker, has also endorsed many humanitarian causes, including the plight of refugees in war-torn countries, and women and children who are victimized by rape and human sex trafficking. She has served as a special envoy for the United Nations High Commissioner for Refugees and has adopted refugee orphans into her own family. When Jolie delivers speeches to the U.N. and other groups, she demonstrates her knowledge of the problems that the poor and oppressed experience, and pleads for support to make a difference. Her trustworthiness is high because she has traveled to many war zones around the world, donated her own money to build schools and shelters, and used her skills as a filmmaker to champion their causes. Her ability as an actor translates into a sincere and compelling presentation of the issues these victims of war must face. Angelina Jolie exhibits all the characteristics of high source credibility: Knowledge; trustworthiness; and charisma.

BOX 3.1

The Face of a Pandemic: Dr. Anthony Fauci

FIGURE 3.4 Dr. Anthony S. Fauci, Director, National Institute of Allergy and Infectious Diseases (NIAID). National Institutes of Health/National Institute of Allergy and Infectious Diseases photo via Wikimedia Commons.

During the COVID-19 pandemic, the world saw the re-emergence of a figure already familiar to many scientists and public health officials, Dr. Anthony Fauci. As the director of the National Institute of Allergy and Infectious Disease of the National Institutes for Health, and advisor to eight U.S. presidents on domestic and global health issues, Dr. Fauci became the most credible and trusted source during this public health emergency. Because of his medical credentials, he demonstrates that he has knowledge of global health and the issues surrounding how society responds to a health crisis. His trustworthiness is high, based on his position and past performance, for example, during the HIV/AIDS crisis. He has lectured and received awards all over the world and has the respect of his peers in the medical community. Finally, Dr. Fauci delivers his messages in a calm, careful, straightforward manner in language even lay people can understand. His charisma leads people to accept his message.

While some sources need to earn credibility, there are some roles that confer credibility upon the person holding that position, whether in the mass media or in face-to-face communication. The president's press secretary, a hospital spokesperson, the city police chief, the local news anchor, and the college professor all exhibit characteristics of source credibility – within their area of expertise, of course. The college professor who teaches media law would have little credibility in a thermodynamics class. Similarly, the physics professor would have low credibility in media law. Additionally, sources might be evaluated differently by different individuals. The Republican president's press secretary may have high credibility among members of his party, but low credibility among Democrats. A TV personality like Dr. Oz has credibility among his many fans; however, his critics cite his promotion of unproven supplements as one of the reasons they might question his credentials.

Understanding the components of source credibility can help media practitioners to craft the most persuasive messages, while recognizing that they can't persuade all the people all the time with a single message, and even a celebrity endorsement does not necessarily sell a product. In fact, Campbell and Warren (2012) found that if a celebrity has any negative associations in the mind of the consumer, those negative feelings will translate to the brand more easily than positive associations. The authors point out that even mostly positive celebrities have some negative qualities that could affect the endorsement. They noted that even using a beloved cartoon character like Garfield or Charlie Brown could have negative associations: Garfield is lazy and Charlie Brown is wimpy (p. 185). Similarly, having an all-star quarterback like Aaron Rogers of the Green Bay Packers endorse Adidas or State Farm might backfire in a market like Chicago with many fans of the Chicago Bears, perennial rivals of the Packers. Media marketing professionals must keep these issues in mind when considering investments in celebrity endorsements.

THEORIES OF BEHAVIORAL CHANGE

Social Learning Theory

How does a child learn to tie her shoes? How does an athlete learn a corner kick in soccer? How does a college student learn how to make chicken parmesan or to speak confidently in an interview? Social learning theory, also referred to as social cognitive theory in the psychology literature, addresses this question.

Chances are that these things and many others were learned through the use of role models. The concept of role models is really the basis behind social learning theory. Individuals are creatures of imitation, and learn to do things by watching and copying the behavior of others. It is also possible to learn what NOT to do by watching others: A child who sees his little sister burned by a hot stove can learn not to put his hand there; a son who watches his father struggle with emphysema may vow not to smoke; or a student whose roommate fails for cheating may resolve to do all her own classwork.

Albert Bandura is the name most frequently associated with social learning or modeling theory. Bandura is a Stanford University psychologist who first achieved a measure of fame for the Bobo doll experiments in the 1960s. Children were exposed to an adult who either played gently or aggressively with a Bobo doll, an inflatable doll that was rounded on the bottom with a weight in the base so it bounced back up when it was knocked down. After the adult left the room, the child was left alone with the doll and was observed through a two-way mirror. Children who saw the doll treated aggressively behaved in an aggressive manner, thereby validating the social learning theory (Box 3.2).

However, Bandura's research went far beyond this experiment. In fact, he is considered one of the top five most influential psychologists of the 20th century, in company with the likes of Sigmund Freud, B.F. Skinner, and Jean Piaget (Haggbloom, 2002, p. 146). Bandura observed that not all learning can be *directly* experienced, that learning comes from a variety of sources. One of those prominent sources is the mass media. Bandura (1994, pp. 70–71) maintained that the media teaches people in three main ways:

1. Through *observation* – individuals can learn how to do things they've never done before because they've seen it in the media. For example, the popularity of cooking shows and competitions has instructed people on new food preparation techniques that they may try in their own kitchens.
2. Through *inhibition* – seeing the negative consequences of behavior in the media can teach people not to engage in such behaviors. For example, seeing reports of the deaths of superstar musicians Prince and Tom Petty from an overdose of prescription opioids might lead someone to be more cautious about using these medications for chronic pain.
3. Through *disinhibition* – people are not afraid of some things because they have seen them being dealt with in the media. For example, a local television anchor had his colonoscopy recorded for broadcast to demonstrate to the public that it was a relatively easy procedure and an important way to detect colon cancer. Many public figures, including the U.S. president and first lady, had their coronavirus shots on camera to demonstrate the safety of the vaccine.

Baran and Davis also note that Bandura's concept of vicarious reinforcement is central to social learning in the mass media. This means that people can learn from reinforcement that is observed and not directly experienced. While learning can occur without reinforcement, individuals choose to engage in the observed behavior based on the positive or negative reinforcement seen (Baran & Davis, 2006, p. 198). For example, many commentators have noted that the rape culture depicted in rap lyrics and videos actually promotes a reinforcement of the violent behavior toward women by men who are fans of the genre (see, for example, Hutchinson, 2015).

Bandura is clearly in sync with other mass media researchers – for example, with George Gerbner, since he sees the media as "cultivating" a certain view of the world, and Everett Rogers, because he sees the role that the media play in diffusing innovation and ideas through society (Bandura, 1994, pp. 75–85). Gerbner and Rogers are discussed in more detail in Chapter 4 with the sociological theories. The key to understanding Bandura is noting the complexity of factors that account for human learning and behavior. The media is a large and important factor, to be sure, but it is not the only means by which cognition occurs.

BOX 3.2

Social Learning Theory on Campus during a Global Pandemic

FIGURE 3.5 Students working in a dorm room while wearing face masks. FatCamera/Getty Images.

Some have called being a resident advisor (RA) the most difficult job on campus during the global pandemic. These students, who are essentially peers of the residents they supervise, were charged with communicating and enforcing strict procedures during the COVID-19 crisis of 2020–2021. While each college set its own policies, at many institutions RAs used interpersonal and media channels to communicate with their residents in an application of Bandura's social learning strategies. The media helped the general public learn to do things they had not done before, most obviously, wearing a mask in public and social distancing. Similarly, testing, masks, social distance, and classroom behavior requirements were communicated to all students via email before their return to campus. RAs had the added burden of communicating the guidelines for communal living to their residents, in a clear application of Bandura's theory.

1. **Observation:** Students who lived on campus were able to observe the protocols in the residence halls through the behavior of their RAs, other residents, as well as the senior residential life staff. They also saw signage demonstrating testing and social distancing, and bulletin boards with illustrations of proper precautions that were required in the residential halls, residents' rooms, and common areas. This was a more difficult change for upper-class students returning to campus after having more freedom with their behavior the year before the pandemic hit. First-year students accepted what they saw as policy since this was their first experience living in a dorm during COVID.

2. **Inhibition:** The penalties for non-compliance with the pandemic policies were clearly communicated to students via email, social media, Zoom sessions, and in-person, distanced meetings with the RAs on each floor. Residents were made aware of the negative consequences of not following the guidelines, including being barred from campus and incurring financial costs for requiring other students to quarantine because of their inappropriate behavior. Students who had been on campus in the early stages of the pandemic realized how difficult it was to be sent back to their homes mid-semester after the virus spread and all classes went online, and they communicated this message to the new students.

3. **Disinhibition:** College students are noted for feeling invincible with regard to things that might be harmful to their well-being. This lack of inhibition with regard to drinking, partying, sex, and social distancing has been the cause of many COVID outbreaks on college campuses. However, RAs have been tasked with laying out and enforcing the rules regardless of their relationships with any of their fellow students. Many campuses instituted hot lines where anyone (faculty, staff, or students) could be reported for disciplinary action for not following the guidelines, and RAs told the authors they used this system. Unlike alcohol or parties in the dorms in the past, there were no warnings given. In addition to threats of punitive action against students during the pandemic, upper class students shared stories of events that led to the campus shutdown and students being sent home.

Source credit: With special thanks to Mary Clare Boyle, St. John Fisher College, resident advisor.

Information Processing and Attitude Change

While earlier in this chapter, the discussion of schemas and processing of news was closely associated with the mass media, psychologist William McGuire suggested his own "information processing theory" that deals with attitude change. The persuasive model offered prescribed steps that needed to be followed in order for attitude change to occur. McGuire's model originally posited six consecutive steps:

1. The persuasive message must be communicated.
2. The receiver will attend to the message.
3. The receiver will comprehend the message.
4. The receiver yields to and is convinced by the arguments presented.
5. The newly adopted position is retained.
6. The desired behavior takes place (McGuire, 1976).

In later versions, McGuire expanded this list to eight steps, and later to 12 steps, but the six presented here explain the sequential process of the theory well. In an application of McGuire's model for planning and conducting public health campaigns, Huhman, Heitzler, and Wong write:

> McGuire's model posits that the impact of persuasive communication is mediated by three broad stages of message processing: Attention, comprehension, and acceptance. Attention depends on exposure and awareness, comprehension is predicated on understanding the message, and acceptance includes intention and, finally, behavior change. In McGuire's model, because of the inherent variability in how people process media messages, a percentage of the audience is lost at each stage. Thus, high levels of exposure and awareness are needed to create measurable population effects (Huhman, Heitzler, & Wong, 2004, p. 5).

For example, a public relations practitioner with the Cystic Fibrosis Society is planning a fund-raising event, a stair climb up to the top of the tallest building in the city, to raise funds for research for a cure for cystic fibrosis. She first needs to get people's attention to the event and the cause. She can do this through a variety of means including social media, news releases, media alerts, celebrity endorsements, and others. This will make the public aware of the event. In the second stage, she needs to get people to understand the cause and the importance of the event to fund the cause. This will require her to separate her message from the other health-related organizations in town and their fund-raisers going on at or near the same time. By emphasizing the strides that have already been made in CF research, she may be able to increase comprehension. In the final stage, the public will accept the message by either participating in the event or sponsoring a participant. She might get this acceptance by enlisting the support of local athletic teams and health clubs, by gaining endorsements from local celebrities affected by CF, or offering desirable prizes for the top fund-raisers.

While McGuire's theory was not originally developed for mass communication, his theory does point up the need for persuasive messages to consider a sequential format

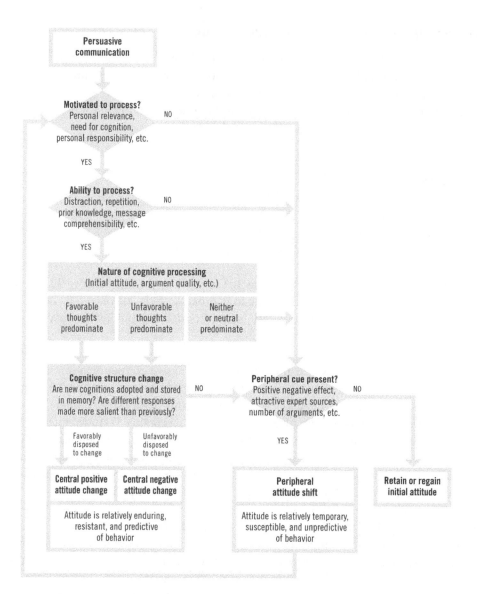

FIGURE 3.6 Elaboration Likelihood Model.

in order for them to be successful. Perry notes that, in the way that the theory views people as processing information in a rational, linear way, it is similar to social learning theory, which was described earlier (Perry, 1996, p. 101). However, what if people are not persuaded through a rational, systematic way? The next theory elaborates on that perspective in considering alternative ways that persuasion occurs.

Elaboration Likelihood Model

A second model that deals with attitude change is the Elaboration Likelihood Model, developed by Petty and Cacioppo (1986). Petty and Cacioppo actually built on

McGuire's work to ask what happens during the message-processing part of the per-suasion process (Perry, 1996, p. 115).

The Elaboration Likelihood Model (ELM) states that there are two routes through which information is processed that can lead to attitudes being changed:

1. The central route, where the information is processed actively and the individual evaluates it in a rational manner.
2. The peripheral route, where the receiver does not actively process the information in a cognitive sense, but instead relies on peripheral cues, such as the style of the message, the credibility of the source, her own mood, etc.

"Elaboration" refers to how much cognitive work is involved in processing the information. When people process information in the central route, they are high in elaboration, relying on their prior experiences and knowledge to analyze the situation, evaluate arguments, and think through their own positions. With peripheral processing, the individual is low in elaboration, and they form attitudes or change ideas based on simple inferences or associations, such as a celebrity endorsement. Attitudes formed on the basis of the central route last longer and are more resistant to change (Perry, 1996, p. 116).

Of course, which route becomes the persuasive one varies depending on several factors related to the individual, starting with their degree of involvement. Individuals are more likely to process via a central route when they are highly involved in the subject and the information coming to them. For example, someone in the market for a new car is more likely to pay attention to the details about price and performance features in a car dealer's TV commercial than someone who just bought a car; that person (who is less involved in the subject of needing a car) might process the commercial peripherally in connection with the brand image or lifestyle represented in the ad. Second, the ELM is more likely to be engaged when an individual perceives the message as personally relevant. This would suggest that a senior will be more interested in the messages from the college Career Center if he is looking for a job after graduation, in comparison to classmates who are planning to attend graduate school or freshmen just completing their first semester at school. Third, the ELM suggests central processing requires a degree of attention and the ability to elaborate on the message. Distractions can weaken the strength of the central message and allow peripheral cues, like the attractiveness of a celebrity endorser, to weigh more heavily in the persuasion (Perry, 1996, p. 116–117). For example, soccer superstar Cristiano Ronaldo endorses Nike, his own clothing and hotel lines (CR7), Herbalife, and Egyptian Steel, among others. While his expertise in recommending athletic footwear may justify his endorsement (and lead a serious soccer player to Ronaldo's endorsements via the central route), advertisers of steel, diet supplements, and high-end clothing are looking for peripheral route persuasion.

Although the ELM suggests that the two routes are mutually exclusive, Petty and Caccioppo stress that they are really points on a cognitive processing continuum that show the degree of effort a person expends when confronted with a message. The more people work to evaluate a message, that is, the more *elaboration* they employ with it, the less they will be influenced by factors not related to the message content (Griffin, 2003, p. 187). Choosing L'Oreal cosmetics because they do the job at a reasonable price employs more elaboration than choosing them because Beyonce endorses the brand.

The elaboration likelihood model brings together a number of attitude change theories. It has excellent application to mass media since mediated messages have the potential to provide both central and peripheral cues. Research has tested ELM most specifically in advertising. Petty and Priester report that studies have shown people are better able to use the central route when processing print sources than those that are more controlled, such as radio and television (1994, p. 104). They note that an important goal of any persuasive strategy aimed at changing attitudes is to increase people's motivation to think about the message. This is true whether one is looking for a long-lasting attitude change, such as safe sex practices, or those where a short-term change is acceptable, such as donating to a dance marathon fundraiser (Petty & Priester, 1994, p. 116).

Later research began to look at some practical applications of the elaboration likelihood model. For example, Angst and Agarwal (2009) found that people who were very reluctant to accept electronic medical records because of privacy concerns could be persuaded to change their minds with carefully developed informative messages about the benefits and advantages of having medical records online. Cheng and Loi (2014) found that the central route can be most persuasive when responding to online reviews. Their study of hotel managers who responded to negative online reviews revealed that if the managers responded promptly with strong, quality arguments (central route), they were more likely to build trust among respondents, who would consider booking at that hotel. They found that using the central route to persuasion would leave a more lasting impression. Users of Yelp! and TripAdvisor would generally support this finding from their own experiences.

Chang, Yu, and Lu (2015) specifically looked at "likes" for Facebook posts and the ELM model to determine what might be important for social media marketing. They determined that social media users are influenced by both the central and peripheral route in their decision to "like" a post. Useful posts tend to address the user's personal needs and have clear content, but images and user comments are also extremely important. It appears from this study that both routes are important in social media.

Most students have learned by now the importance of information technology security at their colleges. At the authors' institution, faculty and students regularly receive "test" messages that look like SPAM (e.g., *your mailbox is almost full, click on the link below to enable more space in your mailbox*). Xu and Warkentin (2020) conducted a literature analysis of security messages and employee motivation to comply, in light of the elaboration likelihood model. They coupled the ELM research with an examination of the role of herd mentality. They found that individuals who are cognitively motivated to comply with the security messages process those messages by the central route. However, those with lower motivation, process the messages peripherally and look to others to suggest what they should do.

CONCLUSION

The psychological theories of mass media illustrate clearly how the discipline has borrowed from allied fields in the social sciences. Social learning theory, perception, and schema theory all came directly from the psychological tradition, and students still study these ideas in introductory psychology classes. Additionally, the theories of persuasion and attitude change, such as social judgment, source credibility, Maguire's information processing theory, and the elaboration likelihood model have their roots in theories of psychology, even though they have also been adopted as part of mass communication's theoretical foundation.

Advertisers, public relations professionals, social media managers, marketers, and journalists are not the only individuals interested in opinion formation and attitude change. In fact, most of the early work in this area (indeed, dating all the way back to Aristotle), focused on how persuasion takes place in interpersonal, group, or face-to-face encounters. However, these theories can be adapted to the mass media because the same dynamics can occur whether an encounter takes place face-to-face, on a social media app, over television, on talk radio, or streamed online.

The uses and gratifications and the media systems dependency theories point up the importance of considering the role of the audience. Researchers are still debating the concept of the active audience, and how purposeful media choices actually are. The value of this perspective, however, is the consideration that has been given to the audience, as a key player in the media landscape. As choices increase and users get more control, the uses and needs of the audience must be taken into account by media practitioners. Further, they need to continue to find ways that they can engage the audience in the media forums, giving them a chance to participate and feel part of the conversation. Instagram, Twitter, blogs, talk radio, reality shows where the audience votes, reader contributions to online news sites – all of these are indicative of the growing role of the user of the mass media in determining programming and content.

These theories focused primarily on the relationship of mass media with the audience at the individual level, although it is assumed that this collection of individuals will impact the larger society. In the next chapter, theories that specifically focus on "mass" or group effects are examined.

Questions for Discussion/Application Exercises

1. Consider some of the media you use in the course of a day – social media, remote learning programs like Zoom, course management systems like Blackboard, news on websites, broadcasting, and others. Looking at the categories of needs in the uses and gratifications theories, how well do the needs match up with your uses?
2. Can you identify your level of dependency on various mass media? Consider a major news story you personally experienced. How did your media use and dependency change as the news emerged?
3. Using Graber's tenets of information processing theory, what factors influence how students consume campus media – whether it's a campus news site, social media messages, a print publication, radio station, TV station, or your college's own news site?

4. What sources can you identify as the most credible as you make important decisions – picking your major, where to look for an internship, how to buy a car? Can you distinguish the impact that personal vs. mass media sources have on your biggest decisions?

5. In social learning theory, Bandura maintains that the media teaches us in three ways: Observation, inhibition, and disinhibition. Find examples of how each of those may be operating to produce learning in children, college students, and adults.

6. As a future media practitioner, what lessons would you take away from the elaboration likelihood model in terms of crafting a persuasive appeal?

NOTE

1 The "Beirut Massacre" referred to the slaughter of thousands of Palestinians and Lebanese Shiites in refugee camps in Lebanon following the Israeli move into Lebanon during the Lebanese civil war in 1982. The killings were done by right-wing Christian Lebanese forces in full-view of the Israeli Defense Forces. Over the years blame for the killings has been the cause of tension between Arabs and Israelis. The extensive media coverage on both sides led the researchers to choose this topic to analyze media bias.

REFERENCES

Angst, C. & Agarwal, R. (2009). Adoption of electronic health records in the presence of privacy concerns: The elaboration likelihood model and individual persuasion. *MIS Quarterly* 33 (2), 339–370.

Axelrod, R. (1973). Schema theory: An information processing model of perception and cognition. *American Political Science Review* 67, 1248–1266.

Baek, T.H. (2017) The value of the third-person effect in theory building. *Review of Communication* 17 (2), 74–86.

Ball-Rokeach, S.J. & DeFleur, M.L. (1976). A dependency model of mass media effects. *Communication Research* 3, 3–21.

Bandura, A. (1994). Social cognitive theory of mass communication. In Bryant, J. & Zillman, D. (Eds.). *Media Effects: Advances in Theory and Research* (pp. 61–90). Hillsdale, NJ: Lawrence Erlbaum Associates.

Baran, S.J. & Davis, D.K. (2006). *Mass communication Theory: Foundations, ferment, and future* (4th ed.). Belmont, CA: Thomson/Wadsworth.

Berelson, B. (1959). The state of communication research. *Public Opinion Quarterly* 23 (1), 1–6.

Bianchi, D. (2020) What can Tweets tell us about this historic moment? Retrieved from https://marketing.twitter.com/en/insights/twitter-conversation-report-black-lives-matter

Campbell, M.C. & Warren, C. (2012). A risk of meaning transfer: Are negative associations more likely to transfer than positive associations? *Social Influence* 7 (3), 172–192.

Chang, Y., Yu, H. & Lu, H. (2015). Persuasive messages, popularity cohesion, and message diffusion in social media marketing. *Journal of Business Research* 68 (4), 777–782.

Cheng, V. & Loi, M. (2014). Handling negative online customer reviews: The effects of elaboration likelihood model and distributive justice. *Journal of Travel & Tourism Marketing*, 31 (1), 1–15.

David. P. & Johnson, M.A. (1998). The role of self in third-person effects about body image. *Journal of Communication* 48 (4), 37–58.

Davison, W.P. (1983). The third person effect in communication. *Public Opinion Quarterly* 47 (1), 1–15.

Davvetas, V. & Diamantopoulos, A. (2016). How product category shapes preferences toward global and local brands: A schema theory perspective. *Journal of International Marketing* 24 (4), 61–81.

Feguson, D.A. & Perse, E.M. (2000). The world wide web as a functional alternative to television. *Journal of Broadcasting and Electronic Media* 44 (2), 155–174.

George Floyd timeline. Retrieved from https://www.nytimes.com/article/george-floyd-protests-timeline.html

Graber, D.A. (1984). *Processing the news: How people tame the information tide.* New York: Longman.

Griffin, E. (2003). *Instructor's manual for A first look at communication theory.* New York: Mc-Graw-Hill.

Haggbloom, S.J. (2002). 100 most eminent psychologists of the 20th century. *Review of General Psychology* 6 (2), 139–152.

Head, A.J., DeFrain, E., Fister, B. & MacMillan, M. (2019, August 5). Across the great divide: How today's college students engage with news. *First Monday*, 24 (8). Retrieved from https://firstmonday.org/ojs/index.php/fm/article/view/10166/8057#:~:text=Nearly%20as%20many%20respondents%20had,at%20least%20once%20a%20day.

Hindman, D.B. (2004). Media system dependency and public support for the press and the president. *Mass Communication and Society* 7 (1), 29–42.

Hovland, C.I. & Weiss, W. (1951). The influence of source credibility on communication effectiveness. *Public Opinion Quarterly* 15 (4), 635–650.

Huhman, M., Heitzler, C. & Wong, F. (2004). The VERB™ campaign logic model: a tool for planning and evaluation. *Preventing Chronic Disease* [serial online]. Retrieved from http://www.cdc.gov/pcd/issues/2004/jul/04_0033.htm.

Hutchinson, S. (2015, August 20). Straight outta rape culture. *Huffington Post*. Retrieved from http://www.huffingtonpost.com/sikivu-hutchinson/straight-outta-rape-cultu_b_7942554.html

Ifinedo, P. (2016). Applying uses and gratifications theory and social influence processes to understand students' pervasive adoption of social networking sites: Perspectives from the Americas. *International Journal of Information Management* 36, 192–206.

Janfaza, R. (2020). TikTok serves as a hub for #blacklivesmatter activism. CNN online. Retrieved from https://www.cnn.com/2020/06/04/politics/tik-tok-black-lives-matter/index.html

Katz, E. (1959). Mass communication research and the study of popular culture. *Studies in Public Communication* 2, 1–6.

Katz, E., Blumler, J.G. & Gurevitch, M. (1974). Utilization of mass communication by the individual. In Blumler, J.G. & Katz, E. (Eds.). *The uses of mass communication* (pp. 19–32). Beverly Hills, CA: Sage Publications.

Katz, E., Gurevich, M. & Haas, H. (1973). On the use of the mass media for important things. *American Sociological Review* 38, 164–181.

Kelchen, R. (2021). Federal financial aid for college will be easier to apply for – and a bit more generous. Retrieved from https://theconversation.com/federal-financial-aid-for-college-will-be-easier-to-apply-for-and-a-bit-more-generous-152785

Klapper, J.T. (1960). *The effects of mass communication.* New York: The Freedom Press.

Lazarsfeld, P.F. & Stanton, F.N. (1944). *Radio research 1942-1943.* New York: Essential Books, Distributed by Duell, Sloan, and Pearce.

Lee, C.S. (2011). Exploring emotional expressions on YouTube through the lens of media systems dependency theory. *New Media & Society* 14 (3), 457–475.

Lin, C.A. (1999). Online-service adoption likelihood. *Journal of Advertising Research* 39 (2), 79–89.

Lin, C.A. (2001). Audience attributes, media supplementation, and likely online service adoption. *Mass Communication and Society* 4 (1), 19–38.

Lo, V.H., & Wei, R. (2000, April). Third-person effect, gender and pornography on the internet. Paper presented at the annual meeting of Broadcast Education Association, Las Vegas, Nevada.

McGuire, W.J. (1976). Some internal psychological factors influencing consumer choice. *Journal of Consumer Research* 2 (4), 302–319.

McLeod, J.M., Kosicki, G.M. & McLeod, D.M. (1994). The expanding boundaries of political communication effects. In Bryant, J. & Zillman, D. (Eds.). *Media effects: Advances in theory and research* (pp. 123–162). Hillsdale, NJ: Lawrence Erlbaum Associates.

Muñiz, C. (2020). Media system dependency and change in risk perception during the COVID-19 pandemic. *Tripodos*, 47 (1), 11–26.

Perks, L.G., Turner, J.S. (2018). Podcasts and productivity: A qualitative uses and gratifications study. *Mass Communication and Society* 22, 96–116.

Perloff, R.M. (2015) A three-decade retrospective on the hostile media effect. *Mass Communication and Society* 18, 701–729.

Perry, D.K. (1996). *Theory and research in mass communication*. Mahwah, NJ: Lawrence Erlbaum Associates.

Petty, R.E. & Cacioppo, J.T. (1986). *The elaboration likelihood model of persuasion*. New York: Academic Press.

Petty, R.E. & Priester, J.R. (1994). Mass media attitude change: Implications of the elaboration likelihood model of persuasion. In Bryant, J. & Zillman, D. (Eds.). *Media effects: Advances in theory and research* (pp. 91–122). Hillsdale, NJ: Lawrence Erlbaum Associates.

Potter, W.J. (1999). *On media violence*. Thousand Oaks, CA: Sage Publications.

Ruggiero, T.E. (2000). Uses and gratifications in the 21st century. *Mass Communication and Society* 3 (1), 3–37.

Schweisberger, V., Billinson, J. & Chock, T.M. (2014). Facebook, the third-person effect, and the differential impact hypothesis. *Journal of Computer Mediated Communication* 19 (3), 403–413.

Severin, W.J. & Tankard, J.W. Jr. (2001). *Communication theories: Origins, methods, and uses in the mass media* (5th ed.). New York: Addison Wesley Longman.

Sherif, C.W. (1963). Social categorization as a function of latitude of acceptance and series range. *Journal of Abnormal Social Psychology* 67, 148–156.

Stewart, E. & Ghaffary, St. (2020). It's not just your feed. Political content has taken over Instagram. *Vox* online. Retrieved from https://www.vox.com/recode/2020/6/24/21300631/instagram-black-lives-matter-politics-blackout-tuesday

Sundar, S.S. & Limperos, A. (2013). Uses and grats 2.0: New gratifications for new media. *Journal of Broadcasting & Electronic Media* 57 (4), 504–525.

Vallone, R., Ross, L. & Lepper, M. (1985). The hostile hedia phenomenon: Biased perceptions of media bias in coverage of the Beirut massacre. *Journal of Personality and Social Psychology* 49 (3), 577–585.

Wang, C.C. & Yang, H.W. (2007). Passion and dependency in online shopping activities. *CyberPsychology & Behavior* 10 (2), 296–298.

Whiting, A. & Williams, D. (2013). Why people use social media: A uses and gratifications approach. *Qualitative Market Research: An International Journal* 16 (4), 362–369.

Xu, F., Warkentin, M. (2020) Integrating elaboration likelihood model and herd theory in information security message persuasiveness. *Computers and Security* 98. Retrieved from https://www.sciencedirect.com/science/article/pii/S0167404820302820

Zhang, L. (2013). Third-person effect and gender in online gaming. *First Monday* 18 (1). Retrieved from http://firstmonday.org/ojs/index.php/fm/article/view/4157/3385.

CHAPTER 4

The Sociological Perspective on Mass Communication Theory

This chapter will:

- Introduce mass media theories that affect society as a whole.
- Consider the impact of agenda setting.
- Trace the development of diffusion of innovation.
- Review the issues associated with the knowledge-gap hypothesis.
- Examine the effect of the spiral of silence.
- Distinguish a variety of cultivation effects, including the effects of television violence.

On Sunday, January 26, 2020, the sports world was rocked by the news of the death of basketball superstar Kobe Bryant in a helicopter crash in Calabasas, California. Headlines announcing the crash included *The New York Times* headline "Helicopter Crash Kills N.B.A. Star Known to All as Kobe," the *Los Angeles Times'* "Kobe Bryant dies in crash" and "Lakers legend, daughter, and 7 others killed in helicopter accident," and an obituary on the front page. Similar coverage was seen across the US and around the world, including a front-page headline in the UK's *Daily Mail*, ten pages of coverage in Canada's *Calgary Sun*, and huge tributes across Asia, especially in China.

Throughout the ordeal of the crash and its aftermath, news media raced to the scene and blanketed the airwaves and online news sites with continuous coverage of the events. Was this a pivotal event in American life? Was this the most important news event occurring at the time? Did the media coverage give more importance to the event than perhaps was warranted? Did the news media give insufficient coverage to other important events occurring at that time, such as the unprecedented bushfires in Australia, the impeachment of the U.S. president, or Billie Eilish sweeping the top awards at the Grammys? How about the newly emerging story of a virus that would become a global pandemic? These questions and the role of the media in choosing to portray what it deems the most newsworthy events are examined in a theory known as agenda setting.

Agenda setting is one of the pivotal theories from the sociological perspective, that is, theories that examine the ways in which the media have been shown to be influential

DOI: 10.4324/9781003121695-4

on large groups or society in general. Chapter 3 examines the psychological theories of the mass media – the theories that look at how media influences affect people at a more individual level. While there is some overlap between these two perspectives, this chapter will focus primarily on the sociological, or group, perspective.

While in strictly chronological terms, agenda setting was not the first of the sociological theories, its origins can actually be traced to Walter Lippmann's *Public Opinion*, written in 1922 (McCombs, 2005, p. 157), so agenda setting will begin this chapter.

AGENDA SETTING

How important is a presidential election? The war against domestic terrorism? Deforestation in the Amazon? The poaching of elephants in Africa? The work of a young climate activist like Sweden's Greta Thunberg? The plight of the Muslim Uighurs in Chinese concentration camps? These are all stories that have received extensive and prolonged coverage by the media, leading the public to know about them and think about them. This is, very simply, agenda setting. Severin and Tankard describe the agenda-setting function of the media as "the media's capability, through repeated news coverage, of raising the importance of an issue in the public's mind" (2001, p. 219). It is clear that the media do this. Twenty-four-hour cable news channels and the explosion of news sites distributing stories through Twitter, Instagram, and other social media have led to coverage of more issues in greater detail than ever before. To fill all those hours, major news outlets such as the BBC, CNN, and Reuters consistently send reporters to provide in-depth and continuing coverage of everything from massive floods to the latest celebrity scandal. Instagram and TikTok stars reach hundreds of thousands of followers and help to elevate the importance of major and even very minor news stories.

Agenda setting is not a recent phenomenon. Chapter 2 notes that as early as 1922 Walter Lippmann was discussing "The World Outside and Pictures in our Heads," and how the press contributed to forming those pictures. Princeton University's Bernard Cohen further refined the concept in 1963 when he noted that the press "may not be successful much of the time in telling people what to think, but it is stunningly successful in telling its readers what to think *about*" (Baran & Davis, 2006, p. 316). While neither Lippmann nor Cohen actually used the term "agenda setting," the concept was essentially the same when mass communication researchers began a systematic study of the press's influence on its audience (McCombs, 2005, p. 157).

The seminal research, known as the Chapel Hill studies, took place during the presidential election of 1968. Maxwell McCombs and Donald Shaw surveyed 100 undecided voters in Chapel Hill, North Carolina, about the issues they considered most important in the upcoming election. They then compared the responses with the stories covered by newspapers, television, radio, and news magazines. The researchers found an almost perfect correlation between the issues that voters thought were the most important and the issues that were most prominently featured in the news media, and described this as "agenda setting" (McCombs & Shaw, 1972). They used the term "salience" to describe the level of importance that becomes attached to an issue; a highly salient issue is one that the audience comes to believe is very important because it gets a lot of media attention. Hundreds of research studies since that time have confirmed this influence.

Agenda Setting Processes

How does agenda setting actually work? There are three main factors that lead to agenda setting: Priming; issue obtrusiveness; and framing.

Priming

In a study of how television newscasts can impact presidential elections, Iyengar, Peters, and Kinder found that the media use a process known as priming. They described this process as "by ignoring some problems and attending to others, television news programs profoundly affect which problems viewers take seriously" (Iyengar, Peters, & Kinder, 1982, p. 855). When the media prime an issue, such as an increase in the minimum wage, over another issue, such as veterans' access to health care, it affects the attention the public gives to the issue and how important it seems to the audience. Iyengar and Simon (1993) investigated priming related to the first Persian Gulf crisis in 1990. They found that the more the story was covered in the news, the more important it appeared in public opinion polls. Further, the research revealed that President George H.W. Bush's approval ratings were more strongly tied to his handling of the war than to any domestic issues. Holbert et al. (2003) investigated the impact that viewing the television program *The West Wing* had on perceptions of the U.S. presidency. In a survey of almost 200 college students, the researchers found that viewing the television program about a fictitious president primed more positive images of the presidency, more positive images of the current president and his predecessor (at the time of the study, George W. Bush and Bill Clinton) and highlighted the importance of being engaged as more important to presidential success. (At the same time, the research also determined that President Josiah Bartlet, the character on the show portrayed by Martin Sheen, was seen by viewers as more popular than either Bush or Clinton.)

News items are primed all the time, whether in stories critical of a presidential candidate, headlining low high school graduation rates in inner city schools, reports of protests against police shootings, or high-profile athletes in trouble with the law. Even an issue such as healthy eating can seem primed in the public's mind if the story shows the first lady planting a White House garden and talking to school children about the benefits of eating vegetables.

In recent years much has been made about the issue of "fake news." While this was a term that U.S. President Donald Trump used to refer to any news story that he disagreed with or portrayed him in a negative light, Van Duyn and Collier (2018) used the term to study priming and news that was actually true or false. They found that subjects who were exposed to false Twitter messages from "elite" sources (i.e., news organizations, public figures, etc.) reported less trust in the media. Priming fake news in the public mind makes it more salient and influential in evaluation of real news (pp. 41–42). It wasn't the exposure to fake news that led to this mistrust; rather, it was getting the information from elite sources. The authors generalize that media discussions of the issue of fake news may actually increase the public's trust in the media itself (p. 43).

Issue Obtrusiveness

A second factor related to agenda setting involves obtrusiveness of issues. Does agenda setting take place with every news story? Zucker (1978) discovered that agenda setting is actually more likely to occur with issues that the public has not experienced, which are known as unobtrusive issues. An issue such as high or low gasoline prices would be considered an obtrusive issue, one which people have direct experience with, as they purchase gas for their automobiles regularly. Contrast that with an issue such as global climate change, the effects of which are less obvious in most people's daily lives. Agenda setting is more powerful in bringing issues that are unobtrusive to the public's agenda. The price of gas will be important to people whether the news media cover it or not, but interest in the topic of global warming increased markedly when young Swedish climate activist Greta Thunberg began her Friday school strike for climate, which turned into a worldwide movement of youth demanding changes in environmental policies. Similarly, while the California drought is obtrusive to people living in that state under tight water restrictions, it became more obtrusive to people on the East coast when news reports linked it with the increasing prices of goods like almonds grown in California.

Another example of an obtrusive issue is parking on college campuses, something most students have much direct experience with and which most students consider to be a real problem on their campuses. While parking problems may be an obtrusive issue for students, most would probably not be aware of how much money the college makes on parking fines or how many students have holds on their academic records because they have not paid their parking tickets. If the student news media did a story on revenue to the college or holds on records, that would make an unobtrusive issue one that is more obtrusive.

Framing

Still, a third factor that affects the public's agenda is the framing of an issue. Is requiring everyone to wear a mask during a global pandemic a violation of their free speech rights or a way to keep them safe during a public health emergency? This is a good example of the framing of an issue almost everyone has experienced.

One of the best-known framing scholars is Robert Entman, who defined framing as, "selecting and highlighting some facets of events or issues, and making connections among them so as to promote a particular interpretation, evaluation, and/or solution" (Entman, 2009, p. 5). Entman noted that framing was one of the theories that was used in both the social sciences and humanities, but often without a central organizing principle. The field of communication, Entman noted, was a good place to provide that framework (Entman, 1993, p. 51-52). Much of his most recognized work has involved identifying and analyzing frames in political crisis situations. For example, after the September 11, 2001, attacks on the World Trade Center towers in New York City, President George W. Bush defined the attacks as an act of war and the attackers as pure evil. He repeated the words "war" and "evil" multiple times in public statements after the attack, and these became the important concepts for the public, making it very unlikely that any action the president wanted to take would be challenged (Entman, 2009, pp. 95-97). The frames that led to the "War on Terror" resonated with the public.

Tankard defines a frame as "the central organizing idea for news content that supplies a context and suggests what the issue is through the use of selection, emphasis, exclusion, and elaboration" (in Sparks, 2002, p. 156). A news frame can be thought of as being like a picture frame or the action of centering/"framing" a photograph with a camera or phone. The viewfinder can capture only a portion of the scene and the photographer has to decide what belongs in the scene and what doesn't. In a similar way, journalists and public relations professionals decide what information to include and what to exclude from a report, and which details deserve the greatest emphasis.

Some theorists question whether frames are consciously placed in a story by the journalist. Whether framing is deliberate or not, it is clear that frames affect the public's perception of an issue. Is gun control a violation of Second Amendment rights or a way to keep the population safe? Is employer-provided contraception a right for all women or can it be denied on religious grounds? Is Alex Rodriquez one of the greatest baseball players of all time or a cheat who should be banned from baseball for using performance enhancing drugs? Do people who live in coastal areas hit by hurricanes deserve insurance protection to rebuild their homes or are they foolish for choosing to live in an unsafe area? A news story about any of these topics could emphasize facts that presented one aspect or the other, providing examples of how frames can affect perception of an issue.

A variety of research studies have shown that the way an issue is framed affects how the public interprets the issue, and who the audience members think is responsible for fixing problems. For example, Maher (1996) looked at the effects of newspaper frames of local environmental problems in Austin, Texas, for his Ph.D. dissertation. He first did a content analysis of the local paper and then surveyed residents about their perceptions of the cause of the problem. He found that the public was influenced by the newspaper coverage of the events, even though there were a number of causes that were not highlighted by the press.

A significant number of media scholars have looked at frames in a wide variety of contexts. Chyi and McCombs examined *The New York Times's* use of frames in coverage of the Columbine High School shootings in 1999. They found that the *Times* kept the story alive for more than 30 days and with 170 articles by changing the frame – e.g., community frame, future frame, society frame (Chyi & McCombs, 2004). Bronstein (2005) examined frames that were being used to describe the new feminist movement to see if journalists were recycling frames from the 1970s. Christopher Martin wrote an entire book on the way the media has framed labor unions. In *Framed: Labor and the Corporate Media*, he maintains that journalists have framed organized labor stories as consumer issues, while ignoring the actual concerns of the union workers (Roush, 2005). Shaffer (2006) examined how frames were used in reporting the case for installation of a municipal wi-fi network in Philadelphia, which was framed as something for the public good by a citizens group and as risky and unnecessary by the telecommunications industry.

It is worth noting that a lot of public relations work is essentially about framing, trying to get news organizations to emphasize certain aspects (i.e., employ certain frames) in their coverage of an organization or an issue. This is a good example of how mass media theory can be relevant at the practitioner level. Long lines at airport security checkpoints can be framed by travelers as incompetence by the screeners, but the TSA (Transportation Safety Administration) can frame those same lines as enhanced security efforts designed to keep passengers safe.

In a study of media framing during the initial two months of the COVID-19 pandemic, Mutua and Ong'ong'a (2020) examined coverage by four international media organizations: BBC; CNN; Al-Jazeera; and the *People's Daily* (China). They identified frames in the coverage including economic consequence, human interest and impact, attribution of responsibility, and health severity. Sinophobia was also identified prominently, as many people, including U.S. President Trump, blamed China for the virus and its spread (p. 5). This led to Asian minorities being the targets of verbal and physical racial attacks. Interestingly, they also identified "fake news" as a frame. (It should be noted that this frame continued throughout the pandemic, especially in the United States, where physicians reported that people dying in the ICU maintained they did not have the disease because it was "a hoax.")

BOX 4.1

Framing and Racism in Native American Athletic Imagery

FIGURE 4.1 Native Americans and supporters protesting the name and logo of the then-Washington Redskins before a game in 2014.

For over 40 years, the National Congress of American Indians (NCAI) waged a battle against athletic teams with American Indian names and mascots, particularly against the Washington Redskins of the National Football League. The NCAI maintained that the imagery of the team name was racist and perpetuated negative stereotypes of native peoples. They cited decades of research that revealed "derogatory 'Indian' sports mascots have serious psychological, social, and cultural consequences for Native Americans, especially Native youth" and have reinforced conditions which have led to the high number of hate crimes against them.

For the NCAI, the issue is framed as one related to the civil rights movement (most closely associated with African Americans in the United States) in general, and a racist move by George Marshall, the original owner of the Washington NFL team, in particular. The term "Redskin" is a racial slur referring to the government's call for the bloody scalps of Indians back in the 1800s, and Marshall himself led the move to segregate the NFL and allow no players of color in the league, a practice that lasted for several decades with his team. While fans who are diehards for the name might frame this issue as political correctness or cancel culture, or while players might frame their play for the team as actually honoring Native Americans, most high school and many college teams have already changed their names.

In 2020, the Redskins owner bowed to the pressure and the team became known as The Washington Football Team. In July 2021, the Cleveland Indians announced that, after over 100 years, they would change the team name from the "Indians" to the "Guardians". At the time of this writing, neither the Kansas City Chiefs football team nor the Atlanta Braves baseball team have any plans to change their names. The Chiefs banned fans from wearing Native American headdresses to the games, but the fans still use the Tomahawk Chop to celebrate the team's successes on the field. As recently as the 2020 Super Bowl, the Kansas City Chiefs entered the field to the chant over the PA system. While the Braves removed the "chop on" sign from their scoreboard, fans still engage in the Tomahawk Chop during the games (Associated Press 2020; Axisa, 2020; Belson, 2021; Bernstein, 2020; National Congress of American Indians, n.d.).

Influences on Agenda Setting

So who is responsible for agenda setting? If the public agenda comes from the press, who sets the press agenda? According to McCombs, the press agenda comes from "the traditions of journalism, the daily interactions among news organizations, and the continuous interactions of news organizations with numerous sources and their agendas, especially including policy makers in government" (2005, p. 164). These influences include:

- The monitoring of what happens at other news organizations. Journalists have always looked to their competitors, as well as to standard-bearers such as *The New York Times* and the *Washington Post*. Students who intern at television or newspaper newsrooms immediately notice the bank of television monitors tuned to all the other stations in town as well as national feeds. 24-hour news coverage and breaking stories on the Web have heightened the sense of competition and monitoring even further.
- Prominent news sources such as public officials, government office holders, administrators, and public relations personnel. These routine sources have significant press access and can be very influential. During elections, especially national elections, political campaigns are particularly successful at setting the press agenda as candidates hold rallies, announce policy positions, and respond to controversial news stories.
- The increase of public relations activities in both the public and private sector has had a significant impact on the press agenda. In 2019 there were over 274,000 public relations professionals, according to the U.S. Bureau of Labor statistics, and the field was projected to grow by 7 percent through 2029 (U.S. Bureau of Labor Statistics, 2019a). By contrast, there were 52,000 reporters, correspondents, and broadcast news analysts, with the job outlook showing an 11 percent decline in the decade (U.S. Bureau of Labor Statistics, 2019b). This discrepancy contributes to issues such as the controversy over video news releases which highlight the press's reliance on business, government, and trade organization sources which sometimes produce stories that look like real news and get aired without editing by television stations (McCombs, 2005, pp. 164–165).

In the early days of agenda setting research, Ray Funkhouser (1973) identified five mechanisms that also influence the amount of media attention an issue might receive. These mechanisms still help to explain how the media sets the agenda:

1. Adaptation of the media to a stream of events: For example, after a time, coverage of wildfires in the West or unrest in the Middle East just seems to be more of the same and ceases to be considered news. Even scenes of COVID testing sites and vaccination clinics seem to be the same media stream when shown on a daily basis.
2. Over-reporting of significant but unusual events: For example, during a military coup against the government of Myanmar in February 2021, a physical education teacher was shown holding a virtual workout class for her students, and she seemed oblivious to military vehicles driving down the roads in the background. The coup and the removal of the government's elected head Aung San Suu Kyi was reported for days by international news organizations, and the video of the woman dancing was often included on social media with the hashtag #Myanmarmilitarycoup and others.
3. Selective reporting of the newsworthy aspects of otherwise non-newsworthy situations: For example, the police answer many calls for domestic disturbances during an average day. However, during one call in Rochester, New York, in January 2021, the police put a 9-year-old girl in handcuffs and pepper-sprayed her

in the back seat of a patrol car. The incident drew national and even international attention when the body camera footage was released, as observers questioned the inappropriate actions of law enforcement toward a child.

4. Pseudo-events, or the manufacturing of events such that they appear to be newsworthy: During the COVID-19 vaccine distribution at Dodger Stadium in Los Angeles, a group of anti-vaxxers showed up to protest the vaccine. They blocked the entrance to the stadium and delayed the vaccine clinic for an hour. Even though it was a manufactured demonstration with a very limited impact, the national media showed up to cover it, late-night comedy made it the target of humor, and thereby gave widespread attention to what might have been a local inconvenience.

5. Event summaries, or situations that portray non-newsworthy events in a news-worthy way: For example, when a video goes viral on social media, both local and national networks will often pick up the story and show it as a human interest feature, such as the video of two polar bears from the National Zoo sliding down a hill in their enclosure during a rare Washington, D.C. snowstorm. This might be an interesting and fun video, but many viewers may have already seen it on TV and social channels.

McCombs concludes that because of its role in agenda setting, the press does exert a major influence on public opinion (2005, p. 166). At the same time, the public also has a role in its interpretation of the media messages as well as sharing on social media. An understanding of information processing (discussed in Chapter 3) may help explain how public agendas are set. In addition, with the media landscape expanding and changing, the nature of agenda setting continues to change. In addition to social media sites such as Instagram, Facebook and Twitter, bloggers, citizen journalists and in-dependent media are all adding more voices that help to set the agenda in society. Some control has been taken from the press, since anyone with internet access can dis-seminate a message. New research is considering these venues for understanding agenda setting.

Agenda Setting and Social Media

When college students are asked where they get their information, most cite social media as the first place they go to find out what is happening (Gottfried & Shearer, 2016). Students at the authors' school mentioned Instagram as their no. 1 social site during focus groups in a data analytics class. Even students' parents and professors are using social media to filter through all the clutter and focus on who and what interests them. The differences in whom individuals are following affect their perceptions of what is happening in the world, and the importance of those things. Social media helps users focus their interests, and thus the agenda setting that comes from this focus. Someone whose Twitter feed was filled with posts from celebrities and athletes would end up with a different agenda from a friend who followed mostly journalists and news organizations. At the same time, social media also can limit the information that is on an individual's agenda. Some students, for example, only follow their friends on social media, and thus they miss out on important news that could impact them, such as the deadline for voter registration or a change in the law affecting student loans.

Has social media (i.e., user-generated content) had an impact on the way the agenda setting theory works? Nearly 50 years after McCombs and Shaw's seminal work, researchers have begun to look at this question.

Meraz (2009) analyzed political blogs that were conservative, liberal, and moderate and were produced by traditional news outlets or citizen journalist-bloggers. She found that traditional media outlets were no longer the sole gatekeeper for what was deemed newsworthy. Indeed, citizen journalists have shifted the balance of power and have as a group impacted the public's agenda. At the same time, she found that traditional media still had the strongest influence.

Grzywinski and Borden (2012) actually studied the impact that social media had on coverage of the Occupy Wall Street movement, a leaderless, non-violent protest against corporate greed and the top wage-earners in the United States, which took place beginning in July 2011. The Occupy movement used Facebook as its primary social media site to plan and organize protest events, and the authors looked at the impact that Facebook had on coverage of the movement in *The New York Times, Washington Post,* and *Los Angeles Times.* They found that social media was a major source of information for participants in the first part of the movement and was also used extensively by traditional media as they picked up and reported on the story.

More recently, Wohn and Bowe (2016) found that young millennials – undergraduate and graduate students at their university – reacted to world and national events based on influence from their social media contacts. The students' perceptions often reflected the attitudes of their online social network, whom the researchers termed, "micro agenda setters," in both positive and negative ways. With so much news being carried by social media, more variability in terms of individuals' agenda awareness might be based on who is in their network.

In an effort to find out just how social media works in agenda setting, Cowart (2020) analyzed the responses of participants who viewed fictitious stories on a Facebook feed and measured their perception of the issue's importance. She found that the greater the number of repetitions of an issue, the greater the subjects perceived its importance (p. 211). Perhaps surprisingly, the order in which the story appeared in the social media feed did not affect the subjects' perception of its importance. Cowart posited that the visual cues represented by traditional media (e.g., newspaper headlines and the top story on the front page) do not impact the reader with issues on social media (p. 212).

The Pew Research Center reported that in 2020, at least half of adults surveyed got their news from social media, with Facebook and YouTube being the top sites (Shearer & Mitchell, 2021). If agenda setting is, indeed, judged differently on social media in comparison to traditional media, the salience of news for the consumer will be an important issue for future research.

Thus, while agenda setting by traditional media outlets is still a real and present phenomenon in telling the public what to think about, the explosion of social media has been affecting that function in an evolving way, sometimes suggesting to people what their views should be and leading them to become more involved both online and offline. A good example of this is the use of the hashtag #BlackLivesMatter on social media beginning in 2013 after George Zimmerman was acquitted in the death of Black teenager Trayvon Martin. The following year, the hashtag drew even more public attention to police interactions with young Black men after the shooting of Michael Brown in Ferguson, Missouri, and it continued to be used in many other high-profile police shootings. As was mentioned in Chapter 3, the hashtag and others such as #BLM became one of the dominant stories of 2020 after the deaths of George Floyd and Breonna Taylor at the hands of the police. Students told the authors that they found out about these events primarily from social media posts, both from their friends and news organizations.

DIFFUSION THEORY

The discussion in Chapter 2 about the early mass communication theories concluded with the two-step flow theory as part of the limited effects paradigm. To recap, the two-step flow theory maintained that information flowed from the media to opinion leaders, who shared the information as well as their perspective with their relevant social contacts. Thus, the media were seen as having more of an indirect rather than a direct effect on society.

For more than two decades, researchers studied the diffusion of political news, social issues, news stories, and even fashion and movie reviews, in an attempt to define the nature and function of these opinion leaders. However, it became clear that there were serious flaws with the two-step flow theory. Among the flaws was the realization that the media were becoming more and more pervasive; in particular, more people had access to more extensive media coverage as television sets became more available and affordable. Thus, it was discovered that people were more likely to receive information directly from the media, rather than from other people. While the two-step flow may still be a valid consideration in special circumstances, such as public relations (where PR professionals may serve as opinion leaders for their media contacts) or small-town news, the research evolved into an examination of how information actually travels through society – diffusion research.

The name most closely associated with diffusion research is Everett Rogers, but the seminal research on diffusion was actually done by Ryan and Gross, who studied the diffusion of hybrid seed among Iowa corn farmers (Ryan & Gross, 1943). The Iowa corn studies were pivotal because they not only looked at the difference between mass media channels and interpersonal channels in spreading news about innovations, but they also identified those people who were likely to be early adopters of an innovation and those who would lag behind (Rogers, 1995). Following his early research and working for more than three decades, Rogers reviewed a wide range of research studies to demonstrate that, when innovations are available to a population, they will pass through a series of stages on their way to becoming adopted. The stages are listed below, along with an example of individuals learning about drones, which is a fairly recent technological development:

- First, people will become aware of the innovation, often through the media; for example, many people learned about the use of drones through news stories and seeing images and videos of drones on social media. The first images related to military use, but commercial and personal drones evolved from this coverage.
- Second, a small group of early adopters will try out the innovation, but because of the cost initially involved and the limited uses, only a few individuals and businesses purchased drones initially, mostly for entertainment.
- Third, opinion leaders learn from the early adopters and try the innovation; for example, a neighbor might bring out his drone during a family picnic and give everyone a chance to try it out or a business may purchase a drone and the employees may experiment with different uses.
- Fourth, if the opinion leaders like the innovation, they may encourage friends to try it, so the drone owner might post pictures and video taken with the drone at the picnic on social media and thus demonstrate how versatile the drone camera might be. An ad agency might have some impressive footage in a television commercial and persuade other clients to consider using a drone for their promotions.
- Fifth, after many people have adopted the innovation, a group called laggards will also make the change; in the future, it is anticipated that drones will deliver packages and even supplies in emergency situations, so their use may become so ubiquitous that it will not seem novel to anyone.

The rate of adoption and number of adopters is often depicted as an S-shaped curve relating number of adopters to the passage of time, as seen in Figure 4.2

Rogers (1983) noted that the innovation decision process generally proceeds through five discrete stages:

1. Knowledge of the innovation (becoming aware of drones).
2. Persuasion by forming an attitude toward the innovation (seeing that drones are superior to radio-controlled toy aircraft).
3. Decision to accept or reject the innovation (everyone agrees that drones take better video for commercials but individuals and businesses will need to decide whether they can make the financial investment).
4. Implementation or trying out the innovation (actually purchasing a drone or borrowing one to experiment with filming).
5. Confirmation: Reinforcing or reversing the decision about the innovation (confirming that this is the best way to shoot video, or returning it after deciding it wasn't worth the investment) (Rogers, 1983).

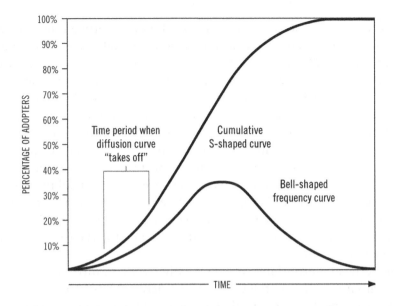

FIGURE 4.2 Diffusion of innovation curve.

In a study of consumer adoption of the ride-sharing service Uber, Min, So, and Jeong (2019) examined the issue in terms of the diffusion of innovation and the technology acceptance model. In addition to other factors proposed by Rogers (described in more detail in Box 4.2), they found that social influence was a big factor in the perceived usefulness and perceived ease of use; however, complexity of using the innovation was also a decision factor for many consumers (pp. 779–780).

While diffusion of technological innovations is one way that diffusion theory can be applied, media practitioners have often been more concerned with how news is diffused through society. Melvin DeFleur summarized more than 40 years of studies about how news flows from media sources through society. Among his findings were that most people get their news directly from a news medium, as opposed to another person. At the same time, news events of deep concern to large numbers of people will move faster and farther within a population, regardless of the source (Severin & Tankard, 2001, pp. 212–213). Events such as the Trump supporters' attack on the U.S. Capitol in early 2021 and the shortage of COVID vaccines during the early days of distribution are examples of news stories that moved swiftly through the population by both media outlets and the two-step flow, as messages often spread from friends and social media contacts, leading people to check out other sources for more information.

From this discussion it may become clear that diffusion of news could be an updated way of examining agenda setting. In 2019, Brosius, Haim, and Weimann examined this very idea, positing that diffusion would provide a good perspective on agenda setting in the age of social media. Since agenda setting examines how news stories spread through society and works well with traditional, mainstream media, diffusion takes into account the way that news spreads through online networks (Brosius, Haim, & Weimann, 2019, p. 124). A single story may appear on a news site, but it might also be spread through social channels by the publication itself, or the author. It may further be shared by readers on other social sites and picked up by other publications. A single user may see the same story in many different places. This dynamic approach is hard to capture through traditional agenda setting strategies, but may be analyzed through diffusion theory, which gives a more prominent role to the news consumers than the focus on the media seen in agenda setting (p. 121). There are some members of the audience who just read the news and move on. However, others may share, like, comment, correct, and in other ways contribute to and sometimes shape the media narrative (pp. 131–132). The authors present this model as a new way to build and refine the theory as well as conduct future research studies.

It would be inappropriate to leave the discussion of diffusion of ideas through society without mentioning the theory of memetics (Yang, 2019), a relatively new theory in mass media but one that comes originally from Darwin's theory of evolution. Social media users are familiar with the term "memes," which can be compared to infectious biological diseases that replicate and spread through society, not unlike the novel coronavirus or the flu. The term has been adopted to describe the spreading of cultural information and, to the readers of this book at least, a form of marketing – and meme marketing is free. Funny videos, images, and GIFs distributed on social media always come from some other media, but memes need to have an identifiable pattern or structure as their defining quality (Lechner, 2021). The goal of a meme is to promote indirectly. For example, during the 2021 inauguration of U.S. President Joseph Biden, with the crowd wearing masks and sitting physically distanced due to COVID, a photo emerged of a masked Senator Bernie Sanders of Vermont sitting alone on a folding chair, arms crossed, holding a manila envelope, and wearing a pair of colorful mittens. The Sanders photo turned into a social media meme that lasted for days and depicted him everywhere from *Star Wars* and *Game of Thrones* scenes to sitting on a bench with Forrest Gump or behind Canadian Prime Minister Justin Trudeau giving a speech. When a new NASA rover sent back photos from Mars about a month after the inauguration, it took only hours before altered images of the Martian landscape with Senator Sanders in the scene began to circulate on social media. How did this happen?

In a study of using artificial intelligence to identify viral memes, Ling et al. (2021) identified three distinct characteristics that cause a meme to go viral. One is the composition of the meme, in this case a close-up image of a single character, Sanders, sitting alone on a folding chair. The second is an image where the character is showing a strong emotion or assumes a particular posture, in this case Sanders appearing cold but comfortable and with his typical Bernie Sanders demeanor. The image is relatable, since everyone knows what it's like to be cold and can put that image into a variety of contexts. The final characteristic is the accessibility of the meme, since Sanders is a recognizable figure and one who is popular among social media users.

BOX 4.2

Diffusion of Innovation and Dockless Electric Scooters

FIGURE 4.3 A bank of electric scooters, ready to be tried by new users.

Everett Rogers examined characteristics that influence whether or how quickly an innovation is adopted. These factors can be applied to a fairly recent innovation, electric scooters. According to surveys in cities where the scooters are available, over 30 percent of respondents had tried them in Portland, Oregon, as well as 45 percent of those surveyed in Denver, Colorado. Men are more likely to ride electric scooters than women, and scooters are more popular among a young demographic, aged 20–39 (Sanders, Branion-Calles, & Nelson, 2020, p. 219). Electric scooters are seen in over 100 cities and most frequently on or around college campuses. Because this is an innovation that is still relatively new for some populations, the use of dockless electric scooters (e-scooters) can illustrate how, using Rogers' categories, a new idea might spread or be diffused through society or among a student population.

1. **Relative advantage:** The degree to which an innovation is perceived as better than the idea it supersedes. In most college towns, e-scooters replace driving and parking a car, taking a ride-sharing service like Lyft or Uber, taking the bus, riding a bicycle, or walking. The e-scooter can be seen as better because it is generally cheaper than a personal car or Uber, access is easy through a smartphone app, payment is convenient (account set up for direct billing through the app), and use can be based on the student's own schedule.

2. **Compatibility:** The degree to which an innovation is perceived as being consistent with the existing values, past experiences, and needs of potential adopters. E-scooters fill a need for transportation options, especially for short trips in a college town. It is consistent with the way college students like to set their own schedules and do as much as possible with their phones. Their past experiences show that it can be difficult to take a bus that has a limited schedule, it's almost impossible to park on campus or park at a reasonable price, and using Uber on a regular basis can be expensive. Walking may not be an option due to distance to campus or the time it takes to walk a mile or two.

3. **Complexity:** The degree to which an innovation is perceived as difficult to understand and use. It is extremely easy to download the app and set up an account with one of the companies that operate scooters near campus. Once the app is installed, users only have to find an available scooter in a large central location or one left within sight on a sidewalk. Once a scooter is located, the user just scans the QR code on the scooter to unlock it. This is not difficult for most college students who are used to downloading and using apps for ride-sharing and food delivery services, among other uses.

4. **Trialability:** The degree to which an innovation may be experimented with on a limited basis. A friend or coworker can demonstrate the app to a potential user, and many first-time users can be observed trying scooters out with a friend before downloading the app themselves. If a user is unhappy with the service or is nervous about the safety of riding an e-scooter in traffic in a city or college town, the app can be uninstalled and the account canceled.

5. **Observability:** The degree to which the results of an innovation are visible to others. It's easy to find many people riding dockless electric scooters around towns and college campuses (in places where they are legal and permitted). In fact, the popularity of this form of transportation, especially for college students, has led to an increased rate of diffusion among the population. This diffusion has also led to laws and regulations in many places, including cities where they have been prohibited, due to safety concerns for both the riders as well as pedestrians and cyclists.

The way information moves through a society is also a significant component of the next theory examined in this chapter.

KNOWLEDGE GAP HYPOTHESIS

Most of today's college students grew up watching *Sesame Street*. At some point, they might have learned it was educational, but they enjoyed it for the entertainment value as well. (Actually, whenever one of the authors brings a clip from *Sesame Street* into the classroom for demonstration purposes, the class always protests when the segment ends. It seems that Cookie Monster, Elmo, and Big Bird bring back happy memories, and college students also get the adult messages underlying much of the program.)

What many students don't know is that *Sesame Street* was actually part of an educational experiment designed to help disadvantaged children become better prepared for kindergarten. The program's original design was aimed at narrowing what was seen as a knowledge gap between children of high and low socioeconomic status. However, the results of extensive research studies and data analysis showed mixed results in terms of its success in meeting that goal. All preschoolers who watched *Sesame Street* on a regular basis did seem to learn from the show, but the program alone did not erase the gap between lower income and higher income children in terms of preparing them for school (Katzman, 1974). In fact, children from better-off families seemed to benefit more from the show than those from poorer homes. Thus, the phenomenon of *Sesame Street* became a significant part of the discussion around the knowledge gap hypothesis.

A hypothesis is basically a research question; the researcher needs to ask questions and answer them in order to formulate theory. The term "hypothesis" also can be used to describe a theory that is still in the development stage or that has not been fully researched and verified. Because of the somewhat contradictory nature of the research findings, the knowledge gap has not yet achieved theory status and is still known as a hypothesis. These research terms are discussed in more detail in Chapter 7.

The names most often associated with the knowledge gap hypothesis are Tichenor, Donohue, and Olien. They stated the knowledge gap in the following way: "As the infusion of mass media information into a social system increases, segments of the population with higher socioeconomic status tend to acquire this information at a faster rate than the lower segments, so that the gap in knowledge between these segments tends to increase rather than decrease" (Tichenor, Donohue, & Olien, 1970, pp. 159–160). Why might there be such a gap in knowledge or information between segments of society at different levels of the socioeconomic scale? Tichenor and his colleagues offered five reasons why this might be so:

- Higher level of communication skills: People with higher socioeconomic status tend to be better educated, so they are better able to read and comprehend material at a high level; for example, in the issue of deciding how to pay for a child's college tuition, people with higher levels of communication skills may be better able to interpret complex information about scholarships, grants, and loans, and seek out additional information, even if it is of a technical nature.

- A greater amount of stored information: Accumulated prior information helps this better-educated population act more capably on new information; for example, the better-educated person probably has made decisions on student financing in the past (for herself or for another child in the family) and can relate any new information about the different options to past experience.
- Relevant social contacts: People from a higher socioeconomic status probably know others who they can call for advice on paying for college. They also may have more access to the information and skill at researching topics, especially online – as well as having a computer and high-speed internet.
- Selective exposure, acceptance, and retention of information; for example, a single mom who thinks she cannot afford her child's education may not pay attention to relevant information or remember details of scholarships and grants, since she considers it so far out of her ability to pay.
- The nature of the mass media system, which has been shown to be aimed at a higher education level (p. 162). Details of college financing are most likely written for someone who understands the college system. Many first-generation college students report that their parents just had no idea how to begin to help them find the information they needed.

The knowledge gap hypothesis can be viewed as a somewhat disturbing theory, pointing up differences in class and privilege in society and proposing that the media contributes to widening the gap. It is true that some of the information gaps are clearly visible today in terms of access to information and technology. Most middle and upper-middle class families have multiple smartphones, computers, mobile devices and high-speed Internet access, which poorer families can't afford. Similarly, high schools in prosperous communities generally have more computers in the classrooms than their inner-city counterparts. With so much emphasis on online classes and remote learning, especially during the global pandemic, these stark differences became even more clear. This technology gap is sometimes known as the "digital divide."

At the same time, research has looked at the impact that this information gap actually had on communities in terms of diffusion of information and issues of local impact. In a follow-up piece of research, Donahue, Tichenor, and Olien (1975) found that the knowledge gap declines when an issue has a strong local impact and when there is conflict in a community; for example, a community that becomes home to a registered sex offender finds ways to spread that information quickly through the society to all members of the community, particularly parents of young children. Additionally, the knowledge gap is likely to be less in smaller communities where there are more limited media channels and much information is shared through informal channels; for example, in a small town where everyone meets at the local diner, in-formation about a newcomer with a questionable background will be shared quickly. In larger communities, with many media outlets for information, the divide among segments of the population is likely to be larger.

Tichenor, Donahue, and Olien also studied the knowledge gap in 19 different cities that were experiencing conflicts over environmental issues (such as wilderness logging and environmental pollution). Their findings regarding the knowledge gap were somewhat reassuring. They found that all segments of society will become informed when there is an important local issue and increased news coverage from local or outside sources provides more and better access to information (Baran & Davis, 2006, pp. 313–314).

In a study of the knowledge gap and presidential elections, Holbrook found that the knowledge gap does not necessarily grow over the course of the election and that forums such as debates actually do help to narrow the knowledge gap among segments of society (Holbrook, 2002). Liu and Eveland found that there was not a clear-cut knowledge gap when voters used newspapers vs. television as their main source of news (Liu & Eveland, 2005). However, in a study of the knowledge gap in transitional democracies' elections (Brazil, Mexico, and Russia), McCann and Lawson found that the knowledge gap widened or stayed the same. While the media resources were there for interested voters, the results were ascribed to the failure of the campaigns and the media to engage the citizens in the process (McCann & Lawson, 2006).

While researchers still try to pinpoint the role of the knowledge gap using traditional media, another segment of the research population is looking at the impact of the digital divide, Internet use, and newer media. For example, Prior (2005) argues that greater media choice makes it easier for people to find the content they most prefer. In a survey of more than 2,300 adults, he found that people who like news and people who like entertainment each take advantage of the increasing number of media channels to watch what they like. As a result of these choices, knowledge gaps have actually widened; those who are interested in the news know more about politics and are more likely to vote, while those who are interested in entertainment know little about politics and are less likely to vote (pp. 585–586). It seems likely that social media has only enhanced this widening of the knowledge gap and increased polarization in society.

In a more recent study conducted in the Netherlands, Boukes and Vliegenthart (2019) found that television played the most important role in narrowing the knowledge gap regarding news consumption by individuals with low education levels. Going to news websites or reading a newspaper did not have the same effect. The modality of the news consumption didn't make a difference for those with a higher level of education (pp. 3665–3666).

It is also clear that consumers self-select the media that corresponds to their philosophical outlook. So, more conservative voters are more likely to choose conservative media outlets such as Fox News, The Ben Shapiro Show, or the *National Review*, while those further to the left might focus on *The Huffington Post, Slate,* and MSNBC. While these choices affirm the voters' political views, they often restrict their exposure to opposing perspectives, thus widening the information gap.

In spite of obvious knowledge gaps due to technology, some media initiatives may contribute to narrowing this gap. Some examples include:

- Corporate donations of Chromebooks and wifi hotspots to students who did not have computers and internet access at home when the global pandemic forced classes online. The authors' institution provided such help to students from rural areas where high-speed internet was not available.
- Public television shows such as *Homework Hotline* and *Dial-a-Teacher*, where students can call in by phone, online chat, or web-based whiteboard, and get help

with their homework when they don't have a parent or after-school program available to assist them.

- High school test review shows, which are broadcast for recording during the overnight hours. In New York State, public television stations produce and broadcast review shows before the Regents exams each spring.
- GED programs which are available online or on television, so that parents or shift workers can earn a high school diploma without having to attend classes in person.
- Distance and online classes offered by most colleges and universities.

Whatever the forum for research into the knowledge gap, the issue of accessibility must play a significant role. The explosion in technology and remote learning, as well working from home, have further highlighted the differences between those with access and those without. Knowledge gaps are partly a function of motivation and interest, but also a function of access to the technology that houses the information.

SPIRAL OF SILENCE

It would be difficult to get through high school without some experience of the impact of peer pressure – to drink, to vape, to have sex, to dress like one's social group, to go along with the crowd. However, every student who has taken introductory psychology knows that this peer pressure extends far beyond adolescence. Individuals are pressured by others to conform to standards of dress, behavior, and attitudes in a wide range of circumstances, even when the groups are not part of their usual social circle.

Elisabeth Noelle-Neumann took the idea of group pressure to conform and added an additional component: The influence of the media. Noelle-Neumann posited that public opinion is formed by a process in which individuals try to determine whether their opinions are in the majority, a process that involves the media because the media is the way that people gauge public opinion. For example, a student from a rural area is a member of the National Rifle Association and opposed to a ban on assault weapons. It is likely that his social group, his friends and family, will also be opposed to such a ban. However, this student will also use information from the media to gauge whether public opinion is for or against gun control. He will then use the knowledge of the public's opinion when he is with a group outside his own immediate social circle, when he is away at college, for example, and that will help him decide whether or not to express his pro-gun opinion on campus. The media publicize which opinions are dominant, which opinions are on the increase, and which opinions may cause social isolation if they are stated in public (Severin & Tankard, 2001, p. 273). So, if this student finds out that public opinion on his campus favors a ban on assault weapons, and he is involved in a discussion on the topic in his political science class, he may be hesitant to express his opinion that would be opposite to the majority view.

It is clear that opinion polls, as reported by the media, play a large part in determining further public opinion. Noelle-Neumann maintains that media reporting helps individuals decide which opinions they might express without being seen as social outcasts and which opinions are in the minority. As individuals self-censor the minority opinions, those opinions do not get expressed, and thus do not get reported in the media. Thus, a spiral effect occurs, because when the majority expresses a dominant opinion and the minority keep silent, that makes the majority opinion seem even *more* dominant and makes the minority view seem even further outside the mainstream.

Glynn and McLeod (1984) conducted research which supported the spiral of silence in their study of 98 Wisconsin voters during the presidential election of 1980 (when Ronald Reagan defeated Jimmy Carter and John Anderson ran as a third-party candidate). They found that individuals were influenced by polls in their willingness to express an opinion that was in the minority; however, even though they did not speak out, they still maintained their minority opinions.

At the same time, not all research on the spiral of silence has supported its view. Glynn, Hayes, and Shanahan (1997) conducted a review of the research studies that had been done on the spiral of silence. They concluded that the evidence supporting the spiral was actually quite weak. The researchers recommended that survey questions that ask individuals if they hypothetically would be willing to express a deviant opinion should be replaced by observations of individuals actually speaking out. However, no studies reviewed for this book followed that recommendation and available research continued to rely on self-reporting surveys.

In 2001, Moy, Domke, and Stamm examined the spiral of silence in relation to people's views on affirmative action. This is considered a sensitive topic, probably more sensitive than one's choice among election candidates, because it affects efforts to promote diversity in education and hiring, but also has resulted in discrimination against people in the majority. Moy and her colleagues found that fear of isolation did influence individuals' willingness to speak out with a minority opinion; however, they found that those with a higher level of education were more likely to speak out. They also found that the most important reference was the opinion of the close circle of friends and family in determining willingness to speak out against the perceived majority opinion (Moy, Domke, & Stamm, 2001, p. 7, pp. 16–17).

Noelle-Neumann viewed the spiral of silence as reflecting a powerful effects model of the media. She maintained that this happens because the media are virtually everywhere, the media tend to repeat stories and perspectives, and the values of journalists influence the content of the news they report (Baran & Davis, 2006, p. 322). This was an almost prophetic observation: At the time when it was made in the early 1970s, the three news networks (ABC, NBC, and CBS) were still dominant. Other outlets such as CNN and Fox News had not yet launched. Almost five decades later, Noelle-Neumann's assertions about media proliferation are more true than ever. Multiple 24-hour cable news channels struggle to fill the hours with repetitive news, an increasing number of opinion pieces, and a focus on features, celebrities, and viral social media. Talk radio surpasses music stations in many markets and has been shown to influence voter opinion during elections and catastrophic events. Pollsters from such organizations as FiveThirtyEight, the American Enterprise Institute, and the Pew Research Center appear regularly on news programs and offer the "pulse" of the country, usually ascertained through overnight polling, and networks and newspapers frequently team up to conduct polls and report their findings. Even visitors to web sites such as Fox News, CNN, and the BBC, and social media channels such as Twitter and

Facebook, can participate in polls and see how their views compare to those of others on the site. The result often is what Eric Alterman called an "echo chamber" of reinforcing opinion from an assortment of media all elaborating on the same idea (Alterman, 2003). As a result, political elections often focus more on the "horse race" rather than the issues. Nowhere was that more obvious than in the U.S. presidential primaries in 2016. Celebrity tycoon Donald Trump initially competed with 16 other candidates for the Republican nomination. Media coverage focused almost exclusively on the polls and Trump's personality, so that more issue-oriented candidates were unable to compete. A Harvard University study documented the boost this gave to Trump's campaign, concluding that "the volume and tone of the coverage helped propel Trump to the top of Republican polls" (Patterson, 2016).

Baran and Davis also provide an example of news coverage in early 2003 as an example of the spiral of silence working to quell public dissent in the run-up to the Iraq War that began in March of that year. In 2004, the editors of *The New York Times* addressed their own inadequacies in investigating and reporting on the George W. Bush administration's claims that Iraq had weapons of mass destruction, the link between Iraq and the September 11 terror attacks, and the assertion that the war would pay for itself with Iraqi oil revenues. The media's unwillingness to challenge the Bush administration's claims on these issues before the war led to public opinion opposing the war being discouraged or even stifled. Questioning the need for war was seen as unpatriotic and not supportive of American troops. The *Times*' acknowledgement that it failed to challenge controversial claims and to investigate reports more aggressively showed that the press had helped to lead the country to a spiral of silence that suppressed dissent on the war (Baran & Davis, 2006, p. 325).

Over the years, the spiral of silence has been somewhat controversial, with studies employing a variety of research designs and producing inconsistent results. Scheufele and Moy (2000) reviewed 25 years of research on the spiral of silence and made several observations and recommendations. Most important, they contend, is the need to consider cultural differences when examining the spiral. Cross-cultural factors are a key variable in the decision to speak out on an issue, and they recommend returning to a more macroscopic view of the theory.

Future research would probably find some interesting perspectives on the spiral of silence and changes in social issues such as gay and transgender rights in American society. It is also important to remember, however, that Noelle-Neumann's theory related to expressing one's ideas directly to others in a face-to-face setting. Social media and comment boards on news sites now allow individuals to offer their perspective in a more anonymous forum. While this participation has become increasingly negative, research shows that users still support anonymity for the comment section (Rosenberry, 2011). At the same time, many news organizations such as CNN, Reuters, the *Chicago Sun-Times*, and others have shut down their comment boards, arguing that they have not elevated the discussion of the issues.

Another study examining how the spiral of silence was manifested in the 2016 presidential election, conducted via an anonymous online survey, on Facebook, or face-to-face by Kushin, Yamamoto, and Dalisay (2019). The authors found that fear of isolation was not a factor in expressing support for either Hillary Clinton or Donald

Trump on Facebook, most likely due to the like-minded people they knew there (p. 8). Respondents seemed more willing to express unpopular opinions with the anonymous online survey, and slightly less willing to express unpopular opinions in a face-to-face survey, leading to the theory of the "shy Trump voter" and explanations of why polls incorrectly showed Clinton was likely to win the election (p. 9).

Does it seem likely that social media would have an impact upon the spiral of silence, that people might be more willing to offer their opinions on Facebook or Twitter? This appears not to be the case. The Pew Research Center reported results of a survey asking 1,801 adults their views on the case of Edward Snowden, the National Security Administration contractor who released secret government documents detailing widespread surveillance of citizens' phone and email records. The survey revealed that people were more likely to discuss their opinions in person and on social media if they thought that their friends and contacts agreed with them. Social media did not provide an alternative platform for expressing views that seemed to differ from those of the majority (Hampton et al., 2014).

It would be inappropriate to leave the discussion of the spiral of silence without comment on the controversy surrounding its originator, Elisabeth Noelle-Neumann. Noelle-Neumann worked as a journalist in Nazi Germany in the 1940s and later became a Nazi apologist (i.e., a person who defended the views and actions of Hitler). Some critics feel that her early views were influential in her writings, including the formation of the spiral of silence. Simpson notes that her writings show hostility toward ethnic and racial diversity in societies and support political reforms that would disenfranchise large segments of the population (Simpson, 1996, p. 166). Simpson also claims that her writings characterize the general population as "ignorant, passive, and incapable of self-rule" and that it is up to the "political and cultural elites...to enforce stability and defend their values and traditions from the onslaught of vulgar democracy" (pp. 166–167). It is questionable whether the personal views of a theorist should affect academic judgment of her theory, but the controversy over this one researcher is noteworthy because of its intensity.

CULTIVATION THEORY

How likely is it that a person will be the victim of a violent crime? Is crime on the increase in society? Are women more likely to be victims of crime? These were some of the questions that George Gerbner's research team asked individuals who were considered light, moderate, and heavy viewers of television (with "heavy" defined as more than four hours of TV time per day). His subjects included U.S. as well as Canadian citizens of all backgrounds, education, and income levels. Gerbner discovered that heavy viewers of television were more likely to overestimate drastically the likelihood that they would be the victims of a violent crime, the lack of safety of their own neighborhoods, and the overall increase of crime in society (Gerbner, Gross, Morgan, & Signorielli, 1980, pp. 222–225). Gerbner called this skewed perception "The Mean World Syndrome." He concluded that people who watch a lot of television inhabit a world that they perceive as meaner and more dangerous than people who watch less television.

George Gerbner has been called "The Man Who Counts the Killings" (Stossel, 1997). The former dean of the Annenberg School of Communications at the University of Pennsylvania became famous for keeping track of the violence on television and projecting how this violence was affecting our society. Gerbner had already been studying violence in the media when, in 1968, U.S. President Lyndon Johnson's National Commission on the Causes and Prevention of Violence tapped him to analyze the content of television news. Thus began the longest running media research project ever (Stossel, 1997), called the Cultural Indicators Project. This project consisted of two components: Message system analysis, which is the monitoring of violence in primetime television; and cultivation analysis, which is the investigation of viewer conceptions of social reality associated with their television viewing (Gerbner et al., 1980, p. 212).

Over the more than 30 years of the project, researchers and the public continued to be astounded at the level of violence shown in television programming, and the amount of television that average Americans consumed. For example, in 1992, the American Medical Association reported that the average child watched television for 27 hours a week and would see more than 40,000 murders by the age of 18 (Stossel, 1997). (This figure is more difficult to measure in today's media environment, given that it is reported more as "screen time" than television time. In 2020, The American Academy of Child and Adolescent Psychiatry [2020] reported that children ages 8–12 in the United States spend four to six hours a day watching or using screens, and teens spend up to nine hours. This has probably increased with the switch to remote learning for most of the country during the COVID crisis.) However, of special interest to mass media researchers, and what Gerbner really wanted to focus on, is how television viewing affected the perceptions of the viewers.

The central tenet of this cultivation theory is that heavy television viewing literally *cultivates* a common view of the world. Just as a farmer cultivates crops to make them develop and grow, media influences also grow and develop over time in people. Thus, cultivation is not the result of a single television program or any short-term exposure to a media message. While Gerbner's research focused exclusively on television violence, it is reasonable to think that this cultivation effect would hold true for social media and other mediated experiences such as video games. Local news stations are often criticized for reporting nothing but bad news, such as crime, fires, and car accidents, which makes it seem like their communities are dangerous places in which to live. Such coverage over time, critics contend, creates a poor image of an area that is nowhere nearly as bad as the reality. Journalist and press critic James Fallows says the same thing happens with coverage of the political process, where emphasis on candidates' weaknesses helps make the public jaded and cynical about politics. By presenting public life as "a depressing spectacle," Fallows says that "the message of today's news coverage is often that the world cannot be understood, shaped or controlled" (Fallows, 1996, p. 140).

Stein, Krause, and Ohler (2019) proposed applying cultivation theory to the social media app Instagram to study young adults' body image, a topic that is often discussed in relation to television programming and fashion magazines. The authors actually found that browsing public Instagram posts of strangers led the subjects to be more critical of these strangers' bodies than their own. It appeared that subjects who viewed the profiles of their friends when browsing Instagram were actually less critical. At the same time, it appeared that Instagram browsing, whether of public or peer profiles, plays a role in leading to eating disorders. The authors suggest that social media cultivates these negative outcomes but could also be used to highlight more positive body image movements that have emerged on social networking (p. 8).

Cultivation Processes

Later in the development of the theory, and in response to some of his critics, Gerbner identified two processes that helped to explain the reactions of different people to the violence they viewed on television. The first was **mainstreaming**, which describes how people from very different social groups come together to share a common perception as a result of their exposure to television; television is the common factor that brings people of different backgrounds and experiences together, that cultivates common perspectives, and that overrides differences among individuals. Indeed, heavy television viewers share high scores on the Mean World Index (Gerbner's survey), which indicates they think most people are looking out for themselves, a person can't be too careful out there, and most people would take advantage of others if they had a chance (Gerbner, Gross, Morgan, & Signorielli, 1986, pp. 30–31). Factors such as age, gender, race or socioeconomic status would not matter, according to Gerbner. All people who watch a lot of television would share the same perceptions.

The second process Gerbner identified to further explain the theory was **resonance**, which describes how some images have an even greater impact for people whose real life situation mirrors that of what happens in the media. Gerbner says "when what people see on television is most congruent with everyday reality (or even perceived reality), the combination may result in a coherent and powerful 'double dose' of the television message and significantly boost cultivation…the congruence of the television world and real life circumstances may 'resonate' and lead to markedly amplified cultivation patterns" (Gerbner et al., 1980, p. 217). For example, everyone who watches the television show *NCIS* gets the impression that there is a significant amount of crime in Washington, D.C. (mainstreaming). However, for people who live in the DC area, the familiar locations and local characters in the show make the level of crime seem more real to them (resonance). Female viewers may have an even higher degree of resonance, since they feel more vulnerable and more likely to be victims of a violent crime.

Gerbner notes that one significant issue that increases the cultivation effect is that the violence that we see on television is "swift, painless, and effective…and always leads to a happy ending." Thus, TV depicts violence as solving many problems without many serious consequences (Stossel, 1997). Gerbner theorizes that this leads people, especially youth, to cultivate a culture of violence and a jaundiced view of the world in which violence is the basis of power as well as the solution to many problems.

Potter and Chang (1990) demonstrated that television viewing does have an impact, but it also matters what type of programming a person is watching. They disagreed with a general cultivation effect for heavy television viewers, but supported a cultivation effect that took into account the type of programming. According to this

argument, someone who watched a lot of crime shows would have a different cultivation effect from someone who watched a lot of reality TV.

In an application of the theory to international students living in the United States,
Woo and Dominick (2003) found very strong support for the cultivation effect.
International students who watched a lot of daytime talk shows that featured topics
such as adultery and other dysfunctional personal relationships had more negative
perceptions of human relationships in the United States and overestimated the incidence of undesirable behaviors in romance, marriage, and families. Even when they
eliminated the softer talk shows (such as *Oprah*) from their analysis, the cultivation
effect was still strong. This was especially true for international students who were new
to the United States and had little other experience with Americans before coming to
study in the U.S. (pp. 122–123). Many students who study abroad can identify with
these findings, hearing from students in other countries that they watch American
television and think everyone here lives like the characters on *Modern Family* or experiences intrigue like the characters on *Homeland*. Research on violent content in
support of cultivation theory continues today, even after the death of George Gerbner.
In 2019, Signorielli, Morgan, and Shanahan reported on five decades of cultural indicators research to see if there were changes in trends in violence on television networks (Signorielli, Morgan, & Shanahan, 2019). They discovered that violence has
been a consistent and central part of programming within major television networks.
While violence decreased during the 1990s when more sitcoms were aired and crime-
related shows like *Law & Order* and *CSI* showed less explicit violence, the trends
increased to historically high levels after that decade (pp. 24–25). The authors contend
that there is no evidence that this culture of violence will change in the coming years.

It is important to recognize that not everyone supported Gerbner's work and
conclusions. Critics faulted his research design, and the fact that he did not differentiate between types of violence. In the Cultural Indicators Project content analyses,
cartoon violence and slapstick comedy were counted the same way as a brutal murder,
without regard to context. Critics maintained that this all-inclusiveness inflated the
violence index. In addition, Gerbner was unable to demonstrate a causal link between
watching violence and viewers' violent behavior (Baran & Davis, 2006, p. 331).

Perhaps most controversial of all is that Gerbner's research attempted to use
quantitative methods to measure a cultural indicator. In doing so, he used empirical
methods to study humanistic assumptions, actually combining social science and humanities (Baran & Davis, 2006, pp. 333–335). This unorthodox approach drew criticism from researchers in both camps (more description of these research methods is
found in Chapters 7, 8 and 9). However, as Newcomb noted, Gerbner was the first to
move his study out of a laboratory setting and examine what was happening in the real
world as well as the impact that television was having upon the culture (Baran & Davis
2006, p. 333).

In an attempt to use cultivation theory in another setting, Melhem and Punyanunt-
Carter (2019) studied the impact of American college students' perceptions of Arabs in
general and on television. In a survey of 429 undergraduates at a large public university
in the southwestern US, the authors found that television had a definite impact on
negative stereotypes of Arabs, describing them in terms such as "terrorists,"

"Muslim," "bad people," and "negative." When asked where they obtained their views, the top three responses all focused on the media (p. 267). The researchers felt that further research on Arab television characters is needed to identify the cultivating impact that these negative impressions have on interpersonal relationships, stereotypes, and perceptions (p. 269).

Other Theories of Media Violence

As cultivation theory illustrates, there is considerable controversy around the issue of media and violence. While Gerbner decried the amount and level of violence in television and the movies, his critics often faulted his failure to show the impact this violence had in terms of society's behavior. Yet thousands of studies have examined the impact of media violence on behavior, much of it focusing on children. These include projects using Albert Bandura's social learning theory (discussed in Chapter 3), which proposed that children imitate role models that they see on television, including aggressive role models.

One of the first scholars to research the impact that television has on children's behavior was Leonard Eron. In 1960, Eron studied third-graders (8- and 9-year-olds) in a suburban community north of New York City. In addition to watching them in the playground, he had their parents fill out questionnaires that included how much and what types of television the child watched. Eron observed that the more violent the programs the children watched, the more aggressive they seemed to be in school. He returned when the children were 19 and found that the boys who watched a lot of television were more likely to get into trouble with the law. Finally, Eron returned to the community in 1982, when his subjects were 30. He found that children who had watched the most violent television programming in their youth were more likely to use violence against their own children, were more likely to be convicted of a crime, and were reported to be more aggressive by their spouses than those who watched less television (Stossel, 1997). In testifying before a U.S. Senate committee on television programming in 1999, Eron estimated that ten percent of all youth violence can be attributed to television (Eron, 1999).

What mass media theories actually help explain the impact that violent programming may have on behavior? There have been many, but three stand out.

The Catharsis Hypothesis

Catharsis is a Greek word that means purification or cleansing. It has also been used to mean tension release. So, the catharsis hypothesis would argue that watching television helps to release tension, a component of the uses and gratifications theory described in Chapter 3. College students often report watching *Jimmy Fallon, Big Brother,* or *The Bachelor* as a way to relax, especially during times of extreme stress such as during finals or the week before a major research project is due. The catharsis hypothesis as applied to media violence, however, would indicate that watching violence on television would help to release violent tendencies in the viewer. Seymour Feshbach was one of the first researchers to propose that viewing TV violence might actually have a positive effect. Feshbach posited that watching other people behave in an aggressive manner would allow an angry and aggressive individual to cleanse their pent-up emotions, calm down, and let them act out aggressive fantasies, so they would be less likely to act on their anger (Sparks, 2002, p. 82). The research in support of this was based on a study done at a detention facility for young boys. The youths in the group that watched the nonviolent programming had higher levels of aggression than the group that watched the violent programming. While the findings initially seemed to support the catharsis hypothesis, it was later discovered that those who weren't allowed to watch their favorite programs were angry and acted out because of this (Sparks, 2002, p. 83). The catharsis hypothesis is not considered a valid explanation of the impact of media violence.

The Disinhibition Hypothesis

A second view of media violence maintains that desensitization to violence occurs in an individual after repeated exposure. People who watch a lot of violence on television are less affected by it, and thus are comfortable with their own aggressive behavior (Perry, 1996, p. 159). This hypothesis has some support from both anecdotal evidence and research studies. For example, Gerbner has noted that the first *Die Hard* movie had 18 deaths, while the second had 264. The first *Robocop* movie had 32 deaths and the second 81 (Stossel, 1997). The implication is that it will take more violence to satisfy the viewers who came to see more of the same in the sequels. The findings are even more blatant in the research studies. Potter (1999) reviewed more than five decades of research on the effects of exposure to media violence. Some of the effects he found were strongly supported in the research findings included:

- Exposure to violent portrayals in the media can lead to subsequent viewer aggression through disinhibition – for example, seeing a TV character use violence to solve a problem, like fighting with the classroom bully, will make the viewer more likely to try violence to solve the problem of the classroom bully in his own school.
- Exposure to violence in the media can lead to desensitization – for example, seeing graphic depictions of violence on shows like *The Walking Dead, The Blacklist*, or *Game of Thrones* may desensitize a person to be less affected by a crime scene in his own neighborhood.
- Long term exposure to media violence is related to aggression in a person's life – i.e., aggression becomes a way to solve all of life's problems.
- Media violence is related to subsequent violence in society – viewers will translate that violence to their lives.
- People exposed to many violent portrayals over a long time will come to be more accepting of violence (p. 26).

Priming

Recall that earlier in this chapter priming was described as a function of agenda setting and a way to describe how agenda setting works. The same term is used in relation to media violence effects as a process of associations. Leonard Berkowitz believes that the mass media are a potent source of images or ideas that can prime people's thoughts and actions. Thus, viewing images of media violence can prime thoughts of hostility and affect the way viewers see others and interpret their actions. It might also prime thoughts that lead one to believe that aggressive behavior might be warranted in certain situations. Violence might even bring benefits and cause people to be more inclined to act violently (Sparks, 2002, p. 83). Research has also discovered that priming can affect the individual for some time after exposure and can operate automatically and even without awareness (Berkowitz & Rogers, 1986, p. 59).

It is worth noting that much of the research on media violence examined television violence, the focus of Gerbner's work that led to cultivation theory. Research has also considered violence in video games. In 2015, an American Psychological Association task force on media violence released a report summarizing their review of all the studies that examined users of violent video games between 2005 and 2013. They concluded that there definitely was a link between increased aggressive behavior and the playing of violent video games. They were unable to determine whether this aggressive behavior actually led to criminal behavior, but expressed concern especially about children younger than ten years of age who play these games (Technical Report on the Review of the Violent Video Game Literature, 2015). These definitive findings provide further support for Gerbner's cultivation theory arising from a violent media culture.

While the theories of media violence may not be considered sociological theories in the strict sense that they affect populations as a whole, they are considered an extension of cultivation theory. Society may be most concerned with the specific case of an individual who views a violent movie or television program and then copies that crime in real life; however, media theorists generally study the question of media violence in terms of the impact it has on a society or culture as a whole.

CONCLUSION

This chapter and the one before it have sought to organize what are known as the effects theories of mass communication according to the level at which they primarily seem to operate, either affecting individual message consumers or affecting larger groups such as members of a community following an election or heavy watchers of television, up to the level of an entire society. Clearly, there is likely some overlap in the nature and results of media effects because large groups and society as a whole are composed of individuals.

The effects theories, however, are not the only way in which researchers seek to explain the influence of the media on modern society. An entirely different way of looking at such influences is discussed in the next chapter, which describes an alternate paradigm of interpretive theories about the connections of media, culture and society.

Questions for Discussion

1. What sorts of topics are on the agendas of students at your university? How

effective are the campus media (newspaper and/or website, radio station, television station, social media accounts of these outlets) in setting the students' agenda? Are students getting their information from these sources or more from each other?

2. How does news spread through your social group? Think of critical news in your life and how you found out about it – which messages came from the media and which came from people? How much comes from social media vs. mainstream media or face-to-face contact?

3. Can you think of a new product or service that you have adopted in the past six months? How did you find out about it? How were you persuaded to try it and use it? Can Everett Rogers's theory apply to your innovation experience?

4. What is the responsibility of the mass media in narrowing the knowledge gap? Are there things that the media is doing or should be doing that help narrow the gap? How important is technology and high-speed internet access in helping to narrow the gap?

5. Can you cite some current examples of how the spiral of silence operates to keep the majority viewpoint and silence the minority? In what ways have you experienced this phenomenon?

6. With the explosion in media choices today, is there really a cultivation effect? Can society as a whole be moving toward a common view when everyone is consuming something different?

REFERENCES

Alterman, E. (2003). *What liberal media?: The truth about bias and the news.* New York: Perseus Books.

American Academy of Child and Adolescent Psychiatry. (2020). *Screen time and children, No. 54.* Retrieved from https://www.aacap.org/AACAP/Families_and_Youth/Facts_for_Families/FFF-Guide/Children-And-Watching-TV-054.aspx

Associated Press. (2020, July 20). Braves remove "Chop On" sign from Truist Park; no call yet on Tomahawk Chop chant. Retrieved from https://www.espn.com/mlb/story/_/id/29503211/braves-remove-chop-sign-truist-park-no-call-tomahawk-chop-chant

Axisa, M. (2020, December 16). Cleveland Indians name change: History of franchise nickname, Chief Wahoo logo and calls for a switch. *CBS Sports* online. Retrieved from https://www.cbssports.com/mlb/news/mlbs-top-10-extension-candidates-fernando-tatis-jr-francisco-lindor-and-key-pieces-for-yankees-dodgers/

Baran, S.J. & Davis, D.K. (2006). *Mass communication theory: Foundations, ferment, and future* (4th ed.). Belmont, CA: Thomson/Wadsworth.

Belson, K. (2021, February 7). The Chiefs enter the field to the sound of the tomahawk chop. *The New York Times* online. Retrieved from https://www.nytimes.com/2021/02/07/sports/football/the-chiefs-enter-the-field-to-the-sound-of-the-tomahawk-chop.html

Bernstein, D. (2020, November 26). Redskins name change timeline: How Daniel Snyder's 'NEVER' gave way to Washington Football Team. *Sporting News* online. Retrieved from https://www.sportingnews.com/us/nfl/news/redskins-name-timeline-washington-football-team/1uk394uouwi631k7poirtq1v1s

Berkowitz, L. & Rogers, K.H. (1986). A priming effect analysis of media influences. In Bryant, J. & Zillman, D. (Eds.). *Perspectives on media effects* (pp. 57–81). Hillsdale, NJ: Lawrence Erlbaum Associates.

Boukes, M. & Vliegenthart, R. (2019). The knowledge gap hypothesis across modality: Differential acquisition of knowledge from television news, newspapers, and news websites. *International Journal of Communication* 13, 3650–3671.

Bronstein, C. (2005). Representing the third wave: Mainstream print media framing of a new feminist movement. *Journalism & Mass Communication Quarterly* 82 (4), 783–804.

Brosius, H-B., Haim, M., & Weimann, G. (2019). Diffusion as a future perspective of agenda setting. *The Agenda Setting Journal* 3 (2), 123–138.

Center for Interactive Advertising (n.d.). Retrieved from http://www.ciadvertising.org/

Chyi, H.I. & McCombs, M. (2004). Media salience and the process of framing: Coverage of the Columbine School shootings. *Journalism & Mass Communication Quarterly* 81 (1), 22–35.

Cowart, H. (2020). What to think about: The applicability of agenda settings in a social media context. *The Agenda Setting Journal* 4 (2), 195–218.

Donahue, G.A., Tichenor, P.J., & Olien, C.N. (1975). Mass media and the knowledge gap: A hypothesis reconsidered. *Communication Research* 2, 3–23.

Entman, R.M. (2009). *Projections of power: Framing news, public opinion, and U.S. foreign policy*. Chicago: University of Chicago Press.

Entman, R.M. (1993). Framing: Toward clarification of a fractured paradigm. *Journal of Communication* 43 (4), 51–58.

Eron, L. D. (1999, May 18). Effects of television violence on children. Testimony before Senate Committee on Science, Commerce and Transportation regarding safe harbor hours in TV programming.

Fallows, J. (1996). *Breaking the news: How the media undermine democracy*. New York: Pantheon Books.

Funkhouser, G.R. (1973). Trends in media coverage of the issues of the '60s. *Journalism Quarterly* 50, 533–538.

Gerbner, G., Gross, L., Morgan, M., & Signorielli, N. (1980). The "mainstreaming" of America: Violence profile No. 11. *Journal of Communication* 30 (3), 212–231.

Gerbner, G., Gross, L., Morgan, M., & Signorielli, N. (1986). Living with television: The dynamics of the cultivation process. In Bryant, J. & Zillman, D. (Eds.). *Perspectives on media effects*. Hillsdale, NJ: Lawrence Erlbaum Associates.

Glynn, J.C. & McLeod, J. (1984). Public opinion du jour: An examination of the spiral of silence. *Public Opinion Quarterly* 48 (4), 731–740.

Glynn, J.C., Hayes, F.A. & Shanahan, J. (1997). Perceived support for one's opinions and willingness to speak out: A meta-analysis of survey studies on the "spiral of silence." *Public Opinion Quarterly* 61 (3), 452–463.

Gottfried, J. & Shearer, E. (2016, May 6). News use across social media platforms 2016. *Pew Research Center*. Retrieved from http://www.journalism.org/2016/05/26/news-use-across-social-media-platforms-2016

Grzywinski, I. & Borden, J. (2012). The impact of social media on traditional media agenda setting theory – the case study of Occupy Wall Street Movement in USA. In Dobek-Ostrowska, B., Łódzki, B., & Wanta, W. (Eds.). *Agenda setting: Old and new problems in the old and new media* (pp. 133–155). Wydawnictwo Uniwersytetu Wrocławskiego.

Hampton, K., Rainie, L., Lu, W., Dwyer, M., Shin, I. & Purcell, K. (2014, August 26). Social media and the "spiral of silence." *Pew Research Center*. Retrieved from http://www.pewinternet.org/2014/08/26/social-media-and-the-spiral-of-silence/

Holbert, R.L., Pillion, O., Tschida, D.A., Armfield, G.G., Kinder, K., Cherry, K.L., & Daulton, A.R. (2003). The West Wing as endorsement of the U.S. presidency: Expanding the bounds of priming in political communication. *Journal of Communication* 53 (3), 427–443.

Holbrook, T.M. (2002). Presidential campaigns and the knowledge gap. *Political Communication* 19, 437–454.

Iyengar, S., Peters, M.D., & Kinger, D.R. (1982). Experimental demonstrations of the "not-so-minimal" consequences of television news programs. *American Political Science Review* 76 (4), 848–858.

Iyengar, S. & Simon, A. (1993). News coverage of the gulf crisis and public opinion. *Communication Research* 20, 365–383.

Katzman, N. (1974). The impact of communication technologies: Promises and prospects. *Journal of Communication* 24 (4), 47–58.

Kushin, M.J., Yamamoto, M. & Dalisay, F. (2019, April–June). Societal majority, Facebook, and the spiral of silence in the 2016 U.S. presidential election. *Social Media + Society* 2019, 1–11.

Lechner, I. (2021). Meme marketing: The next generation of advertising. Retrieved from https://medium.com/magic-media/meme-marketing-the-next-generation-of-advertising-75799c755307

Ling, C., AbuHilal, I., Blackburn, J., De Cristofaro, E., Zannettou, S. & Stringhini, G. (2021). Dissecting the meme magic: Understanding indicators of virality in image memes. Paper presented to the 24th ACM Conference on Computer-Supported Cooperative Work and Social Computing. Retrieved from https://arxiv.org/pdf/2101.06535.pdf

Liu, Y.I. & Eveland, W.P. (2005). Education, need for cognition, and campaign interest as moderators of news effect on political knowledge: An analysis of the knowledge gap. *Journalism & Mass Communication Quarterly* 84 (2), 910–929.

Maher, M. (1996). Media framing and public perception of environmental causality. *Southwestern Mass Communication Journal* 12, 61–73.

McCann, J.A. & Lawson, C. (2006). Presidential campaigns and the knowledge gap in three transitional democracies. *Political Research Quarterly* 59 (1), 13–22.

McCombs, M. & Shaw, D. (1972). The agenda setting function of mass media. *Public Opinion Quarterly* 36 (2), 176–187.

McCombs, M. (2005). The agenda setting function of the press. In Overholser, G. & Jamieson, K.H. (Eds.). *The Press* (pp. 156–168). New York: Oxford University Press.

Melhem, S., Punyanunt-Carter, N. (2019). Using cultivation theory to understand American College Students' perceptions of Arabs in the media. *Journal of Muslim Minority Affairs* 39 (2), 259–271.

Meraz, S. (2009). Is there an elite hold? Traditional media to social media agenda setting influence in blog networks. *Journal of Computer-Mediated Communication* 14 (3), 682–707.

Min, S., So, K., & Jeong, M. (2019). Consumer adoption of the Uber mobile application: Insights from diffusion of innovation theory and technology acceptance model. *Journal of Travel and Tourism Marketing* 36 (7), 770–783.

Moy, P., Domke, D., & Stamm, K. (2001). The spiral of silence and public opinion on affirmative action. *Journalism & Mass Communication Quarterly* 78 (1), 7–25

Mutua, S.N. & Ong'ong'a, D.O. (2020). Online news media framing of COVID-19 pandemic: Probing the initial phases of the disease outbreak in international media. *European Journal of Interactive Multimedia and Education* 1 (2), e0206.

National Congress of American Indians. (n.d.) Ending the era of harmful "Indian" mascots. Retrieved from www.ncai.org/proudtobe

Patterson, T. (2016, June 13). Pre-primary news coverage of the 2016 presidential race: Trump's rise, Sanders' emergence, Clinton's struggle. Shorenstein Center on Media, Politics and Public Policy. Retrieved from http://shorensteincenter.org/pre-primary-news-coverage-2016-trump-clinton-sanders/

Perry, D.K. (1996). *Theory and research in mass communication.* Mahwah, NJ: Lawrence Erlbaum Associates.

Potter, W.J. & Chang, I.C. (1990). Television exposure measures and the cultivation hypothesis. *Journal of Broadcasting and Electronic Media* 34 (3), 313–333.

Potter, W.J. (1999). *On media violence.* Thousand Oaks, CA: Sage Publications.

Prior, M. (2005). News vs. entertainment choice: How increasing media choice widens gaps in political knowledge and turnout. *American Journal of Political Science* 49 (3), 577–592.

Rogers, E. (1983). *Diffusion of innovations* (3rd ed.). New York: Free Press

Rogers, E. (1995). *Diffusion of innovations* (4th ed.). New York: Free Press

Rosenberry, J. (2011). Users support online anonymity despite increasing negativity. *Newspaper Research Journal* 32 (2), 6–19.

Roush, C. (2005). Book review: Framed: Labor and the corporate media. *Journalism & Mass Communication Quarterly* 82 (2), 460–461.

Ryan, B. & Gross, N. (1943). The diffusion of hybrid seed corn in two Iowa communities. *Rural Sociology* 8, 15–24.

Sanders, R.L., Branion-Calles, M. & Nelson, T. (2020). To scoot or not to scoot: Findings from a recent survey about the benefits and barriers of using E-scooters for riders and non-riders. *Transportation Research Part A* 139, 217–227.

Scheufele, D. & Moy, P. (2000). Twenty-five years of the spiral of silence: A conceptual review and empirical outlook. *International Journal of Public Opinion Research* 12 (1), 3–28.

Severin, W.J. & Tankard Jr., J.W. (2001). *Communication theories: Origins, methods, and uses in the mass media* (5th ed.) New York: Addison Wesley Longman.

Shaffer, G. (2006). Frame-up: An analysis of arguments both for and against municipal wi-fi initiatives. Paper presented at the Annual Convention of the Association for Education in Journalism and Mass Communication, San Francisco.

Shearer, E., Mitchell. A. (2021, January 12) New use across social media platforms in 2020. Pew Research Center. Retrieved from https://www.journalism.org/2021/01/12/news-use-across-social-media-platforms-in-2020/

Signorielli, N., Morgan, M. & Shanahan, J. (2019). The violence profile: Five decades of cultural indicators research. *Mass Communication and Society* 22 (1), 1–28.

Simpson, C. (1996). Elizabeth Noelle-Neumann's "spiral of silence" and the historical context of communication theory. *Journal of Communication* 46 (3) 149–171.

Sparks, G.G. (2002). *Mass media effects research*. Belmont, CA: Wadsworth/Thomson Learning.

Stein, J.P., Krause, E. & Ohler, P. (2019, December 12). Every (Insta) Gram counts? Applying cultivation theory to explore the effects of Instagram on young users' body image. *Psychology of Popular Media Culture* 2019, 11–12.

Stossel, S. (1997). The man who counts the killings. *The Atlantic Monthly* 279 (5), 86–104.

Technical Report on the Review of the Violent Video Game Literature (2015). APA Task Force on Violent Media. Retrieved from http://www.apa.org/pi/families/review-video-games.pdf

Tichenor, P., Donahue, G. & Olien, C. (1970). Mass media flow and differential growth in knowledge *Public Opinion Quarterly* 34 (2), 159–170.

U.S. Bureau of Labor Statistics. (2019a). Public Relations Specialists. Retrieved from https://www.bls.gov/ooh/media-and-communication/public-relations-specialists.htm

U.S. Bureau of Labor Statistics. (2019b). Reporters, correspondents, and Broadcast News Analysts. Retrieved from https://www.bls.gov/ooh/media-and-communication/reporters-correspondents-and-broadcast-news-analysts.htm

Van Duyn, E. & Collier, J. (2018). Priming and fake news: The effects of elite discourse on evaluations of news media. *Mass Communication and Society* 22 (1), 29–48.

Wohn, D.Y. & Bowe, B.J. (2016). Micro agenda setters: The effect of social media on young adults' exposure to and attitude toward news. *Social Media + Society* 2 (1), 1–12.

Woo, H.J. & Dominick, J.R. (2003). Acculturation, cultivation, and daytime TV talk shows. *Journalism & Mass Communication Quarterly* 80 (1), 109–127.

Yang, L. (2019). Analysis of fans' cyberwords from the perspective of memetics. *Cross-Cultural Communication* 15 (4), 30–34. Retrieved from http://52.196.142.242/index.php/ccc/article/view/11433.

Zucker, H. (1978). The variable nature of news media influence. *Communication Yearbook* (Vol. 2, pp. 225–245). New Brunswick NJ: Transaction Books.

CHAPTER 5

The Alternative Paradigms of Critical and Cultural Studies

This chapter will:

- Compare and contrast the more traditional communication science paradigm with what communication theorist Denis McQuail has called the "alternative paradigm" of interpretive and critical views of the way media institutions and content affect society and culture.
- Define some of the key terms and concepts used in this area of inquiry, such as ideology, hegemony, and institutional reinforcement of the elite power structure.
- Describe how these different approaches to media study require different research methods and techniques for formulating theory.
- Provide an overview of some of the most popular approaches within this paradigm, including political economy, the Frankfurt and Birmingham (British) schools of cultural studies, postmodernism, and media ecology.

The theories of the effects paradigm investigated through positivist communication science – as described in the two previous chapters – historically have been the main way of theorizing about and researching mass communication. Potter and Riddle (2007) examined 962 articles from 16 communication journals published between 1993 and 2005, and found surveys were the most popular way of conducting the research (32 percent of the studies) with experiments (28 percent) being the next most popular. A more recent study, which analyzed 65 years of research published in the *Journal of Communication*, similarly found positivist inquiries using quantitative methods by far the most common way of conducting communication research. That approach accounted for 80 percent of more than 1,500 published pieces that were reviewed (Walter, Cody, & Ball-Rokeach, 2018). A separate examination of journal articles focused specifically on emerging communication technology, especially Internet communication, found that more than three quarters of them used quantitative empirical approaches, especially content analyses (Borah, 2017).

This style of communication science, however, is not the only way to evaluate how the mass media affect audiences and shape society. Many researchers prefer a non-empirical approach to the topic that comes in different varieties with different labels that share some common underlying themes. Perhaps the most inclusive term comes from Denis McQuail, who refers to it as the "alternative paradigm" (McQuail, 2005, p. 65).

DOI: 10.4324/9781003121695-5

This paradigm encompasses related, but distinct, approaches including cultural studies, symbolic constructivism, critical theory (or critical studies), and media ecology. In their study of the journal articles, Walter et al. described the distinction as, "The critical paradigm referred to studies that revolve around questions of power, status quo, and social structure. Qualitative analyses of everyday practices that create and sustain culture were classified as cultural studies" (Walter et al., 2018, p. 426).

CHARACTERISTICS OF THE PARADIGM

The prevailing theme in this branch of communication inquiry is that knowledge is a form of power, and groups within a society use media institutions to help them exercise and maintain cultural power. This happens through mass media promoting a set of ideas associated with a society's powerful interests, which frequently marginalize or drown out other, non-mainstream ideas. Researchers in this alternative paradigm say that the effects approach is incapable of addressing this issue adequately because effects research tends to be narrowly constructed and focuses on messages and effects of those dominant media. This makes the effects paradigm incapable of looking beyond the status quo toward any sort of reformist stance. By emphasizing quantitative measurement of the existing situation, communication science actually reinforces the status quo and its power arrangements, according to advocates of critical theory. One description of this is "for most administrative research the existing power structure can do no wrong; for most critical research it can do no right" (Melody & Mansell, 1983, p. 106).

Emphasis on Reform

Another characteristic of the interpretive tradition is that its proponents believe theories and research projects should advocate action, specifically actions directed at improving society by helping "outsider" groups overcome the marginalization and domination they face. The dominant theme in critical and cultural studies thus can be seen as giving voice to oppressed groups within the society (Littlejohn, 1999).

This reformist basis is why the approach is called a *critical* one. To understand this better, think about the words "critical" and "criticism" in a generic sense. If a person is being critical of someone or something, what is she doing? Well, she is probably pointing out shortcomings, and possibly also suggesting improvements, about whatever is being criticized. The concept is similar to the "constructive criticism" or "critical feedback" that teachers make on students' assignments. Critical theorists say that is exactly what they are trying to do: offer constructive criticism about both content and control systems for mass media as a social institution. The goal of theory and research in this tradition is to identify ways in which the media system is falling short of its best performance and to suggest ways to improve.

This form of inquiry has its roots in European sociology and its philosophical basis in the ideas of Karl Marx, best known for his theories of politics and economics. Marx was perhaps the original "critical theorist," with criticisms directed at the political and economic power structure of 19th century Europe. In his view, the working class (proletariat) provided the true source of wealth in the newly industrialized society, but the social structure oppressed the workers and allowed that wealth to be unfairly monopolized by the capitalists (bourgeoisie) who owned the factories.

Response to Limited Effects

Scholars at the University of Frankfurt in Germany in the 1930s were among the first to apply variants of Marx's ideas, mixed with psychologist Sigmund Freud's ideas that unconscious impulses are a key part of human behavior, to the operation of mass media and its relation to powerful forces in society. The critical and cultural paradigm really took hold as a reaction to the limited effects paradigm based in social science research and popularized in the United States in the 1950s and early 1960s.

As noted in Chapter 2, the idea of limited effects came about when social scientists such as Paul Lazarsfeld tried to use quantitative methods to test ideas about the powerful, direct, and uniform effects of media associated with propaganda and the "bullet" theory. However, the results of these tests indicated that mass media messages behaved opposite to what theories of powerful effects would predict. According to this research, the media apparently did not strongly or directly influence audience members. Rather, researchers from this era found evidence that the influence of media messages was affected by the audience members' contact with other people (two-step flow theory) and that media messages tended to support ideas that media consumers already had (reinforcement theory).

When Katz, Klapper, and other theorists argued for a view of limited effects, some other media scholars disagreed because they thought that the findings understated media impacts. One of these reactions was further social-science investigation such as agenda-setting and cultivation research (discussed in Chapter 4), which sought to document circumstances under which some type of direct and meaningful effects *could* take place.

Yet another reaction was a more interpretive analysis that took a broader view of media and society together – recognizing how mass media had become a key part of the way ideas were communicated and culture was maintained in modern society. "These new perspectives argued that the media might have the power to intrude on and alter how we make sense of ourselves and our social world ... media affect society because they affect how culture is created, shared, learned and applied" (Baran & Davis, 2006, p. 227). This was the critical/cultural paradigm.

BOX 5.1

Definition of Positivism

Positivism: Using investigative methods of the physical sciences, such as experiments and objective measurement of specified criteria, to address and understand social phenomena. This style of inquiry is associated with the communication science tradition, with research largely based on quantitative measurement of hypotheses. (Often these projects are based in the theories explained in Chapters 3 and 4.) The central idea behind positivism is largely rejected by critical and cultural theorists.

Positivist/Interpretive Differences

The social science approach used in the investigations by scholars such as Lazarsfeld (as described in Chapter 2) is sometimes called the "positivist" or "neo-positivist" method. This term comes from Auguste Comte, an early 19th century sociologist. In Comte's positivist philosophy, the only way "true" knowledge could be developed was through real-world observations. The scientific method and its use as a source of knowledge (as described in Chapter 1) are closely related to this philosophy. From the positivist perspective, "meaning and truth are derived using logical, analytical or empirical rules of verification" (Melody & Mansell, 1983, p. 106).

Interpretive theorists reject the idea that knowledge must always come from scientific proof because they believe that this makes it impossible to consider the context of a situation as part of the research. Additionally, they view human behavior as something that is so complex that it is hard to draw meaningful conclusions about society from things that can be empirically observed and measured (Melody & Mansell, 1983; DeVaus, 2001). Consequently, in terms of research "style," critical and cultural scholars lean heavily toward qualitative methods rather than quantitative ones. In essence, critical and cultural theorists say that studying people requires a different approach than quantitative measurement, and it's more important to go in depth with individual situations than to collect and manipulate statistics from large samplings (see Chapter 9).

Critical researchers believe that this inability of quantitative research to reach accurate conclusions about the impact of media on culture is especially true of long-term developments:

> One of the major problems in that type of (limited effects) research has been that the empirical instruments used were often too crude to note small changes that could be of great significance as they were compounded over time. For instance, it might be hard to detect short-term attitude changes in an audience that result from the content of the network evening news; yet, compounded over years, those effects might be profound (DeSola Pool, 1983, p. 259).

Thus, the critical scholar would maintain that long-term effects of mass communication are best analyzed within individual cases examined over time rather than data collected by surveys, content analyses, and experiments that count the instances of people engaging in particular behaviors at one moment in time. Where a positivist study might document the under-representation of Blacks and other people of color in popular television shows at a particular point in time, a critical view might be more concerned with the cumulative effects of not having such portrayals available to viewers over a matter of years or decades.

In fact, some within the critical school go further, saying that empirical research into human behavior is so narrow and mechanical that it is basically pointless. In this view, "positivists do not merely base their work on that evidence, they enshrine it, making measurable data the definitive goal of research. The result of this slavish devotion to fact is, at best, a narrowing of research sights and, at worst, a view that what is real is measurable and what is measurable is real" (Mosco, 1983, pp. 244–245). Even some quantitative researchers agree on that point. British statistician Denise Lievesley, for example, cautions against doing research based merely on readily available data. Doing so, she says, could result in an outcome that is mathematically significant (according to statistical rules) but not really meaningful relative to the context or larger situation of the topic being investigated. She calls this "hitting the target but missing the point" (Lievesley, 2020).

At the same time, it should be noted that an equally negative view of interpretive research is often held by supporters of traditional social science research. They say the critical/interpretive approach is nothing more than subjective opinion that produces essays instead of research and offers little toward discovery of new knowledge. They further criticize it because it does not allow for precision, falsification and replication and because the same data can yield different but equally plausible interpretations when the criteria are vague (Rosengren, 1983). Some positivist social scientists also say that rather than being truly reform-minded, critical researchers push a narrow, biased agenda based on utopian views that ignore reality and end up merely attacking media practices without any realistic suggestions for reform. While both views have their supporters and detractors, the two traditions have existed together within the discipline for more than half a century. Mixed methods that combine elements of both quantitative AND qualitative approaches are gaining popularity.

GOALS OF CRITICAL AND CULTURAL RESEARCH

In addition to this disagreement over methods of inquiry, quantitative social scientists and critical or cultural theory advocates differ in another important way: Whether to "take sides" in doing research. In the positivist view, social scientists should have a hypothesis – a prediction about how certain variables are related. In order for the research to be reliable, though, scientists should remain objective in their work. This means they should not have a viewpoint, or an idea about how the variables *should* be related, or what relationship among them would be the *best* type of relationship. The goal of social science in the positivist tradition is to investigate and document things *as they are*, not to offer perspectives about how they *should be*.

Critical research takes exactly the opposite stance, dropping the pretense of objectivity, while cultural studies seeks out a middle ground of somewhat more objective analysis through use of qualitative data analysis. Critical tradition researchers deliberately take viewpoints about how they believe the social system should operate and, through their research, set out to illuminate why and how the actual situation varies from their conception of the way things ought to be. Critical research has the goal "to reshape or invent institutions to meet the need of the relevant social community" (Smythe & Van Dinh, 1983, p. 118) and "offers an alternative way of seeing the place of communication in society by focusing on the transformation of social relations" (Mosco, 1983, p. 244). Scholars in this tradition say that research has no real value unless it takes a viewpoint. They further claim that a great deal of empirical research is nothing more than measurement of activities for the sake of measuring them, with findings that serve no real purpose. Rather, "Those who develop critical theories seek social change that will implement their values" (Baran & Davis, 2006, p. 231).

Exploration of Ideology and Hegemony

Two concepts at the heart of these reform-minded approaches are ideology and hegemony. Ideology refers to a dominant way of thinking about how society should be organized, featuring the ideas of those who hold power in the society. For example, both socialism and capitalism are ideologies about how an economic system should be organized. A more technical definition says ideology is "culturally constructed and institutionally reinforced understandings of the world which privilege the positions of the powerful" (Lye, 2004). Hegemony takes the concept of ideology and goes a step further to describe how ideology can become a tool for social control by undermining or crowding out ideas from outside of the mainstream that threaten privileged positions of the powerful.

Hegemony was first defined by Antonio Gramsci, a leftist Italian journalist, who used the term to define a situation in which a large portion of society becomes compliant and consents to a dominant ideology without even realizing it is being imposed on them. This happens because the dominant ideology is made to seem so convincing that even those who end up being exploited by the powerful interests (whom the ideology protects and supports) "buy in" to its ideals. Following on the previous examples, having a capitalist basis for the economy is a hegemonic view in the United States, especially, but also in many other countries, including Japan and Western Europe. Most of the general population in these nations couldn't conceive of how the country would work without a capitalist basis – even poorer people who don't benefit from the system as much as wealthy, more powerful individuals.

In the critical view, the media play a significant role in promoting this consent and compliance. As one scholar puts it, "the concept of hegemony suggests that the ideas of the ruling class in society become the ruling ideas throughout society. The mass media are seen as controlled by the dominant class in society and as aiding in exerting the control of that class over the rest of society" (Severin & Tankard, 2001, p. 282).

BOX 5.2

Definitions of Ideology/Hegemony

Ideology: Dominant way of thinking about how society should be organized, based on the ideas of those who hold power in the society and promoted by those social elites as a way to help them maintain power.

Hegemony: Consent to a dominant ideology by a whole social system, even those who are adversely affected by it and who therefore should be resistant to that ideology being imposed on them.

Focus on Power Structures

To summarize, critical perspectives on ideology, hegemony, and reform of the social structure generally take the form of critiquing power relations within a society's communication system by examining topics such as:

- Which groups hold power, and by what means.
- Which groups are marginalized, oppressed, or cut off from power, and how the more powerful groups keep them marginalized.
- What role communication systems (especially mass media) have in these power relationships.
- How communication structures could be set up differently to address these issues.

TYPES OF CRITICAL AND CULTURAL RESEARCH

So far, the critical, cultural, and interpretive traditions have been described as a single entity, and they have some common goals regarding communication in the exercise of social power (Slack & Allor, 1983). Even within the tradition, though, contrasting approaches examine these social relationships from different perspectives. The fundamental difference is the level of analysis, either at a macroscopic (large-scale) level focusing on social institutions, or at a more micro level about how the culture of everyday life is created and how that culture affects individuals and groups in more personalized ways (Baran & Davis, 2006). (This roughly aligns with the macro and micro perspectives on the effects theories that divided Chapters 3 and 4). The first of these approaches, dealing with social institutions and the structure of society, is more closely aligned with critical theory and the second approach is more common in cultural studies.

Critical Theory

Political Economy

Broadly considered, political economy theory is about how the forces within a society help determine how its economic and social systems operate together. Classical Marxism, with its critique of how the industrial system is controlled by the bourgeoisie or upper class, fits this category with a focus on how that control entrenches elite power within society. Control of the economic base or "structure" is enhanced and reinforced by the control these same elite individuals have over the "superstructure," or social and cultural institutions such as churches, schools, and the media.

As applied to mass communication, political economy theory maintains that "economic institutions shape the media to suit their interests and purposes" (Baran & Davis, 2006, p. 241). Economic control of the means of media production – i.e., ownership of newspapers, magazines, television and radio stations, etc. – by huge corporations limits or alters the forms of mass culture distributed through those media. In its early days, the Internet was seen as a possible counter-influence. However, with the vast majority of Internet content now flowing through only a few large companies –

Apple, Google, Facebook, Amazon – the same economic pattern has developed there as well.

A common implication of this in critical theories of media is that financial imperatives drive content presentations. Product placement in television and movies, sponsored content (also known as native advertising) on news websites, and "labeled" elements of media presentations (e.g., *NBC Sunday Night Football's* "Toyota Halftime Show") are familiar examples. Another increasingly important connection of economic incentives and content presentation is algorithmic determination of social-media content and advertising. Algorithms used by platforms such as Facebook, Twitter, YouTube, and Instagram are designed to keep users engaged by sharing content they can be expected to respond to – by sharing, "liking," or otherwise interacting with it. Keeping users engaged with a site, and showing them algorithmically determined advertising they are likely to be responsive toward, is how the platforms make money. However, this often has unfortunate and unintended side effects such as causing hateful or false content to "go viral" and spread to millions of users, which is profitable for the platforms (DiResta, 2018).

Frankfurt School

The first individuals to apply the "superstructure" aspect of Marxist thought (as mentioned earlier) to media-generated culture and how it created "structures of oppression" (Littlejohn, 1999, p. 9) were a group of scholars in Frankfurt, Germany whose ideas have come to be known as the Frankfurt School of thought. They sought to keep Marxist theory alive during the 1920s and 1930s, at a time when it appeared to be declining because the Communist revolution had not spread from Russia. In fact, Marxism at the time was threatened by the rise of an alternate political/economic philosophy known as fascism that closely aligned the state with commercial interests. (Fascism did in fact take hold across Europe not long after, because it was the political/economic philosophy of Nazi Germany.)

These developments of European history helped to bring the revolutionary appeal of Marxism under control (Bennett, 1982). By using the Marxist view of "superstructure" or control of cultural institutions in society, the Frankfurt scholars theorized that mass culture created by powerful elites was imposed on the masses as a means of social control. Cultural products could help maintain the authority of those powerful individuals by keeping the masses of people distracted and disorganized. Rather than having a cultural system that invites and allows people to participate in the decisions of society, the result is "a generally alienated (rather than emancipated and activated) audience" (Rosengren, 1983, p. 193).

Many of the Frankfurt School's most influential intellectual thinkers were Jewish and actually fled Germany as it came under Nazi control in the 1930s. So, some of what is called the "Frankfurt School's" work actually was done in the United States by these exiled scholars, notably Theodor Adorno, Max Horkheimer, and Herbert Marcuse. Their definitive view of how mass culture promotes social control, *The Dialectic of Enlightenment*, was written in the middle of World War II by Adorno and Horkheimer (1944) while they were living in New York City.

Adorno and Horkheimer describe what happens when production of cultural artifacts moves from an individual-artist basis – illustrated by classical painters such as the Impressionists or musical composers such as Mozart – to an industrial one – illustrated by Hollywood movies and radio music programming. In their view, "the modern culture industry produces safe, standardized products geared to the larger demands of the capitalist economy. It does so by representing 'average' life for purposes of pure entertainment or distraction as seductively and realistically as possible" (During, 1993, p. 31). The result is a market-driven or capitalist set of culture industries, especially producers of Hollywood films, who are not interested in producing art but rather just serving up distractions that would create a conformist society that would accept the values of the capitalist system that produced them. "From every sound film and every broadcast program the social effect can be inferred which is exclusive to none but shared by all alike. The culture industry as a whole has molded men as a type unfailingly reproduced in every product ... The might of industrial society is lodged in men's minds" (Adorno & Horkheimer, 1944, in During, 1993).

The ideas of the Frankfurt School thinkers are an important and influential development in the analysis of media and society because even though they started with a basis in political economy, they transcended pure issues of media ownership to describe how ownership, content production, and social influence mutually reinforced each other with a hegemonic result (i.e., an outcome that supports the continued domination by powerful elites). The Frankfurt School's ideas put ideology at the center of the debate over how media influence society by suggesting that the media "occupy a critical position within the more general Marxist debates concerning the way in which the economic, political and ideological levels of the social formation should be construed as relating to one another" (Bennett, 1982, p. 49).

BOX 5.3

The Frankfurt School and "Indie" Producers

FIGURE 5.1 Klaus Hackenberg via Getty Images.

In their devastating critique of popular culture (Adorno & Horkheimer, 1944) Theodor Adorno and Max Horkheimer wrote that cultural offerings produced by large businesses are all style, with no substance, made with the goal of creating a conformist society while making a lot of money for their creators. Adorno and Horkheimer (1944) compared mass-produced pop culture goods (such as Hollywood movies) unfavorably to works of individual artists such as fine art paintings or the efforts of symphonic composers.

But in a modern adaptation of their thoughts, it could be said that the music and movie industries' emphasis on turning out look-alike and sound-alike productions that will have the greatest popular appeal (think superhero movies) is an example of the same process at work. So is these businesses' associated refusal to distribute the more *avant garde* works of independent filmmakers or non-mainstream musical groups.

This doesn't mean that independent movies or indie musicians can't be successful or popular, especially when online audio and video streaming capabilities help people who produce these works get around the powerful gatekeepers who largely control the industries. And such works arguably do provide more artistic value and substance than the cookie-cutter productions of the big firms. But without the power of a major studio or record label behind them, it is often difficult for these works to find very large audiences.

Commodification of Culture

A logical extension of Adorno and Horkheimer's thinking was developed a couple of decades later by Herbert Schiller, who said the issues of mass-culture hegemony became more significant as the economic system shifted away from an industrial economy toward one that emphasizes production and use of information. The world economy has been following this trend for the past several decades. Just as the trend was taking root, Schiller warned "The accelerating effort to transform information into a good for sale and not primarily for social use is centered directly on its production, accumulation, storage, retrieval, and distribution" (Schiller, 1983, p. 253). It is worth noting that Schiller, who died in 2000, wrote those words before the explosion of current media and expansion of telecommunications offerings such as satellite TV, satellite radio, digital distribution of video and music, or even the Internet and mobile phones. Without question, the "production, accumulation, storage, retrieval and distribution" of information has even more economic value and is controlled by even larger (and fewer) corporations than when he expressed those thoughts in the early 1980s.

Schiller's ideas are referred to as the *commodification of culture* theory. In economics, a commodity is a basic material, such as crude oil or unprocessed grain, that is essentially the same no matter what its source and is therefore sold in large quantities on the basis of price alone. According to Schiller, treating information as a commodity and "selling" it through the mass media explains the simplistic, escapist, and copycat tendencies of television, film, and music. One barrel of oil is identical to another, which is what makes it a commodity. Likewise, many media offerings are so similar that they might as well be identical: Sitcoms, dramas, and reality shows on television; action movies and romantic comedies in the theater; and sound-alike pop singers on Spotify or YouTube Music all are cited as evidence that media offerings also have become a commodity. According to Schiller's theory, commodity-like offerings are created to appeal to the largest audiences possible – which is very lucrative for the corporations that own the media production system. However, it also leads to a less-diverse, poorer-quality set of cultural offerings for the society because all of the commodified goods crowd out higher-quality material, such as important public affairs information, that could lead to social improvement. The latest escapades of popular celebrities can be seen as more important than nuances of government policies about health care or the economy.

BOX 5.4

Copycat Television

Although television shows come in various genres – from soft sitcoms to gritty dramas – a look at the most popular ones demonstrates a surprisingly narrow range of styles.

Out of the 50 most-watched shows from fall 2019 to spring 2020[1], three of the top five were prime-time telecasts of National Football League games (on Sunday, Monday and Thursday nights). Fully half of the shows – 25 out of 50 – were crime or medical dramas. This included 15 police procedural shows such as *NCIS* and *FBI*, which rounded out the top five with the football broadcasts, or *Blue Bloods* and *Chicago PD*, both also in the top ten. Similar shows in the top 50 included four crime dramas, four hospital dramas, and two shows set in fire stations.

Reality shows also were well-represented among the top 50, with seven such programs including five based on music or dance performance. These included *The Masked Singer*, *The Voice*, and rebooted versions of *American Idol* and *America's Got Talent*.

This pattern can be seen throughout American television history. Although none are among top shows today (or even in recent years), westerns such as *Bonanza, Gunsmoke, Wagon Train*, and *Daniel Boone* were immensely popular in the 1950s and early 1960s. The popularity of the James Bond movie franchise helped spur a run of spy shows later in the 1960s such as *I Spy, The Man from U.N.C.L.E, Mission: Impossible*, and the spy parody *Get Smart*.

The current era is not the first time police dramas dominated the ratings, either; the 1970s saw many such shows, including *Colombo, Starsky & Hutch, Baretta, McCloud, Cannon, Kojak, Adam-12, Police Woman*, and *Mannix*. One of the police procedurals in the 2019-20 list, *Hawaii 5-0*, was actually a remake of a show that ran from 1968 to 1980.

Shows that bear such similarities exemplify what Herbert Schiller calls **commodification**. The term comes from economics: A commodity is a good that is identical no matter who the producer is, such as a barrel of oil or a bushel of wheat. Schiller used that metaphor to refer to media offerings that are so similar in form and purpose that they might as well be identical, and are valuable to their producers more for their quantity than their quality. When a show strikes a chord with its audience, producers roll out variants that extend upon the original show's popularity to reach more viewers and also reach the same viewers for more hours in the week.

Commodification also can be seen in the popularity of spinoff shows, which are another way to build off a show's popularity. Counting *Hawaii 5-0*, the top 50 shows include ten spinoffs. Many of them were spun off from other shows on the current list such as three different versions of *NCIS,* or the "Chicago" suite of *Chicago Fire* (the original), *Chicago PD*, and *Chicago Med*.

This tally of ten spinoffs out of 50 doesn't even include the reality performance shows, which were not directly spun off from one another but are all descended from the popularity of the original *American Idol*, which ended a 15-year run in 2016. Even having three prime-time televised NFL games each week traces back to the popularity of the original *Monday Night Football* introduced by ABC in 1970. If the football broadcasts and performance-contest shows are included, about a third of the top-50 list from 2019-20 would be derivatives that were introduced to extend the popularity of a particular style of broadcast.

Chomsky and Herman's Propaganda Model

Another theory that falls under the umbrella of political economy critical theory because it is about media influence exerted by powerful government and business interests is the *propaganda model* of Edward Herman and Noam Chomsky. Herman and Chomsky's ideas aren't quite the same as the theories of propaganda discussed in Chapter 2, which are directed toward deliberate manipulation of public opinion (usually for political purposes). Instead, Herman and Chomsky use the term propaganda in a more generic sense applied to processes that they say provide public-opinion support for powerful interests in society. These theorists describe a system in which most cultural goods are produced by profit-oriented media businesses, which derive most of that profit from advertisers that are also commercial enterprises. These commercial entities look out for the interests of each other. Besides these powerful commercial interests, the power of the government affects the content of the media through the role of government officials as news sources and through tools such as broadcast regulation and licensing.

The model constructed by Herman and Chomsky outlined five influences, which they called filters, that help to determine content in media outlets that are controlled by large commercial enterprises (Herman & Chomsky, 1988, p. 2). The filters are:

Ownership

News and entertainment content tends to be pro-business (or at least favorable to the capitalist system) because media outlets owned by large corporations are not going to report information that would question the basis or legitimacy of how they operate. This trend has accelerated in the three decades since Herman and Chomsky developed their model because media conglomeration has meant progressively greater amounts of media content being produced by a shrinking number of companies. The stranglehold that a handful of large companies – notably Facebook and Google – hold over content distribution via the Internet is another example of ownership significantly affecting content.

Advertising

Media organizations are dependent on advertising, so they have a tendency to avoid coverage that would upset advertisers and also to present information that will draw the largest possible audience to maximize potential advertising revenue. Simple concepts, lots of visuals, and sensational content draw such an audience, especially on television and the Internet (where "clickbait" dominates). This dominance crowds out more in-depth, complicated coverage. Major social media platforms also can serve as an example here, because of the dominance that they have with regard to digital advertising. In 2020, digital advertising was expected to surpass half of all ad spending for the first time, overtaking the cumulative ad spending on legacy media such as newspapers, magazines, television, and radio. Further, Facebook, Google, and Amazon account for almost two-thirds of that spending (Vranica, 2020).

Sourcing

A large volume of news comes from government and business sources (public information officials and public relations representatives), whose job is to present information in terms most favorable to their organizations. To make their point, Chomsky and Herman describe the extensive public relations apparatus of the U.S. Defense Department and how it portrays a particular view of the military. To further illustrate this, the Pew Research Center reported that in 2013, the United States had 4.6 times as many public relations workers as reporters (Williams, 2014). The ratio is undoubtedly higher now because financial pressures have eliminated many newsroom jobs over the past several years (Grieco, 2020).

Flak

Chomsky and Herman use this term to describe the tendency of government and business interests to object vigorously to any information that does not serve their best interests and seeks to offer an opposing view. An outstanding example of flak was U.S. President Donald Trump's frequent attacks on the news media, even going so far as calling reporters "the enemy of the people." An extensive content analysis of his Twitter feed by *The New York Times* found more than 1,300 tweets attacking news organizations during the first three years of his term (Shear et al., 2019).

Us-vs.-Them Framing

A dominant us-vs.-them ideology is used as an organizing scheme for news presentations because powerful interests of government and business want to show the public that they need and deserve its support. In Chomsky and Herman's original formulation, written during the end of the Cold War era of the 1980s, this theme was anti-communism. Now this "us vs. them" concept has taken on a partisan political flavor, with vast amounts of public affairs and cultural news framed in terms of conservative vs. progressive ideology. Demands from Sinclair Broadcasting that the 170 local television stations it owned air segments espousing conservative viewpoints during their local news broadcasts is an example of what this theory would predict (Ember, 2017).

With this theory of propaganda as a tool of corporate information control, Chomsky and Herman sought to update some of the original research into communication and society as described in Chapter 2, demonstrating another way that persuasive communication (or propaganda) supports powerful interests in society. At the same time, Chomsky and Herman's ideas remain controversial because their position that the government and large businesses engage in propaganda goes against the perception that the U.S. media system operates (or at least *should* operate) with freedom of expression as its purpose and goal.

A contemporary media activist whose work builds on Herman and Chomsky's is Robert McChesney, who has written extensively about the negative impacts of media ownership by large conglomerates. McChesney also is active in promoting media reform that emphasizes independent media outlets (such as community radio and Internet campaigns), watchdog groups that confront corporate media, and mobilization of citizens to petition the FCC and other government groups for change. McChesney and some of his associates maintain a Web site, www.freepress.net, with information about these issues and ideas for reforms.

Yet another perspective on commercial influences of media content, one that incorporates the powerful and growing influences of social media platforms on content production and consumption, is provided by Stanford University researcher Renée DiResta. She described how organizations that want to promote a particular viewpoint, or even want to promote the sharing of plainly false disinformation online, can take advantage of algorithms and tools such as "like" and "share" buttons on platforms such as Facebook and Instagram to gain maximum exposure for the content. She calls this process "computational" propaganda. "When manipulators use these tools to push a maligned narrative that goes viral, it can spread far and fast" (DiResta, 2018, p. 14).

Cultural Studies

All of these theoretical approaches, starting with the Frankfurt School, examine production of media content and its relationship to a society's culture. They are generally grouped with critical theory because of their Marxist superstructure approach focused on powerful economic forces seeking to control media content. By emphasizing the importance of ideology, the Frankfurt school also set the stage for a cultural studies tradition to follow that would move away from structural or political economy approaches. This approach to media studies examines the role of ideology in creating and controlling culture through symbolic representation.

Countering Hegemonic Discourse

In a typical cultural studies perspective, multiple ideologies exist, generally including a hegemonic one that a society's mass media helps to keep dominant through repetition and through emphasis of certain aspects of reality and certain points of view to the exclusion of others. As Stuart Hall, one of the scholars most closely associated with cultural studies, has described it, cultural meanings are constructed through use of symbols, especially language. What matters to a cultural scholar is what kinds of meanings become attached to descriptions of people, organizations or situations. "In order for one meaning to be regularly produced, it has to win a kind of credibility, legitimacy or taken-for-grantedness for itself. That involves marginalizing, down-grading or de-legitimating alternative constructions" (Hall, 1982, p. 67).

A major goal of cultural studies research is to counteract portrayals that marginalize segments of society and offer alternatives to them. "The chief aim of cultural studies is to expose how ideologies of powerful groups are unwittingly perpetuated and ways they can be resisted to disrupt the system of power that disenfranchises certain groups" (Littlejohn, 1999, p. 236). Such research employs qualitative social science research techniques, emphasizing evidence gained through examination of human subjects and/or texts, through a process of analyzing large amounts of qualitative data combined with inductive reasoning (making broader generalizations from patterns found in the data). Two key tools for this are semiotics and qualitative (or ethnographic) content analysis, as described in Chapter 9.

Symbolic Interactionism and the Social Construction of Reality

In its emphasis on symbols and signification, cultural studies draws heavily on theories of symbolic interactionism and social construction of reality in examining the influence of ideology. Chapter 2 explains how the earliest developments of mass communication theory focused on what became known as the transmission model, exemplified by Harold Lasswell's functions-of-the-media model (*who* says *what* to *whom* through which *channel* with what *effects*), and Shannon and Weaver's source-message-channel-receiver model. Some theorists, however, proposed an alternative to the functionalist transmission model, which they called interactionism. This was based on the idea that the key determinant of social behavior and organization is the way people react to their surroundings and others around them.

This is literally the opposite perspective of the functionalist theory, which maintains that large-scale social structures and institutions are the driving force behind how people behave and react as social beings. Rather, in this alternative view, media messages shape this reaction arena or social environment through a process of symbolic interactionism. This theory is associated with the work of Herbert Blumer, who coined the term in the 1930s. For Blumer and those who have built upon his work, social behavior – how people act and interact with one another – depends on the meanings they infer or how they interpret what other people say and do. Making these interpretations and attaching these meanings happens entirely through symbolic communication. "We share ideas, rules, goals, values (all symbolic), and these allow us to continue to interact cooperatively with others" (Charon, 2001, p. 90).

The process of interacting and giving meaning to the world around them through reading and interpreting symbolic communication means that people are responsible for constructing the social world that they end up living within. "The human being, because of the symbol, does not respond passively to a reality that imposes itself but actively creates and re-creates the world acted in" (Charon, 2001, p. 90). Consider, for example, the symbolic reality created by fashion. Certain fashions are considered "cool" or hipster while others are more "nerdy" and still others are *avant garde* or even radical. People who dress in certain ways will evoke particular reactions from others in society, part of the reality they create for themselves and by extension for those around them. Social norms – a commonly agreed upon set of standards for what constitutes appropriate reality – play into fashion also, such as dressing nicely for a wedding or a job interview instead of showing up in pajamas or beachwear.

Sociologists Peter Berger and Thomas Luckmann built upon this idea with a theory they called the social construction of reality that takes the interaction from the individual to the sociological level. In this theory, Berger and Luckmann describe how situations created by social interaction come to be seen as "objective" and "real" – in other words, come to be seen as if they were something other than human creations. In an influential essay, Berger and Luckmann (1967) define objective reality as something outside of human control, something that "cannot be wished away." Over time, however, the ongoing interaction of individuals builds up social institutions, in the form of habits, values and roles that people come to adopt. This results in an institutionalized social reality based on shared meanings and understandings that come about through symbolic communication – one that is seen as "objectively" real, even though it was created by people (Berger & Luckmann, 1967, p. 60).

Since people create this reality, they should be able to change it – but that doesn't happen, according to Berger and Luckmann. "The institutions are now experienced as possessing a reality of their own, a reality that confronts the individual as an external and coercive fact … A world so regarded attains a firmness in consciousness; it becomes real in an ever more massive way and can no longer be changed so readily" (Berger & Luckmann, 1967, p. 59). This idea that symbolic expression defines the reality that human beings experience is a central feature of the cultural studies branch of the interpretive paradigm. (Theories of media ecology, described elsewhere in this chapter, also seek to explain how reality is "constructed" from media interactions.)

British Cultural Studies/Birmingham School

One of the first, and most significant, places to develop an alternative paradigm or counterpoint to the limited effects theories generated by U.S. social science researchers was the Centre for Contemporary Cultural Studies at the University of Birmingham, England. (The name of the research center, in fact, gives this branch of the alternative paradigm its name.) Starting in the 1960s, this collection of British scholars in many ways built upon the work of their counterparts in the Frankfurt School. Both sets of researchers were interested in theorizing about how mass culture and mass media helped to create a hegemonic ideology that kept the lower classes from challenging the elites who controlled society. Both schools of thought also believed in the need to construct a critique of the way in which this hegemony came about.

A major difference between the two was that while the Frankfurt School dismissed the idea of mass culture being any sort of positive force in society, the British Cultural Studies school actively focused on ways to "correct" mass culture so that it could counter oppressive ideology. This tradition recognizes the power of elites to promote ideology, but it also maintains that elite domination is not inevitable. It's possible instead to have a more egalitarian and diverse (pluralistic) approach to culture. This happens when people in so-called marginalized groups can be organized in ways for their voices to be heard to change the system. For example, cities with large Latino or African-American communities often have Spanish-language or Black-culture oriented media including newspapers, radio stations and online news sites. Cities with large gay populations sometimes have media devoted to LGBTQ issues; such media were among the first to cover and promote same-sex marriage and transgender rights.

The Birmingham scholars started out with a focus on oppression of working-class people in Great Britain, again similar to the Frankfurt scholars' focus on the class divisions described in Marxist thought. While the Frankfurt school kept its work focused on class struggle, the British school of cultural studies soon expanded to include analysis of texts seen as marginalizing women as well as people of differing races, ethnicities, and sexual orientations. The examples in the previous paragraph would also be examples of these theories in action.

The Frankfurt School was thoroughly Marxist in its approach, while the British School was less clearly so. Stuart Hall, who was director of the Centre for Contemporary Cultural Studies from 1969 to 1979, has said the goal of its research was not to be avowedly pro-Marxist, as the Frankfurt scholars were. Instead, the British scholars just happened to be concerned about the same issues that Marxism helped to highlight: the power and reach of capital in society; relationships between those with social power and exploitation of those without it; and a general theory that would connect different domains of life such as economics, politics and culture. Their work was based around those issues.

In an essay describing the work of the Centre, Hall wrote that application of Gramsci's ideas about hegemony and ideology came closest to describing what the organization was really trying to accomplish (Hall, 1996). He summarized the Centre's work as a consideration of questions of culture through the metaphors of language and textuality and of creating theories about power, history, and politics as matters of representation through language. The British Cultural Studies scholars sought to understand how symbols become a source of cultural power and a way in which people identify themselves. In Hall's words, "Culture is the struggle over meaning, a struggle that takes place over and within" the way things are symbolized (as quoted in Grossberg [1996], p. 157).

A great amount of work in this view of cultural studies concerns the ways in which words, images, symbols, and meanings are used in the portrayal of groups that are outside of the mainstream of social power – especially women and people of different races, ethnic backgrounds, and sexual orientations. For an example of how symbols and meanings can affect portrayals, consider the difference between calling someone a "woman" or a "lady" vs. calling her a "chick," a "honey," or a "babe." Or think about descriptions of individuals as "Black" or "African-American" vs. any one of an unfortunately large number of racial epithets used to describe dark-skinned people (which won't be reprinted here). Insulting words for those of Muslim, Hispanic, Asian, and Jewish backgrounds are also all too common.

The Internet in general and social media in particular have become the main staging area for the "struggle over the sign," as Stuart Hall calls it. This can be seen in the #metoo, #blacklivesmatter, and #oscarssowhite hashtag campaigns to highlight problems of disrespect and mistreatment of women and Blacks. Ways in which derogatory public speech about marginalized groups can cause problems for people and organizations who make such remarks offer another way this is articulated. For example, ABC fired comedian Roseanne Barr from her sitcom after she posted a racist tweet about an African American adviser to President Barack Obama. (Barr also had previously attracted controversy for tweeting about conspiracy theories and anti-semitic comments.) *Saturday Night Live* withdrew an offer to Shane Gillis to join its cast after his racist and homophobic comments in podcasts came to public attention. J.K. Rowling, author of the Harry Potter series, was criticized by fans after comments that seemed to attack transexuals.

These examples demonstrate that symbols (in this case, language) used to describe people and the meanings those symbols convey DO matter, as does the impact that they can have when distributed via media. Cultural theorists, especially ones using the philosophy of the Birmingham School, would further say these examples demonstrate pop-culture media being used to reclaim respect for marginalized groups in the social discourse by pushing back against negative connotations. Not everyone would agree; some might cite the negative reactions to celebrities such as Barr and Rowling as examples of "cancel culture," in which people suffer consequences merely for expressing an opinion. (See Box 5.5 sidebar on cancel culture.)

BOX 5.5

Cancel Culture

The negative reaction that prominent people face in reaction to insensitive comments about race, gender, ethnicity, or sexual orientation is sometimes referred to as an expression of "cancel culture." This happens when people are sanctioned, or "canceled," by angry comments on social media that seek to raise the profile of what they said as a way of shaming them as well as a means to criticize them about it. "Cancellation" means that the criticism includes calls for offenders to be ignored or dismissed from public attention because of the social norms they violated.

While some people see this as a way of countering sexist or racist narratives, as described by the Birmingham cultural studies theorists, others see a darker side to it. As an explanatory article in *Vox* put it, "Is cancel culture an important tool of social justice or a new form of merciless mob intimidation?" (Romano, 2020).

The same *Vox* article explains that the term "cancel" seems to have its origin in hip-hop culture, as a way of exercising grassroots power by withdrawing support for individuals making racist expressions. Stanford University linguist Charity Hudley is quoted as explaining it as "a collective way of saying... 'I may have no power, but the power I have is to [ignore] you'" (Romano, 2020, paragraph 30).

Cancel culture, however, has faced criticism of its own for supposedly causing a chilling effect on expression spurred on by fears of backlash that could lead to self-censorship. A letter to the editor in *Harper's* magazine signed by more than 100 authors, academics and public intellectuals was published to make that point, stating that social shaming that would "weaken our norms of open debate and toleration of differences in favor of ideological conformity ... the result has been to steadily narrow the boundaries of what can be said without the threat of reprisal" (Harpers, 2020). The letter sparked backlash of its own, with criticism of the signers for complaining about comments that often – following Hudley's thinking – come from people with less cultural authority than the signers themselves. Critics further noted that the cultural power the letter-signers hold makes them much more resistant to actual "cancellation," such as loss of their livelihood.

Where cancel culture becomes especially controversial is when the targets of social media criticism are ordinary individuals who suffer real harm such as public humiliation or even loss of their jobs over a comment or action that went viral. A New York City woman who called 911 to report she was being harassed by a Black man in Central Park – who was actually there doing some birdwatching, and simply asked her to keep her dog on its leash – faced public shame after a video of the encounter between them filmed by the birdwatcher on his phone was posted online and viewed millions of times. The woman subsequently was charged with filing a false police report and was fired from her job over the incident. (A few months later the charges were dropped after she completed a restorative justice program [Jacobs, 2021].)

The cancel culture controversy also has political overtones. Social media campaigns that call out prominent people, or even ordinary ones, often originate with and draw the most support from people with progressive/liberal leanings. This means many complaints about such "cancellations" and fears about the danger of cancel culture come from those on the politically conservative end of the spectrum. In a speech during the 2020 Republican National Convention, former United Nations Ambassador Nikki Haley said "political correctness and cancel culture are dangerous and just plain wrong" (Romano, 2020). Even U.S. President Donald Trump characterized criticism of conservative viewpoints as a form of "canceling" (Nakamura, Parker, Itkowitz, & Sacchetti, 2020).

Other Approaches

Much of what McQuail has called the alternative paradigm, generally referred to here as the interpretive paradigm, can be organized under critical or cultural theory approaches. Appropriately for a research tradition that celebrates the varied, subjective nature of scholarly investigation, this paradigm also encompasses other ideas and approaches that cannot be lumped into either of those categories. Descriptions of some of these approaches follow.

Postmodernism

"Postmodern" is a term with broad application in the arts and other areas of contemporary society, and it is possible students have encountered the term in English classes or other humanities subjects. Applied to communication theories, it is sometimes used to describe the fundamental differences in the alternative communication paradigm. Theories that use a structural orientation such as political economy are sometimes called modern approaches because they have to do with traditional organizations of society using the principles of modernity. They are contrasted with the postmodern, sometimes even called "post-structural," views of the cultural studies tradition (Baran & Davis, 2006, p. 8).

To fully understand the term "postmodern" as it applies to social structures, it is necessary first to understand the concept of *modernity* because postmodernism is fundamentally a critique of the modernist ideal and a set of perspectives that offer alternatives to that ideal. Defined in this way, *modernity* is a theory of social organization associated with principles of the 18th century Enlightenment, which said that intellect and reason could be used to understand the universe and solve the problems facing humanity. The Enlightenment philosophy was that knowledge and ideas produced by the rational and knowing self can lead to progress and continuous improvement of human institutions and the human condition. Comte's positivism and the scientific method are direct outgrowths of this perspective.

Most of the ideas used to organize Western society – including capitalism, representative democracy, personal liberty, free flow of information, the rule of law, and the advance of technology – come out of the Enlightenment as a normative theory of social ideals. What Europeans and (especially) Americans think of as "progress" over the past three centuries – the Industrial Revolution, the Information Age, technology-based invention and innovation – all are part of modernity.

Postmodern thinking, on the other hand, questions the benefits of modernity and the philosophy of the Enlightenment that lies behind it. This is because, while modern developments of the past couple of centuries have brought a technologically advanced, more comfortable lifestyle to a portion of the world's inhabitants, notably in North America and Western Europe, many parts of the planet have not shared in the benefits.

Modernity has brought about advanced medical procedures that have saved lives, and technological innovations that have taken humans to the Moon and given us the Internet. It also has led to two world wars in which millions of people died horrible deaths. It has not ended starvation, poverty, pandemic illnesses (such as AIDS or COVID-19), or the tendency for people to be inhumane or cruel to each other. Modernity HAS created pollution, given us nations presided over by brutal dictators who use modern technology to oppress, torture and kill the people they rule, and, for the first time in history, has made it possible for human beings to obliterate life on the planet through the incredible destructive power of nuclear weapons.

So, postmodernist thinking asks: Can this really be called *progress*? As a social philosophy (or theory), the Enlightenment predicts that humans can create a perfect society ultimately by finding the single best approach to social organization through intellect and reason. Is this view a legitimate one? Are people as logical and rational as the theory assumes? Is there a single "right" way to organize an economy or a political system? Will science and technology provide all the answers? Can humans continuously improve themselves and their social systems far enough that the benefits of modernity will outweigh the problems it has created? Postmodernists say that at present the answer to all of these questions is "no," and they doubt that it ever will be possible to answer them "yes."

The general outlines of postmodern thinking are attributed to several French intellectuals, starting with Michel Foucault, who argued that modern life organized around the principles of reason and rationality would necessarily have to exclude from full participation in the social system anyone not capable of being a fully functional, rationally directed member of the society. Those who are incapable of this – the infirmed, disabled, those who chose alternative lifestyles – have no value in the "rationalist" society. Thus, in Foucault's view, rationality and modernity will never lead to the "perfect" society. By definition they will be unjust and dismissive toward a portion of humanity.

Jean Francois Lyotard built upon this foundation (and popularized the word "postmodernism") in a 1979 book in which he argued that the "grand narrative" of modernity no longer had universal value, largely because of the shortcomings of modernist social organizations and some of the negative impacts of modernity as described previously. Rather, he argued that contemporary society should adopt a postmodern view that rejects grand narratives and gives respect and attention to smaller, more individualized narratives with no overall organizing principle. Postmodernism from Lyotard's perspective has been described as "the critique of grand narratives, the awareness that such narratives serve to mask the contradictions and instabilities that are inherent in any social practice" (Klages, 2003).

Thus, postmodernism has come to be defined as a way of looking at society in which there is no unifying, singular way of interpreting any given text, practice or human behavior. There is no "correct" form of government or economic system, no single "correct" way to set up social institutions – and no "correct" (or universal) interpretation of a media message or description of its effects. Knowledge is situationally based and understanding is in the eyes of the beholder.

In the context of the interpretive paradigm, Lyotard's view of postmodernism is very closely associated with cultural studies, which emphasizes the contributions that "marginalized" groups can make to society with their small narratives providing a counterweight to a dominant and hegemonic ideology ("grand narrative") that seeks to keep them oppressed and marginalized. This is further reflected in the differences between proponents of empirical and qualitative research methods. Modernity equates knowledge with science and use of the quantitative, positivist perspective and dismisses the value of individual, subjective narrative. Postmodernism, on the other hand, celebrates such narrower and individual views. This is a fundamental reason why scholars who take a critical or cultural view use methods that reject positivism and instead rely on interpretation and the search for meaning.

For the postmodernist, context is everything and nothing is absolute. However, this attitude that "everything is relative" and everything is open to interpretation opens postmodernism to some criticism as well. If everything is open to interpretation, every viewpoint in scholarly inquiry is potentially valid. If that is the case, then two completely different conclusions drawn from the same set of facts could both be considered equally valid. If that is so, then what is the value of inquiry in the first place? If nothing is ever "wrong," how can anything be "right?" Thus, while postmodernism has many adherents, it also has detractors who dismiss it as a theory with little value or validity.

McLuhan and Media Ecology

As the interpretive or alternative paradigm was growing in popularity in the early 1960s, one of the people who came to be identified with it was Marshall McLuhan, a Canadian media scholar. McLuhan became famous for his analysis of the role of pop culture in society and his formulation of memorable phrases to describe it such as "the global village" and "the medium is the message."

McLuhan built on the ideas of his mentor, Harold Innis, who theorized that forms of communication were directly related to structures in society, a process that Innis called "the biases of communication." This was a classic critical theory/political economy view because he related structures of information control to social structures used in the exercise of power. McLuhan was not a structural theorist in exactly the same way as Innis. Rather, he adapted Innis's ideas to come up with his own theories about how media technologies affect patterns of human thinking and human beings' ways of relating to the world around them. McLuhan's central idea is that historical eras of social structure have each been the product of the dominant communication medium of the time. As communication technology and methods have changed over the course of human history, social organization has changed accordingly (Sparks, 2002).

Thus, the earliest form of human organization in McLuhan's categorization was the tribal paradigm. This existed in the era before written language and mechanical printing, when communication was dominated by real-time oral transmission. The only things people knew about were either from their own experience or from talking to other people about things they had not personally witnessed. In this era, the only way for someone to experience a message was as it happened (i.e., as it was told by another person), and the experiences had to happen in the order in which a person lived his life. According to McLuhan, a culture in which this is the dominant form of communicating is going to be relational and communal.

The tribal paradigm was replaced by the print paradigm, which fostered linear thinking instead of relational thinking and also ended the need for chronological communication. (Some descriptions of McLuhan's work say he divided this "literacy era" into subsegments, with the first tracing back to the invention of the alphabet and written communication and the second beginning with the invention of the printing press.) Unlike oral messages that cannot be preserved, something written can be communicated to someone an hour later, a day later, or many years later. It also, however, creates a need for order and structure in messages; written communication makes sense only if components of the message are in the proper order. In the process of imposing order, linear communication undermines the relational and communal characteristics of tribal-era communication. The Enlightenment, the rise of modernity, and the later stage of the print paradigm are closely related in both time and function.

The linear-print paradigm lasted several hundred years until the invention of the telegraph in the mid-19th century. Then began the electronic paradigm, characterized by how it extended the ability for people to communicate in real time over great distances. Later in this era, radio and television were invented, allowing people to see and hear things from far away in real time and also to experience them as if they were live even if they had been recorded earlier. Communication in this electronic era also used multiple senses and therefore was not as linear as the print style, which gives it something in common with the tribal paradigm, according to McLuhan. For example, someone watching television can hear the telephone ring, and can continue watching the show even as they take the call and talk to the person on the other end. Contrast this with the idea of trying to read a book and a magazine simultaneously. It cannot be done; they would have to be read sequentially, in accord with McLuhan's notion of a linear-oriented print paradigm.

The focal point of McLuhan's ideas is that a society dominated by electronic media will differ from a print-dominated one because people relate to the world around them according to which senses they use to learn about it. This was expressed in one of his well-known sayings that media are "the extensions of man." By this he meant that, as a tool for communication, the media, like other tools, extend human capacities. One of the examples he uses in explaining this is that a person can dig a hole with his hands or dig it with a shovel; the tool of the shovel extends the capacity of the hands and creates conditions under which the hole can be dug faster and more efficiently (McLuhan, 1964). In a similar way, media extend the senses by creating an ability to see and hear things at distance and to experience them at times other than when they were created. According to McLuhan, this "extension" of the senses changes the way people relate to their environment and to each other, altering the social structure in the process.

A related concept is summed up in what is probably McLuhan's best-known saying, that "the medium is the message." In other words, what really matters is not whether or how people react to the content of the messages they receive (as in the effects paradigm), but rather how society is changed by the dominant way in which messages are communicated (oral, print, electronic). Here McLuhan departs dramatically from the effects theorists of the social science tradition and even from most critical and cultural thinkers. In McLuhan's view, it didn't really matter what an individual was watching on television (comedy, violence, news, etc.) or who controlled the content of the broadcast. What mattered was that he was watching television rather than reading a magazine. The effect on the individual and the social system came from the way the message was mediated, not from the content. Contrast this with, for example, Gerbner's cultivation theory (see Chapter 4) about the impact of message content; the difference in perspective is dramatic.

A third famous McLuhan-ism combines these ideas. This was his statement that the electronic media could create a "global village." Even in the 1960s, when these ideas were first presented, technology allowed people to see and hear things from around the world as easily as those nearby. (The BBC is credited with organizing the world's first live global broadcast using satellite technology – called *Our World*, and starring The Beatles and other celebrities – in June 1967.) In McLuhan's view, this technology allowed people to interact in almost the same way they could in the pre-print tribal era, without being limited by geography. He theorized that a new world-wide social order could emerge as electronic media linked the world.

In his time, McLuhan faced stinging criticism from fellow academics, supposedly for ignoring the impact of media content on audiences and also for being a "techno-logical determinist" who would not account for people individually and collectively making the decisions that shape culture. Media ecology theorists dismiss these criticisms as arguments that attack a caricature of McLuhan's ideas rather than anything he actually articulated (Strate, 2008). However, as many of the concepts he predicted came to pass, his ideas earned more respect.

McLuhan died in 1980 but this idea of a new social order based on the media and means of communication has attracted renewed interest in his theories because of the globalization of information through the Internet, satellite delivery of media messages, and other technologies. Even the metaphor of a global village may not be the correct scale to consider these days; perhaps something like a "global household" is more appropriate. This is because mobile devices that allow individual people to instantly and constantly communicate with anyone, anywhere in the world, are having impacts on society that social scientists are only beginning to understand.

BOX 5.6

What Would McLuhan Say about Facebook and Smartphones?

FIGURE 5.2 Smartphones have become a constant presence in most people's lives. Wat'hna Racha / EyeEm via Getty Images.

The focal point of Marshall McLuhan's theory is that the dominant way of communicating in a society affects the way social interactions and social organizations develop and evolve. McLuhan's discussion of how social organization changed with the paradigm shifts from tribal to print to electronic eras has even further meaning and power when thinking about how social media has changed the ways humans connect and communicate.

The Internet in general – and the development of social networking sites such as Facebook, Instagram and Twitter in particular – can be seen as applications of what his ideas would predict because of the way they have changed human behavior and interaction so dramatically.

Mobile communications (voice, text, and video-enabled mobile phones) are another example. Many people today truly live a portion of their lives through their smartphones. Even when face-to-face with someone, the phone becomes a way to stay in constant and instant contact with others. This feature of life is called "ambient awareness" – which a New York Times article described as "very much like being physically near someone and picking up on (their) mood" (Thompson, 2008). Smartphones offering ambient awareness have changed the way social interactions happen online and off, something else that McLuhan's theories predict.

Related to this is the work of Massachusetts Institute of Technology professor Sherry Turkle, who has done extensive research documenting how interpersonal skills are affected by attention to mobile devices; her ideas are summed up nicely in the title of her 2012 book *Alone Together: Why We Expect More from Technology and Less from Each Other*.

Along with personal connection, the smartphone is becoming the tool of choice for surveillance of the environment. A 2015 study by the Knight Foundation discovered that 89 percent of the adult U.S. mobile population (144 million people) access news and information via their mobile device (News Goes Mobile: People Use Smartphones to Access Information, 2016). As McLuhan proposed, the tools of communication that extend human senses of seeing, speaking, and listening dramatically influence how people relate to one another and how ways of interacting across society at large develop.

McLuhan's ideas helped to inspire a new field of study that came to be known as media ecology. During a speech at an academic conference in 1968, New York University professor Neil Postman used that label to describe an emerging set of theories about how technology and media interacted to affect society and culture. Along with McLuhan, Postman became one of the leading theorists in this field of study, founding a graduate program in Media Ecology at NYU in 1972.

Postman said media ecology "looks into the matter of how media of communication affect human perception, understanding, feeling, and value; and how our interaction with media facilitates or impedes our chances of survival.... [it] is the study of media as environments" (Postman, 1970). Lance Strate, one of Postman's students who helped found the Media Ecology Association to organize thinking within the field, on the association's website similarly defines it as "the study of media environments, the idea that technology and techniques, modes of information and codes of communication play a leading role in human affairs" (Strate, 1999). Further reflecting McLuhan's discussion of the shift from tribal culture to literate culture, media ecology puts strong emphasis on the differences in oral and written communication. Another leading media ecologist, Walter Ong, emphasized this contrast, especially in describing how contemporary culture is biased toward visual thought patterns over oral ones (Soukup, 2005).

The choice of the term "ecology" to describe the media as a social environment was a deliberate analogy to biology, which studies how organisms exist in and are affected by the environments around them. Strate notes that Postman even used the metaphor of a biologist's Petri dish as a "medium" being "the substance in which *a culture grows*" (emphasis added). Likewise, communication media are the substance in which social culture – society – grows and develops. Continuing the quote from Postman: "We put the word 'media' in the front of the word 'ecology' to suggest that we were not simply interested in media, but in the ways in which the interaction between media and human beings gives a culture its character and, one might say, helps a culture to maintain symbolic balance" (as quoted in Strate, 2004, p. 3).

The biological metaphor is in fact often extended to contemporary media, such as discussions about how legacy news outlets such as printed newspapers are just one inhabitant of a "news ecosystem" that also includes individual bloggers, community institutions providing public affairs information, online niche news sites, and others collectively providing news for a community (Local News Lab, n.d.). A special issue of a leading academic journal that was focused on new developments in communication described the current state of the media as a "global digital ecosystem" (Mellado, Georgiou, & Nah, 2020, p. 333).

Media ecology, then, is the study of how the *form* that communication takes shapes culture or society as much as the content of messages. Lum (2000) notes that "form" has two different but connected meanings in media ecology. Form can be symbolic, meaning how the information is presented, e.g., spoken words, printed words, or images. Form also is physical, meaning the technology used to deliver the symbols: words spoken in a podcast; words printed in a newspaper; or audio-video transmission via broadcast or the Internet, etc. Different forms have particular biases that "help create the environment or symbolic and cognitive structure in which people symbolically construct the world they come to know and understand" (Lum, 2000, p. 2). Building on that idea, Strate says that "construction begins with raw materials and the tools that shape them. Media are the stuff with which we build our social realities" (Strate, 2008, p. 133).

In the same essay, Strate uses an analogy of different forms of visual art and music to illustrate the concept of form. The same image created in watercolors, oil paints, or a charcoal sketch would have a different impression on the viewer depending on which medium the artist used. Similarly, if the same melody were played on different instruments each would produce a distinct and different piece of music.

Although it was by no means anti-technological, media ecology also sought to critique technology's impacts on society. As one scholar put it, "communication technologies, from writing to digital media, create environments that affect the people who use them" (Scolari, 2012, p. 207). Lum (2000) also points out that, like other forms of cultural studies, media ecology was to some extent a reaction against positivist, behaviorist quantitative research in favor of focusing on how changes in the dominant forms of communication media in society facilitate cultural changes.

CONCLUSION

The alternative paradigm incorporating critical and cultural studies offers a stark contrast to the positivist science/effects tradition in its methods, its goals, and its conclusions about how media and society interact. In many respects the two traditions "talk past" each other. It has been said that quantitative social science emphasizes reliability over validity, while the alternative approach focuses on validity at the expense of reliability; in both cases, the results are incomplete. To put it another way, positivist communication scholars say that critical and cultural theories are opinions without verification; critical and cultural scholars say that empirical research is measurement without meaning. These divisions often seem difficult to reconcile because they lie at the core of what each tradition values most.

Both traditions have a contribution for communication study. Critical theory and cultural theory raise interesting and important questions about the role of the media and its impact on culture in contemporary society, even if it lacks the means to answer them definitively. In the process, cultural studies has diverged somewhat from the critical paradigm. It has increasingly turned to qualitative analysis of media texts and text-audience interaction in the interpretation of meaning, using interviews, focus groups, and ethnography to better understand the nature of these influences in modern society. However, its focus on interpretation and understanding still limits its ability to make definitive general claims about the nature of media effects. On the other hand, the traditional paradigm of quantitative social science research consists of tools that can provide verifiable, credible evidence to answer questions. Its critics from the interpretive paradigm are correct in saying that positivist social scientists frequently are content with narrow, quantifiable research projects that seldom even ask important questions much less try to answer them (Rosengren, 1983).

However, using all of these perspectives can offer a more comprehensive picture of media and culture than might be provided by only using one paradigm. For example, a common theme in cultural studies is the tendency of the media to promote a hegemonic perspective on gender, through such practices as sexualized portrayals of women in movies, music videos, television and magazines. This same bias is reflected in greater media attention to topics with more of a male audience, such as the prominence of male-dominated professional sports in television. A political economy analysis would look at the impact of corporate control on creating these outcomes; a cultural theorist's concern would be interpreting meanings of the content that is produced.

The same issue can be addressed, however, through effects theories such as Bandura's social learning theory, which might ask: "Are the body-image problems many young women have developed through what they learn from sexualized images in the media?" Conversely, an agenda setting perspective could be used, such as "How many male-oriented topics do the mass media present vs. female-oriented ones?" Identifying issues such as these and describing why they matter to society can be best analyzed from a critical perspective. Once that problem definition is made, such topics also can be investigated with quantitative social-science methods such as attitude surveys or content analyses.

The net effect could be likened to multi-channel sound for music and video production, which provide more audio information to create a fuller, richer, and more complete reproduction of a soundtrack by literally surrounding the viewer with audio.

Increased richness and detail are developed when multiple paradigms are applied to an analysis, similar to the increased richness and detail that a multi-channel home theater system can provide, as opposed to a conventional two-channel stereo. Likewise, the interpretive and social science paradigms, when used in harmony with each other, can offer a more complete picture of the impact of media on society and culture.

Questions for Discussion/Application Exercises

1. Students who've done internships at media outlets can probably identify ways in which they were confronted with the political economy model. Can you identify specific examples of filters identified by Herman and Chomsky that you have experienced?
2. After considering the contributions of Marshall McLuhan from this chapter, visit the following Web site from the Canadian Broadcasting Corporation. After viewing some of the links in the archives, how have your views of McLuhan changed? Is there a lesson for today's media practitioners in his message? http://www.cbc.ca/archives/tag/marshall+mcluhan/
3. Identify some areas of mass media or issues involving the media that might be addressed more appropriately by the critical or cultural perspective than by the effects tradition described in chapters 3 and 4. Then see if you can identify some research questions that would use this approach to study them.

NOTE

1 From A.C. Neilsen reports of average viewership from Sept. 23, 2019, to May 20, 2020, for series that aired four or more episodes, as reported in USA Today (Levin, 2020).

REFERENCES

Adorno, T. & Horkheimer, M. (1944). The culture industry: Enlightenment as mass deception [Chapter 1 of *The dialectic of enlightenment*]. In During, S. (Ed.). *The cultural studies reader* (2nd ed.) (pp. 31–41). New York: Routledge.

Baran, S. & Davis, D. (2006). *Mass communication theory: Foundations, ferment and future* (4th ed.). Belmont, CA: Thompson Wadworth.

Bennett, T. (1982). Theories of the media, theories of society. In Gurevitch, M., Bennett, T., Curran J. & Woollacott, J. (Eds.). *Culture, society and the media* (pp. 30–55). London: Methuen & Co. Ltd.

Berger, P. & Luckmann T. (1967). *The social construction of reality*. New York: Anchor Books.

Borah, P. (2017). Emerging communication technology research: Theoretical and methodological variables in the last 16 years and future directions. *New Media & Society* 19 (4), 616–636.

Charon, J. (2001). The importance of the symbol. In O'Brien, J. & Kollock, P. (Eds.). *The production of reality: Essays and readings on social interaction* (3rd ed.) (pp. 89–96). Thousand Oaks, CA: Pine Forge Press.

DeSola Pool, I. (1983, Summer). What ferment? A challenge for empirical research. *Journal of Communication* 33 (3), 258–261.

DeVaus, D.A. (2001). *Research Design in Social Research*. London: Sage.

DiResta, R. (2018). Computational propaganda: If you make it trend, you make it true. *The Yale*

Review 106 (4) October 2018, 12-19. Retrieved from https://yalereview.yale.edu/computational-propaganda

During, S. (1993). Introduction. In During, S. (Ed.). *The cultural studies reader* (2nd ed.) (pp. 1–30). New York: Routledge.

Ember, S. (2017, May 12). Sinclair requires TV stations to air segments that tilt to the right. The New York Times online. Retrieved from https://www.nytimes.com/2017/05/12/business/media/sinclair-broadcast-komo-conservative-media.html

Grieco, E. (2020, April 20). U.S. newspapers have shed half of their newsroom employees since 2008. Pew Research Center. Retrieved from https://www.pewresearch.org/fact-tank/2020/04/20/u-s-newsroom-employment-has-dropped-by-a-quarter-since-2008/

Grossberg, L. (1996). History, politics and postmodernism: Stuart Hall and cultural studies. In Morley, D. & Chen, K.-H. (Eds.). *Stuart Hall: Critical dialogues in cultural studies* (pp. 151–173). New York: Routledge.

Hall, S. (1982). The rediscovery of ideology: return of the repressed in media studies. In Gurevitch, M., Bennett, T., Curran J. & Woollacott, J. (Eds.). *Culture, society and the media* (pp. 56–90). London: Methuen & Co. Ltd.

Hall, S. (1996). Cultural studies and its theoretical legacies. In Morley, D. & Chen, K.-H. (Eds.). *Stuart Hall: Critical dialogues in cultural studies* (pp. 262–275). New York: Routledge.

Harpers. (2020, July 7). A Letter on Justice and Open Debate. Harpers online. Retrieved from https://harpers.org/a-letter-on-justice-and-open-debate/

Herman, E. & Chomsky, N. (1988). *Manufacturing consent: The political economy of the mass media*. New York: Pantheon Books.

Jacobs, S. (2021, February 16). Case dismissed against Amy Cooper, who called police on Black birdwatcher in viral Central Park video. Washington Post online edition. Retrieved from https://www.washingtonpost.com/national-security/case-dismissed-against-amy-cooper-who-called-police-on-black-birdwatcher-in-viral-central-park-video/2021/02/16/d7f026d6–7069-11eb-93be-c10813e358a2_story.html.

Klages, M. (2003). Postmodernism. Retrieved from http://www.colorado.edu/English/courses/ENGL2012Klages/pomo.html.

Lievesley, D. (2020, May 20). A guide to statistics for journalists. Webinar presented by Reuters Institute for the Study of Journalism, Oxford University, United Kingdom. Retrieved from: https://reutersinstitute.politics.ox.ac.uk/calendar/guide-statistics-journalists.

Littlejohn, S. (1999). *Theories of human communication*. Belmont, CA: Wadsworth Publishing Co.

Local News Lab. (n.d.). What is a news ecosystem? Retrieved from https://localnewslab.org/what-is-a-news-ecosystem/.

Lum, C.M.K. (2000). Introduction: The intellectual roots of media ecology. *The New Jersey Journal of Communication* 8 (1), 1–7.

Lye, J. (2004). Who controls the media and their meanings? Retrieved from http://www.brocku.ca/english/jlye/control.html.

Mellado, C., Georgiou, M. & Nah, S. (2020). Advancing journalism and communication research: New concepts, theories, and pathways. *Journalism & Mass Communication Quarterly* 97 (2), 333–341.

McLuhan, M. (1964). *Understanding media: The extensions of man*. Excerpt republished in Hanson. J. & Maxcy, D. (1999). *Sources: Notable Selections in Mass Media* (2nd ed.) (pp. 117–123). Guilford, CT: Dushkin/McGraw-Hill.

McQuail, D. (2005). *McQuail's mass communication theory* (5th ed.). London: Sage Publications Ltd.

Melody, W. & Mansell, R. (1983). The debate over critical vs. administrative research: circularity or challenge. *Journal of Communication* 33 (3), 103–116.

Mosco, V. (1983). Critical research and the role of labor. *Journal of Communication* 33 (3), 237–248.

Nakamura, D., Parker, A., Itkowitz, C. & Sacchetti, M. (2020, July 4). At Mount Rushmore, Trump exploits social divisions, warns of 'left-wing cultural revolution' in dark speech ahead of Independence Day. Washington Post online edition. Retrieved from https://www.washingtonpost.com/politics/trump-mount-rushmore-fireworks/2020/07/03/af2e84f6-bd25-11ea-bdaf-a129f921026f_story.html

News Goes Mobile: People Use Smartphones to Access Information (2016, May). Knight Foundation. Retrieved from https://medium.com/mobile-first-news-how-people-use-smartphones-to

Postman, N. (1970). The reformed English curriculum. In Eurich, A.C. (Ed.). *High school 1980: The shape of the future in American secondary education* (pp. 160–168). New York: Pitman. Quoted matter retrieved from https://www.media-ecology.org/What-Is-Media-Ecology.

Potter, W.J. & Riddle, K. (2007). A content analysis of the media effects literature. *Journalism & Mass Communication Quarterly 84* (1), 90–104

Romano, A. (2020, August 25). Why we can't stop fighting about cancel culture. Vox online. Retrieved from https://www.vox.com/culture/2019/12/30/20879720/what-is-cancel-culture-explained-history-debate

Rosengren, K. (1983). Communication research: One paradigm or four? *Journal of Communication 33* (3), 185–207.

Schiller, H. (1983). Critical research in the information age. *Journal of Communication 33* (3), 249–257.

Scolari. C. (2012). Media ecology: Exploring the metaphor to expand the theory. *Communication Theory 22*, 204–225.

Severin, W.J. & Tankard, J.W. (2001). *Communication theories: Origins, methods, and uses in the mass media* (5th ed.). New York: Addison Wesley Longman.

Shear, M., Haberman, M., Confessore, M., Yourish, K., Buchanan, L. & Collins, K. (2019, November 2). How Trump Reshaped the Presidency in Over 11,000 Tweets. The New York Times online. Retrieved from https://www.nytimes.com/interactive/2019/11/02/us/politics/trump-twitter-presidency.html

Slack, J. & Allor, M. (1983). The political and epistemological constituents of critical communication research. *Journal of Communication 33* (3), 208–218.

Smythe, D. & Van Dinh, T. (1983). On critical and administrative research: A new critical analysis. *Journal of Communication 33* (3), 117–127.

Soukup, P. (2005). Looking is not enough: Reflections on Walter J. Ong and media ecology. *Proceedings of the Media Ecology Association 6*, 1–9.

Sparks, G. (2002). *Media effects research: A basic overview*. Belmont, CA: Wadsworth Publishing Co.

Strate, L. (1999). Understanding MEA. *In Medias Res 1* (1), Fall 1999. Retrieved from https://www.media-ecology.org/What-Is-Media-Ecology.

Strate, L. (2004). A media ecology review. *Communication Research Trends 23* (2), 3–48.

Strate, L. (2008). Studying media as media: McLuhan and the media ecology approach. *MediaTropes eJournal 1*, 127–142.

Thompson, C. (2008, September 7). Brave new world of digital intimacy. New York Times Magazine online. Retrieved from www.nytimes.com/2008/09/07/magazine/07awareness-t.html

Vranica, S. (2020, December 1). Google, Facebook and Amazon Gain as Coronavirus Reshapes Ad Spending. The Wall Street Journal Online. Retrieved from https://www.wsj.com/articles/google-facebook-and-amazon-gain-as-coronavirus-reshapes-ad-spending-11606831201

Walter, N., Cody, M. & Ball-Rokeach, S. (2018). The Ebb and flow of communication research: Seven decades of publication trends and research priorities. *Journal of Communication 68*, 424–440.

Williams, A. (2014, August 11). The growing pay gap between journalism and public relations. Pew Research Center. Retrieved from http://www.pewresearch.org/fact-tank/2014/08/11/the-growing-pay-gap-between-journalism-and-public-relations/

CHAPTER 6

International Communication Theories

In a world that is continually more globalized, it is increasingly important to understand implications of communicatiFn across national borders. Perhaps the most valuable aspect of this is that studying media systems from other places can lead to a better understanding of one's own media system. With that in mind, this chapter reviews some of the history of theories about international communication and explores the two major paradigms used to study communication around the world: the flow of information model and the comparative media model:

- Information flow was the first of these to be developed, largely focused on hegemonic influences of large, powerful countries over the information flows of smaller ones in the post-World War II (post-colonial) era.
- Comparative media analysis, which was developed later, places international communication in a global context with local influences. It has become a more popular and productive approach since the end of the Cold War and resulting obsolescence of the Three Worlds geopolitical model, which led to the growth of globalized flows of information, goods, and financial services. Comparative study can also help people understand their own media systems better.

The statement that the world has shrunk is no longer a cliché. Arguably, we have come to live in what Marshall McLuhan described as a global village (see Chapter 5). We can see, hear, and in some ways experience events that happen around the world as readily as if they happened in our home towns.

For example, the author of this chapter spent a semester teaching in Ireland and was able to keep in touch daily with friends and family in the United States via social media and internet video chats, a phenomenon sometimes called the "death of distance." He was able to consume U.S. media, including his hometown newspaper and U.S. national news, through Internet apps. (He was also able to continue following Irish media in the same way upon returning home.) One of the semester's highlights was a trip to a conference in London, where he was able to meet,

DOI: 10.4324/9781003121695-6

in person, several U.K. journalists whom he had "met" only in the virtual world before then.

This is an outcome of a phenomenon often called globalization, defined as "a social system with the capacity to work as a unit on a planetary scale in real or chosen time" (Castells, 2008). Globalization and related trends make it worthwhile to develop an understanding of theories that can predict and explain international communication practices and their implications.

As with some of this book's other chapters, a historical approach will be used to explore the realm of international communication theories. Information flow across national borders was the first international communication phenomenon to be studied, and for many years was the dominant way to theorize about it. Theories centered on information flow originally were formed to explain how communication technology and practices unfolded as new nations were created after World War II from what had been the colonies of early-20th century European powers.

Now, the more recently developed comparative studies approach – such as the model developed by Daniel Hallin and Paolo Mancini, which is explored in depth later in this chapter – is the leading paradigm. This addresses differences in cultures, media practices, and media systems that remain intact even in a shrunken world. It also is valuable because examining differences in media across international borders helps people understand their own national systems more completely. For instance, Shaw and Tan (2014) looked at advertising portrayals of Western vs. Asian male models in magazine advertising to examine how masculinity was portrayed differently for each race. Further, communication flows have become so globalized that it no longer makes sense to confine media study just to the activities within one nation's borders (Livingstone, 2012). Esser (2013) calls this expansion "deterritorialism."

The starting point for studying international communication is realizing that different nations have different political structures that influence their media systems, especially through different policies of media regulation. The U.S. system, for example, is based on freedom of expression and freedom of information flows, with strong constraints on government regulation of media content. Many countries, however, are not as strong in that tradition as the United States and have laws that regulate media more strictly. This means American understandings of media regulation may not always be helpful in interpreting how media from other nations operate and interact with their societies. This is especially true in the online digital realm. European Union constraints on things such as digital privacy, articulated in its General Data Protection Regulation (GDPR) rules safeguarding personal data, differ substantially from U.S. regulations, for example (Burgess, 2020; Palmer, 2019).

BOX 6.1

Why Is This Website Asking Me about Cookies?

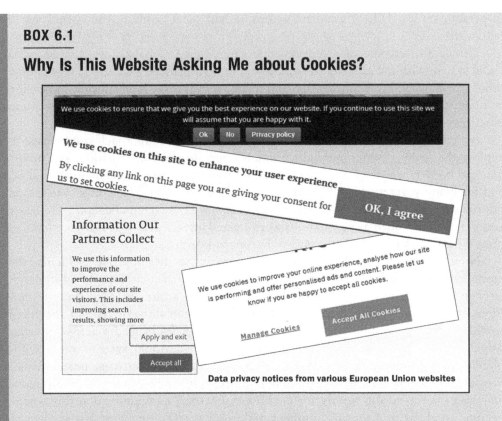

Data privacy notices from various European Union websites

FIGURE 6.1 Warnings about cookies address data privacy.

It's become common now when visiting a website to find a pop-up box with a warning about how the site handles cookies, which are small pieces of software code left on a user's computer by sites that are visited. Usually, cookies are left to help the site "remember" the user, and are a vital part of things such as recommendations, return logins, and shopping carts.

Websites that use these digital identifiers face requirements about disclosure and opt-out policies under European Union regulations meant to give EU citizens more control over their personal data. The cookie controls are part of the General Data Protection Regulation (GDPR), which was adopted in April 2016 after four years of planning, and took full effect in May 2018.

GDPR's main purpose is limiting how businesses and other organizations collect and use digital information that can directly or indirectly identify people. It applies to European organizations but also to businesses outside of Europe that operate in the EU or interact with EU citizens. Data that is affected, of course, includes things such as names, addresses, credit card numbers and other personal information. The regulations also classify IP addresses and cookies as personal data, leading to limitations around them as well. (Another key provision of the GDPR is the so-called "right to be forgotten," which gives EU citizens control over personal information about them that can be found with Internet search engines.)

Although the GDPR codifies things further, the EU regulated cookies with earlier policies dating to 2002 and 2009, called the ePrivacy Directive (EPD). Regulations that must be followed to comply with the EPD include, among others, that websites must receive users' consent to use cookies, must describe what the cookies track to help consumers decide whether to give consent, and must document and store records of consent given by users.

The pop-up boxes that have become so common are the way this consent is managed. They serve as a good example of globalization of media regulation because they appear to web users worldwide who access sites based in Europe or who visit sites of organizations with a strong presence there.

(In addition to cited sources, material was taken from various sections of the "Complete guide to GDPR compliance" published by the EU, including https://gdpr.eu/; https://gdpr.eu/what-is-gdpr/; and https://gdpr.eu/cookies/.)

As a corollary, communication theories that reflect Western thought patterns may not necessarily apply to non-Western societies such as those in Asia and Africa. This notion of whether Western normative theories are valuable or relevant in other cultural contexts is a major consideration in theorizing about communication on a global scale. For example, because of cultural similarities based on historical immigration patterns, the U.S. and European media systems are fairly similar. Even here, though, differences can be found, as documented in Hallin and Mancini's work.

EVOLUTION OF INTERNATIONAL COMMUNICATION THEORIES

Eminent international communication scholar Oliver Boyd-Barrett describes the traditional development of international communication theory as beginning with propaganda studies in the World War I era (see Chapter 2), and from there moving on to modernization and free-flow of information as normative theories in the post-colonial era after World War II. Questioning and critiques of those theories – especially whether they should be considered normative – led to development of theories with opposing perspectives such as dependency, cultural imperialism, and media imperialism. Finally, discourses of globalization have developed more recently (Boyd-Barrett & Rantanen, 1998).

Globalization includes not only the technology that can "selectively connect anyone and anything throughout the world" (Castells, 2008) but, also accompanying institutional and organizational arrangements. In short, Castells maintains, all core economic, communication and cultural activity has become globalized including: finance (investments and banking); production and distribution of goods such as clothing and electronic hardware; and media and cultural goods.

Global exchange of media has a particular significance, however, that goes beyond trade in things such as agricultural commodities or manufactured goods. This is because messages presented in media such as news reports, books, magazines, music, movies, and television shows can "export" cultural values. Such messages can influence social behaviors and organization far from their society of origin, especially if they come from a large and powerful place. For example, Bhattacharjee (2017) studied the impact of European advertising in India while Fitzgerald (2019) examined the growth of Western streaming video services such as Netflix there. These impacts can even include globalization of public opinion and social movements through spontaneous organization on social networks. An example of this would be how #BlackLivesMatter protests in the wake of George Floyd's death at the hands of police officers spread from U.S. cities to London, Berlin, and other European cities, and even as far away as New Zealand (Rahim & Picheta, 2020).

Communication Infrastructure and Political Power

Global communication infrastructure was a critical element for 19th and early 20th century European colonial empires to maintain control of far-flung territories. The telegraph, developed in the mid-1800s, was an early tool for Great Britain to communicate to territories as far away as India, Singapore, and Hong Kong. Other European powers such as France, Germany, and Belgium did the same with colonies in Africa, Asia, South America, and elsewhere. Later, long distance voice communication through telephone and radio served the same purpose. A parallel development of international media using similar infrastructure was the growth of international news agencies, notably Reuters (United Kingdom), Agence France Presse (France) and the Associated Press (United States). The early- to mid-20th century saw global spread of media such as advertising, audio recording, films and, eventually, television.

In the current globalized era, nation-states are no longer the only players on the field; in fact, they may not be the most significant ones. Transnational corporations have come to dominate not only news as in the days of Reuters and Associated Press (both still around, as it happens) but nearly all aspects of international communication, starting with the hardware used to produce and consume it. The most popular mobile phones, for instance, come from Apple, an American firm that manufactures a large share of its iPhones in China, and Samsung, a Korean corporation. They have supplanted Scandinavian suppliers – Sweden's Ericsson and Finland's Nokia – that were the market leaders when mobile phones first became popular in the 1990s. Similarly, top television brands sold worldwide are Korean (LG, and Samsung again) and Japanese (Sony). All of these companies sell all of their devices worldwide.

While Asian companies dominate in hardware, American and European firms tend to dominate content production, such as America's Disney, Warner Brothers, Paramount, and Universal in movies and Twentieth Century Fox, ABC, and NBC in television. That is not meant to imply that U.S. firms are the only sources of such content. America's CNN is probably the world's most recognized news brand, but news from the British Broadcasting Corp. is respected around the globe. Also, Japan's Sony owns a major movie studio, and productions such as Indian "Bollywood" films, Korean "K-pop" music recordings, and South American telenovela dramas have global audiences as well. Still, top selling movies and TV shows around the globe tend to originate from U.S.-based transnational companies. Meanwhile, the world's top book publishers are European, including Penguin-Random House (jointly owned by U.K. and German interests), Hachette Livre (France), Harper-Collins (a subsidiary of U.K.-based News Corp.), and Macmillan (a subsidiary of the German Holtzbrinck Publishing). The most popular social media platforms and apps – Facebook, YouTube (owned by Google), Instagram (owned by Facebook), Twitter, Reddit, Snapchat, LinkedIn, and WhatsApp – are U.S. based. Newcomer TikTok, founded in 2016, is based in China and by one accounting was the seventh-most popular social media platform in the world by mid-2020, with 800 million users (dataportal.com).

STRUCTURE AND FLOW OF INTERNATIONAL COMMUNICATION

The interconnection of media and political power that began in the imperial era is still a common starting point for theorizing about international communication. Thussu (2006) says the discipline has two main schools of thought, one that analyzes communication in relation to economic and political structures (a political economy approach) and another rooted in cultural studies, or how media create shared meanings and values. (Chapter 5 explores other differences in these two approaches.) The political economy branch can be further divided into Marxist and non-Marxist schools of thought.

A Divided World

Around the time that many of the theories described here were developed, especially the ones built around hegemony (or imperialism) of the developed world over the developing world, the global community of nations was generally described with the "Three Worlds" model. The terms First World, Second World, and Third World referred to geopolitical relationships during the time of the Cold War that followed World War II. The breakup of the Soviet Union in the 1990s made these divisions less meaningful. It is, however, useful to know this history relative to the development of international communication theories from the era.

The concept of a "Cold War" meant that even though the shooting across Europe had ended in 1945, the continent was still at war because two large, powerful military complexes led by the United States and the Soviet Union faced each other in the region. The U.S. had allies among Western European nations such as France and Great Britain, while the Soviet allies were Eastern European states such as Poland, Hungary, and Romania. The dividing line, labeled the "Iron Curtain" in a post-war speech by former British Prime Minister Winston Churchill, was in Germany. It was determined roughly by the territory the Western Allies and Soviets controlled when Nazi Germany surrendered. Germany itself was divided into two countries (West and East) each with its own government allied with the U.S. and the Soviets, respectively. This state of affairs lasted into the early 1990s, when the Berlin Wall was removed and Germany was able to reunite.

Within this political arrangement, the term "First World" referred to developed, capitalist, industrial countries led by the United States with generally common political and economic interests. Geographically this meant North America, Western Europe, Japan, and Australia. The "Second World" consisted of communist-socialist industrial states of the Soviet Union, Eastern Europe, The People's Republic of China and a few other nations such as Cuba and North Korea. That left all other countries as the "Third World," notably developing countries of Africa, Asia, and Latin America.

These Third World countries were characterized by low economic development, high levels of poverty, and heavy dependence on industrialized nations. They often had high rates of illiteracy and disease, along with unstable governments. Many were former colonies of European powers that had gained independence after the war and were seen by First World leaders as needing economic, political, and cultural modernization.

Non-Marxist Theories of Political Economy

Modernization Theory

This theory developed in this post World War II era, stating that political and economic modernization of underdeveloped Third World countries to improve their living standards should also incorporate modern Western-style media as a normative model. Recall that a normative theory or model is one that supposedly offers the most beneficial way of establishing social systems. This theory stated that media with a liberal, Westernized philosophy of commercial control and a free-flow-of-information approach could help developing post-colonial countries shed old, traditional (backward) ways and help them aspire to a new, modern (i.e., Westernized) way of living.

One of modernization theory's chief proponents, Daniel Lerner, said the media assisted this process by helping citizens develop aspirations for what their nation could become. "The modernization process begins with new public communication… new ideas and new information which stimulate people to want to behave in new ways" (Lerner, 1963, p. 86). This mediated process of illustrating individual and collective aspirations would in turn create new social and political institutions that could support economic modernization.

However, this theory is now seen as outdated and largely invalid. It was popular from the 1960s to 1980s, especially as the Western world sought to influence the development of South American, African, and Asian nations. It lost favor because of its assumption that a Westernized lifestyle based in capitalist industrialism was the "right" model for every society. This approach assumed that traditional cultural customs *required* modernization, failing to recognize their value, and also assumed that a modern economy and traditional lifestyles were mutually exclusive (Thussu, 2006, pp. 44–45). The theory also failed to address unequal distribution of economic growth, reinforcement of elite hegemony by media, and the uniqueness of local political/social/cultural contexts. It was even seen as a variant on propaganda theory in that its purpose seemed to be manipulation of people's opinions, attitudes and behaviours. Because of these shortcomings, especially the way it dismisses the value of indigenous cultures, modernization is no longer considered a viable theory.

Free Flow of Information

The philosophical underpinning of media behavior in modernization theory was an approach known as free flow of information theory. The U.S. media system based in the First Amendment falls within this category. "Free flow" as a theoretical construct proposes minimal state influence over media content or ownership for all countries, as well as no barriers to information flow across borders. In this model, an individual's freedom to write or speak whatever he or she desires is raised to the level of a fundamental human right. A further principle in this approach is that all other freedoms within a society must be supported by free expression, or a "marketplace of ideas." According to this theory, without free expression it is impossible to have political, social, and economic freedom that allows a society to develop to its fullest potential.

Free flow of information is seen as particularly valuable in the political arena for two reasons. First, it creates conditions for having the media serve as a watchdog or check on the government. In contrast, one of the main features of an authoritarian environment is controls on the media to prevent the spread of criticism against the government. Even more importantly, the free flow of information theory maintains that it is not possible to have effective self-governance unless the public has substantial knowledge about government officials, activities, and policies. Citizens need such information to make intelligent choices in self-governance; if the government can exercise control of the media, this flow of information will be reduced and biased in favor of government viewpoints.

Marxist Political Economy Theories

The central feature of Marxist political economy theories is examination of the connection between media systems and political power within a society (also described in Chapter 5). Marxist theory developed first as a critique of the intertwined interests of the state and capitalist economic interests. Marxism says these connections provide a structure that allows powerful elite forces (and people) in a society to oppress the lower classes. However, cultural institutions, including the media, are also seen as aligned with capitalist interests in what Marx called a "superstructure" that supports or maintains an ideology that capitalist values are normative. Some theories that use this basis to explain how the media relate to the political-economic structure were developed specifically regarding global communication patterns.

Dependency Theory

Dependency theory states that transnational corporations with support of their home governments (especially from the United States and Europe) set the agenda for world economic development. As part of this, they seek to keep developing countries economically and culturally dependent upon the involvement of the transnational corporations in those countries. Transnational control of the media, for its part, helps maintain an ideology that supports this relationship in a dependent country (Straubhaar, 2003). Transnational firms gain this by getting the support of the government for their operations, and in turn help maintain public opinion favorable to the government. This theory emerged to explain economic and media activities in Latin America in the 1960s, and was in part a reaction to modernization theory. Dependency was a forerunner of other theories that proposed an imperialistic relationship between the developed and developing worlds.

Structural Imperialism

This theory states that people of higher political and social status (elites) in the developed world of "core" countries build structural relationships to elites in developing "peripheral" countries. In this context the core refers to developed Western nations, primarily the United States and European countries, while the periphery lies mostly in Africa, Latin America and southern Asia. (The term "Global South" is sometimes used to describe this collection of countries because that is their geographic position relative to the United States and Western Europe.) Not coincidentally, the "core" is mostly colonial imperial powers and the "periphery" former colonies.

Through these relationships, dominance of the core countries over the peripheral countries is maintained by a harmony of interest between the power elite on both sides. In other words, the elite individuals of peripheral countries have more in common with and are more strongly connected to the elite of the core nations than they are to lower-class people and interests in their own countries. The structural result is beneficial primarily to the core countries in the relationships (Galtung, 1971). Structural imperialism is not strictly a media theory, since it also concerns social, political, and economic relationships. The theory also states that flow of news and other information is a key component of maintaining these structural relationships, similar to the Marxist concept of superstructure. As a result, in peripheral countries, the general (non-elite) population knows more about affiliated core countries than they do about neighboring countries (Galtung & Ruge, 1965).

Cultural Imperialism

This theory was proposed by Herbert Schiller in 1976 to describe and explain the way in which large multinational corporations from developed countries, including media companies, dominated developing countries. (Schiller's related commodification of culture theory is covered in Chapter 5.) Cultural imperialism proposes that a society is brought into the modern world system when it is attracted, pressured, forced, or sometimes bribed into shaping its social institutions to correspond to the values and structures of the dominating center of the system (Schiller, 1976). Cultural imperialism further maintains that U.S.-based transnational corporations undermined cultural autonomy of countries in the Global South and created dependencies in communication hardware (equipment) and software (content) (Thussu, 2006, p. 47). The popularity of U.S. television shows, movies, Internet platforms, and celebrities abroad is one example of this.

Media Imperialism

This idea related to cultural imperialism was proposed by British scholar J. Oliver Boyd-Barrett, who defined it as "the process whereby the ownership, structure, distribution, or content of the media in any country are singly or together subject to substantial external pressures from the media interests of any other country or countries, without proportionate reciprocation of influence by the country so affected" (Boyd-Barrett, 1977, p. 117). This means that while Hollywood blockbusters are popular around the world, many of the films produced by studios in other countries are never screened in the United States. Those that do reach the U.S. market generally have limited release in art-house cinemas rather than on hundreds of screens at the multiplexes around the country. This theory overlaps with Schiller's, of course, but is addressed a little more narrowly to the influences of media exports by powerful media producers (especially the United States). These exports influence the media content available in less-developed countries, providing Western media for consumption in those countries that replaces or crowds out indigenous media.

Reaction from the Periphery

Dependency, cultural imperialism and media imperialism theories all relate to the phenomenon of information flow primarily from a Third World perspective, contending that imbalances have a negative impact on the less-developed countries. As Galtung described it, control of the major international media by core countries means that most of the news in smaller, less-developed countries is about large, rich nations and that smaller countries read the most about nations to which they are structurally tied. To put it another way, most people in, say, a post-colonial African country would get more news and information about their former imperialist "masters" than they would of other countries on their own continent.

This "imbalanced" news flow into and among the Third World nations was seen as a problem in the developing world. Not only was the news available in many Third World nations mostly provided *by* core nations *about* core nations, but news about the Third World that did reach core countries was mostly negative, and focused on war, political strife, and natural disasters. (This was sometimes described as news about "coups and earthquakes.") Stevenson and Cole (1984) demonstrated that such an imbalance of information and domination of news flow by core countries created distorted perceptions on both sides of the core-periphery divide.

This led to a reaction in the mid- to late 1970s through the United Nations Educational, Scientific and Cultural Organization (UNESCO) to counter cultural and economic hegemony in the flow of information around the world through two related initiatives. The first was UNESCO's International Commission for the Study of Communication Problems, commonly known as the MacBride Commission after its chairman, Irish diplomat Sean MacBride. The Commission's 1980 report said the world's commercial media system was dominated by transnational corporations that championed a free flow of information – but that this mostly benefited the information "haves" of the core at the expense of information "have nots" in the periphery. The MacBride Commission report listed 82 recommendations for reforming the international communication system in ways that would help Third World countries strengthen their independence, self-determination, and cultural identity by shifting greater control of media resources to the local level.

This prepared the way for a resolution adopted by UNESCO in 1980 that called for a New World Information and Communication Order (NWICO). This would encompass, among other things, "elimination of the imbalances and inequalities [of information exchanges] which characterize the present situation" and "respect for each people's cultural identity and for the right of each nation to inform the world public about its interests, its aspirations and its social and cultural values" (UNESCO 21st General Conference Resolution, in Thussu, [2009], pp. 471–72).

The NWICO proposal, however, was not readily accepted by the Western world. Western news organizations said that, contrary to the report's findings, they were not purposely making poorer countries look bad. Rather, the news organizations said, they were just reporting on realities of the difficult economic, political, and social conditions in many Third World countries – and that undemocratic governments didn't like this news reporting because it reflected badly on them. Western authorities and media companies also argued that the NWICO movement was a Soviet-inspired design to justify government control of media throughout the Third World. They further said it contradicted freedom of information so important in Western society, a viewpoint based in free flow of information as a normative theory. In 1984 the United States withdrew its membership from UNESCO over the matter, and in 1985 the United Kingdom left UNESCO also. (The United States rejoined the organization in 2002, but left again in 2019, this time after accusing the agency of being biased against U.S. ally Israel.)

The Wall Falls, and Globalization Rises

While the UNESCO debates about the need for new world information orders played out, geopolitical forces were at work that would shortly lead to the shattering of the old world order anyway. The fall of the Berlin Wall in November 1989 signaled the beginning of the end of the Three Worlds geopolitical model, and was a catalyst for the emergence of a truly new world political order – with impacts for economics, culture, and media as well.

The Cold War had kept Eastern Europe secluded behind what former U.K. Prime Minister Winston Churchill described as "an Iron Curtain," with totalitarian domination by the Soviet Union. But after 1989, the nations of Eastern Europe were able to become more fully integrated into the world community of nations. With the dismantling of the Soviet Union two years later, the idea of a "Second World" disappeared. This didn't end cultural or economic hegemony in the world; in many ways, transnational media companies have actually become more powerful in the decades since then. It did, however, mean the end of an era in which Third World nations too often became pawns in a global chess match by the U.S. and Soviet superpowers. This in turn led to more freedom of movement for people, goods – and information.

The tensions of the old world order helped lead to theories such as modernization, and reactions to it such as dependency theories and the UNESCO movements. These competing ideas largely grew as an extension of former colonial nations' drives for independence after World War II; the media theories extended these anti-colonial efforts in political and economic spheres into cultural ones as well (Sparks, 2012). Sparks calls the set of imperialistic theories largely obsolete today. Globalization, he says "has tended to discount the role of the state in favor of the relations between the global and the local" (p. 282). Larger nations still seek to wield influence, sometimes in competition with each other, but do not act with outright imperialism. In this perspective, there is no single core dominating a periphery in the globalized world. White makes similar arguments, saying that theories such as cultural imperialism applied well to the time in which they were proposed, but further notes that "with the advent of advanced communication technologies that allow for a multi-directional as opposed to a unidirectional flow of information between countries, cultural imperialism is no longer a useful framework for explaining the same phenomena that it was applied to in the 1970s" (White, 2001, paragraph 8).

Other theorists disagree, and say that imperialist perspectives on world communication flows are still highly relevant because of the power that transnational media corporations hold. One such theorist is Oliver Boyd-Barrett, who argues media imperialism is as valuable as ever to understanding the post-1989 world. While recognizing that the decline of Marxist Eastern Europe led to skepticism about the validity and relevance of dependency and imperialist theory, Boyd-Barrett says those theories still help to explain "the relationship between national economies and the global capitalist economy, and the role of culture and media in helping to sustain and reinvigorate that relationship" (Boyd-Barrett & Rantanen, 1998, p. 151). Another is Schiller, who argues that "The domination that exists today [in the early 1990s] … is better understood as transnational corporate cultural domination (Schiller, 1991, p. 14).

1989 also was the year that British scientist Tim Berners Lee, who was working at a research institute in Switzerland, proposed the idea of a computer network using a tool he called hypertext to link documents and information. His idea was the foundation for the World Wide Web. As the Web grew it became the most efficient way ever invented for information to flow freely around the world, creating a truly global and borderless media system. So, 1989 can be seen as a watershed year for both world politics and international communication that saw the first steps taken on a path leading to our current globalized, interdependent world.

Development of the Web contributed to the phenomenon of media systems that were primarily national in 1990 being largely global by the turn of the 21st century ten years later. "Today, one must first grasp the nature and logic of the global commercial system and then determine how the local and national media deviate" (McChesney, 1999, p. 78). Similar to Boyd-Barrett and Schiller, McChesney notes that this global media system is encouraged by and in turn supportive of global capitalism, especially the interests of transnational corporations. He also notes that transnational groups such as the World Trade Organization as well as the globalization of the advertising industry provide further support for the related interests of global media and global capitalism.

CONTEMPORARY PARADIGM: COMPARATIVE MEDIA MODELS

Schiller's discussion of the interplay of global, national and local forces illustrates that despite the growth and expansion of a global information system, important political and cultural differences do remain at the national level. This is why the most prominent and popular theoretical framework for examining international communication has become comparative studies, which analyzes the similarities and differences of media systems in different nations or regions (groups of nations). Cultural and national settings for media systems – laws, geography, language, politics, economics and technology – shape those systems (Trappel, 2011).

Esser (2013) notes that a comparative approach helps improve awareness that there are no one-size-fits-all media models. Comparing systems also brings attention to things about them that are not readily apparent or have not previously been noticed. "Virtually no other approach has the potential to bring communication studies further forward in the age of transnationalization than the comparative approach" (Esser, 2013, p. 113).

He cautions, however, that the approach will be valid only if theoretical frameworks and concepts are equivalent for each case (country or region). Esser points to a set of models developed by Daniel Hallin and Paolo Mancini as an example of a comparative framework that meets these criteria. Trappel also cites Hallin and Mancini's approach as a productive one because it doesn't use the East/West power conflict or other ideologies as a starting point but rather seeks to make analyses based on empirical characteristics of countries' media systems.

A Comparative Framework

In doing this, Hallin and Mancini (2004) built on Siebert, Peterson and Schramm's "Four Theories of the Press" model (Siebert, Peterson, & Schramm, 1956). (These are presented, in more detail, in Chapter 2.) The models they developed, called the Four Theories of the Press, are:

Libertarian Model

This model supposes an almost pure form of free press with no government regulation. In it, the media are privately owned and fulfill functions of informing and entertaining their audiences, and keeping a check on government. The United States is said to come closest to embodying this approach because of the First Amendment to its Constitution, which restricts government interference in the content media may produce. Even the U.S. system has certain constraints, however. Therefore, pure libertarian models exist in theory only and not at all in practice. In fact, the United States falls behind most of Europe, Canada, Australia, and even some African and South American countries in rankings of press freedom (see Box 6.2).

Social Responsibility Model

This model also presumes freedom of expression is a core value for a country, but with an underlying principle that freedom carries obligations for the media to act in ways that benefit society. This happens through two processes. First, media organizations exercise voluntary restraint to act in the social interest. Second, government regulation is both legitimate and necessary to control excesses.

As described in Chapter 2, a mix of government regulation and voluntary industry restrictions place the U.S. media system in this category. However, the national public broadcasting service models of the British Broadcasting Corp. (BBC) in the United Kingdom, Raidió Teilifis Éireann (RTÉ) in Ireland and the Canadian Broadcasting Corp. (CBC) are often said to embody this approach even more fully. These and other media organizations in Great Britain, Canada, and Ireland have great freedom of operation. However, the BBC, RTÉ, and CBC are wholly or partially funded by their

BOX 6.2

World Press Freedom Rankings

Americans like to think they live in the most free and open society in the world. Freedom, though, is relative, and an organization called Reporters Sans Frontières (Reporters Without Borders) publishes an annual ranking of press freedom around the world. It is based on a survey of press experts and its own tally of violent activity toward journalists. Factors the index takes into account are pluralism, media independence, self-censorship, government regulation, and transparency of government and other major institutions that journalists cover.

In 2019, the group ranked the United States 45th out of 180 countries in its index. Major Western powers ranked ahead of it included the United Kingdom, Germany, and Canada. RSF attributed this relatively low U.S. ranking to a general lack of transparency from the government along with arrests, assaults, and harassment faced by U.S. journalists in 2019. "Much of that ire has come from President Trump and his associates in the federal government, who have demonstrated the United States is no longer a champion of press freedom at home or abroad," the agency reported on its website.

Reporters Without Borders ranked Western Europe as the region with the greatest press freedom, particularly countries that Hallin and Mancini say follow a "democratic corporatist" approach such as those in Scandinavia. (Although the rankings were shuffled slightly, nine of the top 10 countries on the 2019 list were the same ones as in 2015, listed in a previous edition of this book, with five of them from Scandinavia.) By contrast, the countries at the bottom of the list in both 2015 and 2019 were China, Eritrea, Turkmenistan, and North Korea.

Top Ten Countries for Press Freedom in 2019
(according to Reporters Without Borders):

Norway
Finland
Denmark
Sweden
Netherlands
Jamaica
Costa Rica
Switzerland
New Zealand
Portugal

Source: https://rsf.org/en/ranking

national governments and answerable to them. That means they have both financial incentives and government regulations and policies encouraging them to create programming "in the public interest."

Authoritarian Model

In this approach, the media must support policies of the government and they are punished if they do not. Media are not owned and operated by the government, but are tightly controlled by it through prior restraint (censorship), subsequent sanction (punishment for presenting content that the government finds objectionable), and sometimes through licensing of media outlets. China stands out as an example in the contemporary world. Goh (2015) studied another authoritarian system – Singapore – and discovered that social media there helped to provide citizens with alternatives to the closely controlled mainstream press during a general election.

Totalitarian Model

This approach also features strict control of the media, so that it can serve the purposes of the state as a propaganda tool. Siebert, Peterson & Schramm referred to this as the "Soviet communist theory of the press" because of how the Soviet Union media operated in the 1950s when the Four Theories book was published. Perhaps the best current example of this model is North Korea.

Like Siebert, Peterson and Schramm did, Hallin and Mancini (2004) seek to show the interrelationship of media models with the specific social and political structures of the nations in which they operate. In doing so, their theories fit firmly within the political economy approach. They state that their purpose is to "develop a framework for comparing media systems and a set of hypotheses for how they are linked structurally and historically to the development of the political system" (p. 5). For example, the United States, Canada, the United Kingdom and Ireland have common cultural and political histories and comparable levels of economic development. A comparative approach analyzes how those commonalities help to predict/explain the media systems each country has, but also sheds light on differences that exist despite their common heritage. Hallin and Mancini focus on news media and press regulation along four major dimensions, which are:

The contemporary situation and historical development of a country's **media marketplace**, especially the presence and growth of mass circulation newspapers and commercial broadcasting. For example, they say that the most distinctive historical characteristic of the North Atlantic countries (United States, United Kingdom, Ireland, and Canada) "is the early and strong development of commercial newspapers" (p. 202). In the United States commercial media began to replace the partisan press in the mid-19th century (1840s) with development of the penny press. Similar developments occurred in the U.K. in the 1850s and Canada in 1880s, in line with the shift from a rural population and agricultural economy to an urban, industrialized one. Ireland, which industrialized later, saw its commercial media system begin to develop a few decades later, in the early 20th century. On the other hand, southern Europe (Spain, Portugal, France, Italy, Greece), saw its commercial press develop later still, and even today news media there have an elite audience rather than a mass one.

The state of **political parallelism** in a country or region, which is how closely news media are related to political divisions in society. This is measured especially by the number and prominence of partisan publications, including ones affiliated with political parties and also with trade unions and other social institutions.

The level of **journalistic professionalism** found in a country, by which they primarily mean level of independence and public service orientation. One way to think of this is how thoroughly journalists follow the characteristics set out by Siebert, Peterson and Schramm's social responsibility theory.

Finally, Hallin and Mancini examine the **degree of state intervention** in the media system, which varies dramatically around the world. The United States arguably has the lowest level of government authority to intervene or regulate the media of any country in the world because of the First Amendment to the U.S. Constitution and the way it has been interpreted by the courts. (Although, as Box 6.2 describes, factors other than legal authority affect levels of press freedom.) As noted earlier, Canada, Ireland, and the United Kingdom also have national public-service broadcasting systems funded wholly or in part by the government and operating under a government charter or authority. Although the U.S. Public Broadcasting System does receive a small amount of government funding (through the Corporation for Public Broadcasting), nothing like the BBC exists in the United States. Furthermore, a government charter such as the one the British government grants for the BBC probably could *not* exist in the United States without violating the First Amendment.

Applying the framework to countries across North America and Western Europe, Hallin and Mancini developed three primary models, consisting of countries that have similar characteristics along these dimensions but also fall into geographic groupings, as follows:

- **Liberal (North Atlantic) model**, in which commercial media dominate while political parallelism and government intervention are low. This model exists in the United States, United Kingdom, Canada, and Ireland.
- **Democratic Corporatist model**, where commercial media co-exist with ones closely affiliated with social and political groups. These countries also have a tradition of the state playing an active but limited role. The most common location for this set of characteristics is northern Europe, including Germany, Austria, The Netherlands, and Scandinavia.
- **Polarized Pluralist Model**, which is found in countries with weaker commercial media, greater integration of media into party politics, and a stronger legal role for the state in regulating the media. This model is associated with southern Europe, notably Spain, Portugal, Italy, and Greece.

Generalizing about these models, Hallin and Mancini (2004, p. 76) make the following observations:

- In the Liberal (North Atlantic) countries, the media are closest to business interests and furthest from political influences. It's not a coincidence that so many large multinational media corporations such as Disney (U.S.) and News Corp. (U.K.) are based in the North Atlantic region since media systems there are friendliest to commercial enterprises.

- The Polarized Pluralist countries of southern Europe are just the opposite. Media are closely integrated with political interests, and operate from less of a commercial basis.
- The Democratic Corporatist model in Northern Europe demonstrates relatively strong ties of media both to commercial *and* political entities.
- The trend over time has been away from political control and more toward commercial control, i.e., a gradual shift toward alignment with the liberal model, in all regions of Europe.

Hallin and Mancini emphasize that these are not "pure" forms. Their point is not to provide a taxonomy or classification system but instead to identify patterns and relationships that can be used as a basis for comparing the systems. The four dimensions of market structure, political parallelism, professionalism, and state intervention can be evaluated independently for any particular analysis. For example, countries within the North Atlantic model are highly similar but still have differences, especially between the United States and the United Kingdom. The United States is closest to a libertarian model (though not wholly) while the United Kingdom has elements of the democratic corporatist model with a blend of commercial and state-chartered media and a generally more politicized media system. Ireland and Canada are somewhere in between. However, it could be argued that the growing influence of conservative right-wing media outlets in recent years has made the U.S. media system more politicized, closing some of the differences Hallin and Mancini cite.

Hallin and Mancini also warn against seeing any of these as normative models. Their liberal model is sometimes talked about as the normative ideal; certainly it is viewed that way in the free flow of information and modernization theories. (Not by everyone, though, as the NWICO movement and MacBride reports illustrated.) Hallin and Mancini are not trying to endorse a normative *approach*, but rather seek to devise a framework that can be used to help understand normative *questions* such as the proper relationship of the state to the media and impact of commercialization and regulation on media independence.

The Hallin and Mancini model has become a popular way to study social and political influences on media systems, especially in Europe; a Google Scholar search in late 2020 showed about 7,600 citations of their 2004 book. These included studies of populist rhetoric by politicians in different Western democracies (Blassnig, Büchel, & Ernst, 2019), descriptive comparison of Nordic news audiences (Schrøder, Blach-Ørsten, & Kæmsgaard Eberholst, 2020), a comparative review of whether people in different countries will take political action in response to media content they perceive to be biased against them (Barnidge, Rojas, Beck, & Schmitt-Beck, 2020), and a study of how audiences react to media disinformation (Humprecht, Esser, & Van Aelst, 2020).

CONCLUSION

Greater international information flow and the "death of distance" unquestionably make it seem as if the world is smaller than it was a generation ago. People can e-mail or connect on social media or video chat to others literally anywhere at any time. They consume news and entertainment programs from distant countries as easily as those created in their own towns. The days when people were marginalized and kept down by a small group of elite actors maintaining a stranglehold on information flow are largely in the past, although transnational media companies such as Disney and News Corp. do maintain a commercial dominance that gives them a great influence in many countries around the world.

More efficient flow of more types of information in greater volumes does not mean it is homogenized, however. Political, social, and economic systems still vary around the world, and their associated media systems differ accordingly. Everyone lives in a place where the media system has certain characteristics, but one way to develop a better understanding of one's own system is to examine systems from different settings. (That's also a rationale for why semester study abroad programs have become increasingly popular.) Comparative media frameworks such as the popular one developed by Hallin and Mancini have real value for the same reason. Knowing more about other people and other cultures leads to greater self-awareness and self-understanding.

Discussion Questions/Application Exercises

1. Visit the home page of the British Broadcasting Corp.'s news operations at http://www.bbc.com/news and look at the mix of stories there. How many or what proportion are coverage of U.S. news or issues?
2. If you have the language skills to do so, examine the main national broadcaster's website for a country such as Spain, Italy, Portugal or Greece and review news stories there. Recall that Hallin and Mancini group together these Mediterranean nations as having a "polarized pluralist" media system that would reflect partisan views more strongly. Does that seem to have an impact on their coverage as compared to news from outlets in the United States or United Kingdom (two representatives of the liberal/North Atlantic model)?
3. If you have access to it,[1] watch a broadcast of the BBC World News and compare the content to a U.S. nightly network news show. This can start with which topics or issues are covered, looking especially for differences in "local" stories (meaning U.K. news for the BBC and U.S. news for the U.S. outlets) vs. international ones. Also look at the format and style of how the news stories are constructed and how they are delivered by the presenters.
4. As question 3 suggested with regard to news, compare and contrast U.S. vs. BBC programming in another genre of programming such as comedies, dramas, talk shows, or reality TV.
5. Are you, or any of your friends, fans of K-pop music groups, Latin American telenovelas, Bollywood films, or European art-house cinema? How much of this media content do you consume compared to American offerings?

NOTE

1 Available on many cable systems, and also on some PBS stations and via streaming options

REFERENCES

Barnidge, M., Rojas, H., Beck, P.A. & Schmitt-Beck, R. (2020). Comparative corrective action: Perceived media bias and political action in 17 countries. *International Journal of Public Opinion Research* 32(4). doi: 10.1093/ijpor/edz043

Bhattacharjee, A. (2017, November). Impact of "cultural imperialism" on advertising and marketing. *Journal of Intercultural Communication* 45. Retrieved from http://mail.immi.se/intercultural/nr45/bhattacharjee.html

Blassnig, S., Büchel, F., Ernst, N. & Engesser, S. (2019). Populism and informal fallacies: An analysis of right-wing populist rhetoric in election campaigns. *Argumentation* 33, 107–136. Retrieved from https://doi.org/10.1007/s10503-018-9461-2

Boyd-Barrett, O. (1977). Media imperialism: Towards an international framework for the analysis of media systems. In Curran, J., Gurevitch, M., & Woollacott, J. (Eds.). *Mass communication and society* (pp. 116–135). London: Edward Arnold.

Boyd-Barrett, O. & Rantanen, T. (1998). *The globalisation of news*. Sage Publications Ltd.

Burgess, M. (2020, March 24). What is GDPR? The summary guide to GDPR compliance in the UK. *Wired UK* online. Retrieved from https://www.wired.co.uk/article/what-is-gdpr-uk-eu-legislation-compliance-summary-fines-2018

Castells, M. (2008). The new public sphere: Global civil society, communication networks, and global governance. *Annals of the American Academy of Political and Social Science* 616, 78–93. doi: 10.1177/0002716207311877

Esser, F. (2013). The emerging paradigm of comparative communication enquiry: Advancing cross-national research in times of globalization. *International Journal of Communication* 7, 113–128.

Fitzgerald, S. (2019). Over-the-top (OTT) video services in India: Media imperialism after globalization. *Media Industries Journal* 6 (2). Retrieved from https://quod.lib.umich.edu/m/mij/15031809.0006.206/--over-the-top-video-services-in-india-media-imperialism-after?rgn=main;view=fulltext;q1=Fitzgerald

Galtung, J. (1971). A structural theory of imperialism. *Journal of Peace Research* 8 (2), 81–117.

Galtung, J. & Ruge, M.H. (1965). The structure of foreign news. *Journal of Peace Research* 2 (1), 64–91.

Goh, D. (2015). Narrowing the knowledge gap: The role of alternative online media in an authoritarian press system. *Journalism & Mass Communication Quarterly* 92 (4), 877–897.

Hallin, D.C., & Mancini, P. (2004). *Comparing media systems: Three models of media and politics*. New York: Cambridge University Press.

Humprecht, E., Esser, F., & Van Aelst, P. (2020). Resilience to online disinformation: a framework for cross-national comparative research. *The International Journal of Press/Politics* 25 (3), 493–516.

Lerner, D. (1963). Toward a communication theory of modernization: A set of considerations. In Pye, L. (Ed.). *Communications and political development* (pp. 327–350). Princeton: Princeton University Press.

Livingstone, S. (2012). Challenges to comparative research in a globalizing media landscape. In Esser, F. & Hanitzsch, T. (Eds.). *Handbook of comparative communication research* (pp. 415–429). London, UK: Routledge.

McChesney, R. (1999). *Rich Media, Poor Democracy*. Urbana: University of Illinois Press.

Palmer, D. (2019, May 17). What is GDPR? Everything you need to know about the new general data protection regulations. *ZDNet* online. Retrieved from https://www.zdnet.com/article/gdpr-an-executive-guide-to-what-you-need-to-know/

Rahim, Z. & Picheta, R. (2020, June 1). *CNN* online. Retrieved from https://www.cnn.com/2020/06/01/world/george-floyd-global-protests-intl/index.html

Recommendations from the MacBride Report 1980. (2009). In Thussu, D.K. (Ed.) *International communication: A reader* (pp. 473–477). New York: Routledge.

Schiller, H. (1976). *Communication and cultural domination*. White Plains, NY: ME Sharpe.

Schiller, H. (1991). Not yet the post-imperialist era. *Critical Studies in Mass Communication* 8, 13–28.

Schrøder, K.C., Blach-Ørsten, M., & Kæmsgaard Eberholst, M. (2020). Is there a Nordic news media system? *Nordic Journal of Media Studies* 2 (1), 23–35. doi: https://doi.org/10.2478/njms-2020-0003

Shaw, P. & Tan, Y. (2014). Race and masculinity: A comparison of Asian and Western models in men's lifestyle magazine advertisements. *Journalism & Mass Communication Quarterly* 91 (1), 118–138.

Siebert, F.S., Peterson, T., & Schramm, W. (1956). *Four theories of the press: The authoritarian, libertarian, social responsibility, and Soviet communist concepts of what the press should be and do*. University of Illinois Press.

Sparks, C. (2012, September). Media and cultural imperialism reconsidered. *Chinese Journal of Communication* 5 (3), 281–299.

Straubhaar, J.D. (2003). Globalization, media imperialism and dependency as communication frameworks. In Anokwa, K., Lin, C.A. & Salwen, M.B. (Eds.). *International communication: Concepts and cases* (pp. 225–238). Belmont: Wadsworth/Thomson Lear.

Stevenson, R.L. & Cole, R. (1984). Issues in foreign news. In Stevenson, R.L. & Shaw, D.L. (Eds.). *Foreign news and the New World information order* (pp. 5–20). Ames, IA: Iowa State University Press.

Thussu, D.K. (2006). *International communication: Continuity and change*. London: Hodder Arnold.

Trappel, J. (2011). *Media in Europe today*. Bristol, UK: Intellect Books.

"UNESCO 21st general conference resolution on NWICO" (2009). In Thussu, D.K. (Ed.). *International communication: A reader* (pp. 471–472). New York: Routledge.

White, L.A. (2001). Reconsidering cultural imperialism theory. *Transnational Broadcasting Studies* 6, 1–17. Retrieved from http://tbsjournal.arabmediasociety.com/Archives/Spring01/white3.html, paragraph 8.

CHAPTER 7

Research Principles and Practices

This chapter will:

- Examine several dimensions in which qualitative and quantitative research differ along a spectrum of complementary principles, such as more general to more specific.
- Provide an overview of the research process and design of theory-based research in both the positivist and interpretive traditions.

Theory and research work together to help develop new insights about human activity through the systematic process of developing and testing explanations (theories) about how phenomena relate to one another. Developing this knowledge about mass media influences on individuals and society entails theory-driven research using many of the ideas and theories from Chapters 2 through 6.

The actual research can take different forms, depending on the style of theory involved. Communication science-styled research is systematic and objective in its collection, processing, analysis, and reporting of information (Poindexter & McCombs, 2000). This is also known as the positivist method, a term coined by sociologist Auguste Comte in the early 1800s. "Positivism," as Comte defined it, adapts the scientific method and numerical measurements as used in the natural sciences to reach conclusions about human behavior. Methods to employ this research style are described in Chapter 8.

Some researchers, however, rely on qualitative methods rather than quantitative ones. They use ideas and evidence drawn from sources such as interviews and observations, augmented by the researcher's own ideas and interpretations. Positivist researchers seek to generalize and explain phenomena across a variety of settings whereas interpretive scholars prefer to provide unique explanations about specific situations to develop deeper understandings. As Wimmer and Dominick put it, "whereas positivist researchers strive for breadth, interpretive researchers strive for depth" (2000, p. 104). Methods appropriate to this style of research are covered in Chapter 9.

The positivist approach is the oldest and most widely used method of inquiry in communication research; the most popular theories that researchers rely upon follow this tradition as well (Walter, Cody, & Ball-Rokeach, 2018). The interpretive paradigm has become an important part of the discipline as well, starting in the 1950s and gaining in recognition throughout the last quarter of the 20th century (Wimmer & Dominick, 2000).

DOI: 10.4324/9781003121695-7

The positivist, quantitative research tradition and the qualitative, interpretive tradition differ on several dimensions with characteristics that are described in ways that make them seem to be opposites, but on closer review actually are more complementary than opposed to one another.

EXPLANATORY VS. DESCRIPTIVE RESEARCH

The first of these divisions to discuss is rooted in the nature of quantitative vs. qualitative work, but goes beyond those styles somewhat. That is because it represents a fundamental distinction of its own that can be pursued with either research style. This distinction is between descriptive and explanatory research. In fact, deciding whether a project is meant to be explanatory or descriptive is one of the first and most basic decisions a researcher must make. Descriptive research is addressed toward **what** is happening while explanatory research seeks to answer **why** something is happening. The path a researcher follows toward one of these approaches or the other depends on the purpose of the project. Sometimes a combination of these styles can create the most meaningful understanding of all.

Effective description is a fundamental part of good research because it improves people's understanding of the world around them. For example, careful and thorough description of social problems can be an important first step toward addressing them (De Vaus, 2001). Government statistics such as the U.S. Census are an example of descriptive work that could have that type of impact. Before policies addressing problems such as poverty or public health can be deployed, the people making those policies need good descriptions about the extent and details of the problem.

While descriptive research can have useful purposes, gaining deeper understanding of a phenomenon often requires examining the causes behind it, which requires explanatory research. This is where the two approaches to research are truly complementary, because descriptive work can be a starting point for developing the "why" questions that are answered with explanatory research. Extending the example, a detailed description of a social problem such as crime or poverty is important on its own. Understanding why particular regions or ethnic groups tend to be more impoverished than others or more likely than others to be crime victims, however, requires explanatory research that digs into the question of why the situation exists as it does.

Generally speaking, descriptive research is associated more with qualitative research, which often is based on observations and uses narrative discussions to relate its findings. Explanatory research tends to be more quantitative, using specific measurements to explain why something is happening in a more precise fashion.

DIFFERENCES IN APPROACH AND VIEWPOINT

Three other dimensions in which the qualitative and quantitative research traditions differ reflect how each is approached and presented, along a spectrum of general to specific and whether the researcher takes a neutral standpoint or a subjective one.

The first of these distinctions concerns whether the approach to a project is inductive or deductive, which are distinguished by a bottom-up or top-down way of researching the matter. An inductive approach, the bottom-up method, begins with detailed observations that then are used to generate broader ideas or perspectives on the subject. In other words, it moves from specific observations to general conclusions. A deductive, or top-down approach, goes in the opposite direction. It starts with the broad ideas and then seeks out specific observations to support (or sometimes refute) them. The inductive approach often merges data interpretation and collection, while deductive approaches separate the two, first collecting the data then analyzing it later. These differences mean inductive approaches lend themselves to qualitative research, while deductive research tends to be quantitative. Quantitative deductions that can demonstrate some level of cause and effect are one way that explanatory research can answer the "Why did this happen?" question in many projects (Morgan, 2014).

Another way in which this spectrum about specificity shows differences between the research traditions is whether a project is meant to be applied as generally as possible or whether it is meant to offer the kind of context and detail that comes from examining situations more closely. Qualitative research tends to explore specific situations in depth and detail, providing insight into those situations and the contexts in which they take place. Quantitative research, on the other hand, uses large numbers of observations, such as hundreds or even thousands of responses to a survey, in order to create a general overview that relates to things as broadly as possible (Morgan, 2014).

A third dimension separating these research styles concerns how the researcher approaches the work, whether from a subjective stance of trying to make a point about something, or from a more neutral or objective viewpoint. Qualitative researchers often have a more subjective approach both in purpose – the topic and research question under investigation – and procedure, or willingness to interact with research subjects and offer interpretations about the findings. Quantitative researchers, on the other hand, rely on procedures that are designed to take their viewpoints out of the research as much as possible (Morgan, 2014). This is also manifested in the way critical or cultural researchers generally approach their work as contrasted with effects-tradition researchers. (See discussion in Chapter 5.)

To summarize:

- Qualitative research uses an inductive (specific-to-general) approach to contextualize the study in detail, with the researcher's viewpoints and interpretation as part of the results.
- Quantitative research uses the deductive method to create broad, general understandings from a neutral standpoint.

WHY THESE DISTINCTIONS MATTER

Effective research depends on gathering the correct type of information, and enough of it, to answer the research question adequately. Effective research design means figuring out the best ways to get that information. Research that is meant to be descriptive requires collecting different types of information from research intended to offer an explanation such as a cause-effect relationship. The information also is analyzed and presented differently. Research meant to build theories or generate hypotheses proceeds differently from that meant to test theories. At the same time, it is important not to confuse methods with designs, or to equate a style of data collection (e.g., quantitative survey) with design of a project, which should be seen as "a logical task undertaken to ensure that the evidence collected enables us to answer questions or to test theories as unambiguously as possible" (De Vaus, 2001, p. 16). In other words, research design requires figuring out what type of evidence is needed to answer a research question, or sometimes test a hypothesis, in a convincing way. Principles and practices for doing that are explored in the remainder of this chapter.

BOX 7.1

Definitions of Qualitative and Quantitative Research

Qualitative research: Based on ideas and evidence drawn from personal observations, interviews or texts (other published work) that is augmented by the researcher's own ideas and logic.

Quantitative (empirical) research: Based on hypotheses and research designs yielding numerically stated values of observed data.

THEORY AND RESEARCH IN THE POSITIVIST TRADITION

Successful research projects of either paradigm require both a meaningful research question and an appropriate way to answer that question. Choosing research methods that can accomplish those research goals requires knowing both what your options are and how to evaluate those options (Morgan, 2014). In quantitative or positivist social science research, this generally consists of stating either a research question or a hypothesis. A research question is just what the name says it is: A question that can be answered with some type of research such as "What happens when people view violent movies and television?" or "Do people get a greater awareness about political issues from following social media or from traditional media such as newspapers and television news?"

BOX 7.2

Definition of Positivism

Positivism: Using investigative methods of the physical sciences, such as experiments and objective measurement of specified criteria, to address and understand social phenomena.

Some research questions are open-ended and explorative. A hypothesis, however, is a particular type of research question, which states the question in a particular way. Specifically, a hypothesis makes a prediction that can be tested by observing and analyzing some type of evidence. Turning the research question mentioned earlier about legacy news vs. social media news sharing into a hypothesis could be done by rewording to make it into a testable proposition: "People who rely on social media as a news source will have a greater awareness of political issues than those who rely on traditional news sources."

The fact that it can be *tested* is what makes a hypothesis a valuable and powerful research tool. What makes it testable is that it makes a prediction about how things are related. As Kerlinger and Lee point out, facts cannot be tested but relationships can (2000). In the example, the hypothesis relates "news source" and "awareness of political issues" to each other; the strength of this relationship can then be observed so that the prediction can be shown to be either correct or incorrect. (Box 7.3 follows the progression of this research design.)

BOX 7.3

Theory-to-research Example

Paradigm	Moderate effects (communication science basis)
Theory	Agenda setting
Hypothesis	People who rely on social media referral as their primary news source will have greater awareness of political issues than those who rely on traditional media (newspaper or TV news)
Variables	Independent Variable = news source (social media vs. legacy media) Dependent Variable = awareness
Hypothesis (restated with variables)	Social media used more than legacy = higher issue awareness Social media used less than legacy = lower issue awareness
Measurement (Operationalization)	Independent variables: • Number times/week watching news. • Number times/week reading paper. • Number of political news "shares" on social media reviewed during week. (Use raw numbers to calculate proportion or comparison value as variable for calculations) Dependent variable: • Questionnaire with 1–5 scale of awareness for 20 top issues in the news.

> **BOX 7.4**
>
> ## Definition of Hypothesis
>
> *Hypothesis:* A prediction about how certain things are related that can be tested by observing and analyzing evidence that will illustrate whether or not the prediction is correct.

Scope of the Research

As with theories from which they are often derived, good hypotheses are neither too narrow nor too broad. If a problem is too general or too vague, the researcher will have great difficulty gathering and evaluating enough good evidence to reach a conclusion about it. An example of an overly vague research question might be: "What impact does smartphone ownership have on college students?" Today's college students have literally grown up with their phones, and use of phones affects many aspects of their lives. Where would an investigation about "impact on college students" start, and what could it hope to conclude? On the other hand, if the research topic is too narrow or specific, the research will end up being inconsequential because the answers it produces just will not matter to enough people. An example of that might be: "Do 19-year-olds prefer Android phones or iPhones?" Focusing on 19-year-olds isn't all that useful because their phone decisions would not be that much different from 18-year-olds or 20-year-olds. The artificially narrow age demographic makes the research question too specific. Also, the type of phone people own is a pretty mundane question; what people do with their phones or the impact those activities have on their lives would be much more interesting than which operating system they prefer.

A more effective research scope might investigate a specific aspect of students' use of some medium and how it affects a particular aspect of their lives in a way that could predict or explain the impact on many students rather than just a narrow group. For example, a researcher with an interest in social networks such as Snapchat, Twitter, and Instagram could develop a hypothesis that explores the relationship of student interaction on those applications with their friendships and personal networks in the "real world." The researcher might then try to answer the question: "Are students with large virtual networks in Snapchat also likely to join in more student clubs or activities? Or are they less likely to be real-world 'joiners' because their online friendships substitute for real-world ones?" This question is small enough in scope that the researcher can answer it effectively, but large enough to be interesting to many people.

Establishing "Proof" and Causality

A further connection between theories and hypotheses is that testing the hypothesis can help to validate or "prove" a theory. ("Prove" is in quotes because social scientists generally think that theories can never be really proved beyond all doubts; more commonly they say that theories are either *supported* or *challenged* by investigations into them. The individual and social behavior of human beings is complicated and has so many conditions and variables that "deterministic" proof for questions about how people react or behave is essentially impossible [De Vaus, 2001]). This support for a theory often comes from a hypothesis about a causal relationship, when one condition can reasonably be said to *cause* another at least some of the time. The Snapchat (or Twitter or Instagram) example is not stated as a causal relationship, but the news media example used previously is causal because it proposes that greater attention to politics on social media can be seen as *causing* a difference in issue awareness on the part of readers.

BOX 7.5

Look-Alike Terms: Causal vs. Casual

Researchers write a lot about causal circumstances and causality. It's important to note the spelling there, which places the "u" before the "s." Both are derived from the word cause, which the dictionary defines as "to bring about or to make happen." A causal condition is one that brings about change in another condition (or, more directly stated, causes changes). It is very easy when seeing the word in print to read it as *casual* (note that here the "s" is before the "u"). This word, of course, means "informal" or "relaxed" (e.g., business casual clothing, or a casual get-together). Just two letters trading places creates two words that are almost exact opposites. Students who see either of these words in a research report should look carefully to make sure they are considering the correct meaning of the word they are reading.

Establishing a causal relationship requires that three specific conditions be met, however. First, the effect that is being observed and the condition that is thought to be causing the effect must be somehow related, such as both increasing or both decreasing in a coordinated fashion. Finding evidence of such coordination is a major part of many research projects. The second condition is that the cause must happen before the effect. The third is that other potential causes must be ruled out. This is often a key consideration in the research design as well. In trying to say that paying greater attention to social media causes people to be more aware of political issues, the researcher would have to be sure that a factor such as being a political activist wasn't the real reason a respondent had more awareness of politics.

To recap, theories are *general* statements that seek to predict or explain how certain phenomena are related to one another. Hypotheses are *specific* predictions that can be tested by collecting and analyzing observations to illustrate whether or not the prediction is correct. When the general ideas of the theory are used to create the specific predictions represented in the hypothesis, showing support for the hypothesis is a way of validating the theory.

Constructs, Variables, and Measurements

Answering research questions or testing hypotheses involves the use of tools called concepts, constructs and variables. These three terms are related but not interchangeable, and cover a spectrum from most abstract (concept) to most specific (variable). Kerlinger and Lee (2000) draw the distinction by saying that a *concept* is an abstract idea that the researcher is interested in, such as "political awareness" in the previous example. A *construct* is a concept that is more precisely defined in connection with a specific research question or hypothesis. Continuing the social media/issue awareness example, the concept of "awareness" could mean almost anything. A researcher could define it as simply knowing something – anything – about an election, taxes, or social issue such as transgender rights (general awareness). It also could be defined as knowing the details and differences among various ideas that government officials and political parties are proposing to address those concerns (detailed awareness). Turning "awareness" from a concept into a construct means that the researcher has to describe and define exactly what it means for someone to be "aware."

BOX 7.6

Definitions of Construct, Operationalization, and Variable

Construct: An abstract concept defined in such a way that it has a specific purpose for a research hypothesis.

Operationalization: Process of establishing the rules for how a construct will be observed and measured.

Variable: The operational definition of a construct, with the rules of measurement and observation defined in such a way that it can take on different numerical values to be used in the analysis.

Operationalizing a Construct

Creating such a description is called making an *operational definition* of the construct, or *operationalizing* it, and is a key part of determining which variables will be researched and how the research will go forward. The word *operationalize* seems complicated, but it simply means setting up the rules for how the construct is going to be observed and measured. For example, suppose a researcher (who also was a teacher) wanted to operationalize "class participation" for a particular course. What guidelines could be used for deciding whether students were participating, or measuring how much they were participating? The teacher could just look at attendance statistics; showing up for class is one way students participate. He could observe the class and count the number of times students raise their hands to ask a question or offer a comment as another way of defining participation. He could give a quiz at the beginning of every class designed to measure what the students recall from the previous class since paying attention is also a component of participation. He even could use a combination of those approaches. The point is that any of these *could* be used to measure participation. It would be up to the researcher to decide which way was best for the specific research project he was conducting, and then to specify exactly how the measurement would be made, or operationalized.

Once the operational definitions have been made and the rules for measurement have been decided, the construct then can be measured as a *variable*. Continuing the politics-and-media example, the researcher may decide to operationalize "issue awareness" by having a questionnaire that measures what individuals know about national politics. This questionnaire could be constructed in such a way that a high score would indicate a highly aware person and a low score would represent someone with less awareness. In one study, this exact procedure was used, with a survey that asked questions about the respondents' understanding of the U.S. Constitution, knowledge of which political party controlled Congress, and ability to identify political figures. The more the respondents knew, the more "politically aware" they were said to be (Koch, 1998).

Measurement and Human Behavior

Making such definitions and decisions about measurement can be challenging for social science research, including communication. As mentioned previously, the problem comes from trying to apply "hard-science" methods to activities involving people. Chemists and physicists have reliable and precise ways to measure properties of the things they study such as the temperature of a reaction or the wavelengths of light. Such exactness can be difficult to obtain when studying people, however. A chemist can stick a thermometer in a beaker to take a reaction's temperature, but the social scientist doesn't have a comparable tool to precisely measure a characteristic such as "motivation" or "anxiety," or even "political awareness." A communication researcher may want to study people who "regularly" view the television news, but what does "regularly" mean? Every day? A few times a week? Defining "regular viewing" does not have a firm standard the way that, say, the boiling point of water does. In practice, social science researchers must decide what measures will be used and explain why they are appropriate for the construct that is being studied. For example, in his studies of cultivation theory George Gerbner defined a "heavy" television viewer as one who watched four or more hours of television per day.

The inability to directly and precisely measure human behavior and attitudes is only part of the problem communication scientists face in trying to use positivist methods. Collecting and evaluating such data also is complicated because people think about their actions and have decision-making ability. One beaker of water cannot "decide" that it wants to boil at a different temperature than the one next to it on the lab bench, or "learn" about boiling so that it boils faster next time. Humans, however, can and do react differently even in very similar circumstances, and their responses to situations do change over time. These two characteristics make human behavior difficult to measure with the kind of precision that social scientists would like to have.

Using mass media and their messages as an area of study complicates things further. For example, would a researcher studying violent images in the media classify violent acts in an R-rated action movie or war movie, which could be quite graphic, the same as violence on broadcast television, which is more implied? What about cartoon violence, comedic violence or depiction of the victims of violence on the television news? Those are all ways in which the media are showing violent acts, but the nature of what is shown and the context in which it is shown varies significantly. Using the media and their messages as variables makes mass media research more complex in many ways than other types of research.

Dependent vs. Independent Variables

Nevertheless, quantitative social science research relies on such measurements, and a key part of any research project is carefully defining the constructs and setting up the measurement rules that apply to them, even while acknowledging that the measurements will lack a certain degree of precision. This includes selecting and operationalizing the variables on both sides of the hypothesis, referred to as the independent and dependent variables. As described earlier, the point of many research studies is to determine whether one construct can reasonably be said to cause changes in the other. The characteristic that appears to be causing the changes under observation is called the *independent variable*; the one that is being affected is called the *dependent variable*. A good way to remember this is that what happens to the dependent variable *depends on* changes in the other one. Continuing the news/awareness example, news sources (social media and news viewing on traditional platforms) are the independent variables and level of political awareness is the dependent variable. The hypothesis says that the level of awareness is caused by (or depends on) the amount and type of media exposure.

BOX 7.7

Definitions of Dependent, Independent Variables

Independent variable: The construct that appears to be causing the changes under observation.

Dependent variable: The construct that is being affected by the independent variable (i.e., whose characteristics depend on the other variable). Often, examining changes in a dependent variable and conditions under which they occur is the main point of a research study.

Levels of Measurement

Operationalizing a construct, or establishing guidelines for assigning values to a it, can be challenging in social science research not only because of the variability of human behavior but also because of the inability to observe a construct, such as "awareness" directly. This means values assigned to the construct often must be inferred indirectly, from observations of other characteristics. In the example described previously, subjects' knowledge of things such as control of Congress and information about the Constitution were used as indirect indicators of their level of political awareness.

Just as the researcher must establish guidelines for operationalizing constructs, so too must he specify the ways the data can be measured. Quantitative social science data can be measured in one of four ways, which form a hierarchy from the broadest or least specific up to the most specific. They are:

Nominal Measurement (Categorization)

This is commonly used because researchers frequently want to examine similarities or differences between groups of people who differ in some respect. Such categories often are used to define the independent variables in a research study, such as those who watch television vs. those who don't, or people who affiliate with a particular political party. Nominal measurement also is used for demographic classification, categorizing research subjects by gender, age, or race, for example.

Ordinal Measurement

In this scale, the values of the variable are put in some sort of ranked order (hence, the name: order = ordinal). Think of a list of social media sites in order of membership, for example, or a list of most-watched TV shows or most popular songs. An important, and limiting, characteristic of this level of measurement is that it does not have a common space or "distance" between the values. Picture ten items in rank order, such as ten people arranged by height. Would number ten (the tallest) be twice as tall as number five? He might be, if he was a 6-foot-tall adult and the fifth person in line was a 3-foot-tall kindergartner. The same, though, would not hold true for a lineup of ten average adults of roughly similar height. Rank order thus cannot be used to distinguish differences of magnitude in the lists.

Differences in "distance" between real and ordinal values can be seen in the accompanying graphic (Figure 7.1) showing television ratings from 2019-2020. The top-ranked show from September 2019 to May 2020 was NBC's *Sunday Night Football*, with an average of around 20 million viewers a week. The second and third place shows had about 15 million viewers on average and the fourth-place show, *Monday Night Football*, close to 13 million. From there, the numbers drop off more gradually with much smaller differences. In fact, the difference between fourth place and 15th is only about 2 million viewers, compared to almost 7 million between first and fourth. A discussion focused just on rankings (ordinal values) might obscure the degree of actual difference.

Interval Measurement

As with an ordinal scale, interval measurement takes place when variables are evaluated as greater or lesser than one another. Unlike other ordinals, this scale has equal steps in the interval: The distance between 1 and 2 is the same as the distance between 5 and 6, or any other two values. Interval measurement may seem like the typical way that things are measured, but it has an important limitation in that an interval scale has no true zero point. The classic example of this is temperature measurement. The difference between 25 and 30 degrees Fahrenheit is the same as the difference between 55

Rank Show and Network	Avg. Viewers (in millions)
1 Sunday Night Football (NBC)	20.1
2 NCIS (CBS)	15.3
3 Thursday Night Football (Fox)	15.0
4 Monday Night Football (ESPN)	12.8
5 FBI (CBS)	12.6
6 Blue Bloods (CBS)	12.0
7 Chicago Fire (NBC)	11.7
8 This is Us (NBC)	11.5
9 Young Sheldon (CBS)	11.4
10 Chicago PD (NBC)	11.2
11 Chicago Med (NBC)	11.2
12 The Good Doctor (ABC)	10.8
13 The Masked Singer (Fox)	10.7
14 Bull (CBS)	10.5
15 60 Minutes (CBS)	10.5

Comparing Ordinal & Ratio Measurements

In the 2019-20 television season, NBC's *Sunday Night Football* was the top-ranked regular broadcast with about 20 million viewers each week. The top 15 average shows are presented in rank order (at left), which is an ordinal value.

This chart illustrates how ordinal values may not show relationships as precisely as ratio values, illustrated with actual viewership (shown on a consistent scale at right). The gap of 4.8 million viewers between the first and second ranked shows is identical to the gap between the second- ranked and 15th-ranked shows (also 4.8 million).

From A.C. Neilsen reports of average viewership from Sept. 23, 2019, to May 20, 2020, for series airing four or more episodes, as reported in *USA Today*

Levin, G. (2020, June 8). Here are the top 100 shows of the 2019-20 TV season. USA Online. Retrieved from https://www.usatoday.com/story/entertainment/tv/2020/06/08/ratings-top-100-shows-2019-2020-tv-season/3144382001/

Millions of viewers

FIGURE 7.1 TV rankings as example of ordinal and ratio measurement

and 60 degrees, so the interval is meaningful. The zero on a temperature scale, however, is purely arbitrary – remember, zero is different in the Fahrenheit, Celsius, and Kelvin scales; zero Celsius is equal to 32 degrees Fahrenheit. Additionally, for that matter, the scales have different intervals; a change of 45 degrees in the Fahrenheit system would be a movement of only 25 degrees Celsius. Because of this, it's not possible to say that 60 degrees is "twice as warm" as 30 in either system.

Perhaps the most common instance of interval scales in social science research are Likert scales, which are used to evaluate items along a range of values. These measurement tools, named for the psychologist who developed them, typically have symmetrical 5- or 7-point scales with assigned levels such as "strongly agree" to "strongly disagree" or "highly satisfied" to "highly dissatisfied." Social science research often assigns numerical values to these ratings (e.g., 5 = "strongly agree") that can be used in statistical evaluations. Such calculations assume that there are equal intervals between the values, which is why a Likert scale is considered an interval scale. Many students experience these types of scales when they complete course evaluations at the end of a semester.

Ratio Measurement

This is similar to interval measurement but it has the additional characteristic of a meaningful zero point, which allows numbers to be compared to each other as ratios. It may be impossible to describe today's temperature as "twice as warm" as yesterday's but it is possible to say a 160-pound man weighs twice as much as his 80-pound child, or that a business executive with a $90,000 salary makes three times as much as the $30,000-a-year entry-level workers in her company. Most of the routine measurements of life – distances, heights, weights, salaries, ages, etc. – take place with ratio measurements. An important type of ratio measure used in social science research is proportions, usually expressed as percentages. If 70 percent of 60-year-olds watch the network news but only 35 percent of 20-year-olds do, it can be said that the viewing rate of young people is only half that of the older generation.

Why Measurement Scales Are Important

An important characteristic of these measurement systems that students should remember is that they are hierarchical – higher-order systems can be used to derive lower-order measurements, but the process does not work in the other direction. In other words, data about a variable that is expressed in interval or ratio terms could be used to create an ordinal scale or a nominal classification, but not the other way around.

One helpful way to think about this distinction is in terms of numerical, letter and pass/fail grades. Numerical assessments follow a ratio scale, letter grades represent the ordinal scale, and pass/fail is a nominal measurement (the student is in one of two categories). A teacher who graded all assignments numerically could then use a grade curve, such as 90 or more for an A, 80-89 for a B, etc., to assign letter grades or even pass/fail grades. However, a teacher who graded each assignment as "pass" or "fail" could not return after the fact to assign a numerical result. The limited detail of the initial data would prevent that.

Understanding measurement scales is valuable for students who are doing research because the time will come in any project when it is necessary to operationalize the constructs – to decide which data are necessary to answer a research question or test a hypothesis, and to establish the guidelines for collecting it and comparing it. For example, a student doing a survey might want to classify the survey respondents *nominally* (by gender, age, or some other demographic characteristic), but collect the survey responses in *interval* form (on a 1 to 5 point Likert scale, perhaps). A student doing a content analysis of television shows, on the other hand, might employ *ratio-level* data, such as minutes of airtime for a particular character or number of times a product placement happens. Thinking about the different ways that data can be measured will help students think more systematically about how to assign measurement rules for the variables in their projects.

The types of variables used to collect data also will affect analysis of that data, especially if statistical tests are used. A project with a nominal classification for the dependent variable and numerical (ratio or interval) data for the dependent variable would use one type of statistical test while a comparison of categorical variables on each side of the hypothesis would require a different test. Finally, understanding the ways data are measured will help students understand projects that use quantitative data when the students encounter them during a literature review for their own projects. This book's Appendix provides more specific advice about how to conduct a research project.

Reliability and Validity

No matter which level of measurement is used, the adequacy of a measurement rests on two primary criteria:

- Reliability, or the degree to which the rules for measurement will yield the same results if repeated.
- Validity, or the degree to which the variable actually measures what it is supposed to measure.

BOX 7.8

Definitions of Reliability and Validity

Reliability: The degree of accuracy and consistency in measurement, such that the measurements made according to the guidelines will end up with the same results if repeated or used by different researchers.

Validity: Degree to which the variable actually measures what it is supposed to measure (internal validity) and can be extended to cases outside the test set (external validity).

A reliable measurement is one that is both accurate and consistent. For example, consider three scales and a pile of weights (such as the ones used in a weightlifting set) that are accurately labeled:

Scale No. 1. With this scale, when plates totaling a certain stated weight are piled on it, the scale reads out a total weight that matches the totals on the weight plates. Different stacks are always weighed at their stated value. When a stack is taken off and then put back on, the scale gives the same reading. This scale is both accurate and consistent.

Scale No. 2. This scale tends to read out a weight about 10 pounds less than the labeled value of the plates. When two 25-pound plates are laid on the scale, it reads 40 pounds, not 50. When three 10-pounders are piled on it, it reads 20 pounds instead of 30.

When a particular stack of weights is taken off and put back, the same weight is reported each time. No matter how much the stack weighs, though, the scale's measurement is always 10 pounds lower than what the stated value on the plates totals. This scale is consistent, but not accurate. It suffers from what is called *systematic error*, or bias.

Scale No. 3. This one sometimes reads a stack correctly, but other times reports too heavy or too light. This one also, oddly, will take an identical stack that is placed on it three times in a row and report three different weights. It is neither accurate nor consistent, and suffers from what is called *random error*.

This concept of measurement error is especially important to quantitative social science research because of the abstract nature of what must be measured and how it is measured, as discussed above. As a practical matter, nearly any measurement is going to have some degree of error. Even the "true" scale in the example above will have some random variability in how it measures. As long as the fluctuations are small and truly random – sometimes high, sometimes low – the measurement is reliable. In the example above, scale one is reliable. The second scale, however, is not a reliable measurement tool because even though its random error seems small (it is consistent), it has a strong systematic error component or bias in that it measures 10 pounds too light. The third scale's large random error makes it unreliable as well.

Defining the rules for measurement in such a way that the measurements can be done as accurately and consistently as possible is the core of both reliability and validity in positivist research. For a measurement to be valid, it must first be reliable, but simply because a measurement is reliable does not necessarily make it valid. Some other considerations go into assessing a variable's validity.

To start with, in order to have valid measurement a variable must be operationalized in a way that is truly capable of measuring the construct the way it should. The example was given previously about operationalizing the variable known as "temperature" in a chemistry experiment. This can easily be done because there are standard ways of evaluating it and precise tools to make the measurement. To make a valid measurement the scientist would need to have the proper tool. A physics time-and-motion experiment that needed precise measurements of time (down to, say, 1/10 of a second) couldn't be measured with a wall clock that only ticked away the minutes. More precise measurements would require a stopwatch with the proper calibration; failure to use that would lead to invalid results. Similarly, a scale cannot measure temperature (that requires a thermometer) and a thermometer cannot measure atmospheric pressure (a barometer is necessary for that). Using the wrong tool for a purpose would clearly result in an invalid measurement, no matter how reliable, accurate, and consistent the device was.

At the same time, as described elsewhere, measuring social sciences constructs is trickier than collecting data for natural sciences. Selecting the correct measurement scale and correct tool to evaluate natural phenomena usually are fairly obvious, such as a thermometer for temperature readings. Finding the correct scales and tools for measuring human characteristics is more difficult. For example, what constitutes a valid measure of "intelligence?" Could it be operationalized by shoe size – people with bigger feet are more intelligent? Obviously not; such a measurement would certainly be invalid. How about by a student's grade point average? That is certainly more valid than shoe size; how smart a person is and the grades she attains might have something to do with each other. However, many other factors influence a student's GPA, so it is not a valid measure of intelligence, either. How about a score from a standardized intelligence test? While some people even take issue with these instruments, they still can be seen as a more valid way of measuring the construct "intelligence" than either shoe size or GPA.

Ensuring that the measurement accurately represents the construct it is supposed to, such as using someone's shoe size to operationalize the size of his or her feet or a well-regarded standard test to measure intelligence, is called internal validity. Another issue, however, is external validity, which is whether the results of a measurement can be generalized beyond the subjects actually being measured. For an example, consider two classes – two sections of the same course, actually, with similar exams and assignments – taught by professors with dramatically different grading curves:

Prof. Tuff	Prof. Softie
A = 98–100	A = 70–100
B = 90–97	B = 60–69
C = 85–89	C = 50–59
D = 80–84	D = 30–49
F = 79 or lower	F = 29 or lower

Assuming the tests were graded fairly, a student would know that anything in the 70s would earn a particular score. (An A from Softie, an F from Tuff.). Thus, the scores could have perfect *internal* validity: The grade matches the numerical score exactly as the curve defines it and would be an accurate comparison of students *within* the course. However, the "F" that appears on the transcripts of many students who were unfortunate enough to take Professor Tuff and the A's that go to Professor Softie's class don't have the same meaning as the A's and F's of other students in the school (or even of those same students' grades in other courses). Thus, the grades would be said to lack *external* validity: An A or an F should have similar meaning across the college regardless of the course, but Tuff and Softie grades have little to do with the students' actual performance compared to classmates in other courses.

Unless a measurement is reliable (consistent and accurate) and valid (both internally and externally), it has little value in any type of research that involves quantitative measurement. The corollary of that statement also is true: Research that is based on unreliable or invalid measures has little value, either. Creating good hypotheses, defining proper constructs, and making operationalizations that result in valid, reliable measurements are at the heart of any effective communication science research project.

Quantitative Research Approaches

Chapter 8 describes in detail common research methods used in quantitative media studies. This section briefly reviews those methods with suggestions for how they might be applied to typical projects in positivist communication research, and discusses how concepts such as reliability, validity and types of variables are part of the design considerations.

Surveys

Surveys involve collecting information from people in a structured way. The main components of a survey include:

- Topic: The research question or hypothesis based on the theory being investigated.
- Sample: Who will be asked to respond to the survey? How will they be located? Why are these people rather than others being selected as respondents? How the sample is operationalized – the rules defining how it will be selected – affects the reliability and validity of the research.
- Survey instrument/Questionnaire: A broad research topic is broken down into specific questions for the study, either objective or open-ended. Questions must be presented and written in a way that ensures they will generate data to answer the research question, with reliable and valid measurements of independent and dependent variables. This is where consideration of variable types (categorical or numerical) comes into play when designing the survey. Researchers also must consider internal and external validity, making sure that the questions collect data truly capable of measuring characteristics of the variables.
- Findings: Analysis of survey answers should show relationships among variables as described in the hypothesis.

Content Analysis

Content analysis is the systematic collection and analysis of messages as they appear in media, usually done by assigning particular content items to particular categories. Components of quantitative content analysis include:

- Topic: What data will be collected? For what purpose? The research question should be the key to defining the topic and how the content analysis will answer the question.
- Units of analysis: At what level will data be collected? Content can be considered broadly or narrowly, and how it is defined will affect the type of data collected.
- Sample: How will units to be analyzed be determined? Are enough units of analysis included to provide meaningful results?
- Operationalization: What categories will be created? What rules will determine which items go into which categories? This step is important to ensure consistency among those who will code the research (see discussion of coder reliability in Chapter 8), which is the main way reliability and validity are assessed in quantitative content analysis.
- Analysis and findings: Similar to how surveys are presented, the research findings should explain what relationship among variables in the hypothesis was discovered.

Experiment

When a researcher conducts an experiment, data is gathered under controlled conditions. Key features of an experiment include:

- Random assignment. Subjects in an experiment are assigned either to a group that receives the experimental effect or a control group, which does not receive the effect. This assignment must be done randomly to make the experiment reliable and valid.
- Manipulation of a key variable for one (experimental) group vs. no manipulation for a second (control) group. With the exception of the experimental effect, each group should be treated essentially the same way.
- Post-experiment evaluation. Experiments typically test subjects after the fact to see if the experimental treatment caused any changes. This is often coupled with a pre-test, to determine a baseline for the subjects before any treatment took place. These evaluations can be either quantitative (something like a survey, given only to experiment participants), or qualitative, often done with either individual or focus-group interviews.
- Presentation of findings and analysis depends on the technique used. If quantitative data is generated, this is presented in the findings through data charts and descriptive text, similar to the techniques used for surveys and content analysis. However, focus groups often yield more qualitative data that may be reported in descriptive text.

THEORY AND RESEARCH IN THE INTERPRETIVE TRADITION

The value and effectiveness of positivist communication-science research largely depends on the quality of the measurements to test a stated hypothesis, as explained in the previous section. Theory and research in the interpretive tradition, though, have different purposes. Here, the main goal is understanding the meanings behind communication and the viewpoints of the actors in the situation rather than seeking evidence to test a hypothesis. The goal of the interpretive researcher is "to understand how people in everyday natural settings create meanings and interpret the events of the world" (Wimmer & Dominick, 2000, p. 103). This embodies the inductive, contextualized, and interpretive characteristics described near the beginning of the chapter. The point is to see the possibilities for what could be learned from the data rather than trying to measure or refute the existence of something specified ahead of time (such as the data that would "prove" a hypothesis in positivist research).

Typically, qualitative research seeks to answer questions about *what* is happening, *how* it is happening, or *what it means* rather than *why* it is happening. Quantitative studies frequently search for causality – proof that X causes Y – but this is not common in qualitative work. (Earlier this was presented as descriptive vs. explanatory research.) Whether searching for causes or just underlying relationships, quantitative research tends to be deductive, using a theory to derive a hypothesis, then testing it. Qualitative research tends to be more inductive, which means the principles and relationships it establishes are unknown in advance and are derived from the process of collecting and analyzing the data

In adopting this approach, qualitative researchers are not looking for sweeping generalizations that describe widespread effects or implications of a social activity. Often, such generalizability is the goal of quantitative studies, which is why statistical precision and techniques such as probability sampling are so important to success with those methods. Qualitative research, on the other hand, is more interested in deeper understanding of specific instances. Many qualitative projects are case studies that examine a small number of situations – sometimes a single instance – where the concepts the researcher wants to study can be found. Gathering and examining a wide body of evidence about the specific situation allows the researcher to do this. A weakness of case studies is that they cannot be generalized, except through the logic of "if it happened here, it can happen elsewhere." This is not a guarantee or a prediction that characteristics observed in the case study definitely do exist elsewhere, but it is a way of documenting that they *could*, which often is an important conclusion in its own right.

Observing and collecting data in their natural environments and proper contexts is important for credibility and validation in qualitative research. Therefore, a researcher wishing to observe reporters constructing their stories would want to see them doing it in the newsroom rather than bringing them on campus and observing them in a computer lab. Spending time in the reporters' workplace is exactly what Elizabeth Hindman (1998) did to study the newsroom culture of an inner-city neighborhood newspaper and what Tracy Everbach (2006) did for a similar study at a Florida newspaper.

Origins of Qualitative Research

The idea of studying the human condition through observation can be traced to the work of cultural anthropologists in the early 20th century. These researchers lived among the populations they were trying to learn more about, making detailed records of what they saw and later writing research reports about it. Perhaps the most famous of them was Margaret Mead, who did pioneering work in the field with her studies of the indigenous population of Samoa in the 1920s. (The type of study she conducted has come to be known as ethnography, and is described in Chapter 9.)

Around the same time that Mead was off in Samoa, the University of Chicago became known for similar sorts of field-observation work. Researchers there used the city of Chicago around them as a "natural laboratory for sociological investigation" (Rogers, 1994), especially with regard to immigrant populations. Interestingly, much of their work involved the media. Robert Park, a newspaper reporter who became a researcher, studied the immigrant press in the city, among his other work. Morris Janowitz (1952) studied neighborhood newspapers with both quantitative tools (neighborhood demographics, content analysis, and reader surveys) and qualitative ones (in-depth interviews with the newspaper executives and residents of the neighborhoods they served). In doing so, he sought to determine how the content and function of the community press were linked to the social requirements of the community. His approach embodied what is probably the key characteristic of qualitative research, which is studying people in their natural settings.

Characteristics of Qualitative Research

Janowitz's work, in fact, is a good example of several characteristics of qualitative research as identified by Miles and Huberman. They say that qualitative data is meant to "offer descriptions and explanations ... in identifiable local contexts" (Miles & Huberman, 1994, p. 1), which is exactly what Janowitz sought with regard to contributions of the local media to community identity and structure. Other characteristics of qualitative research Miles and Huberman identify are that it:

- Is conducted through field study.
- Seeks a holistic or integrated view of the situation under study and contexts for it.
- Captures data from inside the setting.
- Establishes meaning from identifying themes and patterns in the collected data.

Overall, the main task for the qualitative researcher is understanding the way in which people manage the situations in which they find themselves.

Qualitative Research Approaches

Chapter 9 describes common qualitative research methods in more detail. This section briefly reviews those methods.

Focus Groups

A common qualitative method for gathering opinions is the use of focus groups. Focus groups are personal interviews, but instead of interviewing individuals one at a time, six to twelve people are interviewed together. The purpose is to get in-depth opinions on a topic and allow the focus group members to build on the ideas of each other.

Case Studies

A case study is a descriptive analysis of characteristics surrounding a particular case or situation, seeking to learn as much about it as possible over a period of time. They often employ participant observation, in-depth individual interviews or focus-group interviews to gather data.

CONCLUSION

Theory and research are two powerful tools for learning more about the way the world around us works, including important aspects of how people communicate in that world and what happens to them when they do. Communication research can take various theoretical orientations, but the most common approach is communication science, or the study of communication activities with observable, empirical measurements similar to other social sciences such as psychology. Social scientific research of this nature poses some challenges because of the difficulty in measuring intangible concepts of human behavior that cannot be directly observed, such as attitudes and personal characteristics.

Nevertheless, communication researchers in the positivist tradition frequently conduct their projects by formulating a hypothesis (making a testable prediction about the relationship of two variables), stating the rules for measurement and evaluation of the variables in the hypothesis, and trying to collect the data in the most systematic, reliable, and valid way possible. Alternatively, interpretive researchers craft research questions that get at a deeper understanding of the meaning of a situation with extensive, in-depth collection of qualitative data and painstaking analysis of it. Some of the specific methods for engaging in both practices are described in the next two chapters: The positivist tradition in Chapter 8, and the interpretive tradition in Chapter 9.

Questions for Discussion/Application Exercises

1. Figuring out how to measure abstract concepts is one of the most important – and most challenging – aspects of effective research. In this chapter, examples of this process were given for the concepts of *political awareness* and *class participation*. Take one or more of the concepts listed at the end of this question and define it as a construct, then operationalize it (state how it would be observed and measured). Topics to conceptualize and operationalize: Campus involvement; community service; alcohol abuse; or sexual activity.
2. "Coarse culture" is a popular topic of complaint about the media: Vulgar song lyrics and demeaning images of women in music videos, excessive and gratuitous use of sex and violence in movies and on television, etc. Develop a research hypothesis that examines some aspect of this. Remember, it's not a real hypothesis unless it states some sort of relationship that can be tested. Once you have the hypothesis, try to operationalize the constructs: Just how would you observe and measure the "items of interest" that your hypothesis relates to each other?

REFERENCES

De Vaus, D.A. (2001). *Research design in social research*. London: Sage.

Everbach, T. (2006). The culture of a women-led newspaper: An ethnographic study of the Sarasota Herald-Tribune. *Journalism & Mass Communication Quarterly* 83 (3), 477–493.

Hindman, E.B. (1998). "Spectacles of the poor": Conventions of alternative news. *Journalism & Mass Communication Quarterly* 75 (1), 177–193.

Janowitz, M. (1952). *The community press in an urban setting: The social elements of urbanism*. Chicago: University of Chicago Press.

Kerlinger, F. & Lee, H. (2000). *Foundations of behavioral research* (4th ed.). Fort Worth, TX: Harcourt College Publishers

Koch, J. (1998). Political rhetoric and political persuasion: The changing structure of citizens' preferences on health insurance during policy debate. *Public Opinion Quarterly* 62 (2), 209–230.

Miles, M.B. & Huberman, A.M. (1994). *Qualitative data analysis* (2nd ed.). Thousand Oaks, CA: Sage Publications.

Morgan, D.L. (2014). *Integrating qualitative and quantitative methods: A pragmatic approach.* Los Angeles: Sage.

Poindexter, P. & McCombs, M. (2000). *Research in mass communication: A practical guide.* Boston: Bedford/St. Martins.

Rogers, E.M. (1994). *A history of communication study: A biographical approach.* New York: The Free Press.

Walter, N., Cody, M. & Ball-Rokeach, S. (2018). The ebb and flow of communication research: Seven decades of publication trends and research priorities. *Journal of Communication 68,* 424–440.

Wimmer, R.D. & Dominick, J.R. (2000). Mass media research: An introduction (6th ed.). Belmont, CA: Wadsworth Publishing Co.

CHAPTER 8

Quantitative Research Methods

This chapter will:

Build on the general description of research from Chapter 7 to describe specific communication research using quantitative methodologies:

- Surveys.
- Content analysis.
- Experiments.

The heart of this book is the relationship of research and theory, as introduced in Chapter 1 and elaborated upon in Chapter 7. Research and theory are used together to develop knowledge. In the interpretive tradition, this comes about in the form of new understandings of the meanings of communication and its impact on society from in-depth study of particular situations. In the positivist tradition – the subject of this chapter – it comes about through application of the scientific method.

This process starts with a hypothesis that can be used to test or validate theories; research then documents the evidence that illustrates whether things really are related to each other in the way that the hypothesis supposes. This process of turning a research *idea* into a research *project* requires one final stage: Selecting and implementing a set of methods to collect and evaluate the evidence. In communication science research, this usually involves two elements.

The first is showing that the dependent and independent variables in the hypothesis are somehow related or connected. For example, the project might investigate whether both variables increase or decrease at the same time, a characteristic called correlation; or the project might determine that different independent variables have different impacts on a common dependent variable. Sometimes the relationship is even inverse: As one quantity increases, the other *decreases* in a similar fashion. (One example of an inverse relationship might be the amount of time spent binge-watching Netflix as related to a student's academic performance: The *more* time spent with streaming video [independent variable] the *lower* the student's grades [dependent variable] will be because too little time gets spent on homework!)

The second element is demonstrating that the changes in the dependent variable cannot be attributed to something other than the changes in the independent variable.

DOI: 10.4324/9781003121695-8

This is done by ruling out other potential causes, so that the only likely cause of variation in the independent variable is the impact on it by the dependent variable. (In the previous example, if the researcher really wanted to show a relationship between academic performance and binge-watching, the research design would somehow have to account for all of the other things that affect a student's grades. This might be difficult or even impossible because there are so many potential factors affecting that.)

Importantly, **both** of these points must be demonstrated. Theories and hypotheses by definition are based on relationships of certain phenomena, so failing to show a relationship or connection between the variables obviously means there is no "proof" for the hypothesis. Showing that there is a relationship but failing to rule out other potential influences means it is not possible to claim that the independent variable really is causing the observed effects in the dependent variable. Thus, successful quantitative research requires selection of a methodology that will give the researcher the strongest tools to demonstrate both a relationship between the variables and the absence of outside influences that could be causing the observed connection.

Empirical or quantitative research conducted in the manner described above uses numerical measurements of the variables as evidence of the relationship at the center of the hypothesis, such as the percentage of heavy TV watchers (or even binge-streamers) who behave in a certain way compared to people whose media usage is not as heavy. Within mass communication, this is the most common way of doing research, labeled as "communication science" by Chaffee and Berger (1987). In the same study cited in Chapter 7 that documented some of the most popular theories used in research, Walter, Cody, and Ball-Rokeach (2018) also investigated the most popular research methods. They reported that about 80 percent of the nearly 1,600 articles from the *Journal of Communication* that they surveyed used one of three quantitative methods. They were:

- Surveys, used in 24 percent of the articles in their study.
- Content analysis, used 26 percent of the time.
- Experiments, used 30 percent of the time.

The remaining 20 percent of the research projects used a qualitative approach to analysis or mixtures of the methods. This chapter will introduce quantitative methods; qualitative methods are covered in more detail in Chapter 9.

SURVEY RESEARCH

Surveys are not only the most common technique for researching mass communication, but one of the most familiar methods for nearly any research purpose. Surveys are the basis of television and radio ratings. They are used to collect the data used to report voters' preferences in an election and the popularity of officials once they are elected. Many readers of this book likely have participated in a survey, either by being called on the telephone or being the target of an email solicitation or pop-up survey on some websites or in some apps. Even course evaluations at the end of a semester are a form of survey research.

BOX 8.1

Definition of Survey

Survey: A research technique for collecting information from people by asking them a structured series of questions

A survey is defined as a research technique for collecting information from people by asking them a structured series of questions. Breaking down the definition helps to identify the key issues in designing survey research:

- Collecting information: What questions will be asked? How do they relate to the hypothesis? What data are needed to evaluate the hypothesis?
- From people: Who will be questioned, and how many subjects should be included? How will the researcher determine whom to include? How will the subjects be reached to participate in the survey?
- In a structured way: How will questions be put to the respondents? This applies to both the format of the questions – e.g., will they be multiple choice, or open-ended? – and the circumstances under which they will be asked. Will interviews take place in person? Over the phone? Online? The structure of the survey with regard to both the style of the questions and the circumstances in which they are asked is closely related to the project's credibility because the way the survey is designed affects both its reliability (consistency of measurement) and its validity, which is defined as gathering enough verifiable data to truly answer the question.

Fink and Kosecoff (1998, p. 3) list the following steps for designing surveys:

- Deciding how the survey will be administered (phone, face-to-face, online, another method).
- Selecting the content and writing the questions.
- Selecting respondents.
- Administering the survey to collect the data.
- Processing, analyzing, and interpreting the results.
- Reporting the results.

Fink and Kosecoff also recommend that the last of these steps – how the data will be used in the analysis and how the results will be reported – should be the first thing the researcher considers. This is because selection of the respondents, administration of the survey, and wording of the questions all should be done with the end results in mind. Training the interviewers who will conduct the surveys is also an important part of the process, because if questions are asked improperly, the survey's results may not be valid.

Survey Administration

Surveys are a popular way of gathering information, but they also can be a resource-intensive way of collecting it because for a survey to be worthwhile it must include a large number of responses. Furthermore, each respondent must be contacted individually and the information must be collected and recorded from each individually. Because of the large number of respondents required, this process takes time; time frequently translates into money because people must be hired both to conduct interviews and to tabulate the data.

How the survey is administered also affects the response rate among the pool of potential respondents and the amount of time and money it takes to collect the data. The most common ways to administer surveys have tradeoffs in how time-consuming/expensive the process is for the researcher vs. the response rate and the timeliness of data collection.

Collection Methods

Data can be gathered from respondents in a variety of ways. These methods and their strengths and weakness are:

Mail Surveys

These are the least time-consuming for the researcher because respondents complete them without assistance or intervention. They are, however, the slowest in terms of time it takes to gather and compile all the data and also have the worst response rate because it is easy for potential respondents to ignore them. The low response rate can add to the overall cost because of the need to find a larger potential response pool and the need to send out more contact letters, which adds to printing and postage expenses.

Online Surveys

These are written and administered nearly the same way as mail surveys, the only difference being that respondents fill them in with a mouse and keyboard through an online interface rather than a pencil or pen on paper. Usually, potential respondents are emailed a link to a Web site such as Survey Monkey or Google Forms where the survey can be completed. If respondents act quickly on the call to participate, these surveys can collect data in a more timely way than waiting for "snail mail" to go out and be returned. As an added bonus, online survey tools often will compile the results automatically and report them as tables or charts. They suffer, though, from the same drawback as surveys through the regular mail: A low response rate because it is just as easy (or maybe easier) to ignore an email as it is to ignore a letter. The solicitation also may not reach some of those to whom it is directed because of spam filtering and outdated email addresses. Sometimes survey responses can be collected by posting a link to the collection form on a social media site; however, even a good response rate to this method might yield a very skewed group of respondents, since they are friends with – and probably similar to – the researcher.

Face-to-Face Interviews

This has a better response rate and faster data collection than mail or e-mail surveys. It is the most time consuming/expensive way of doing a survey, however, because the researchers – or individuals paid to work with them – must locate and meet with each respondent, then take the time to do the interview and record the responses.

Phone Interviews

This has the same advantages as individual personal interviewing for things such as response rate and timeliness, and is nearly as time consuming since trained interviewers still must go through a questionnaire with each respondent. Phone contact is more efficient in that interviewers spend a greater portion of their time with the respondents. Making the next phone call takes just seconds compared to, for example, having to travel to a location and wait for someone to come to the door for a personal interview. In recent years, however, it has become more difficult to find a representative sample to respond to phone interviews, due to more people screening their calls with answering machines and caller ID, and more people getting rid of landlines in their homes in favor of using only their mobile phones to screen calls and block unwanted numbers. Of course, some people simply will not participate even if the researcher does reach them because they don't want to take the time, are shy about expressing their views, and various other reasons for refusal.

BOX 8.2

Definition of Cross-Sectional vs. Longitudinal

Cross-sectional survey: One done with all of the data collected at a single point in time.

Longitudinal survey: One with multiple data collection points at different times. Longitudinal data allow for comparisons of how the respondents' ideas, attitudes or knowledge changed as time passed.

Time Frames

In addition to the question of how to approach respondents, another decision to be made when designing a survey is what time frame it will cover. Surveys can be done either at a single point in time, known as a cross-sectional survey, or at different times, known as a longitudinal approach. Longitudinal data allow for comparisons of how the respondents' ideas, attitudes or knowledge changed as time passed. They can take one of three forms:

Trend surveys ask the same questions of a similar group at a different time, but not necessarily the same individuals. A good example of this type of survey is recurring polls of political popularity or voting preference where the similar grouping is members of a particular political party, people who identify themselves as likely voters, or a particular demographic group within the electorate.

Cohort surveys also survey different individuals, but take the passage of time into account and control for it by "aging" the respondent pool accordingly, but not necessarily interviewing the same people at both points in time. For example, a survey of college freshmen about a particular topic that was followed up by a survey of seniors three years later to see whether their ideas on the subject had changed during their first three years in college would be a cohort study.

Panel studies also take before and after measurements, but are different from cohorts because the surveys are given to the same individuals at both points in time.

Survey Instruments

The actual questionnaire or survey instrument must include the questions themselves, the response options, and the guidelines for administering it. These instructions are addressed to the respondent for a self-administered survey and to the interviewer for a phone or face-to-face data collection.

Key Components

Poindexter and McCombs (2000) note that a survey instrument should have the following components:

Record Keeping

Who did the interview, and what were its circumstances such as date and time, location (for a personal interview), or phone number called (for a phone interview). A survey record sometimes also has interviewer comments.

Introduction

This includes a brief statement indicating the purpose and sponsor of the research, an estimate of how long it will take to complete the survey, a promise of confidentiality of the information provided, and possibly a screening question to determine whether the person being interviewed is qualified to respond. An example Poindexter and McCombs use is that for a survey about cable television, a screening question to make sure the potential respondent subscribes to or regularly watches cable should be included. They further point out that the introduction should assume the respondents are going to answer the survey and not give them a chance to decline, as this will depress the response rate (Poindexter & McCombs, 2000, p. 58).

Content/Questions

The content of the survey obviously is the largest element in it and the most important. Format and wording of questions are discussed in the next section.

Closing

A statement that notifies the respondents that the questioning is completed and thanks them for their participation

Questions

The central feature of a survey, of course, is the questions that are directed to the respondents. Exactly what questions are asked, what form they take, and how many are asked all depend on the purpose of the project: Exactly what is the researcher trying to find out? A clear answer to that question is vital for properly constructing the question set.

For example, this book's authors once did a survey about capstone courses in communication programs. This research was not a hypothesis test, but rather a piece of descriptive work designed to answer the research question: What characteristics are common in mass communication capstone courses?

The first thing the researchers wanted to know was how common such courses were, so the very first question in the survey was "Does your school or department offer a capstone course?" (This also served as a filter question, which is described shortly.) From reading scholarly articles about capstone courses done by other researchers, the authors knew that issues such as whether or not the course is required, how many students are in a typical class, and how many different faculty members teach the course can differ from college to college, so they wanted to find out what the trends in each of these areas were in mass communication departments. They decided the research would be most effective if it could describe the purposes that capstone courses were meant to serve, what strategies instructors used to teach them and grade them, and which topics were most commonly covered in them. The researchers also were curious about whether capstone teachers were satisfied with the courses, or had ideas for changing them.

All of these different purposes of the research went into construction of the survey instrument, which ultimately contained 18 questions to gather the data. It was administered online, with e-mail solicitations to college faculty and administrators who might be involved with capstone courses.

BOX 8.3

Closed-end vs. Open-ended Questions

Closed-ended questions offer a limited range of responses, usually answered with a check-the-item response.

Open-ended questions are answered with a few words (or a sentence, or more) as the respondents see fit. In survey research, data generated from open-ended questions requires additional analysis, perhaps using qualitative methods.

Question Formats

Questions themselves can take one of two primary forms: Closed-ended questions (sometimes called forced-choice questions) and open-ended ones. In an open-ended question, the respondents can answer in any way they see fit. In the capstone-course survey one of the open-ended questions was "If you see a need for change in the capstone course, what would be your top priority?" and respondents answered with a sentence or two describing that.

In a closed-ended question, the researcher provides responses and an instruction to the respondent about selecting them such as "Check just one response" or "Check all that apply." Closed-ended questions can take a variety of common forms including either/or (yes/no), checklists, and ranked comparisons or range of agreement responses (Fink & Kosecoff, 1998). The authors' survey included single-check responses for questions such as "Does your school or department offer a capstone course? (1) Yes (2) No," and a range-of-agreement response about course satisfaction in which respondents checked one of five levels ranging from "very satisfied" to "very dissatisfied." An example of a check-all-that-apply option was "Which of the following content areas are included in your capstone course?" with respondents given a choice of nine different course subjects, including theory, research, ethics, law, and others.

Any sort of question with a check-only-one-response limitation must be carefully worded to ensure that the answer choices are both *mutually exclusive* (the respondent can logically pick only one) and *exhaustive* (a wide enough range of choices that the respondent will be able to pick *something*). For example, take the following hypothetical survey question:

Which source do you use for news?
A. Television
B. Newspaper
C. Internet

This is not mutually exclusive, because some people might use two or even all three news sources, so which one would they check? It is also not exhaustive, because other news sources such as magazines and radio are not on the list.
A better way of wording the question would

*Which of the following news sources do you use the **most**?*
A. Newspaper
B. Online news site
C. Network broadcast news
D. Local affiliate broadcast news
E. Cable news channels
F. Radio
G. Social media
H. Other (please specify) _____

This wording of the question, by asking for the respondents to pick their *most-used* source, makes the choices mutually exclusive. Even if people use more than one item on the list, only one can be used the *most*, and the question directs respondents to select that one. The question also is exhaustive, both by providing a more complete set of common choices and by inclusion of the category "other." If a respondent really doesn't get news from any of the A through G choices, she is free to fill in what she does use (perhaps a timely podcast?) as response H.

BOX 8.4

Mutual Exclusivity and Exhaustiveness

Survey questions that require a single answer need to be both mutually exclusive and exhaustive to be meaningful. These terms are defined as:

- Mutually exclusive: Respondents can reasonably select only one possible choice.
- Exhaustive: The range of choices is wide enough that all respondents can select something.

For example, suppose a survey question asked whether someone:

- Worked at a store.
- Worked at a restaurant.
- Worked at a factory.
- Attended school.

This would not be mutually exclusive, because many college students – who would be eligible to check "attended school" – also work at stores and restaurants (and some may even work in factories, at least during the summer). It would therefore be impossible for many people to make a single choice. It also is not exhaustive. People can work for the government, for non-profit agencies, and many other types of organizations, or may not work at all, and none of those choices is on the list.

When survey questions (or content analysis categories) are not mutually exclusive or exhaustive, respondents can be confused and the data that are collected can be unreliable.

A special type of question included in many surveys is the filter or screening question, which is used to determine whether a respondent meets qualifications that the researcher has in mind for answering a particular question. As mentioned earlier, a screen might be included in the introduction to qualify a respondent for the entire survey. As respondents work their way through, such filters can be applied elsewhere as well. They require an instruction about what to do next based on the answer to the filter question, such as "If you answered 'yes' to question 12, go on to question 13; if you answered 'no', skip questions 13 to 15 and go to question 16." These may be directed either straight to the respondent in a self-administered survey such as a mail questionnaire, or given as an instruction to the interviewer for a phone survey. Many online survey tools have a feature known as "skip logic" that will do this automatically. In such a survey, if someone selected "no" for question 12, the survey software would not display questions 13, 14 or 15 and would automatically skip to number 16. One of the authors of this book did a survey of communication majors and wanted to differentiate between transfer students and those students who came to their schools as freshmen. A filter question asked how they entered their college, and transfer students were given a different set of questions from so-called "native" students.

Question Wording

Students planning a career in mass communication must be good writers; communication researchers need this skill as well, particularly when it comes to writing survey questions. Poorly worded questions can undermine the survey and make its results less valuable because they can confuse respondents.

Poindexter and McCombs (2000, pp. 49–51) provide a list of ideas for making sure survey questions are worded properly. According to these researchers, questions should be:

- Short, specific and limited to a single idea to avoid confusion.
- Phrased clearly.
- Unbiased, meaning they avoid wording that might cause respondents to select a particular answer.

The responses that a survey offers for respondents to select should be:

- Uncomplicated.
- Appropriate to the question.
- Mutually exclusive and exhaustive if a single-choice response is required.

Furthermore, questions should avoid:

- Jargon and terms that would be unfamiliar to respondents.
- Emotionally loaded words and phrases that might bias the responses.
- Asking about multiple things in one question.
- Use of the word "not" or other formulations that state ideas in the negative. For example, the following negatively worded question – "Is it ethically better for journalists not to practice deceptive news gathering?" – could be reworded "Should ethical journalists avoid deceptive news gathering?"

A check on the quality of the survey instrument, including instructions, question wording, and potential difficulty with responses, can be made by testing it before it is used. Such a pre-test is absolutely necessary, according to experts in the craft, so that questions and responses can be rewritten if necessary to correct problems with them before actual data collection begins (Poindexter & McCombs, 2000, p. 74; Fink & Kosecoff, 1998, p. 33). Poindexter and McCombs suggest that if 1/3 or more of the respondents in the pretest have difficulty with a particular question or instruction then it should be revised. The pre-test also gives the researcher an idea of how long it will take to do the survey.

BOX 8.5

Typical Wording of Category Scales in Surveys

Strongly approve
Approve
Neither approve nor disapprove
Disapprove
Strongly disapprove

Definitely agree
Probably agree
Neither agree nor disagree
Probably don't agree
Definitely don't agree

Frequently
Sometimes
Almost never

Very favorable
Favorable
Neither favorable nor unfavorable
Unfavorable
Very unfavorable

Pre-testing the Survey

Once a survey has been developed, researchers always pre-test it, preferably with a small group of respondents similar to the group that will be part of the actual research. The purpose of the pretest is to make sure there is no confusion or bias in the questions, and to make sure that all the responses work properly in an online survey. For example, when the authors of this book finished with the design of their survey on capstone courses, they asked a small group of colleagues (who would not be in the respondent pool) to take the survey and report back on any issues or problems that they had. Their responses helped to make the survey better and more focused on the questions the researchers wanted to answer.

Survey Respondents

This section of the chapter has so far addressed the first and third points of the original description of survey research, elaborating on "collection of information" and "in a structured way." That middle part – "from people" – is another special concern in survey research. The researcher must decide how many people will be questioned, who they will be, and how to get access to them so they can participate.

One way to conduct a survey is to complete a census, which would question every member of a population. The United States government does this every ten years to document the nation's demographics. It is an expensive, complicated process to collect information about more than 128 million households and more than 330 million individuals, which was the country's approximate population during the 2020 census. (The data, which are sometimes used in social science research, can be found at www.census.gov.) Usually, a census survey is not realistic except for small, well-defined populations such as all the members of a school's graduating class. Researchers frequently rely on a sample survey, administered to just part of the population.

Samples come in two varieties, probability samples (also known as random samples) and non-probability samples. Which type of sample is used greatly affects interpretation of their results.

Random (Probability) Sampling

The basis of a random sample is that it assumes every element of the population has an equal probability of being included. When this is done, the principles of statistical probability allow the researcher to specify a sampling error and make valid inferences from the sample to the entire population. This is common in political polling, for example, when journalists (based on a survey researcher's work) will report something like: "55 percent of people surveyed say they are likely to vote for candidate X, with a margin of error of plus or minus 3 percentage points at a confidence level of 95 percent." What this means is that even though not all of the potential voters were actually questioned, the researcher can say with some certainty (only a 5 percent chance of being incorrect) that the true proportion of the candidate's support within the larger population is between 52 and 58 percent (55 percent plus 3 points, and 55 percent minus 3 points).

Effective random or probability sampling requires a list of potential people to be surveyed, called a sampling frame. The frame should be as comprehensive and current as possible to represent the population and should include the information necessary to contact individuals within it, such as e-mail addresses for an online survey or phone numbers for a phone survey. Once the frame is in hand, the researcher then must select elements for the sample with a procedure that meets the assumption that every element of the population has an equal probability of being included. Some of the ways this can be accomplished include:

Simple Random Sampling

This approach to identifying respondents has elements literally drawn at random. For example, suppose the population of interest was a class of 60 students and the desired sample was 12 individuals. The frame is simply the class list. A simple random sampling procedure could be done by putting the 60 names on slips of paper in a box and drawing out 12. This works with such a small population and sample frame but obviously would not be efficient in selecting, for example, several hundred names out of 100,000 voters in a particular district or 1,000 voters out of more than 1 million residents of a city. Therefore, other methods have been devised that can have the same equal-probability result.

Systematic Random Sampling

In this procedure, elements from the population or sample frame are methodically selected at a regular interval after starting at a random point. Using the class example above, the desired sample was one fifth of the individuals. To make a systematic random sample, the names would be placed in a 60-item list, a starting point would be selected randomly, and every fifth person after that would be used in the sample; e.g., starting with the fifth name on the list and continuing with the 10th, 15th, 20th, etc. One of the authors once used this technique to select a sample of 60 newspapers from the listing of approximately 1,500 in a directory of every daily newspaper in the United States. The sample was about 1/25th of the entire population, so a random starting point was selected and every 25th paper was selected after that through the end of the list.

Stratified Random Sampling

This approach uses a random method such as one of the two described. Before the random selection is applied, the population is divided into various strata or subdivisions to ensure some sort of equivalent representation of the divisions. For example, suppose instead of one class, the survey was meant to apply to the entire campus – but the campus has unequal gender balance (60 percent women and 40 percent men) and the researcher wants to know that men and women are fairly represented in the sample. Separate random selections would be done of women and men to select a final number of each such that the sample would preserve the 60-40 ratio, such as 30 women and 20 men in a 50-person sample.

Cluster Sampling

This method has some similarities to stratified sampling but involves administering the survey by clusters or groups of respondents selected at random. For example, in a campus-wide survey it would be easier to give questionnaires to entire rooms of students all at once rather than do a simple random sample that might pick a small number of students from each classroom to take the survey. Entire classes of students typically are selected to be surveyed, but on a random basis such as using the semester's course schedule as a frame and applying a random-selection method to choose the required number of classes.

Sampling without a Frame

In all of the examples given so far, the population has been well-defined and known for use as a sampling frame. This is sometimes the case in survey research. In the various school examples, enrollment data would provide names and contact information for all the students in the population. Or, a publication that wanted to survey its subscribers would have names, addresses and other contact information about them. Many surveys, though, use all the residents of a city, state or other defined area as their population. Comprehensive lists of all the residents of such an area are harder to come by, although sometimes things such as voter registration records are used in political polling.

In these cases, where the surveys are typically conducted by telephone, random telephone dialing is often used to reach potential respondents. This technique meets the test of being a probability sampling method by giving everyone in the area with a telephone an equal likelihood of being included. Often this is done by randomly generating four-digit values that are paired with the various prefixes or exchanges in an area. A drawback is that this will generate some non-working numbers. That is less of a problem for the survey's validity, however, than deliberately excluding a certain subset of the population, such as using a directory of landline numbers, which would exclude people who rely on mobile phones.

BOX 8.6

Probability vs. Non Probability Sample

Probability (random) sampling: every element of the sample frame has an equal likelihood of being selected. This is important if the researcher wants to use the sample for inferences to a larger population, such as an opinion poll designed to represent public opinion in general.

Non-probability sampling: elements for the sample are selected by the researcher according to convenience or for a specific purpose. These can still be useful samples, but cannot be used to infer information for a larger group.

Non-Probability (Convenience and Purposive) Sampling

Any time the researcher wants to make mathematically valid inferences about a large population based on the results of a sample, a probability sample must be used. For various reasons, ranging from simple convenience to sheer impossibility of doing a true probability survey, many surveys rely on non-probability samples. These types of samples still can produce interesting and useful data and give insight into the larger population from which they are drawn, even though they lack statistical "proof." Many researchers do not see this as a major problem, since even probability samples are subject to random error and interpretation of what the numbers mean, so, a well-constructed non-probability sample is often suitable for conducting a survey.

Two common types of non-probability sampling are self-selection surveys and convenience samples. Self-selection is just what the name implies: The researcher publicizes the survey and invites responses, and respondents decide whether to include themselves in the survey. Examples of this include online polls found through links posted on a website or sent through social media channels, and the telephone and text-message surveys associated with some television shows in which viewers can vote for a particular outcome. The definition of a convenience sample also is built into the name, because it means respondents are included primarily because the researcher has easy, convenient access to them. So-called "intercept" surveys done in public settings such as a school's student union, where people employed by a researcher ask any willing passer-by to take the survey, are good examples of a convenience sample.

A third type of convenience sample is the quota sample, which has some similarities to stratified random sampling in its effort to make sure all groups from a population are represented according to a quota system in which the researcher specifies in advance how many respondents are needed from each classification. A quota sampling of students at a college might, for example, set the numbers of freshmen, sophomores, juniors, seniors, and graduate students according to their ratio in the overall school population. The difference is that after the quotas are set, the specific respondents are chosen by the convenience method rather than any random method directed toward equal likelihood of inclusion for all members of the population. For example, in one class project, students wanted to interview seniors in different majors about their use of the career center. They decided to ask the teachers in the capstone courses in Management, Communications, Biology, and Nursing if they could survey their classes, to get their quotas of seniors in a range of majors.

Sample Size

The general rule on how many individuals should be included in the sample to ensure good results can be summarized as: The bigger, the better – up to a point. In other words, researchers want enough respondents to give the results meaning but don't want to lose sight of the idea that the survey is coming from a sample, not a census.

For an idea of how important sample size can be, consider a survey about television viewing with a ridiculously small sample of three individuals. If all three of them report that they watch a particular show, would it be reasonable to assume that the show had 100 percent viewing among the general population? If none of them watched, would it mean the show had zero ratings? Clearly the answer is "no" in both cases, and the reason is pretty obvious: Three people can't adequately represent a television audience of millions of viewers. The same principle that prevents this unusually small sample from accurately representing the larger group applies to any sample of less-than-adequate size.

Sample size is especially important with probability samples because it is directly related to the size of the sampling error – that plus/minus figure that is used to adjust the sample mean from the survey. Larger samples result in smaller error intervals and more precise results.

Take the example from earlier in the chapter, in which a hypothetical political poll reported that one candidate had support from 55 percent of the voters, ± 3 percentage points. This meant the researcher could report with some confidence that the candidate's actual support among the whole voting population was somewhere in a range of 52 to 58 percent. If the sample were smaller, however, and the sampling error were larger, such as ± 6 percentage points, then the range would expand to actual support being somewhere between 49 and 61 percent of the voters (55 percent, ± 6 points). Since the same range applies to the other candidate who received 45 percent support in the poll, it means his "true" support is somewhere between 39 and 51 percent. Even though the poll shows one candidate ten points ahead of the other, the sampling error makes the race too close to call because the intervals overlap – there is a reasonable possibility that the two candidates actually may be splitting the vote close to 50-50.

So what *is* a good sample size for a survey? With non-probability sampling it has to be large enough that the researcher can logically say that the results are meaningful. Clearly, that would not be possible with the three-person sample used as an example earlier. Whether a sufficient number is 50, 100, or 1,500 respondents depends on the nature of the research, the logic of the researcher, and the size of the population from which it is drawn.

With probability sampling, the sample has to be large enough to minimize the sampling error to a reasonable level. As the example illustrates, ± 6 percentage points is not really sufficient for political polling data, and probably would not be sufficient for many other types of surveys, either. Bigger is better only up to a point, though, because every extra respondent adds time, effort and cost to the collection process. After a while the additional precision that another 1,000, 500, or 100 responses would add to a project is not important enough to go to the trouble of obtaining them.

With large-scale surveys such as national political polls, the "sweet spot" is about 1,500 respondents selected through probabilistic random methods, which typically yields a sampling error of around ± 2.5 percentage points with 95 percent confidence of being within the stated interval. News stories about presidential popularity and other issues frequently report that the results were based on surveys with approximately this number of respondents and sampling error (See Box 8.7).

As the sample sizes decline from this typical level, the margins of error increase. A sample of 1,000 individuals would have a sampling error of ± 3.0 percentage points, while a sample of 500 would have an error of ± 4.4 percentage points (both still at the 95 percent confidence level). Sampling 200 individuals would result in a sampling error of ± 6.9 percentage points and a sample of just 10 would have an error of ± 30.1 percentage points. (Figures taken from chart in Poindexter & McCombs, 2000, p. 84).

Another consideration in sampling, however, is sub-groups about which the researcher may want to report. Suppose that a 1,000-response sample was about equally split between men and women, and the researcher wanted to investigate whether certain responses differed by gender. The overall error for 1,000 respondents is ± 3 points. Since the inferences would be made from a set of only about 500 responses for each sex, the sampling error would be larger (± 4.4 percentage points) for those subgroups. In general, the more sub-groups a survey researcher wants to report about, the larger the overall sample needs to be so that each sub-group has sufficient numbers to make reporting on the results that apply to that group meaningful.

BOX 8.7

News Reporting of Error Margins in Polls

Polls are one of the most common topics of news reporting about elections and politics, and news organizations often report data-collection details and margins of error when reporting on such surveys. For example, in a report on public attitudes toward impeaching U.S. President Donald Trump for a second time near the end of his term in early 2021, CBS News described the poll methodology as follows:

> *This CBS News survey was conducted by YouGov using a nationally representative sample of 1,521 U.S. residents interviewed between January 11–12, 2021. This sample was weighted according to gender, age, race and education based on the American Community Survey, conducted by the U.S. Bureau of the Census, as well as the 2020 presidential vote and registration status. The margin of error is ±2.9 points* (Salvanto et al., 2021).

Analysis of Survey Results

Reporting on the results of a survey again comes back to the matter of whether it was done with a probability or non-probability sample. With a convenience sample or other type of non-probability selection, results can be reported *for the survey respondents only*. Strictly speaking, the results cannot be used to imply that similar characteristics or relationships exist in the larger population; such extrapolation can be done only with probability samples. Nevertheless, non-probability samples are frequently used and can develop useful data that can be inferred to apply to larger groups using logic in combination with other supporting data that help the researcher explain the significance of the results.

Fink and Kosecoff (1998, p. 5) list some of the common types of results drawn from surveys for a researcher's report:

- Proportions of the sample reporting each response, e.g., presidential approval ratings and other political poll results used as examples throughout this chapter.
- Comparison of groups, e.g., the number of men vs. women watching a particular type of television show. This can be done either proportionally (55 percent of a show's audience is women, 45 percent are men) or with raw numbers (the show's viewers included 3.2 million women and 2.6 million men).
- Relationship of items surveyed about, again with either proportions or actual scores, e.g., the percentage of teens who use a particular social media platform.
- Changes over time (for longitudinal surveys only), e.g., the proportion of the U.S. population that subscribes to cable or satellite TV now as compared to five years ago. (In other words, a survey to document the phenomenon of "cord cutting.")

Ultimately, what the researcher decides to report from the survey is directly related to the original research question or hypothesis. The whole point of the survey construction, administration, and analysis, after all, is to document evidence that illustrates how the variables that the survey researcher is interested in are related to one another.

CONTENT ANALYSIS

Surveys are clearly a popular and powerful way for social-science researchers to collect data about their interests. At the same time, Walter et al. (2018) found that content analysis was equally popular, with each approach used in about a quarter of the nearly 1,600 projects included in their analysis.

The classic definition of content analysis is generally attributed to Bernard Berelson, who described it as "a research technique for objective, systematic and quantitative description of the manifest content of communication" (Stempel, 2003, p. 210). Generally this has come to mean sorting messages into different categories according to some set of classification criteria. Content analysis can be applied to any form of communication, such as categorizing statements made in conversations as part of studying interpersonal communication. As applied to mass communication, it usually means evaluating and categorizing elements of media messages such as newspaper and magazine articles and advertisements (either in print or online), television shows and commercials, and social media messages. A major benefit of content analysis is data reduction – the ability to take large amounts of material and organize it into a manageable number of groups or categories for analysis.

BOX 8.8

Definition of Content Analysis

Content analysis: Objective, systematic and quantitative description of the manifest content of communication.

Stempel (2003) deconstructs Berelson's definition of content analysis as follows:

- **Objective,** meaning the classification criteria are defined in such a way that different people would classify the same messages in the same way.
- **Systematic,** meaning that all content is evaluated in the same way. In other words, categories are set up in such a way that nothing is overlooked in the analysis, and the results are organized in ways that make them useful as research data.
- **Quantitative,** meaning that the end product of the analysis is numerical values used for the analysis. Usually, these are either frequencies (raw counts) or proportions of content in the various categories.
- **Manifest,** meaning analysis is focused on the content as it appears, not on any interpretation the analyst reads into it.

Neuendorf (2002) says this systematic quantification makes content analysis different from other types of text interpretation such as rhetorical analysis, semiotics (analysis of symbols and their meanings), and critical analysis, all of which are methods of qualitative study that are discussed in the next chapter. Nevertheless, those who are not familiar with the content-analysis process sometimes confuse a descriptive content review for a quantitative content analysis. In other words, simply describing media messages in narrative terms – such as a student writing in a research report that "A content analysis of *The Office* shows ongoing tension and disrespect among employees of the fictional Dunder-Mifflin Paper Company" – does not constitute actual content analysis. Such a conclusion might be reached from qualitative content analysis, but that would entail much more rigor and in-depth review of the content than given in this example; that technique is discussed in Chapter 9.

To complete an effective quantitative content analysis, the researcher would want to create categories and count instances, then report in the research paper something like: "Over its first seven seasons, *Game of Thrones* included a cumulative 46 minutes of male nudity and 30 minutes of female nudity, and cumulatively more than three hours of violent acts." Elsewhere in the paper she would have to describe the procedures and definitions used to create the categories and do the measurements, such as specifying how she decided that a particular scene included nudity or what constituted a "violent act." This section of the chapter is intended to explain how defining such categories and measurements is done. (As an aside, these statistics about *Game of Thrones* are not made up, but were taken from a content analysis of the show posted on a television blog [Welsh, 2019].)

Components of Content Analysis

Neuendorf (2002) provides a nine-step process for developing an effective content analysis. It includes:

1. Developing the research question or hypothesis.
2. Defining the constructs, which is what the analysis intends to measure, and describing how each of them relates to the hypothesis or research question.
3. Operationalizing the constructs, which means specifying the categories and the rules for assigning content to fit within them.
4. Writing a codebook that explains all of the operationalizations in detail.
5. Selecting the items to be analyzed, which often entails taking a sample of all available content. As with surveys, if the researcher wishes to make valid statistical inferences that go beyond the sample, the selection must be done in ways that create a random or probability sample.
6. Training coders and doing reliability trials.
7. Doing the actual coding. For the best and most reliable results, any project should include multiple coders with some overlap of the coding work to provide a second reliability check.
8. Judging the final reliability.
9. Tabulating and reporting the results. Because content analysis by definition generates numerical results, this often involves statistical analysis.

Units of Analysis

As with surveys and, indeed, all social science research, a content analysis project starts with a specific research question or hypothesis. While surveys are designed to collect information from people, content analysis is designed to describe the attributes of messages based on what is in them. This is what Berelson meant by *manifest* content; Neuendorf calls this measuring the variables as they "reside within the message" (2002, p. 96).

Defining and operationalizing the constructs to be measured first requires selecting a *unit of analysis*, which is an identifiable component that:

- Helps to identify the population to be studied.
- Provides a way to measure the variables.
- Can be used as the basis for reporting the analysis (Neuendorf, 2002, p. 71).

In the previous *Game of Thrones* example, the unit of analysis was the entire content of 67 episodes; the researcher's goal was to measure the total screen time devoted to nudity and violence within the show.

The unit of analysis can be as general as the entire website of an online publication, an entire television show (as with the GoT example), or at least several episodes of it. It also can be as detailed as individual words within an online article or television script. Often it is somewhere in between, such as a series of individual articles or specific scenes within a show. The unit of analysis should be selected with regard for what needs to be examined to understand the message pool in the medium that is being studied (Neuendorf, 2002, p. 96). For example, if the goal of the content analysis is to seek out bias in TV news broadcasts, the entire show might be the effective unit of analysis if the researcher were trying to show that certain *networks* were biased in certain ways. If the goal is to show biased word choices *within* the news pieces, however, the analytical frame would be the script of a news package.

Defining the unit of analysis provides a starting point for doing the measurement. For example, if the purpose of a content analysis is to determine characteristics of a news organization's political coverage, then the number of articles that include certain characteristics might be counted to help determine that. Likewise, if the purpose of a television show's content analysis is to evaluate its portrayal of African-American or Hispanic characters, then counting the number of scenes or the total screen time in which characters with that description appear and comparing that to the total number of scenes/total running time would be one way to gather and evaluate data about that question.

Finely-grained content analyses might even reach to the paragraph or individual-word level; for example, defining a list of words that are considered to be racist or sexist and counting the number of times they appear in an article or television script or in the social media posts of a particular organization. An analysis might, on the other hand, examine paragraphs of text to classify them as having positive, neutral or negative implications about a person or group as a way of determining whether the coverage was balanced or slanted with regard to that person or group.

Sampling Content

As with surveys, content analyses may be done on either an entire population of message units or some subset (sample) of it. Which level the researcher chooses to analyze depends mostly on the size of the population.

If the point of the research is to draw implications about "streaming video," a census would be impossible and some sort of sample would be used instead because there are hundreds of hours of such programming every month on the major services such as Netflix and Hulu alone, and thousands of hours if every streaming provider were included. If the target of the study were a particular show, it might be possible to analyze an entire population, such as the episodes from a full season of the show. The population of interest sometimes is defined by boundaries set by the researcher. For example, a project might seek to analyze all the stories on a particular topic on a news website during a set time frame; the total might range from a few dozen to a few hundred. A television content analysis might concern itself with a specific show during a specific season of a dozen or so episodes. With a population that small, every element could be subjected to analysis.

More frequently, content is sampled from a larger population. As with surveys, sampling for content analysis can be either probabilistic (random) or non-probabilistic (convenience) based. The same statistical principle described in the section of this chapter about surveys applies to content analyses: If the researcher wishes to generalize to the larger population, the sample must be selected in such a way that each element of the population has the same likelihood of being included in the sample. In the example given previously about using systematic random sampling to select 60 newspapers from a list of approximately 1,500, the purpose was to obtain a representative, probability-based sample of the U.S. daily newspaper population for detailed content analysis. A second randomization was done to select the actual days to be analyzed.

Many content analyses are done on convenience samples; sometimes these are even based on which materials happen to be available and accessible to the researcher. One of the authors, for example, once did a trend study to see whether the wording of newspaper leads (first paragraphs) had changed over time. The content selection was done by means of purposive sampling, which is selecting a convenience sample but choosing it in a deliberate way with a specific purpose in mind (hence, the name *purposive*). In this case, the four newspapers used in the study were selected partly because they were from similar cities all in the same state (that was one purpose of selection). These papers also were selected partly because the researcher had access to microfilm copies of them during the time frame under study (a convenience factor).

Categorizing Content

After deciding on a unit of analysis and deciding whether to sample or analyze all of the units in the population, the next decision in designing a content analysis project is establishing the categories into which the content will be classified. Stempel (2003, p. 212) lists three criteria for a good classification system:

- Categories must be pertinent and closely related to the hypothesis or research question.
- Categories must be functional, meaning the data gathered about them ought to be useful in evaluating the hypothesis or research question.
- The overall system must be manageable.

A key feature of content analysis categories is that they must be *exhaustive* and *mutually exclusive*, two concepts discussed previously in relation to writing survey questions. Applied to content analysis, this means a particular content item logically can be placed in just one of the categories (mutually exclusive) and there is a wide enough range of choices that everything should be able to go somewhere (exhaustive). In surveys, some questions are mutually exclusive and exhaustive while others are written in a "check all that apply" manner or are open ended. Content analysis categorization, however, cannot have any "all that apply" classifications. The categories must use the principles of mutual exclusivity and exhaustiveness, or else the coders will be confused and the results collected will not be valid.

Sometimes, coding categories are set up to capture multiple dimensions at the same time, but these principles of exclusivity and exhaustiveness still apply. For example, a content analysis that sought to characterize the types of statements made by minority characters in a TV drama might code both the race or ethnicity of the character as well as the emotional nature of the statement (friendly, angry, or neutral, for example). Within each dimension, however, every statement should have only one place in which it can logically be categorized.

Coding Reliability and Validity

Reliability and validity both are as important to content analysis as they are to surveys, and the same principles apply: A project's conclusions cannot be considered valid unless they are first reliable. Even with reliability – consistency of results – other considerations come into play in determining whether results of a content analysis are valid, especially whether the constructs were selected in such a way that they actually measure what they are intended to measure and whether they provide data relevant to the research question. A word of caution that researchers often issue about validity is that quantitative content analysis cannot be used to infer meanings about the content under study; recall what Berelson meant by *manifest* content. Content analysis is most effectively and properly used to describe characteristics of messages or to identify relationships among them (Neuendorf, 2002). A valid coding scheme should do this rather than trying to find hidden meanings, or asking coders to "read between the lines" in assigning content to categories. For example, a study designed to look at political partisanship might count words with partisan overtones such as "liberal," "conservative," "left wing," "right wing," etc. It might ask coders to look for positive or negative words – as defined in the code book – applied to particular politicians or concepts (e.g., gun control or same-sex marriage). A *quantitative* study, though, would not go beyond this manifest content and ask coders to interpret whether a message was positive or negative, or partisan or non-partisan, because that could compromise data integrity.

Reliability is largely related to how consistently the material is coded. Recall that one of the elements listed by Berelson in the classic definition of the process was objectivity, which Stempel further defined as establishing classification criteria in such a way that different people would classify the same messages in the same way (2003, p. 210). Common threats to this type of reliability, according to Neuendorf (2002, p. 145) are:

- Poorly designed coding schemes.
- Inadequate coder training.

- Coder fatigue.
- Coders who either cannot or will not act in a reliable fashion.

The best way to address the first two of these problems is to create a codebook, a detailed document in which the coding scheme is meticulously spelled out. This means including all of the rules defining the units of measurement and guidelines for classifying each of them into one of the content categories. "The goal in creating codebooks and coding forms is to make the set so complete and unambiguous as to almost eliminate the individual differences among the coders" (Neuendorf, 2002, p. 132).

In the same way that survey instruments should be tested to discover and eliminate problem questions, coding rules should be tried out to see whether any of them are confusing, incomplete or have other problems. This is done by having coders undergo training in use of the codebook and categories. During this developmental phase, many things about the project will be in flux as the codebook is revised and individuals who will be doing the coding learn more about the project and the process.

Intercoder Reliability

At some point in the process when the coding rules have been revised to a workable level and the coders seem to have a good grasp of their assignments, a trial run for reliability typically is conducted. This is done by having coders go through the procedure and then checking the results to see how closely they agree on categorization of the material. Usually this is done with material that is similar to – but not a part of – the actual data set. For example, if certain episodes of a television show were going to be analyzed, the reliability trial would include different episodes of the same show. If agreement among the coders seems sufficient at that stage, then coding of the actual data can begin. If agreement is insufficient, further coder training and/or codebook revision are needed until the researcher decides the team is ready for another trial. In addition to the reliability trial that is done before actual coding begins, on many projects some of the material will be coded by multiple coders and used for a second reliability test.

This intercoder reliability is usually reported as the percent of cases in which coders agree on an evaluation. For example, suppose two coders were categorizing a series of 10 news articles as positive, negative or neutral to a certain position (such as LGBTQ rights), and these were the results:

	Coder A	Coder B	Agree
Article 1	Positive	Positive	Yes
Article 2	Positive	Neutral	No
Article 3	Negative	Negative	Yes
Article 4	Positive	Positive	Yes
Article 5	Neutral	Positive	No
Article 6	Negative	Negative	Yes
Article 7	Positive	Positive	Yes
Article 8	Neutral	Neutral	Yes
Article 9	Positive	Neutral	No
Article 10	Positive	Positive	Yes

The intercoder agreement in this case is 70 percent, or .70 (they reached the same conclusion 7 out of 10 times, indicated in bold). Is that sufficient? Some people might say so, although the answer is not clear-cut. According to Neuendorf, who summarized discussions from several content analysis guidebooks, there is no firm agreement among researchers about what constitutes sufficient intercoder agreement. But taking the general themes of what other scholars said, she concluded that "reliability coefficients of .90 or greater would be acceptable to all, .80 or greater would be acceptable in most cases and, below that, there exists great disagreement" (2002, p. 143).

Content analysts have developed a variety of statistical measures that modify simple percent agreement to take into account the likelihood of chance agreement. For instance, in the example above, suppose an unethical and lazy coder decided not to read all of the articles assigned to him and just marked "neutral" on the coding forms for every one of them. Then the results of the agreement test would look like this:

	Coder A	Coder B	Agree
Article 1	Neutral	Positive	No
Article 2	**Neutral**	**Neutral**	**Yes**
Article 3	Neutral	Negative	No
Article 4	Neutral	Positive	No
Article 5	Neutral	Positive	No
Article 6	Neutral	Negative	No
Article 7	Neutral	Positive	No
Article 8	**Neutral**	**Neutral**	**Yes**
Article 9	**Neutral**	**Neutral**	**Yes**
Article 10	Neutral	Positive	No

As the chart shows, the coders agree 30 percent of the time even when one of the coders is behaving in a fashion that should make him 100 percent unreliable. (As they say, even a stopped clock is correct twice a day.) Because of this, any sort of intercoder reliability check must take into account the possibilities that coders will categorize material in the same way purely by accident. Even when coders are behaving carefully and conscientiously, there are times when this chance agreement will happen because they are classifying content into a limited number of categories and one or both of them makes an honest mistake in judgment. This happens more with a small number of categories, which increases the probability of chance agreement.

An assortment of intercoder reliability statistics have been developed that content analysts frequently use in addition to (or sometimes instead of) simple percent agreement. These procedures, named after the researchers who developed them – such as Scott's pi, Cohen's kappa, and Krippendorf's alpha – generally take the raw percent agreement figure and make it lower to adjust for the likelihood of chance agreement. In a project done by one of the authors, he and a student assistant coded more than 1,400 online news articles according to their topic: politics; crime; business; sports; etc. An overlapping 110 items in the data set were analyzed by both of them. Their simple percentage agreement on these items was approximately 76 percent, but the adjusted agreement rate using both Cohen's kappa and Scott's pi was .714. (This outcome was on the low end of what conventional wisdom says is a good value to reach, as previously described.) Statistics about intercoder reliability are usually reported as part of the research, in the same way that sampling error is reported in survey research. It is an admission of some margin for error, which means the results can't be taken exactly as stated. It also is an attempt to quantify how large that error might be, which adds credibility to the results that are reported.

Reporting Results

The final stage of a content analysis, again the same as survey research, is tabulation and reporting of the results. Depending on the design of the research, the content measurements might be either the independent or the dependent variable, and the frequencies or percentages observed in the various categories are used to illustrate the relationship of those variables.

In another project by one of the authors, also involving online community news sites, the goal was to see what factors helped to determine how active such news sites were on social media. To do this, activity on Facebook and Twitter by the organizations themselves and by audience members interacting with them on those platforms was measured with content analysis; this became the *dependent* variable. The independent variables were the size (population) of the community served by the website and size (circulation) of the print newspaper associated with the online site. The project found evidence that these variables were related; larger papers serving larger communities tended to have more social media engagement with their audiences (Rosenberry, 2013). Another older but similar project categorized newspaper content by topic, such as how much of a paper's coverage was political news, how much was sports news, etc. After compiling the data, a statistical analysis was used to determine whether newspapers with different news mixes would have differences in circulation performance of the paper. Here, the content categories were used as the *independent* variables, while circulation performance was the *dependent* variable (Rosenberry, 2005).

Exactly how the researcher uses the content analysis depends largely on what results the project is designed to show. Differences or similarities are often evaluated with statistical tests that allow the researcher to state at a certain confidence level that two measurements are either similar or significantly different. In the project about social media usage by online news sites, the published paper used tables and charts showing the results of a statistical test called regression to illustrate how closely the two sets of variables were related to each other (Rosenberry, 2013).

EXPERIMENTS

The third common way of conducting quantitative research is one that many readers will be familiar with from classes in the natural sciences, at least in elementary and high school, if not in college. This is the experiment.

> ### BOX 8.9
>
> ## Definition of Experiment
>
> *Experiment*: A research technique in which the independent variable is intentionally manipulated by the researcher under controlled conditions so that effects on the dependent variable can be observed.

The key aspect of an experiment is the control under which it takes place. An experiment can be defined as a research technique in which the independent variable is intentionally manipulated by the researcher under controlled conditions so that effects on the dependent variable can be observed. Sparks (2002, p. 33) specifies three features that create this sense of control:

- **Manipulation of a key variable,** one that the researcher thinks might be the cause of impacts on another variable. This manipulated variable often is called the experimental treatment.
- **Random assignment of subjects** to groupings that will either (a) be manipulated or (b) not be manipulated. Random here has the same meaning as random selection in a probability sample for a survey or content analysis: Each subject in the experiment has an equal probability of being selected to face the experimental treatment or not face it. The subjects that do not face the treatment are called a control group.
- **Identical treatment** of these different groupings except for the intentional manipulation.

Grabe and Westley (2003) assert that experiments are the strongest tool researchers have for showing causes of impact and making predictions because experiments give the researcher the greatest control over alternative explanations (or alternative causes) of the changes observed in the dependent variable. This allows the researcher to predict more confidently that changes in the independent variable truly are causing those changes in the dependent variable. This means experiments have great internal validity. However, to get this they make a tradeoff in external validity, or the ability to generalize the results of the experiment to a larger population. Experiments are often conducted with relatively small numbers of individual subjects and the overall pool of subjects rarely is selected by a random/ probability method that would allow the experimenter to say they represent the larger population. In fact, a great many experiments conducted by college professors use the students at their institutions as a conveniently accessible pool of research subjects,

In addition to having small, non-representative samples, Poindexter and McCombs (2000, p. 224) say that the conditions under which experiments are conducted often reduce the ability to say that the results apply to a larger group. One of these characteristics is pre-testing of subjects. Many experimental designs include some sort of evaluation of subjects before the treatment takes place, often some form of questionnaire to measure knowledge or attitudes related to the topic that is being studied. Anyone who hasn't participated in the experiment has not had this experience, so the results of the experiment may not apply to them. Also, experiments often happen under artificial conditions, which means the findings may not apply to people doing the same activities in more natural settings.

For example, much experimentation about news media and advertising has involved having subjects watch newscasts, read news articles, or view advertising messages that are altered in some way to reflect the experimental manipulation. Experimenters try to be careful and subtle about the manipulation and the questions that are asked about it so that it won't be obvious to the experimental subjects what they should be looking for. Watching a newscast or viewing a news website at home, though, is still different from watching it with a group of other people in a college classroom or computer lab, especially when the watchers know that they are involved in some sort of experiment and either know or suspect that they will be asked questions about what they have seen. One of the authors of this book was involved in a research project on what happens to people physically when they deliver presentations. She had to speak in front of a group of researchers while wearing electrodes over much of her body and a blood pressure cuff – which clearly are conditions most people don't face when giving a speech or presentation.

To counter this, experimenters sometimes conduct field experiments, in which subjects are observed in natural settings rather than in the artificial environment of a lab. This reduces the ability to put strict physical controls on the process but researchers often try to still maintain a sense of controlling the process through selection of the subjects, making sure some have experienced the conditions (treatment) that the experimenter is interested in studying and others have not (for a control group).

When consumer-goods manufacturers test new marketing procedures, they often conduct field experiments. That is to say, rather than bringing people into a lab to evaluate the marketing message, they distribute it in one or more actual markets and vary the conditions under which the marketing takes place. In a field experiment for the advertising and promotion of a new breakfast cereal, for example, one market might get heavy TV and radio advertising, while a second market receives print advertising with coupons for the cereal and a third is offered events coupled with social media messages in an attempt to get viral word-of-mouth recommendations about the product to spread. In a fourth market the cereal would be introduced with no advertising to serve as a control group. Note that what makes this an experiment is the deliberate manipulation of message exposure for the different groups. Results across the markets then can be compared to determine the most effective media-message strategy.

Experimental Designs

Experiments may be designed differently in terms of pre- and post-testing of subjects, delivery of treatments, and the number of experimental groupings. Some of the most common designs are:

Single-group: A group of individuals is evaluated before experimental treatment, exposed to the treatment, and evaluated again to see if any changes can be detected. Although this is the simplest design, it also has the weakest internal validity because it does not control for the possibility of outside influences causing the changes that are observed.

Single test with control group: Two groups are created through random assignment, but only one is exposed to the experimental treatment. After that exposure, both are tested and the results are compared to see whether the treatment seems to have had an impact on those exposed to it.

Pre- and post-test with control group: In this format, two groups again are created through random assignment, but both are evaluated at the beginning *and* end of the experiment. Comparison of the pre-tests and post-tests should show whether there was a change in the experimental group that did not happen in the control group. Use of the control group in this fashion helps to control for exterior influences.

Four-group design: One concern in some experiments is that the pre-test may somehow influence the results by creating an awareness or sensitivity about the topic of the experiment among the subjects. The four-group design seeks to control for this by having control groups for both the pre-test and the experimental treatment itself, as follows:

- An experimental group undergoes pre-testing, treatment and post-testing.
- A control group undergoes pre- and post-testing without treatment.
- A third group is not pre-tested but is given the experimental treatment and post-test.
- A fourth group is given the post-test only.

Notice that in this design, the first two groups are identical to a standard two-group design, but adding the third and fourth groups helps the experimenter to control for the impact of the pre-test. Because neither of those groups undergoes pre-testing, their post-test responses help the researcher determine what effect, if any, the pre-test may have had on the first two groups.

A four-group design to test the impact of an advertisement might be organized as follows:

Group 1. This group would receive a pre-test to evaluate their knowledge of the product being advertised, view the advertisement, then undergo a post-test to determine whether they have additional knowledge or information gained from exposure to the ad. So that it won't be obvious to the subjects exactly what the researcher is trying to find out, both the before and after questionnaires will contain a variety of questions, some related to the advertisement or product and some unrelated. The advertisement most likely would be shown with other advertisements, and maybe even shown in the context of a popular television show to make the viewing more realistic. This is another way to reduce testing effects and get more accurate results.

Group 2. This group would face a pre-test and post-test questionnaire – identical instruments to the ones given to Group 1 – but would not be exposed to the advertisement. They most likely would see the same show as the experimental group, with most of the same ads, but minus the "treatment" ad. This is a traditional control group.

Group 3. This group would not be pre-tested, but would view the show and advertisements and get the post-test to evaluate their knowledge about the product.

Group 4. This group would get the post-test only. Their response to it would be compared to the response of Group 2 members – the traditional control group – to see whether Group 2 was affected in some way by undergoing the pre-test.

Evaluating Experiments

How does the researcher determine whether or not the results of one group really are different from another? Often, it is done with the same types of statistical tests described at the end of the content analysis section that can be used to say, with some level of confidence, that measurements from one group are substantially different (called a statistically significant difference) from the others. If the experimental group changes in a significant way and the control group does not, the researcher can reasonably conclude that the independent variable is influencing the dependent variable.

CONCLUSION

Quantitative methods as described in this chapter are popular and dominant in communication research. They are not, however, the only way of conducting research, and Chapter 9 will explore the alternative approach, known as qualitative research.

The fundamental difference between qualitative and quantitative research is what "counts" as evidence or data – a term that may be taken literally. The three empirical social science data-collection techniques described in this chapter all have a common end result, namely, producing a set of numbers that represent or describe the variables under study. These numerical results are usually evaluated with statistical tools that highlight similarities and differences among those sets of numbers. When the samples to be evaluated are selected in a random, probabilistic manner, these statistical tools can be used for valid inferences to the larger population from which the sample was drawn. Even non-probability samples can be used to obtain useful knowledge about mass media phenomena. Qualitative research uses no such numerical representation and no such methods of mathematical inference. It rests instead on descriptions of situations, behaviors or texts.

Communication research, whether from a quantitative/positivist perspective or a more qualitative/interpretive perspective, ultimately seeks to provide the evidence that supports a researcher's claims. In either case, the carefulness of the researcher and the rigor of the methods used to collect, compile, and analyze the data are intricately related to the quality and outcome of the research project.

Discussion Questions/Application Exercises

1. Search a database of news articles (or even conduct a Google search) for stories about political poll results. Find three different articles and note the following about each, if it is reported:

    * What size sample was the poll based on?
    * How was the poll conducted (mail, phone, online)?
    * What was the time frame in which it was conducted?
    * What sampling error do the poll results have?

2. Look through several editions of a scholarly journal that publishes research about media topics, such as *Journalism & Mass Communication Quarterly,* to find one example of each of the methods outlined in this chapter (survey, content analysis, experiment). Then try to find articles that use a combination of methods, particularly a quantitative approach combined with a qualitative one.

REFERENCES

Chaffee, S.H. & Berger, C.R. (1987). The study of communication as a science. In Berger, C.R. & Chaffee, S.H. (Eds.). *Handbook of communication science* (pp. 15–19). Newbury Park, CA: Sage Publications.

Fink, A. & Kosecoff, J. (1998). *How to conduct surveys: A step-by-step guide* (2nd ed.). Thousand Oaks, CA: Sage Publications.

Grabe, M.E. & Westley, B. (2003). The controlled experiment. In Stempel, G., Weaver, D. & Wilhoit, G.C. (Eds.). *Mass communication research and theory* (pp. 267–298). Boston: Allyn & Bacon.

Neuendorf, K. (2002). *The content analysis guidebook*. Thousand Oaks, CA: Sage Publications.

Poindexter, P. & McCombs, M. (2000). *Research in mass communication: A practical guide*. Boston: Bedford/St. Martins.

Rosenberry, J. (2005). The effect of content mix on circulation penetration for U.S. daily newspapers. *Journalism & Mass Communication Quarterly* 82 (2), 377–397.

Rosenberry, J. (2013, Summer). Circulation and community population are factors in newspapers' use of social media. *Newspaper Research Journal* 34 (3), 86–100.

Salvanto, A., De Pinto, J., Backus, F. & Khanna, K. (2021, January 13). Majority back impeachment and are concerned about more D.C. violence. *CBS News* online. Retrieved from https://www.cbsnews.com/news/opinion-poll-impeachment-donald-trump/

Sparks, G. (2002). *Media effects research: A basic overview*. Belmont, CA: Wadsworth Publishing Co.

Stempel, G. (2003). Content analysis. In Stempel, G., Weaver, D. & Wilhoit, G.C. (Eds.). *Mass communication research and theory* (pp. 209–219). Boston: Allyn & Bacon.

Walter, N., Cody, M. & Ball-Rokeach, S. (2018). The ebb and flow of communication research: Seven decades of publication trends and research priorities. *Journal of Communication* 68, 424–440.

Welsh, D. (2019). Game of Thrones research reveals new data about the show's sex and violence. *Huffpost UK* online. Retrieved from https://www.huffingtonpost.co.uk/entry/game-of-thrones-sex-nudity-violence_uk_5cb0a88fe4b082aab084fe20

CHAPTER 9

Qualitative Research Methods

This chapter will build on the general description of communication research principles from Chapter 7 and draw contrasts with quantitative methods presented in Chapter 8 to describe principles and techniques of using qualitative research methodologies, including:

- Characteristics and origins of the practice.
- Styles or genres of qualitative research, including:
  - Ethnography.
  - Phenomenology.
  - Socio-linguistics.
- Procedures for conducting qualitative research, including:
  - Designing studies.
  - Collecting data in the field with observation and interviews.
  - Analyzing the collected data to reach valid conclusions.

Although research in the positivist tradition using methods as outlined in Chapter 8 – what Chaffee and Berger (1987) called "communication science" – is the dominant approach in mass communication research, the use of qualitative methods to understand communication phenomena has grown in prominence and popularity.

The point of all social science research, including communication studies, is to understand the human experience more completely by asking good questions about it (Marshall & Rossman, 2011). Within that, qualitative research "represents a broad view that to understand human affairs it is insufficient to rely on quantitative surveys and statistics, and necessary to delve deep into the subjective qualities that govern behavior" (Holliday, 2002, p. 7).

Using an example from outside of communication, consider two different approaches to investigating poverty. Demographic statistics – collected through quantitative means such as surveys of the population – can tell researchers a lot about the topic. This approach could determine what proportion of a population lives in poverty, what their approximate level of income is, and whether poverty affects some groups of the population more than others. Measured at different points in time, such statistics can even indicate whether more or fewer people are living in poverty now as compared to previously. Indicators of such a

DOI: 10.4324/9781003121695-9

change could offer insight into the effectiveness of anti-poverty policies and practices. One thing a statistical approach cannot do, however, is describe what it is like to live in a poor neighborhood, to be hungry, or suffer food insecurity. Numerical descriptions cannot help someone understand the challenges faced by a poor single mother trying to do the best she can for her family. Only qualitative research – interviewing or directly observing people affected by poverty – can offer insights about those topics. It is interesting to note that many news reports begin with a qualitative approach, such as the profile of someone struggling to make ends meet for her family, and then proceed to include quantitative statistics about poverty. In this way, the coverage gives a human face to a larger social issue using both qualitative and quantitative indicators.

In adopting this qualitative approach, researchers are not looking for sweeping generalizations but rather seek deeper understanding of specific instances. "Qualitative research places an emphasis on understanding through looking closely at people's words, actions and records" (Maykut & Morehouse, 1994). Typically, qualitative research seeks to answer questions about *what* is happening rather than *why* it is happening, and especially what is happening in a particular natural setting that the researcher selects for study. One definition describes qualitative research as:

> A process of understanding based on distinct methodological traditions of inquiry that explore a social or human problem. The researcher builds a complex, holistic picture; analyzes words; reports detailed views of informants; and conducts the study in a natural setting (Creswell, 1998, p. 15).

BOX 9.1

Definition of Qualitative Research

Qualitative research: A process that seeks better understanding of a social or human problem based on analyses conducted in natural settings.

As noted in Chapter 7, qualitative research tends to use an inductive, subjective, and contextualized approach in contrast with the deductive, neutral, and generalized approach of quantitative studies (Morgan, 2014). Another way of contrasting the research styles is that quantitative researchers work with a few variables and many cases, whereas qualitative researchers rely on a few cases but study many variables within each of them. Those "variables" come in the form of practically anything research subjects do or say that the researcher can observe or ask about. Overall, the main task for the qualitative researcher is understanding the social environment and how people make their way within it.

STYLES OF QUALITATIVE RESEARCH

Perhaps appropriately for a practice with no predetermined principles (other than inquiry in natural settings), there is no single or universally agreed-upon way to classify the various approaches to qualitative research that are commonly used. For example, some researchers list case study as a genre or tradition of qualitative research (e.g., Creswell, 1998); others would consider it a level of study that can be explored through various techniques (an ethnographic case study, a sociolinguistic case study). Marshall and Rossman describe the process of conducting qualitative research as "confusing, messy, intensely frustrating and fundamentally nonlinear" (2011, p. 55). Attempting to classify the ways it is done can be described with the same terms. However, because of the increasing interest in qualitative research and its importance in the study of mass media, this chapter presents a (hopefully) less confusing, less messy, and less frustrating way to think about studying the media using specific areas or genres of qualitative research.

BOX 9.2

Styles of Qualitative Research

Ethnography: Study of cultures.
Phenomenology: Study of people's lived experiences.
Socio-linguistics: Study of spoken, written or image-based communication.

For their part, Marshall and Rossman outline three major genres of qualitative research as:

- Ethnography, or cultural study.
- Phenomenology, or examination of people's lived experiences.
- Sociolinguistic review, which is analyzing the contents of communication as it is said, written, or presented as images.

These categories correspond to the three types of data most commonly used in qualitative research: observation, interviews, and written documents (Trochim, 2005). Berger (2000) describes a similar typology, saying that the three primary ways of getting information about people are by watching them (observation), by asking them things (interviewing), and by examining the documents and artifacts they produce (documentary analysis). This chapter reviews these main types of research and then describes procedures for conducting research in these areas.

Ethnography

In reviewing various ways of conducting qualitative research, it makes sense to begin with ethnography both for historical reasons – the importance of cultural anthropology to the development of qualitative research in general – and because it embodies key characteristics of the practice, especially making unstructured inquiry in a natural setting. Ethnography may be defined as:

Description and interpretation of a cultural or social group or system, usually with data developed by participant observation in which the researcher is immersed in day-to-day lives of the people under study, or collected in one-on-one interviews with them (Creswell, 1998).

BOX 9.3

Definition of Ethnography

Ethnography: Description and interpretation of a cultural or social group or system, usually with data developed by participant observation or collected in one-on-one interviews with research subjects.

Ethnography can be conducted for various purposes, including just to describe characteristics of the culture under study, or to probe deeper to understand its structure and customs. Ethnographies can highlight culturally unique beliefs or practices, or sometimes even critique problems with the culture. An example of such a critique – constructive criticism would be another way to put it – might be a researcher in a health-care setting studying the organizational culture there. As part of the work, the researcher might document staff/patient interactions, a key aspect of the organizational culture, in order to offer suggestions for improving them.

A famous organizational ethnography involving the mass media was done by Harvard Business School professor Chris Argyris, who wrote a book about the culture of a major metropolitan newspaper (*Behind the Front Page*, 1974) after spending several months in the newsroom alongside the journalists. More recently, Everbach (2006) used an ethnographic study of a Florida newspaper to document how the newsroom culture was affected by the fact that all of the top editors were women, and Ryfe (2009) also studied a newspaper to evaluate the impact of changes in how reporters were assigned to cover their community.

The term "ethnography" applies not just to a type of qualitative research, however, but also a technique by which it is done. It is, as Singer (2009) puts it, both a process and a product (Box 9.4). With that in mind, Warren and Karner define the process of ethnography as "present-time face-to-face interaction in a [specific] setting" (2015, p. 2).

As both a style of research and a technique for conducting it, ethnography forces certain considerations on researchers who want to do it. As Warren and Karner further point out, talking and interacting in a setting can be more complicated than it sounds. Some of the things researchers may need to take into account are finding and defining the setting, getting access to it, deciding what to do (and avoid doing) when conducting research in the setting, and how deeply involved they should get with the research subjects.

The final point is probably the most crucial one. Effective ethnography means getting close to subjects; Margaret Mead lived with her subjects in Samoa for years. At

BOX 9.4

Journalism and Ethnography

Qualitative research, especially ethnography, has a good deal of similarity to journalism because with both practices, researchers (reporters) go into the field and use essentially the same tools: observation and interviews. However, as scholar Jane Singer (2009) points out, they are not the same thing, because the methodological rigor of academic studies goes deeper than the descriptive narrative of news reporting. Singer cites those academic characteristics as:

- Work that probes for meaning rather than merely doing transcription.
- Acknowledgement of the researcher's interpretive relationship to the subjects, content, and context of the study.
- Methodological richness and appropriate contextualization of data.
- Extensive time in the research environment and a nuanced understanding of what was encountered there.
- Connections to a framework of knowledge and interpretation that extends beyond the immediate study.
- Meaning extracted from the usual patterns of social life exhibited by those being studied.
- Evidence that researchers have been sensitive in interacting with sources and in presenting information.

the same time, the researcher is there as an outsider, not a full member of the group, so a balance of closeness and distance must be maintained as the relationship between the researcher and his or her subjects develops. Often, researchers do become part of the group in at least some activities. Warren and Karner document one anecdote of a researcher investigating work in restaurant kitchens who was put to work preparing food and cleaning up as part of the bargain (2015, p. 86). At an extreme, researchers can "go native" and become so involved with the group that it compromises their work, so researchers must be cautious as to how involved they can get without having it affect their work.

Personal characteristics – especially age, race, and gender – can have impacts on the relationship between the researcher and subjects as well. A Black researcher, for example, would have great difficulty incorporating with a white supremacy group to observe it. A more realistic example might be a young woman wanting to conduct an ethnographic study of an all-male sports team by hanging around before and after practices and games to document the team's culture. It is likely she would be treated differently than a male researcher in the same environment. Her presence could, in fact, cause team members to behave differently from how they would if she were not around, or at least differently from how they might act in the presence of another man. Such "unnatural" behavior could compromise the effectiveness of the research. (This is not meant to suggest that female researchers could never investigate all-male environments, or vice versa, but merely to offer an example of how personal markers such as gender can have an impact on a researcher's ability to become integrated with subjects in a setting.)

Finally, as Warren and Karner point out, when observing something "Your ethnographic agenda does not protect you as a person" (2015, p. 91). From emotional issues to physical discomfort or even possible danger, field experiences can sometimes be challenging. Imagine, for example, being a researcher working alongside TV journalists and traveling with them to a gruesome auto accident or murder scene they were assigned to cover. Most likely the gory elements wouldn't make the 11 p.m. news, but that doesn't mean the journalists and researchers wouldn't be exposed to them. "Fieldwork occurs in a social setting … and has all of the opportunities for emotional response that are present in everyday life" (Warren & Karner, 2015, p. 92).

Phenomenology

Documenting and describing lived experiences, often the shared reactions of individuals who have experienced something in common, is called phenomenology. Basic features of a phenomenological study include defining the phenomenon to be studied and its essential structure – the components of the experience as shared by all of the group under study. This focus on shared experiences related to a single phenomenon is what makes this different from the ethnographic study of a full culture of a society as Mead did, or a workplace as in the previous newsroom examples, or an organization such as the sports team example. When the phenomenon in question is mass media exposure, phenomenology becomes one way to study social impacts of that exposure.

BOX 9.5

Definition of phenomenology

Phenomenology: Documenting and describing lived experiences, often the shared reactions of individuals who have experienced something in common, including media exposure.

An important aspect of phenomenology is the idea that what people experience as "reality" is fundamentally a social construction. In other words, there is no objective, universally-experienced reality. What makes something real to those who experience it is the common set of interactions they have with others who experience the same phenomenon. Holliday calls this the progressivist school of social research, in which there is no naturally occurring state of society to be observed. All facets of the world are socially constructed, and researchers' interpretations are part of the construction process (Holliday, 2002, p. 20).

Like ethnography, phenomenology is both process and product, and is closely associated with some of the theorists and theories described elsewhere in the book.

Joseph Klapper's ideas about how the media reinforce viewpoints more than create them (as discussed in Chapter 2) is sometimes called phenomenistic because he is theorizing about the common lived experience of particular types of media exposure. Berger and Luckman's hypothesis about the social construction of reality (covered in Chapter 5) also has phenomenology as its basis. Media events such as a widely watched event (e.g., the Super Bowl, or season finale of a popular show) are a shared life experience for the viewers that can be investigated on a phenomenistic basis. This is especially true when the experience is enhanced through social media, such as following the #TheBachelor hashtag and contributing to the conversation while watching an episode.

Sociolinguistic Analysis

In addition to ethnographic study of a culture and investigations of the impacts of shared experiences around common phenomena (including media), another approach to qualitative research involves examination of documents or *texts*. This can entail analysis of written documents that are personal (such as diaries and correspondence) or public (newspapers, magazines, TV and movie scripts, websites, and collections of social media posts). As the examples show, this area of qualitative research offers rich prospects for mass media researchers.

However, it is important not to take the term *text* literally here, as it does not always mean words written out as sentences or paragraphs. A "text" might be constructed that way, of course, but it might also be an advertisement that is mostly visual or an audiovisual presentation such as a film or television show. All of these can be subjected to qualitative analysis, and the subject of such analysis is usually referred to as a "text." A collection of items, such as all of the advertisements in one magazine, or all of the ads across several platforms by a single company, also can serve as the "text" for this type of analysis.

BOX 9.6

Definition of Sociolinguistics

Sociolinguistics: Examination of documents or texts to discern their meaning and contexts. The word "text" is not meant literally because it does not always mean written words. A "text" might be mostly visual images or even an audiovisual such as a film or television show.

Unlike the numerical measurements done in objective content analysis (as described in Chapter 8), qualitative investigation of documents is focused on their meanings and contexts. Altheide defines this as a process for "locating, identifying, retrieving and analyzing documents for their relevance, significance and meaning" (1996, p. 2). This type of analysis also goes beyond the manifest content of the document to consider it as a cultural artifact. Commonly asked questions in this regard are: Who produced it? For what purpose? What does its existence mean or accomplish? Common types of document-based investigation that help to answer these and other questions about documents and texts include qualitative content analysis, to evaluate and describe meanings within the text, and semiotic analysis, which examines symbols used within the text and their meanings.

Qualitative Content Analysis

In qualitative content analysis, the researcher "interacts" with the documentary materials to analyze the documents and better understand their meanings in context. It's sometimes called ethnographic content analysis because of the parallels to how a participant-observer doing an ethnographic study interacts with his or her environment. "Good qualitative content analysis requires an open-minded researcher, a specific research question and a systematic way of looking at whatever content is chosen" (Priest, 1996, p. 114).

Exactly which documents the researcher examines are selected for conceptually or theoretically relevant reasons (Altheide, 1996, p. 34). After that, the analysis starts with a protocol, or list of questions, ideas, or categories about which the investigator seeks to learn more from the documents. The main emphasis is capturing definitions, meanings and themes of the narrative, descriptions, and possibly images in the text. The process involves "extensive reading, sorting and searching through materials, comparing within categories, coding and adding keywords and concepts," then summarizing the results according to the research questions as identified in the original protocol (Altheide, 1996, p. 43). For example, an assignment in a class taught by one of the authors has all class members examine the same website and list approximately ten characteristics about its usability: Organization; text presentation; use of graphics, etc. All of these observations are then compiled into one long list of as many as 200 individual items. The second part of the exercise then has the students examine the whole body of items for common themes or trends, putting into practice the sorting and summarization approach Altheide describes.

Semiotics

On an even more detail-focused level, semiotics is the study of signs and symbols and how they relate to concepts and objects that they signify as part of social life. The basis of semiotics is that studying these relationships can provide a greater understanding of how meaning is created by a particular symbol or a collection of them, such as the words and images in a book, magazine, movie, television show, or advertisement. Semiotics seeks to analyze media texts as structured wholes with a focus on the system of rules governing the "discourse" they present, stressing the role of semiotic context in shaping meaning (Chandler, 2002). Put another way, "Semiotics helps us understand how to decipher the messages we are sent and understand better the messages we send" (Berger, 2000, p. 43).

This technique for understanding the meanings of a text is based in linguistics, especially the work of Swiss linguist Ferdinand de Saussure, who developed a form of semiotic analysis known as structuralism. Saussure defined a sign as being composed of a "signifier," which is the form that the sign takes, and the "signified," or the concept it represents.

As semiotics has developed, the structuralist approach pioneered by Saussure has been augmented with social semiotics, which is how the meanings of texts – especially mass media messages – have an impact on society around them. "Signs do not just 'convey' meanings, but constitute a medium in which meanings are constructed. Semiotics helps us to realize that meaning is not passively absorbed but arises only in the active process of interpretation" (Chandler, 2002, p. 217). Emphasizing sense-making using these ideas has particular appeal for media theorists who stress the importance of how audiences actively interpret media messages.

Often, these meanings and their impacts on an audience member's life are not obvious to the individual consumer of the message; one goal of semiotic analysis is to help to reveal the deeper meanings. "Semiotics is important because it can help us not to take 'reality' for granted as something having a purely objective existence which is independent of human interpretation. It teaches us that reality is a system of signs. ... It can help us to realize that ... meaning is not 'transmitted' to us – we actively create it according to a complex interplay of codes or conventions of which we are normally unaware" (Chandler, 2002, p. 9).

This is especially important because the "reality" most people experience is NOT from personal experience but from what they experience through signs and symbols – such as reading about or seeing videos of people they do not know who live in another part of the country or the world. Most Americans have never lived in or even been part of a war zone (aside from soldiers). Everyone, though, has seen war movies and coverage of wars around the world on television news, or played realistic video games set in a war zone. The experience of "war," then, for most Americans is purely through symbols, which is vastly different from lived experience. As Chandler further puts it, "Although things may exist independently of signs, we know them only through the mediation of signs. We see only what our sign systems allow us to see" (2002, p. 216).

One area of mass media research in which semiotic analysis is widely used is investigation of meanings conveyed by advertising texts. Examples of this include projects that examined the meanings found in advertising for antidepressant medications (Grow, Park, & Han, 2006) and of how Nike ads were presented toward women (Grow, 2006). Anido Freire (2014) examined how advertising by luxury fashion brands created coherent global identities to reinforce their brand images. Away from advertising, Felicia (2019) used semiotics to examine how gender was presented in Nigerian political cartoons and Polidoro (2016) used textual analysis to examine how class ideology, centered on portrayal of the aristocracy, was presented in the British television show *Downton Abbey*.

Semiotics also has a valuable role to play in understanding how encoding and decoding of mass media texts contribute to certain ideas becoming dominant in society and preventing non-mainstream ideas from becoming better understood. This has been done through the research tradition known as cultural studies, as described further in Chapter 5.

CONDUCTING QUALITATIVE RESEARCH

A qualitative research project – like any research project – starts with an idea to investigate a topic of interest to the researcher. As noted in Chapter 7, it helps for the idea to be right-sized – small enough in scope to make for a manageable project but large enough to have some significance to the field and other researchers within it. Projects that are too big become impossible to complete while those that are too small or too specific usually fail to contribute new insights and therefore are not very valuable.

Research Design

Qualitative research starts in a more open-ended way than its quantitative cousin. Quantitative research often starts with a specific, theoretically-derived hypothesis to be empirically tested with data collection and analysis. Qualitative projects, on the other hand, start with a more general question to be researched, or what Creswell (1998) calls a purpose statement. Marshall and Rossman (2011) recommend finding this purpose by filling in the answers to statements such as "I would like to know more about…" or "I would like a better understanding of …" Beginning the inquiry this way adds some focus without being overly narrow. Creswell notes that research questions driving qualitative research often address *what* is happening in an area or *how* it is happening rather than *why*, which is often a topic for quantitative research. (In Chapter 7, this is presented as descriptive vs. explanatory research.) Miles and Huberman (1994) suggest augmenting the purpose statement with a research framework that will set out the main things to be studied: Key factors; key constructs or variables; and presumed relationships among them.

While it is helpful to be open-ended at this stage to allow the inductive process and spirit of inquiry that animate qualitative research to take root, the researcher also should not operate on too wide a scope. Doing that will make subsequent parts of the process inefficient and subject to wasted effort. Once the overall purpose statement is developed, it can be used to craft a small number of more specific research questions that will lie at the heart of the data collection and analysis. As De Vaus (2001) points out, a research design is only effective if it can ensure that the evidence obtained will answer the research question. However, it also is important to recognize that the specific questions may change along the way as information is discovered that leads the researcher to think about the topic in different ways.

Maykut and Morehouse recommend that effective research design have the following characteristics (1994, pp. 43–47):

- Exploratory and descriptive focus that allows for a deeper understanding of the subjects under study.
- Flexibility so that as leads are discovered in the early phases, new questions can emerge.
- Purposive sample of subjects that are selected because of good fit with the topic of inquiry.

- Collection of data in natural settings.
- Dual role for the researcher as both the collector and interpreter of the data.
- Appropriate methodology for the task, usually either participant observation, interviews, or review of relevant documents.
- Early and ongoing inductive data analysis, so that as patterns emerge they can help develop additional research questions.

One final consideration in designing the study is setting boundaries for the work. This makes the project more manageable overall and also helps define the context for data that is collected. This involves answering the question(s) "What information will be sought, from which people, by which procedures?" Often the boundary is culturally determined, such as a particular social group, organization or workplace in an ethnography, a particular occupation or social demographic for a phenomenological study, or a particular media genre (e.g., fashion magazines) for a socio-linguistic analysis.

Data Collection

Armed with a purpose for the research and an initial set of open-ended questions – which may change as the study progresses – a qualitative researcher is ready to move into data-collection for the project. While all phases of the project are important, this is perhaps the most crucial because without effective data, a project is essentially worthless. "The backbone of qualitative research is extensive collection of data, typically from multiple sources of information" (Creswell, 1998, p. 19).

Setting a Sample

Drawing samples of items to study for qualitative purposes is usually the exact opposite of finding a sample for a quantitative study. Numerical research emphasizes use of large samples and (often) a random probability method to ensure statistical validity. A qualitative study, on the other hand, seeks a purposive sample that provides the best likelihood of gaining a deep understanding about a topic that is the goal of such research. This is logical given that the research often focuses on individuals in a particular setting or who have had a common experience, which means a large segment of the population would be inappropriate for the sample. A researcher who was interested in studying media-streaming preferences of a college-age audience, for example, would need to focus on people in that narrow range of the population. Collecting information from older audience members wouldn't be valuable to the project; it would be similarly unproductive to get data from people who only follow broadcast media rather than online streaming services.

No particular sample size needs to be determined at the outset, and a "snowball" technique of asking initial subjects to recommend others who may be observed or interviewed can help build the subject pool. It is important in selecting a sample to have what Maykut and Morehouse (1994) call maximum variation sampling, or a set of individuals who represent as wide a range as feasible of those experiencing the phenomenon under study. Returning to the college-audience media-streaming example, this would mean trying to find individuals for the sample from a variety of institutions (large and small, public and private), a variety of academic majors or programs, and different demographics (men and women, as well as people from different geographic, social, economic, ethnic, and racial backgrounds). The reason for this should be intuitive. Even though qualitative research doesn't seek representative samples from which generalizations can be drawn, it requires diverse perspectives to get the deepest possible understanding of the phenomenon under study. Sampling a non-diverse group of people from just one or two demographics would limit the perspectives available to the researcher and lead to a weaker pool of data to analyze for valid conclusions.

Of course, this example assumes a broad base for the study. The researcher might be interested in a narrower pool, such as media streaming preferences of college-age Black women. In this case, the sample would be composed entirely of young Black women. Still, the principle of maximum variability means they should come from a variety of economic backgrounds, academic majors, and institutions to offer a sufficiently wide range of experiences.

Types of Data

In qualitative research, what "counts" as data covers a wide range of human experiences and productions. According to Holliday (2002, pp. 71–72) some of the things it can consist of are:

- Descriptions of behaviors, settings, appearances or events that the researcher sees.
- Listening observations by the researcher of things he or she hears or overhears.
- Accounts of what people say to the researcher, either informally or in a formally structured interview.
- Documents and other artifacts that illustrate aspects of the environment under study.

Similar to the idea of maximum variation in selecting a sample, researchers will end up with better information if it is collected across a range of data types. For example, when Paterson (2011) wanted to study the newsroom cultures of two international television networks based in London, he relied on document analysis, video content analysis, participant observation of the newsrooms, and interviews.

Qualitative research is always done within the boundaries of a particular social setting or in connection with a particular social phenomenon, and all data that is collected must fit within those boundaries. Collecting as wide a range of data as possible within those boundaries is critical to conducting the research effectively. As Holliday puts it, "Data alone is not enough. Collecting the right interconnected data is necessary" (2002, p. 81).

Documenting the Data

An old proverb holds that "the faintest ink is more powerful than the strongest memory." This is a worthwhile adage to keep in mind when recording data, especially when documenting observations with field notes. Accurate recording of direct interviews is important also, but the more controlled setting of a one-on-one or focus-group interview means it's often possible to record them for preservation – either an audio recording or sometimes even on video. Such recordings are seldom possible in field observations.

Field Notes

Crafting effective field notes is a vital skill for any qualitative researcher. They are the equivalent of the raw data collected by quantitative researchers for later analysis (Warren & Karner, 2015). These notes, which document what researchers see and hear during observations, should be full narrative instead of just phrases and bullet points. Notes should be composed, to the degree possible, as the observations are being made. Sometimes a researcher might be able to use a recorder to make voice memos, but many situations will not be feasible for that and notes will need to be written out. Sometimes it may not even be possible to write notes at the exact time of the observation, simply because some settings are inappropriate or inefficient for having a notebook out. In that case, recording should be done as soon as possible after the observations so that details are fresh in the researcher's mind.

Field notes should use neutral language and contain as much detail as possible, even though it's neither possible nor desirable to record everything. An analogy for striking this balance that some students may relate to is annotating a textbook by underlining or highlighting to prepare for a test. If very little is highlighted, there may not be enough material to study effectively. On the other hand, if everything is underlined, the markings are worthless since they don't direct the reader's attention to the important points. Likewise, striking that proper balance in recording observations is one of the main challenges for researchers in the field. The guideline Holliday (2002) provides is that the researcher should focus on collecting enough data that individual observations have a systematic relationship in which they reinforce or corroborate one another. Like variability in sampling, this increases the validity of the data by creating multiple perceptions of the same phenomena. At the same time, the researcher must be careful not to filter or edit too much because it is impossible to know as things are unfolding what will be important later on. Special attention should be paid to things that are confusing, surprising, or interesting to the researcher since such occurrences often turn out to be important (Priest, 1996).

Having the notes in narrative form, richly detailed and created as close as possible to the same time as the observation creates the best conditions for having what sociologist Clifford Geertz calls "thick" description of an event that not only documents the event but adds context and meaning (Warren & Karner, 2015, p. 103). Thick description shows the complexity and variety in the data, which also helps in assessing its cultural meaning (Holliday, 2002).

Interviews

Interviews come in a variety of purposes and formats. Everyone has seen or heard a broadcast interview on a news show, or during a sporting event or entertainment talk show. Many radio shows, especially on National Public Radio (NPR), are built entirely around such interviews. Most college students have been through an internship or job interview, and many mass communication students conduct interviews for campus news organizations. Some students may even have experience at informational interviews to learn about career prospects before trying to secure that job or internship interview and build their professional network of contacts. (More information about this is in Chapter 10.)

An interview as part of a qualitative research project, however, has some special characteristics. These include both a formal structure and a focus on probing subjects' thoughts and feelings to gain a deep understanding of the phenomena they are experiencing or the social setting they inhabit that the researcher is investigating. "At its best, the qualitative interview creates an event in which one person (the interviewer) encourages another person to articulate interests or experiences freely" (Lindlof, 1995, p. 163). Often, these interviews last an hour or more; on occasion, subjects are interviewed multiple times to cover all the material the researcher hopes to acquire from them. Warren and Karner (2015) say such interviews can involve as much social interaction between researcher and subject as ethnographic immersion.

Whether an interview should be used in the research depends on the specific questions under investigation and type of data that must be collected to address them. A rule of thumb provided by Warren and Karner (2015) is that when researchers are more interested in behaviors and social interactions, ethnographic observation is the best technique. Personal accounts of how people managed a social setting are best gathered in interviews. Of course, the techniques are not mutually exclusive; researchers sometimes use both in a single project to gather different types of data that could reinforce or corroborate one another.

Once the decision has been made to include interview data, the general research questions for the study are used to formulate specific questions that are incorporated into an interview framework or schedule that can vary from a less-structured, more open-ended approach to a tightly scripted series of questions that the researcher wants answered. Berger (2000) listed interview techniques based on the amount of structure that is built into them as:

- **Informal interviews,** which are essentially general conversation with no set agenda, and often are used just to help the researcher and the subjects become familiar with each other. They might be used in the initial, exploratory phase of a project.
- **Unstructured interviews,** in which the researcher has a focus or agenda but proceeds in an informal manner and exercises little control over the respondents' answers.
- **Semi-structured interviews,** in which the researcher starts with a detailed agenda or list of questions, but tries to maintain an informal approach and is free to explore avenues apart from the agenda if they seem interesting or worthwhile.
- **Structured interviews,** in which the interviewer has a detailed list of questions and follow-ups, all of which must be covered according to the way they were prepared in advance.

Like so many other decisions in the qualitative research process, the level of structure in the interview is rooted mostly in the type of study and the type of data that is needed. Whatever the level of detail in the schedule or framework, the researcher has some important things to keep in mind in developing the questions. Questions always should be open-ended; in other words, they should not be questions that can be answered "yes" or "no" or with just a few words. They should be specific; a vague question will result in a vague answer that will be of little use. They should be simple because an overly complex question could be misunderstood by the subject and lead to an unproductive answer. Patton (1990) offers a taxonomy of question types that qualitative researchers often draw on in formulating an interview:

- **Knowledge**: What facts or understandings do subjects have about a topic?
- **Opinion/value questions**: What do subjects think about a topic or what opinions do they hold about it?
- **Affective questions**: How do subjects feel about a topic? What emotional reactions do they have to it?
- **Experience/behavioral questions**: What have subjects done?
- **Sensory questions**: What have subjects seen, heard, touched or otherwise experienced with their senses about the phenomenon under study?
- **Background/demographics**. This is the one category of questions in qualitative in-depth interviewing that may be closed-ended since the answers are often answerable in just a few words giving a subject's gender, age, occupation, and the like. Sometimes this data is even collected with a written survey instrument where subjects fill in blanks or check multiple-choice answers to collect basic information without bringing it into the questions asked by the researcher as part of the interview.

Researchers also must give thought to the logistics of the interview and what information must be given to subjects to prepare them for it. Maykut and Morehouse (1994) recommend that the interview framework or schedule also include:

- Personal introduction from whomever is conducting the interview.
- Statement of purpose for the interview: why it is being conducted and how the information gathered will fit into the research.
- Statement about confidentiality.
- Plans for documentation, including permission from the subject to record the interview on audio or video, if such recording is planned.

In actually conducting the interview, it is important for the interviewer to stay focused and on task, to ask clear questions, to prompt respondents for elaboration when necessary, to be non-judgmental, and to ask questions in a way that doesn't "lead" the respondent or prompt any particular answer (Berger, 2000). Listening carefully to what the subjects are saying also is critical to being able to ask appropriate follow-up questions. "The main event of the interview is dialogue. Chance, surprise and persistence contribute at least as much to the happy results of an interview as advance planning" (Lindlof, 1995, p. 194).

Focus Groups

In-depth interviewing of a small group of people rather than single individuals is often called a focus-group study. All of the guidelines about question development covered in the last section apply to this approach as well. In addition to being used in qualitative academic research, focus groups are extremely common in the worlds of advertising and marketing. Students with career interests in those areas should take a special interest in this research method.

Focus group research involves a trained moderator leading the group through a series of questions comparable to an unstructured or semi-structured interview. This methodology "uses open-ended, follow-up and probing questions to scratch below the surface of a small group of participants' attitudes, opinions and behaviors to understand motivations, feelings and reactions" (Poindexter & McCombs, 2000, p. 240). Much of the value of a focus group comes from the interaction among the group members as they elaborate on, question or challenge each other's statements. The goal is to have interaction "creating a richer set of data than can sometimes result from a single interviewer's interaction with a single respondent" (Priest, 1996 p. 109). Many colleges use focus groups to determine what motivated students to apply to and decide to attend their school. Serving on one of these focus groups gives many students an opportunity to experience a focus group firsthand, especially if it is conducted by a professional.

The researcher usually doesn't try for any sort of probabilistic or random sampling for those included in the group; rather, subjects are chosen because of their background or knowledge about a topic. If, for example, the purpose of a group is to explore reactions to the advertisements that typically appear on reality shows or in televised professional sports, the researcher would want focus-group participants who were regular watchers of the reality shows or the games, respectively. This makes focus groups easier to organize and administer than a large-scale probabilistic survey. This, plus their flexibility in exploring topics in unstructured or semi-structured ways, makes them especially useful for exploratory research although they also are used for research in other stages of projects as well.

The size of the group has an impact on its effectiveness. Experts recommend at least six but no more than 12 participants because the group needs to be large enough that participants react to each other's statements, but not so large that it becomes unmanageable and not everyone has a chance to be heard. In fact, it is the job of the focus group moderator to be sure that everyone's opinion is heard, as well as to guide the group back to the specific topic if they stray to tangents unrelated to the research study. As with some individual interviews, the focus-group session may be recorded with video or audio for transcription and later analysis, and may be observed by researchers other than the moderator.

Documents and Artifacts: Discourse and Semiotic Analysis

As with observational and interview opportunities, when a documentary analysis is conducted, the researcher considers what should be selected on the basis of appropriateness to the particular element of human experience or culture that the researcher is studying. Mass media products – especially television shows and magazines – have a long history of being examined as cultural indicators for topics such as gender roles and stereotypes. Media portrayals of women, especially regarding sexual objectification, have been the subject of much investigation through movies, music videos, television and magazines as artifacts. Magazines have proved to be a rich source in this regard because of the wide variety of often narrow topics and demographics that they address (Warren & Karner, 2015). It's easy to find magazines targeted specifically to men, or women, or teens, or even teen women/girls to conduct these studies. Music videos, especially by rap artists, have been used extensively for studies of misogyny and what has been called "rape culture." (See, for example, Thaller & Messing, 2014.)

As with the selection of bounded cultural settings for ethnography or subjects for interviews, selection of media artifacts for a project is not done randomly but rather done purposely to get a data set that will be most effective in answering the research questions. Warren and Karner (2015) call this theoretical sampling, or using items that address the broad themes the research is meant to investigate. Even with this sort of sampling, however, it is important also to be specific in defining constructs and content that serve as a cultural marker. A study of sexual objectification in advertising, for instance, would require a definition of what was considered sexy, and details about what sorts of images or portrayals counted as objectification.

These characteristics are what semioticians call signifiers, and their associated features of denotations and connotations. Extending from de Saussure's original definitions, contemporary semioticians refer to the creation and interpretation of texts as "encoding" and "decoding" respectively. Decoding involves not simply recognizing and comprehending what a text says, but also interpreting and evaluating its meaning. Semiotic researchers are especially concerned with the differences in denotations (literal meanings) and connotations (implied meanings) of words, and how that difference affects the meaning of communication.

For example, the letters C-A-T form a common English word that is a symbol for something else, namely a mammal of the feline genus. That is its denotation, or "signifier" to use de Saussure's term. Different people who read or hear the word "cat" might have different reactions to it or understandings of it – different connotations. A cat owner might think of her own pet, someone who loved seeing the "big cats"¹ at the zoo might think of a lion or tiger, and someone who is allergic to cats might think of the last case of hives he had when he came into contact with one. An avid reader of the newspaper comics might think of Garfield, while a fan of reality TV might think of Tiger King. Which of these varying connotations did the author most likely have in mind when "encoding" the text by using the word "cat," and how can the potentially different "decodings" affect the meaning of the text for the reader? Semiotics would look at the symbol (the word "cat") in its context (other words and images around it) to try and make that determination, recognizing that the number of ways to decode it is limited only by the number of people who see the symbol, but also using the principle that other context clues around it can provide a surer sense of its meaning. In semiotics "the critical emphasis is on trying to unravel the author's assumptions, motives and consequences as revealed by analysis of the document" (Altheide, 1996, p. 7).

In a segment of his book called "D.I.Y. Semiotic Analysis: Advice to My Own Students," Chandler (2002) identifies several considerations in using semiotics to probe meanings. These start with identifying the text and the purpose for conducting the analysis and then identifying the signifiers within it. The analysis should then account for a symbol's modality, or its representation of truth or accuracy. In describing how a term could have different modalities, Chandler uses the example of a statement such as "The weather is wonderful." This statement could exist in any of several modes, including an accurate or factual one (the weather really is pleasant), an untruthful one (weather is bad, and the statement is meant to mislead), or an ironic one (the weather is bad, but the statement is made with sarcasm). Anyone who has ever misread a sarcastic or ironic message in an email or social media post has experienced a "decoding" problem with regard to message modality.

The semiotician also needs to analyze the general context and structural elements of the text, which are known respectively as paradigmatic and syntagmatic analyses. This helps to situate the signifiers within the text and better understand their meaning in the context surrounding them. Paradigmatic analysis means identifying a set of related symbols, but ones that are not interchangeable with ones from different paradigms. This analysis examines signifiers in their overall contexts by comparing and contrasting them with others that might have been chosen, and by considering the significance of the choices made – and then assessing what the implications are for the related connotations. This analysis may include something called a commutation test, which is to imagine what meaning might result if a substitute was used for one of the signifiers in the analysis. Syntagmatic analysis involves studying a text's structure and the relationships between its parts. In the most literal interpretation of text, say a magazine article or movie script, this analysis might examine the narrative or story arc in the writing. Paradigmatic and syntagmatic analysis taken together can be used to infer meanings more deeply because of how the signifiers at each level interact and reinforce each other.

One of the examples used by Chandler, and other semioticians, to explain how paradigms and syntagmatic structures work together is to consider a clothing ensemble. (The example isn't even far-fetched, because the way people dress does have connotations for the impression they make on those around them.) The paradigms in this example are different categories of clothing that can't substitute for one another, such as tops, bottoms, and shoes. A variety of individual "signs" can exist within a given paradigm; in this metaphorical example, those could be t-shirts, hoodies, fancy shirts/blouses, flannel button-downs, etc. that people can wear on their torsos and arms. The syntagmatic structure, or narrative, is the message conveyed when different signifiers from each paradigm are presented together. Sandals, shorts, and a t-shirt convey a different message than a skirt, blouse, and pumps. Incoherence in the syntagmatic structure – such as wearing bedroom slippers with a three-piece suit, or a dressy blouse with cutoff jean shorts – sends a different message entirely. (Those substitution examples help to illustrate how a commutation test that substitutes signifiers for one another can shed insight into the meaning of a sign. The fact that nice shoes rather than fuzzy slippers are usually worn with a suit provides insight into the connotations of wearing such shoes.)

The semiotic analysis also should account for how the subject text relates to other texts, either within its own genre or as referring to other genres, in which semiotic codes (frames of reference that give a sign meaning) are employed around it, and what social context it seems to portray. This can be addressed by considering questions such as: Who created the sign? For whom was it intended? Whose realities does it represent and whose does it exclude? (Chandler, 2002).

Process and Ethics in Data Collection

Creswell (1998) says that data collection consists of a series of steps as outlined here, from locating the data-collection site and gaining access to it, to creating a purposive sample, to recording and storing the data, and finally analyzing and interpreting it. Anywhere along the way the qualitative researcher may need to resolve issues that arise in the field in relation to the process. Most importantly, Creswell emphasizes, is that the process is not linear. Often, the researcher will reach the end of this process and loop back to the beginning – or even re-enter the sequence somewhere other than the beginning – to add to the sample, or collect more data, or return to a previously visited field site to record additional details.

One final note that anyone interested in collecting qualitative data from individual subjects must keep in mind is that nearly all colleges and universities have detailed policies for how researchers and their subjects should interact, especially with the type of research described here. Often these policies are set and enforced by a campus committee called an institutional review board, or similar title. Even research done by students is often subject to what is known as "IRB approval."

These policies are usually meant to serve three purposes for research subjects. The first is to ensure that participants who are involved in a study do so under conditions of informed consent. In other words, they are told about the researcher's expectations for them (are informed) and participate willingly (give consent). Second, research subjects are usually entitled to some measure of confidentiality that must be spelled out for them as part of securing their informed consent. Finally, research ethics (as enforced by review boards) insist that no harm come to research subjects. It's easy to imagine types of research that might put research subjects significantly in harm's way, such as medical research or drug trials. Even in communication research, though, questions of harm can enter the discussion, and the standard for "harm" might be fairly low. For example, questions that could cause emotional difficulty for a subject, such as asking them about bad childhood memories or family trauma, could be considered harmful and a researcher might be restricted in collecting or using such data because of the potential impacts on the interviewees. Most research projects that would use the types of methods described in this chapter will need approval of the researcher's institutional review board before proceeding into the project.

Data Analysis

So what does it all *mean*? That is the essential question every researcher faces on every project when the time comes to evaluate all of the processes that have been followed and all of the data that have been collected. Without an effective answer to that question, the project cannot be called a success.

The time for assessing meaning is another point of difference between qualitative and quantitative research. Quantitative analysis must wait until all of the data has been collected. The results of a survey cannot be analyzed properly until the survey has closed and the last of its responses are logged in some sort of database because statistical analysis done without all of the cases in hand would be meaningless. Similarly, all of the stages of an experiment (pre-test, treatment, post-test) have to be finished and the data from them compiled before the results can be evaluated.

Qualitative data analysis proceeds similarly to Creswell's description of the data collection process as a "loop" that researchers might pass through multiple times. Warren and Karner (2015) note that analysis can start as soon as the first bits of data are in hand. They also say effective data analysis requires:

- "Thick" description in field notes or interview results, gathered over time.
- Good organization of the collected data to contextualize and retrieve it.
- Deep familiarity of the researcher with the data itself and the setting(s) in which it was collected.
- Ample time to engage with the data and conduct the analysis stage.

The central activity in analyzing qualitative data is identification of recurrent patterns or themes that give meaning to it by connecting with ideas or themes identified in the study's purpose and research questions. Marshall and Rossman say this process is "messy, ambiguous, time-consuming, creative and fascinating. It does not proceed in a linear fashion; it is not neat" (2011, p. 207). They lay out a six-step process for managing some of the ambiguity and messiness, which entails:

- Organizing the data.
- Reading and re-reading it.
- Generating categories and themes.
- Coding individual units (e.g., observations of particular events, snippets of interviews) according to those categories or themes.
- Interpreting meanings as this categorization takes place.
- Searching for alternate interpretations as a validity check.

A technique for inductively deriving categories and patterns recommended by Maykut and Morehouse (1994) is the constant comparative method, which works something like this:

Data are first organized and broken down into individual "units of meaning," such as single observations or clusters of related ones. These are then grouped according to category or theme on a rolling basis. In other words, the categories or themes are not predetermined but take shape as individual units are reviewed and categorized similarly based on loose criteria for association. If the researcher wants to create new categories, or collapse them, he or she is free to do so.

This "gut feel" assignment process will start to give shape to the data and tentatively identify associations and patterns. After a time, however, the reviewer should look back more closely at the items that have been associated with each other to identify common characteristics more precisely. This will help the researcher create more formal rules for categorization. Once all categories have these more formal criteria and all of the units have been categorized according to them, the search can begin for relationships and connections within the data to find the broader understandings that will address the research questions and purpose of the study.

In addition to the search for meaning in data, a key concern of any social science researcher is validity of the findings. Quantitative researchers rely on statistics to demonstrate this, with well-established procedures for precision of statistical estimates and things such as reliability of inter-coder agreement (as described in Chapter 8). Lacking such numerical validation, qualitative researchers rely on a different set of techniques to make sure the data support their interpretation and that they "haven't 'discovered' in their data only what [they] wanted to see" (Warren & Karner, 2015, p. 236). In a somewhat ironic analogy, Holliday says this process is akin to "showing the work" when solving a math problem. "Where the quantitative researcher needs to report details of established procedure, the qualitative researcher needs to justify every move – demonstrating particularly how the overall strategy is appropriate to the social setting and the researcher-subject relationship within it" (2002, p. 9). For example, clearly stating the formalized rules for categorization that the researcher developed at the sorting stage, and explaining how they emerged, are something the project report must include as part of "showing the work."

More recently, some qualitative researchers have begun to use special software to help with their data analysis. This can be helpful to organize information; for example, lengthy interviews can be entered into the software, which then searches for particular words and phrases that the subject used. Field notes, images, and videos can also be organized this way. Some of the more popular software includes NVivo, Atlas.ti, MAXQDA, and HyperRESEARCH. Students may have access to these and other similar tools through their school's computer services, and free programs and trials also are available. It should be noted, however, that most mass communication qualitative researchers are still employing the data analysis procedures described in this chapter.

Gathering data under authentic conditions, following systematic procedures so that important details are not missed, and being aware of the potential for the researcher to affect the results (if he or she is not careful) are other ways that qualitative researchers seek to improve the validity of their work. "Good qualitative work proceeds from an open mind, takes all available data into account as systematically as possible, is guided by a carefully chosen research question rather than the impulses of the researcher and makes a contribution to theory. ... In other words, qualitative work is as rigorous as quantitative work. Doing qualitative work is not the same as writing an opinion piece!" (Priest, 1996, p. 181).

CONCLUSION

Communication research, whether from a quantitative scientific-method perspective or a more qualitative/interpretive perspective, has a primary goal of providing the evidence that supports a researcher's claims, either stated through a formal hypothesis testable with empirical data or through an analytical, qualitative framework in which discovery of meaning is the primary goal. In either case, the carefulness of the researcher and the methods used to collect, compile and analyze the data are intricately related to the quality and outcome of the research project.

BOX 9.7

Mixed Methods Approach

The Tow Center for Digital Journalism at Columbia University's Graduate School of Journalism used a combination of qualitative and quantitative research to investigate how newsrooms are adapting to the rising influence of technology companies, specifically by partnering with sites such as Facebook, Google, Snapchat, and Twitter for news distribution. The qualitative portion consisted of interviews and a focus group; the quantitative part was a content analysis.

The research found that the shift to news distribution on social platforms had advanced further and faster than people in the news industry had expected over a short time span, concluding that "The increasing influence of a handful of West Coast [technology] companies is shaping every aspect of news production, distribution, and monetization." Lead researcher Emily Bell described the methodology that led to these findings this way:

> We spoke to more than 60 people who work in news organizations and platform companies, the majority through interviews, and a group of 15 social media managers through a round table[1] held at Columbia Journalism School. Interviewees and roundtable participants were all directly involved in the social distribution of news. We also conducted a week-long quantitative analysis of how publishers posted links or full articles across different platforms. (Bell, 2016)

Neither quantitative nor qualitative methods have a monopoly on wisdom in the field. Both are used widely, and the proper method to be employed depends on the nature of the project and what the researcher hopes to demonstrate. Numerical analyses and hypothesis testing remain the most popular ways of conducting communication research, but not everything can or should be researched that way. One of the first things the researcher must do in designing a project is think about exactly what he or she hopes to learn from it, then select the methods that will be the best ones for that purpose.

Effective research can use multiple methodologies as well. Morris Janowitz's ground-breaking research (1952) about the urban community press in Chicago combined surveys, content analyses, and in-depth interviews of two different types of subjects (journalists and readers). Paterson's similar, but more recent (2011), study did the same for international news media. One of the authors of this book actually combined these methods in a study of how to engage transfer students in mass communication programs. She did a survey of more than 600 communication majors from colleges and universities across the country asking about whether they were native students (came in as freshmen) or transfer students. The survey also asked what communication organizations they were involved in, such as the campus radio station, PRSSA, internships, etc. At the end of the survey, students were asked if they would be willing to be interviewed by the researcher. In the second part of the study, 30 students had conversations lasting between 15 and 30 minutes with the researcher about their experiences and their ideas for getting more transfer students involved in their major in the future (Vicker, 2015).

While mixed methods can be a productive approach, Morgan (2014) points out that because relatively few studies follow this approach, researchers often will need to explain why they have adopted it. The best way to do this is to explain why the integration of the two methods is superior to a single approach by itself. Most surveys are quantitative instruments, with meaning in the data determined by numerical tallies and statistical analysis. Many surveys also include open-ended responses, which are a form of qualitative data and can augment and deepen the researcher's understanding about what the numbers from the closed-ended questions really mean. Likewise, a numerical content analysis could document evidence of stereotyping with quantities or proportions of statements that reflect stereotypical views. Defining and operationalizing what constitutes a stereotype or the impacts on people who are stereotyped, however, is a job for qualitative analysis. Thus, research that combines quantitative and qualitative methods can yield insights that neither approach can reveal on its own.

Discussion Questions/Application Exercises

1.. Conduct a qualitative observation exercise by visiting a dining hall, student union, residence hall lounge, or some other place where people gather and interact. Spend about an hour observing and making detailed notes on your observations. Afterward, re-read your notes several times and try to identify some themes that would summarize the activity you observed.

2.. The chapter offers several examples of published research using the techniques of qualitative research. Look through several editions of a scholarly journal that publishes research about media topics, such as *Journalism & Mass Communication Quarterly*, to find additional examples. Try to locate articles that employ each of the data collection methods outlined in this chapter (participant observation, in-depth individual interviews, focus group interviews and qualitative content analysis). In what ways are the methods appropriate for getting data that answer the research questions? What sorts of points do the authors make in validating their findings?

NOTE

1 What Bell calls a round table would have worked very much like a focus group.

REFERENCES

Altheide, D. (1996). *Qualitative media analysis*. Thousand Oaks, CA: Sage Publications.

Anido Freire, N. (2014). When luxury advertising adds the identitary values of luxury: A semiotic analysis. *Journal of Business Research 67*, 2666–2675. doi: 10.1016/j.jbusres.2014.04.004

Argyris, C. (1974). *Behind the front page: Organizational self-renewal in a metropolitan newspaper*. Jossey-Bass.

Bell, E. (2016, June 21). Who owns the news consumer: Social media platforms or publishers? Retrieved from http://www.cjr.org/tow_center/platforms_and_publishers_new_research_from_the_tow_center.php#.

Berger, A.A. (2000). *Media and communication research methods*. Thousand Oaks, CA: Sage Publications.

Chaffee, S.H. & Berger, C.R. (1987). The study of communication as a science. In Berger, C.R. & Chaffee, S.H. (Eds.). *Handbook of communication science* (pp. 15–19). Newbury Park, CA: Sage Publications.

Chandler, D. (2002). *Semiotics: The basics*. New York: Routledge.

Creswell, J.W. (1998). *Qualitative inquiry and design: Choosing among five traditions*. Thousand Oaks, CA: Sage.

De Vaus, D.A. (2001). *Research design in social research*. London: Sage.

Everbach, T. (2006) The culture of a women-led newspaper: An ethnographic study of the Sarasota Herald-Tribune. *Journalism & Mass Communication Quarterly 83* (3), 477–493.

Felicia, O. (2019). A social semiotic analysis of gender power in Nigeria's newspaper political cartoons. *Social Semiotics 31*(1), 1–16.

Grow, J.M. (2006). Stories of community: The first ten years of Nike women's advertising. *The American Journal of Semiotics 22* (1-4), 167–198.

Grow, J.M., Park, J.S. & Han X. (2006, April). Your life is waiting!: Symbolic meanings in direct-to-consumer antidepressant advertising. *The Journal of Communication Inquiry 30* (2), 163ff.

Holliday, A. (2002). *Doing and writing qualitative research*. London: Sage Publications.

Janowitz, M. (1952). *The community press in an urban setting: The social elements of urbanism*. Chicago: University of Chicago Press.

Lindlof, T.R. (1995). *Qualitative communication research methods*. Thousand Oaks, CA: Sage Publications.

Marshall, C. & Rossman, G.B. (2011). *Designing qualitative research* (5th ed.). Thousand Oaks, CA: Sage Publications.

Maykut, P. & Morehouse, R. (1994). *Beginning qualitative research: A philosophical and practical guide*. London: Routledge/Falmer.

Miles, M.B. & Huberman, A.M. (1994). *Qualitative data analysis* (2nd ed.). Thousand Oaks, CA: Sage Publications.

Morgan, D. (2014). *Integrating qualitative and quantitative methods: A pragmatic approach*. Los Angeles: Sage.

Paterson, C. (2011). *The international television news agencies: The world from London*. New York: Peter Lang.

Patton, M.Q. (1990). *Qualitative evaluation and research methods* (2nd ed.). Beverly Hills CA: Sage Publications.

Poindexter, P. & McCombs, M. (2000). *Research in mass communication: A practical guide.* Boston: Bedford/St. Martins.

Polidoro, P. (2016). Serial sacrifices: A semiotic analysis of Downton Abbey ideology. *Between* 6(11).

Priest, S.H. (1996). *Doing media research: An introduction.* Thousand Oaks, CA: Sage Publications.

Ryfe, D.M. (2009). Broader and deeper: A study of newsroom culture in a time of change. *Journalism* 10 (2), 197–216.

Singer, J.B. (2009). Ethnography. *Journalism & Mass Communication Quarterly* 86 (1), 191–198.

Thaller, J. & Messing, J.T. (2014). (Mis)perceptions around intimate partner violence in the music video and lyrics for "Love the Way You Lie." *Feminist Media Studies* 14 (4), 623–639.

Trochim, W. (2005). *The research methods knowledge base* (2nd ed.). Retrieved from http://www.socialresearchmethods.net/kb/qual.htm.

Vicker, L. (2015). Revisiting "Entering the game at halftime:" An examination of how we engage mass communication students in internships and co-curricular activities. Paper presented to the annual meeting of the Association for Education in Journalism and Mass Communication, San Francisco.

Warren, C.A.B. & Karner T.X. (2015). *Discovering qualitative methods: Ethnography, documents, and images.* New York: Oxford University Press.

CHAPTER 10

Beyond Theory and Research

Taking What You've Learned to the Real World of Work

A generation ago, media and communication students found it fairly straightforward to use the skills and knowledge from their college work to find a meaningful career after graduation. Some students developed an interest in working as journalists for newspapers, magazines, radio, or television. In broadcasting, this could mean working as "talent" (the on-air reporters) or in production (the behind-the-scenes workers for the news show). Other students went to work in ad agencies, either on the creative side (developing the content of print and broadcast ads) or on the client-services side (helping the agency plan and execute campaigns). Still others found jobs with public relations agencies that were structured pretty much the same way. Some with interests in PR went to work for organizations, from major corporations to government agencies to small non-profit outfits, helping to craft the image for those employers. Some students found careers in book publishing, entertainment television, documentary or entertainment filmmaking, or sports broadcasting, to name a few popular destinations.

The work was varied but in each of these cases, the pathway of education to career was fairly well-defined because it led into distinct, robust organizations such as newspapers, TV stations, PR or advertising agencies, corporate communications departments, etc. The idea of "convergence," either of the content offered by media organizations or of the skills needed by media workers, had not yet emerged. That didn't mean there were no overlaps; the writing-based education of a journalism student created a skillset that was valuable in public relations. Knowing how to shoot and edit video could be a qualification for working on a movie set or for a sports broadcast. Jobs did, though, tend to exist in certain "silos;" media education was oriented around those silos, and students found work in them fairly readily.

All of this changed with the disruptive emergence of the Internet in the late 20th and early 21st centuries. In 1990, few people had heard of the Internet. At that time, it mostly connected computers on a few dozen college campuses and was just a few years removed from its beginnings as a U.S. Defense Department experiment in communicating over a computer network. The World Wide Web had been created only a year earlier, in 1989, so only a few hundred websites existed. By the mid-1990s, though, the

DOI: 10.4324/9781003121695-10

Internet started to reach the general public through new services such as America Online. These providers allowed people to access the web from their home computers via telephone lines. By the turn of the century just a few years later, the first "dot.com boom" had begun to change the way people accessed and shared information. Suddenly, content could be produced and distributed in new and different ways, and shared over great distances with minimal costs or friction. This was destined to have major implications for old-line media industries, especially those supported by advertising. That was because the Internet also gave advertisers new and different ways to reach audiences.

Then came the real game-changer: The rise of the mobile internet. Mobile telephony began in the 1970s with the development of technology that let phones connect to different short-distance transmitting towers as they came into range, and then be "handed off" to a different tower as they moved without interrupting the call. (These short-distance transmitters were called "cells," leading to the terms "cell phone" and "cellular service.") Power needs meant most early mobile phones were installed in cars, although an iconic scene from the 1987 movie *Wall Street* shows the central character, a wealthy stock trader, walking on a beach with a mobile phone that looks like a World War II-era "walkie-talkie" radio. Fast-forward 20 years from that image to 2007, and Apple introduced the iPhone, the first true "smartphone" that could do more than make voice calls and send text messages. A year later, in 2008, the first phones running the alternative Android system appeared. Having Internet-enabled devices with them most of the time meant people spent even more time online and within ten years, by 2017, half of all Internet traffic was coming from mobile devices (Clement, 2020). It was clear that for many people, technology had shifted "from some devices and platforms we use to an entire environment in which we function" (Rushkoff, 2019).

The implications of this for today's study of media and communication and the career choices for those who pursue that study are profound. This chapter examines contemporary trends in media businesses and operations to help students understand that environment better, followed by some practical advice for landing that first job or internship.

A (VERY) BRIEF HISTORY OF COMMERCIAL MEDIA

While many students find interesting and fulfilling careers in the non-profit sector, the vast majority of career opportunities are with commercial enterprises, from major transnational corporations down to small local ones or even startups. (Some students may even aspire to launch a startup themselves; media entrepreneurship is discussed later in the chapter). As with other places in this book, the discussion starts with some historical precedents that offer context for the contemporary situation.

Advertising-Supported Content

The beginnings of commercial media trace to the rise of the "penny press" in the mid-19th century, so-called because it consisted of newspapers that cost just one cent. The commercial innovation of the penny papers was that they appealed to a wide range of readers, in contrast with other newspapers of the era directed toward readers with a particular political viewpoint (called partisan press) or ones meant for wealthy, elite readers, such as business owners, who paid significantly more than a penny a copy for publications that provided specialized information. As the penny papers began to serve a mass market, those business owners came to realize it could be worthwhile to partner with the publishers to get their messages to that large audience, which is how advertising first developed.

When electronic media emerged a few decades later, in the 1920s, different ideas for how to support it developed on opposite sides of the Atlantic Ocean. In the United Kingdom, the British Broadcasting Corp. (BBC) was granted a royal charter and other government support so that it could operate without advertising, which holds true to this day. Other European public-service broadcasters were established soon after, following the same model of government charter and support although some, such as Ireland's Raidió Teilifís Éireann (RTÉ), have hybrid models that accept advertising. In the United States, however, a purely commercial system formed. The Federal Communications Commission (FCC) provided some degree of regulation, mostly of the broadcast technology, to allocate the spectrum so radio and television stations could operate without interfering with each other. The government didn't fund the outlets or regulate them financially, however, leading to a system in which nearly all U.S. radio and, later, television programming was supported by advertising.

For nearly 150 years from the founding of the penny press through the early years of the Internet, businesses selling everything from cars to clothes to personal care products used primarily print and broadcast advertising to inform people of what they had to offer and persuade them to buy it. Some money went to promotion methods such as mailed catalogs or billboards, but the majority of advertising dollars went to mass media outlets for ads to appear alongside news and entertainment content. It was a mutually beneficial relationship: Print or broadcast outlets gathered the audience for the advertisers, and the revenue from advertisements supported the work of creating the content that drew those audiences. Advertising agencies were founded to help match outlets and advertisers by creating and placing ads in exchange for a commission. This system also proved to be lucrative for the publishers and the agencies. It was worthwhile for the advertisers, too, even if not very efficient. Department store owner John Wanamaker supposedly quipped "Half the money I spend on advertising is wasted; the trouble is I don't know which half" (Bradt, 2016).

Even though newspapers and magazines had people paying for subscriptions, they still derived most of their revenue from advertising – money that helped pay the salaries of reporters and editors, among other things, and still left a tidy profit for the publishers. Radio and television were essentially 100 percent advertising supported until cable television emerged, adding subscription revenue for some broadcast offerings. Even then, free broadcast TV was available alongside cable with ad revenue covering the production costs of everything from local news and talk shows to sitcoms, dramas, news, sports, and other shows on the national networks. For most of these businesses, profit margins were large, and jobs for media students were plentiful. Life was good.

Commercial Growth

President Calvin Coolidge once famously remarked that "The business of the American people is business" (Bartlett, 1980, p. 736). Ironically, he made this statement during an address to the American Society of Newspaper Editors at a time when the media really were *not* major business operations. When Coolidge said this in 1925, television had not been commercialized and radio was in its infancy, a small industry of local operators. Among the dominant mass medium of the day – newspapers – most were family-owned enterprises serving local markets. Newspaper chains and other media conglomerates would not develop for several decades.

Since Coolidge's day, however, media industries have become more corporate, more diversified (as new technologies created new media forms), and much larger. When journalist and media critic Ben Bagdikian published the first edition of his classic work *The Media Monopoly* in 1983, he warned of growing media concentration by noting that about 50 major corporations – newspaper chains, magazine groups, TV networks – controlled most mass media production in the United States. The book was revised through seven editions over 21 years and with each revision, the number shrank from 50 to progressively smaller numbers. In the final version, Bagdikian (2004) identified a "big five" set of conglomerates that each owned operations across the media spectrum: Broadcast, cable, and satellite TV; newspapers and magazines; movie studios; and radio-station groups.

A similarly small number of companies dominate today's media environment, but in a different way. The "big five" that Bagdikian identified are still recognizable as major players in media, including Disney, Viacom (now Viacom/CBS), and Fox. Nowhere on that 2004 list would readers have found Facebook (which was founded that year), Apple (still a maker of desktop computers at that point), Google (which became a public company that year), or Amazon (then largely an online book retailer). Now, those are the household names with more market power than the ones Bagdikian identified in 2004.

This growth and conglomeration of traditional media documented by Bagdikian was facilitated in part by passage of the Telecommunications Act of 1996. This major rewrite of federal communication law substantially changed regulation of media ownership in general, and broadcast-station ownership in particular. It also contained a regulation, known as Section 230, giving broad authority to Internet content providers to operate largely in their own best interest. This stood in sharp contrast to the FCC requiring broadcasters to act "in the public interest, convenience and necessity."

Before the 1996 law was enacted, the government had strict limits on the types of communication operations that could be owned or controlled by a single business. For example, federal law required telephone, cable, and Internet providers to remain separate from each other. Even though all three industries ran wires into people's homes, none of them could offer multiple services. Companies in those industries couldn't own broadcast stations, either. In fact, FCC regulations strictly controlled the number of radio and TV stations one owner could have in a single market, and also capped the number that could be held nationwide. However, under the 1996 Telecom Act, these structural regulations were relaxed or in some cases eliminated, leading to the current phenomenon of most markets having a dominant local company offering bundled phone, Internet, and cable television service and creating situations where one or two large conglomerates own most of the radio and TV stations operating in a local broadcast market.

The important thing to recognize about this for college students thinking about a career is how many organizations that seem to be local might really be part of one of these major conglomerates. In the authors' home area, for example, local TV stations are a popular destination for students with an interest in journalism and video work; all of the local network-affiliate stations employ graduates of the school where the authors teach. However, these local outlets actually are owned by some of the largest companies in the industry. Three of the four network affiliates at the time of this writing were associated with either the Nexstar Broadcasting Group or Sinclair Broadcast Group, both among the nation's largest TV station ownership groups. Similarly, the local daily newspaper and several weekly papers are part of the USA Today Network (Gannett Corp.), the nation's largest, and most of the radio stations in the market are owned by the country's two largest radio groups, Entercom and iHeartRadio. (All affiliations are current as of early 2021.) Many students will find the markets where they grew up or where their school is located have similar structures. The same pattern holds in many other industries aside from journalism and broadcasting, especially book publishing, which is dominated by a handful of European firms, and entertainment media such as movies, television, and music.

Digital Disruption of Business Models

The Internet has changed how media firms develop and share content, but the implications go further because of the disruption it has brought to the dominant paradigm of advertising paying for content production across most media industries. This traditional model has been upended by targeted digital advertising that can be distributed with precision and tracked with online metrics. As social media led people to spend progressively more time online, advertisers became even more interested in this way of reaching the public. Students who fail to understand these changing business models do so at their own peril.

The disruption began with newspapers, whose classified advertising sections were almost literally a license to print money. For around 100 years, from the late 19th to the late 20th century, newspapers universally featured page upon page of densely packed, text-only ads selling cars, real estate, household merchandise, and more. Because individual ads could be purchased relatively cheaply, yet still reach all of the newspaper's readers, they were the main way individuals with something to sell, such as a used car, could advertise. Businesses also used classifieds to advertise job openings (often called "help wanted" ads) and some products and services. Although each individual ad was relatively inexpensive, collectively they meant big money for the newspapers simply because they were purchased in such great volume.

In 1996, however, entrepreneur Craig Newmark began offering an online version of this community marketplace, first in San Francisco and later in markets around the United States and the rest of the world. Newmark's key innovation was that ads could be placed at no cost to the person taking the ad unless the merchandise was sold, in which case Craigslist (as the service was known) took a commission. Businesses could purchase ads, like they did in the newspaper. The online format also allowed ads to be sorted and searched more easily. The combination of being free for most users, and the searchability, made Craigslist hugely popular. It quickly siphoned off a great amount of newspaper advertising as people with a bicycle or bed frame to sell turned to Craigslist rather than buying a newspaper classified. Newmark became a billionaire, and online listings soon supplanted newspaper classifieds as the main source of consumer-to-consumer advertising. Later, consumer marketplace sites such as eBay and Facebook Marketplace developed, along with niche sites that functioned similar to Craigslist for areas that had once dominated the newspaper classifieds. These included ads for vehicles (Cars.com and Autotrader), employment (Monster.com and Indeed), and real estate (HomeFinder and Zillow). Today, it's rare to find more than a handful of classified ads in most print newspapers.

More disruptive still – to all media, not just newspapers – was digital advertising associated with search engines and social media platforms. Early digital advertising was primarily display placements, similar to newspaper and magazine ads, and pop-up ads. Advertisers found the static ads ineffective, because they were too easily ignored, while site users hated pop-ups because they were annoying. Both of these styles of digital ads still exist, but by far the dominant way that advertisers now reach their audiences is with targeted advertising that appears with content that has already drawn a user's attention. The leaders in this are Google and Facebook, which use algorithms to target ads ever more precisely to their users, based on information derived from tracking a user's activity. Everyone who has done a Google search has seen the "related ads" atop or alongside the results, and many young people (especially women) who have changed their Facebook status to "engaged" have suddenly begun to see wedding planning ads alongside their news feed.

These changes in the market for advertising dramatically affected the ad-revenue-based business models for traditional media. They also affect students interested in entering advertising, and the related fields of marketing and strategic communication, because workers who understand how to target audiences and interpret the analytics of audience behavior are in high demand. Targeted search and social ads have become the dominant way for advertisers to reach their audiences today, accounting for more than half of all U.S. advertising spending in 2020. Approximately two thirds of that money – meaning one third of all U.S. advertising revenue – went to just three firms: Google, Facebook and Amazon (Soto Reyes, 2020). Similarly, the United Kingdom's Competition and Markets Authority reports that Google accounts for more than 90 percent of the country's search-advertising revenues and Facebook for half the value of all its display ads (Schumpeter, 2020).

Summary

The combination of factors described in this section – consolidated ownership of media outlets into large corporations offering an assortment of content, combined with digital disruption of traditional content approaches and also of the advertising models that funded those organizations – has dramatically changed the nature of media work available today. The types of jobs and career paths described at the beginning of this chapter, for all practical purposes, no longer exist. The next section explores the technology of this disruption further and describes some of the specific impacts on journalism, advertising/public relations, and other types of media work.

MEDIA WORK IN THE INTERCONNECTED AGE

Young people today, including most college students, are often described as "digital natives" because the environment they live in has always included the Internet and online communication. Most have literally grown up with a smart phone in their hands and have integrated it into their lives (Rushkoff, 2019). This can make it difficult for them to examine the implications of online technology and social media from an independent perspective because they have no frame of reference to any time when the environment was different. Even digital natives, though, should be aware of some things about modern media technology that might not be readily apparent.

Technology and Media

An important, but sometimes underrated, implication of the hyperconnected world of the Internet is that for the first time in human history social sharing allows anyone to create content that – hypothetically, at least – can be seen by millions of people. Of course, most online postings don't have that much reach unless they are made by a celebrity user who has millions of followers on a social site such as Twitter or Instagram. A.J. Liebling, a mid-20th century American journalist, was famously quoted as saying that freedom of the press belonged to the person who owned it. He meant this literally, as in a newspaper printing press. He was, moreover, correct for his era; at that time printing and broadcast facilities were rare and expensive, meaning those who controlled them controlled the reach of most media messages. (Critical theories of media based in a political economy approach as discussed in Chapter 5 are built on this idea.) Today, any post by anyone could be widely seen if it goes viral. Swedish teenager Greta Thunberg, who became world famous for her advocacy against climate change on social media, stands out as an example. Emma Gonzalez, David Hogg and some of their classmates are another example, for the attention they received for their advocacy against gun violence after a shooting at their school in Parkland, Florida (Bromwich, 2018).

More commonly, this development opens up the media system to a platform for user-generated content to become part of everyone's media mix. This same open access to media content production also means the process of "gatekeeping," in which those with access to the means of production control what can be published, has been eroded. It's not quite correct to say gatekeeping has ended because large traditional media outlets such as major newspapers and national broadcast networks still exist, and also because individuals and organizations with massive social media followings exert powerful influence over what many people see and experience online. An Instagram post by Ariana Grande, Kylie Jenner, or Selena Gomez (all with more than 200 million followers) is going to be viewed more than a post by an average college sophomore. Even still, unlike in Liebling's time, the sophomore has the ability to post content for the whole world potentially to see – as Greta Thunberg and the Parkland students demonstrated.

Another powerful influence is the impact of social media algorithms on the content of individual feeds and topics or items that "trend" or go viral. These algorithms are designed to promote emotionally engaging content, because those characteristics are more likely to draw a reaction from a recipient. Those reactions cause further sharing, creating a snowball effect that leads to something "going viral" through sharing far beyond the followers of the person who posted it.

The key concept implicit in all of this discussion is that online technology has become a tool of disintermediation. As noted in the introductory discussion of mass media in Chapter 1, the term "media" means "in between." The term is appropriate for print or broadcast content producers because they are the "middlemen" through which people learn about the world outside their direct experience. Traditional media – often referred to as "legacy" media – still do that, but not as completely or powerfully as they once did because they no longer have a monopoly on gatekeeping when peer-to-peer online capacity lets individual users reach audiences in new ways. An Instagram "influencer" can draw as much or more attention to an idea or product than an entire ad campaign in print or broadcast might have a generation ago. The development of technology that allows widespread content sharing without the complicated and expensive hardware of legacy media and the resulting diminishment of gatekeeping has had profound effects.

An expanded range of devices and places for consuming content is another development whose importance has perhaps been under-appreciated. It is no longer necessary to be seated in front of a television or near a radio, at a particular time, to see and hear favorite programming, or even to be seated at a computer to enjoy digital entertainment. The combination of on-demand access to content on mobile devices is another major disruption from earlier years, giving new meaning and relevance to the concept of the active audience discussed in Chapter 3. These new patterns of media access and consumption have important implications for the media-production work that is central to careers most communication students are interested in pursuing.

Considering Careers in Journalism

Special concern about the impact of online content and digital disruption of legacy media has been focused on journalism. This is largely because of the important role journalism plays in society, as discussed by Siebert, Peterson and Schramm's Social Responsibility Theory (Peterson, 1956). All legacy media have suffered declining revenue as Google and Facebook have pulled so much advertising spending away from traditional outlets. However, starting with the impact of Craigslist on classifieds, and continuing through the growth of targeted online spending, the loss of advertising support has changed journalism's business model most of all. Even though newspapers sold copies to readers, most of the revenue they earned to pay the costs of producing the news came from advertising. Compounding this, greater reliance on social platforms for news gathering makes audience members reluctant to pay for news as they once did; the expectation is that news content should be free, the same as other posts in their feed. So, despite the use of "paywalls" that require readers to pay for access, most legacy news organizations have had difficulty replacing lost print-ad revenue with enough earnings from subscriptions or digital ads to pay for producing the amount of news that was common from them in years past.

These forces have affected journalism in two main ways. First, a significant number of local newspapers – more than 2,000 of them between 2004 and 2019 – have simply gone out of business because they could no longer afford to operate (McIntyre, 2019). In addition, surviving papers have suffered from a hollowing out of their newsrooms because they cannot afford to employ as many reporters and editors. Data from the Pew Research Center documented that the number of newsroom jobs in 2020 was only about half of what existed in 2008 (Grieco, 2020). This has led to the rise of "news deserts," where no local news source can be found, and "ghost papers" that still publish, but with little meaningful news content (Abernathy, 2020).

Two counter-trends that have emerged in reaction to this could help journalism, providing hopeful signs for students interested in careers as journalists. One is a growth of alternate funding sources to offset the decline of advertising revenue. These include subscription or membership models that have emerged to support the work of journalists financially, although these have been most effective for certain major organizations such as *The New York Times, Washington Post,* and *Wall Street Journal.* Other news organizations, including the U.K.-based *Guardian,* have had some success with volunteer payments supplementing subscription revenue. Importantly, these approaches only work for outlets that provide substantial content that audiences think is valuable and therefore worth the cost; smaller local and regional publishers have not had much success with these strategies.

Another growing source of support for journalism comes from non-profit approaches. Some news organizations, such as *ProPublica,* the *Texas Tribune,* and even the *Philadelphia Inquirer* are operated as non-profit organizations. *The 19th* is a non-profit online newsroom focused on coverage of women, people of color and the LGBTQ+ communities. Report for America is a non-profit organization that recruits and pays some of the costs for reporters that are then placed in local newsrooms around the country. Much of its funding comes from organizations such as the Lenfest Foundation, Knight Foundation, and Craig Newmark Foundation. The Institute for Nonprofit News (https://inn.org) has a roster of more than 240 affiliated organizations. Outside of the U.S., the European Journalism Centre has worked with 230 media partners to make more than €4 million worth of grants that support creative reporting projects and spent €1.2 million to strengthen the watchdog role of investigative journalism in Europe (ejc.net/grants). Foundation support is augmented by some corporate support as well, such as the Google News Initiative, which has made grants to more than 5,000 newsrooms in Latin America, Africa, Asia, Europe and the United States (Schiffrin, 2021).

A second trend in journalism that's rested on the growth of the Internet is outlets that publish only online, which can be done far more cheaply than print media. They still have the cost of paying the journalists producing the content, but overall operate at far lower cost because they don't pay for printing presses, paper, or distribution costs. Examples of these at the national level include *Vox, Axios,* and *Buzzfeed.* A growing number of such organizations are also emerging at the local level. In the United States, the trade association Local Independent Online News (LION) Publishers lists more than 300 members, while in the United Kingdom the Independent Community News Network based at Cardiff University in Wales lists more than 125 local news sites as members.

Online access also makes it easier to review news from a wider geographic range of outlets than in decades past. Few printed newspapers are delivered outside of a radius of about 50 miles from their home cities, making it impractical to read news published far from where the reader lives. Until *USA Today* was launched in 1982, the United States did not have a truly national newspaper. National print papers were and are more common in Europe, where countries are geographically smaller. Now, because virtually every newspaper regardless of size or location has a website, that geographic barrier no longer exists. The *Washington Post* and *The New York Times* have become truly national (even international) news outlets online, especially with regard to their public affairs coverage. Many U.S. news consumers in return look to international online sources such as *The Guardian* or the BBC for an international perspective on domestic affairs.

In summary, while the online environment's impact on advertising support of legacy media has damaged journalism's business model, new ideas are emerging to help fulfill journalism's social responsibility role. In a famous essay, New York University professor Clay Shirky speculated on the end of the legacy newspaper business as its advertising model collapsed because of the Internet. At the time, the idea that newspapers could disappear was feared and lamented. As Shirky observed, "Society doesn't need newspapers. What we need is journalism" (Shirky, 2009, p. 29). His suggestion for preserving journalism was that "nothing will work, but everything might" (p. 29). What he meant was that no single thing was likely to emerge to replace the public service function newspapers had served, but that experimentation in the field could create many new approaches, each doing a portion of the work – and collectively meeting society's information needs the way that newspaper journalism had for much of the 20th century. With the rise of subscription and membership models, non-profit support, and entrepreneurial efforts represented by the LION and ICNN groups, what Shirky predicted in 2009 may be coming to pass. Disintermediation also creates opportunities for free-lance writers or videographers with journalistic interests to create and post work independently, and new formats such as podcasts and email newsletters provide ways to reach audiences who aren't inclined to visit a website. These changes make for a different career path than the one straight to a print or broadcast newsroom a couple of decades ago, but the changes offer new and different opportunities for students who want to work as journalists.

Considering Careers in Advertising and Public Relations

As previously discussed, one of the most significant impacts of the growth of online media over the past couple of decades has been a shift to search-based and social media ads as the main magnets for advertising revenue. Advertisers (and their spending) migrated to those locations because platform algorithms focused on engagement and virality can reach huge audiences while also delivering relevant, targeted ads. In 2020, for the first time, online advertising accounted for more than half of all U.S. ad spending, with two-thirds of that (or about one third of total spending) going to Google, Facebook, and Amazon (Soto Reyes, 2020). This has caused a change in the advertising agency business model that for many decades was based on taking a commission for advertisements produced and placed into legacy media on clients' behalf. However, the use of algorithms has created new opportunities for agencies to design and deliver more precisely targeted ads and also created new roles within the agencies for individuals with an understanding of web analytics to design the targeted campaigns and track their results.

The disintermediated peer-to-peer aspect of online sharing also creates new ways for using advertising to pay for content creation. A good example is YouTube entertainment stars or "influencers," who single-handedly draw enough of an audience to earn money from ads that appear with the videos they produce. The more popular the videos are, the more the ads are viewed – with each new view adding to the video creator's total take. It's now possible to make a career from getting enough of a YouTube or Instagram following to monetize the content work with advertisements, brand-affiliation deals, and product placements.

Online virality also can spread clever advertising messages in effective ways. One of the most noteworthy examples of this was when a power outage at the stadium delayed the 2013 Super Bowl for more than 30 minutes. Quick thinking advertising managers for Oreo cookies created a photo captioned "You can still dunk in the dark" and posted it on Oreo's social media sites while the blackout was underway. It won the Internet that night, being retweeted almost 15,000 times and increasing Oreo's Twitter following by about 8,000. It also got nearly 20,000 likes on Facebook and helped build the brand's Instagram followers from 2,000 to 36,000 literally overnight (Rooney, 2013).

The emergence and growth of social media also has had a major impact on public relations practice. The Public Relations Society of America, an organization for PR practitioners, defines public relations as "a strategic communication process that builds mutually beneficial relationships between organizations and their publics" (PRSA, 2012). In other words, it's all about connection and engagement, which the online environment has changed dramatically.

The most traditional function of public relations work was – and still is – the quest for "earned media," or coverage by news outlets. PR practitioners cultivate what the definition calls "mutually beneficial relationships" with journalists because news coverage can affect the image or public perception of an organization. Because of this, knowing how the online environment has disrupted journalism, as explained in the previous section, is also important for students interested in PR work. Even more importantly, online tools can reach key publics directly, which means public relations efforts no longer need to rely as much on third parties such as journalists. News releases, blogs, podcasts, and videos posted on organizations' websites and sent through social media channels allow for distribution of messages without legacy media involvement. An increasing share of public relations efforts are going into this work.

Social media, in particular, offers both benefits and challenges for contemporary public relations work. Increasingly, in-house public relations staff and agencies working on behalf of clients focus their efforts on managing an organization's social media presence across multiple platforms. This offers real-time, peer-to-peer prospects for building engagement with members of those key publics. It also can be an important source of feedback about how the PR effort is succeeding by hearing directly from members of the public. Social media sharing, however, can present a challenge for those charged with promoting and managing an organization's image when negative information starts circulating. A standard part of every public relations staff's repertoire is crisis communications, or reacting to minimize the damage when something happens that could hurt the organization's reputation. However, the viral nature of social media can cause bad information to be shared so widely and so rapidly that an organization's PR staff might be unable to keep pace.

One recent example of an organization facing a crisis response was Boeing, which needed to address production flaws that had caused fatal crashes of its new 737 Max airplane, leading to the plane being grounded for months (Kitterman, 2019). In the age of COVID, many organizations, including many colleges and universities, also have had to address crises in their reporting of positive cases on campus as well as procedures for keeping students, faculty, and staff safe. In a lighter vein, Kentucky Fried Chicken had a crisis to manage when its restaurants across the United Kingdom and Ireland ran out of … chicken. The KFC example though, came to be seen as a model response to such a crisis because it demonstrated how a social media campaign can lessen the impact of bad news. In this case, KFC used social media to keep customers posted on its efforts to restock the restaurants. The campaign had a humorous edge, using modified images of the company's KFC logo – on an empty bucket – to identify what happened as a "FCK" up (Petroff, 2018).

As noted in the discussion of career prospects at the end of the previous section on journalism, students interested in advertising, public relations, or marketing – which are increasingly studied together under the umbrella of strategic communication – may not find obvious paths into an entry-level agency or corporate communication role as their predecessors were able to do a few years ago. Understanding how the nature of online communication has changed the roles and functions of advertising and PR organizations and those who work in them can help them find the route to such careers.

Considering Careers in Entertainment media

When Harold Lasswell developed one of the earliest theories of mass media, he described its social functions as surveillance of the environment, correlation of responses to that environment, and transmission of cultural heritage. These fall squarely within the work of journalism. Lasswell's protege Charles Wright later expanded the theory, adding entertainment as a key function. This made the theory far more robust and complete, because people spend far more time using media for entertainment than for any of the original three purposes Lasswell had outlined.

From their earliest days, newspapers provided not only the news (fulfilling the surveillance function), but puzzles, comics, and serialized novels to entertain readers as well. The first "non-print" mass media to be developed, movies and phonographs, also had entertainment as their central purpose. When radio, and later television, came on the scene, news was part of the programming. However, far more airtime was devoted to music, dramas, comedies, quiz shows, and the like. Even today, the major broadcast networks air three to four hours of primetime entertainment programs every night, but only 30 minutes of news. Some of the thousands of radio stations in the United States have news or news-talk formats, but far more play mostly music across many styles to keep listeners entertained. A few influential news magazines have had strong reader-ship, but they were far outnumbered by magazines devoted to fashion, hobbies, and other entertaining topics. Clearly, without entertainment in the list, a functional de-scription of mass-media purposes would be incomplete. Yet, like other forms of communication, the online environment has changed entertainment as well.

The Internet's disruption of the entertainment space was preceded by another form of technological disruption, which was the development of cable television in the 1970s. Prior to cable's arrival, broadcast content – still focused largely on entertain-ment – came over the airwaves, free to the user. Aside from a few non-profit outlets, such as public broadcasting affiliates, these broadcasts were 100 percent advertising supported. However, the choices were limited. Strict FCC control of broadcast licenses meant most markets had only a handful of radio and televisions stations, mostly airing similar entertainment programming geared toward the broadest possible audiences. (See discussion of commoditized television in Chapter 5). Cable had the bandwidth to deliver far more programming options, at a price. Many people willingly paid that price to expand their entertainment choices, creating a hybrid subscription-advertising revenue stream like print media of the time. A typical roster of cable offerings included network broadcast affiliates but also specialty channels devoted to news, sports, mo-vies, shopping, and niche interests such as history, cooking, or travel programs.

The first entertainment medium to be disrupted specifically by the Internet was music, where digital music files allowed for the separation of the content (songs) from the physical media needed to play them (vinyl albums, cassette tapes, or digital com-pact discs). The end result was far more flexible listening. This started with peer-to-peer sharing of digitized tunes, followed by unbundled purchases via iTunes, and later expanded into streaming services such as Pandora and Spotify. Now, this model of unbundled, on-demand offerings that was pioneered with music has expanded into other types of entertainment content, most notably streaming video and podcasts.

The single-subscription cable model for a bundle of programming choices the consumer did not control has lost popularity, replaced by many consumers with a la carte subscriptions to streaming services that meet their needs more precisely. The success of Netflix established this model. Netflix started as a service to get movie DVDs delivered by the U.S. Mail, while offering some content via on-demand streaming. The streaming component in time became Netflix's main business. The popularity of streamed offerings led to new entrants in the field, including Hulu, Disney Plus, Apple TV, and Amazon to name a few. Now, even traditional media organizations such as the broadcast television networks (ABC, CBS, Fox, NBC) offer streaming services of their own. Subscriptions come in different levels, with premium charges to see ex-clusive content and programming without ads. Other cable programmers such as ESPN for sports and HBO and Showtime for movies have "over the top" ways for consumers to access their content without a cable subscription. Some services, such as Sling TV, bundle popular cable channels such as ESPN, Discovery, and news channels into a single subscription streaming service. With live streaming and on-demand offerings, the Internet offers hundreds of ways to find entertainment, and often multiple ways to access a single program. (See Box 10.1).

BOX 10.1

Where to Watch? Inauguration Shown in a Variety of Ways

FIGURE 10.1 Joe Biden is inaugurated on Jan. 20, 2021.
Credit: whitehouse.gov YouTube channel

One key feature of the online media environment is vastly more, and more diverse, ways to consume content. This leads to a corresponding growth in opportunities for ways to create content, in different ways for different purposes; awareness of those opportunities is how students of media can locate career opportunities.

As an example of this fractured environment for media consumption, anyone who wanted to watch live as Joe Biden was inaugurated as the 46th U.S. president could have chosen among more than a dozen sources, including:

- Four traditional broadcast networks (ABC, CBS, NBC, and PBS).
- Four cable news networks (CNN, C-SPAN, Fox, and MSNBC).
- Five sources of an official live stream from the Biden Inaugural Committee (its website, YouTube, Facebook, Twitter, and Twitch). The stream also appeared on the White House website.
- Live streamed video from *The New York Times*, *Washington Post* and other major news organizations.
- Streams from several news outlets on The Roku Channel and Newsy.

In addition, an inauguration livestream for children was broadcast on Nickelodeon and Discovery Education and streamed on YouTube.

Source: New York Times, Jan. 20, 2021.

This, of course, describes how the online environment has affected major corporate content producers. Aside from them, Internet audiences can turn to individual musicians and other artists who have global reach by using streaming on YouTube and similar sites to bypass traditional distribution channels. Sometimes this content is monetized with advertising, as described previously. These entertainers also can take advantage of online payment services including crowdfunding and subscription services such as Kickstarter, Patreon, and Indiegogo to earn from their work. Another popular entertainment diversion is computer games, which have advanced from being rooted to a gaming console or computer to becoming online social experiences. And even beyond entertainment programming, many people today entertain and amuse themselves by scrolling through social media feeds for messages and small pieces of content (such as memes, GIFs, and quirky TikTok videos) shared by friends.

In short, media entertainment has never been so diverse and fractured, with literally hundreds if not thousands of places anyone with a computer or even a mobile smartphone can turn to for momentary distraction or uninterrupted hours of entertainment. More organizations, and individuals, are creating more diverse content than ever in history. The competition for attention has, in some respects, drawn out higher quality in the content being produced. Unlike the 1960s when the choice of nighttime TV was limited to formulaic sitcoms and dramas available on just three national networks, the high quality shows available on cable and Internet streaming have been called a new "golden age" for entertainment (Thompson, 2013). These include critically acclaimed and popular offerings such as *The Sopranos, Breaking Bad, House of Cards, Game of Thrones,* and *The Crown.*

What does this mean for media students interested in careers producing entertainment programming – music, films, television, and the like? For starters, it means more places to find a job using those skills. The path may not be as clear or direct as going to a handful of major production companies, but the options are greater. The nature of this diverse arena includes more opportunity for freelance and gig work, including the option of people making their own productions shared via venues such as YouTube and monetized through crowd funding or digital advertising.

A Few Other Key Concepts to Consider

Another way to understand the disruption and evolution of the media business in the Internet age is through three key concepts that affect all of the genres described in the last section. They are convergence, engagement, and entrepreneurship.

Convergence

Convergence means coming together, and the replacement of traditional media "silos" with a more converged environment has a lot to do with how the media system has changed since the beginning of the 21st century. Two different types of convergence are important to understand: Organizational and technological. As an example of the latter, no one talks about, or works as, a "print" journalist anymore; even reporters whose work appears in print also have work posted as online text, or maybe even as a podcast or video. And the places they work often are "convergent" ones where different operations with different outputs or products all operate under one business organization. This used to be called "backpack journalism" because that is how many journalists carried the gear to produce the stories, but now most of the work is done with a smartphone. Advertising, public relations, and marketing also have become more converged, often under the umbrella of strategic communications. This approach means a single organization – sometimes a small to medium sized agency representing a variety of clients – performs all those functions. Further, the professionals working for such organizations need to be fluent across a variety of media, as on any given day they might be called upon to write a text news release or newsletter, or produce a podcast or a video for the client's social media channels, or design and implement social media strategies to help those messages spread effectively. This places a premium on students learning a variety of skills and also developing critical thinking and analytic ability that makes them more adaptable in converged environments.

Engagement

Every media genre today has some degree of focus on connecting or engaging with the audience as a way of building trust and support. As noted in the discussion of advertising and public relations, using online tools, especially social media, to engage with customers is a key task of professionals in those areas today. In a slightly broader perspective, marketers using similar approaches seek to create a "brand experience" and get customers to develop a relationship with their products. Digital marketer Pam Moore, who urges a strategic approach to social media marketing, offers a list of more than 30 "social media truths." Topping the list is "People don't buy things, they join things" (Moore, 2012). In similar fashion, John Goldman, CEO of a content sharing site, notes that "User experience becomes the key to locking onto and growing a real, loyal audience" (Goldman, 2010). These principles are at the heart of using online capacity to engage with an audience from a public relations or marketing perspective.

The concept of engagement also has taken a prominent place in journalism. Legacy news organizations mostly use it to describe audience interaction with online content, primarily clicks, shares, and comments. In other contexts – especially relating to innovative, emerging digital presentations – the term refers to a fundamental re-thinking of the relationship between the news organization and news consumers. In a strategy report for the American Press Institute, researcher Monica Guzman said engagement means collaboration between journalists and their audiences in defining and producing the news. Engagement is "making sure your work matters to your audience … [it] is not about what your audience can do for you, but what you can do with your audience" (Guzman, 2016). In another prescription using similar language, Josh Stearns of the Democracy Fund wrote of the need "to be more intentional about finding spaces and places across journalism to build with, rather than for, our communities" (Stearns, 2015). The European Journalism Centre has a program called the Engaged Journalism Accelerator that aims to help news organizations put community engagement at the heart of their strategies. And journalism professor Jake Batsell literally wrote the book on this practice (Batsell, 2015), based on interviews with journalists in more than 20 news organizations that describe how news providers should listen to, interact with, and fulfill the needs of their audiences. Effective performance in all media genres today requires an attitude of building trusting engagement with audiences rather than relying on the mass-produced one-way flow typical of legacy media for most of mass media's history.

Entrepreneurship

Both within organizations and in new stand-alone operations, people entering the media and communications world will find it beneficial to have an entrepreneurial approach of seeking new and different ways to fill audience needs. This is not especially new; entrepreneurship has been a part of media culture going back to Benjamin Day founding the New York *Sun* as the first "penny press" newspaper in the 19th century, David Sarnoff founding the National Broadcasting Corp. (NBC), and Edward Bernays creating new techniques as the "father of public relations" in the early 20th century. The companies that are today's media behemoths, in fact, began as entrepreneurial enterprises, with stories that are now familiar: Facebook was started in a Harvard dorm room; Google began in a graduate student office at Stanford; Apple was started in a garage in Cupertino, California. Not everyone who starts their own media business will make it as successful as those companies, of course. According to Jan Schaffer, director of the J-Lab media innovation center, "A growing number of journalism, advertising and public relations students are starting their careers either in media startups launched by others or in entrepreneurial ventures they are starting themselves" (Schaffer, 2016a). Respondents to a survey conducted by the Tow-Knight Center for Entrepreneurial Journalism at City University of New York offered the following characteristics of media entrepreneurship with a journalistic focus:

- Starting an operation that can be monetized.
- Going into business for oneself.
- Figuring out how to generate revenue to pay for journalism that matters.
- Learning how to think like a businessperson while also thinking as a journalist.
- Acquiring the ability to plan a digital news/info startup and develop a sustainable business model (Schaffer, 2016b).

Innovation is crucial for larger organizations, too (where it is sometimes called "intrapreneurship"). In a report for the World Association of Newspaper Publishers, a researcher from the Craig Newmark School of Journalism at City University of New York reported that user-centered product development was the focus for news organizations around the world in 2020. Among her examples of this were a CNN podcast featuring the network's chief medical correspondent Dr. Sanjay Gupta, a coronavirus newsletter from Quartz, and a German news site's use of an online map of Munich that would help readers find, and use the services of, small shops and restaurants that had been hurt by the pandemic (Gupta, 2021).

The introduction to this book's first edition described it as "not your parents' theory textbook." The same could be said about the contemporary media landscape: The impact of online communications has fundamentally changed it in ways that make finding a career within it both more complicated and more exciting than it was a generation ago at the turn of the 21st century. The landscape is more complicated because potential jobs and possible employers are not as well defined. The manageable set of direct career paths into media a generation ago are now a kaleidoscope of entry points and interconnected pathways. The skills needed to navigate them are more complicated, too. Those same circumstances make it more open and exciting because these new ways of creating and distributing media content, and earning revenue from it, create far broader and more diverse opportunities for media work. And despite the volume and pace of change in the media world over the past few years, the evolution is not finished; in fact, new and different types of media work and places to do it are likely to keep emerging as today's students graduate, begin their careers, and progress through them. Many of today's students at some point in their careers will be doing jobs that literally have not been invented yet.

This situation underscores the central idea about this book, which is that a firm grounding in media theory can help people predict and explain things that happen in the real world around them, including novel and unexpected ones. This is a key component of preparing students for careers that don't even exist now. However, even in this new, emerging world some tried-and-true best practices can help in landing that first post-graduation job, and the next ones along the career ladder. The next part of this chapter explores them.

PLANNING YOUR CAREER IN THE MASS MEDIA

"I'm a graduating senior and I still don't know what I want to do..."

Usually by graduation time, most students have a good idea of what their career path might look like, but not always. At the same time, we meet some first-year students who feel pressured to know exactly what they want to do as soon as they begin college. In some fields, this is important. If a student wants to be a nurse or an accountant, for example, they would need to commit before they begin their sophomore year, to be sure they can complete all the course requirements along with the practical experiences. While this may also be true in some communication programs, mass media programs are often more flexible. And students can take advantage of this flexibility to try some different areas of the field and see what interests them the most. At the same time, employers are often looking for "jacks of all trade," graduates who know about a lot of different areas rather than someone who specializes in one thing. This is an example of how times have changed in mass communication. One of the authors of this book spent more than 20 years working for newspapers. At the time, there were reporters, editors, photographers, page designers, and graphic artists, and their job responsibilities seldom crossed. Now, new graduates interested in positions with news organizations must be what is known as "backpack journalists." They need to be able to report and write and take their own pictures (both still and video) and edit their own work, often without setting foot in the office. In today's digital age, a journalist needs to know how to write for the web, how to post his own stories and photos, maintain social media accounts, and more often how to shoot and edit video to go along with the story. All those jobs are now often done by one person.

So it's actually good when students do not focus too narrowly, especially in the beginning of their academic programs. Having a diverse skill set will be helpful. At the same time, a student's focus should not be so diffused that they have difficulty articulating what they have to offer to an employer. The most important things to keep in mind during the college years can be summed up in two words: Career preparation. The main components of this career preparation, in addition to academic coursework, are:

- Getting involved in co-curricular activities.
- Keeping a portfolio of work.
- Creating a resume and a LinkedIn profile.
- Networking.
- Internships, internships, internships.

Co-curricular Activities

A college campus can be a great place to start a career as a media professional. In addition to classes, media skills can be acquired and grown through campus broadcasting (radio, television), news outlets (newspaper, magazine, website, social media), professional groups such as PRSSA (Public Relations Student Society of America) and AMA (American Marketing Association), in-house firms, and many others depending on the size and scope of the campus and mass communication program. And mass media skills can also be applied to other campus organizations. For example, a student at the authors' institution became the social media manager for the campus theater group. Another did all the event planning for the Latino Student Union. Still more students might get on-campus jobs in the college communications office, working directly under media professionals. The key is to get involved, and do it early in one's college career. Communications has always been a very competitive field, so building up experience to supplement class work will help to make a student more marketable when they begin to look for a professional position. Getting this experience will help focus a student's interests and skill sets, weed out the things that they don't want to do, and begin to build a professional resume to help land an internship and, ultimately, a job. Additionally, co-curricular activities help students to network with individuals who could be valuable assets in their professional networks. Communication majors work on projects that put them in touch with college administrators, members of the board of trustees, and people in the community who are well-connected. It's also wise to remember that fellow students are also part of their professional networks. Many alumni stay in touch with one another and use their former classmates as links to new job opportunities, new companies, and new locations.

Building a Portfolio of Work

Many mass media jobs, and even some internships, require that students present a portfolio of their work, and it's never too early to begin saving and organizing samples from class assignments and projects from co-curricular activities. When you are presenting your portfolio, you want everything to be flawless, but get in the habit of saving everything and then you can decide what stays and what goes when it's time to bring your portfolio to an interview. In some colleges and universities, students are encouraged or required to begin saving items to their e-portfolios beginning in their first-semester classes. This is helpful to have the work organized in one place, for easy reference to it throughout college. Also, you may realize that work you have done in non-communication classes may be relevant for a communications portfolio. For example, a marketing proposal or a political science analysis may be appropriate for some jobs in advertising, public relations, or journalism.

For print/online journalism, advertising, and public relations majors, a portfolio means a collection of writing samples – news stories, ad copy, news releases, media alerts, social media reports – as well as other items specific to career interest – brochure designs, flyers and invitations, photography, graphic designs, video editing, analytics, and social media posts, among others. While most employers no longer ask for a hard copy of a portfolio – a black binder with plastic sheets protecting work samples – job sites like Indeed.com advise that bringing a hard copy portfolio to an interview can impress the hiring manager (https://www.indeed.com/career-advice/interviewing/portfolio-interview). Portfolio samples should be flawless, consisting of only a student's best work. Page 1 of the portfolio should be a resume. Reference letters may also be included, but the key is to organize everything so it is easy to follow. A portfolio is taken to interviews, but should not be left behind. Rather than reading every word of every piece, interviewers usually browse through the portfolio during an interview to get a sense of the range of work the student has accomplished.

More and more, however, employers like to see an online portfolio of the student's work. This might be a site the student designs using a relatively simple tool like WordPress (wordpress.com) or Wix (wix.com), a more complex design site such as Carbonmade (carbonmade.com) or Behance (behance.net), Adobe Dreamweaver CC, Weebly, Visual Studio Code, or even a site for which the student himself writes the code, which is a skill more and more employers are looking for. (Another thing employers are saying, especially in journalism, is that it's helpful for graduating students to have some familiarity with coding.) Online portfolios can be sent as a link to the prospective employer, but a student can also present it on a laptop or tablet during an interview.

For broadcasting and new media students, a portfolio is likely a personal web page containing digital work samples. It can even be a digital resume with a link to work samples uploaded to YouTube or Vimeo. These samples may include television news and feature packages, radio spots, production examples, podcasts, or new media work such as websites and online newsletters as well as examples of using social media for professional purposes (e.g., live-tweeting a news or sporting event). However the portfolio is presented, it is the responsibility of the applicant to make it as easy as possible for a prospective employer to see the work, so students should make sure any instructions provided with the job listing are followed to the letter. One of our alums who works as an executive producer at a local television station advises that it's a good idea to bring the portfolio on a flash drive to an interview, just in case questions arise and it will be easy to check out the work samples.

Given the media convergence described in detail earlier in this chapter, it is wise for students to consider work samples outside of communication courses, co-curricular activities, and internships. For example, one of the top skills all employers are looking for is the ability to work in teams. A student who did a team project for a class in any subject – psychology, marketing, biology, etc. – might include that project in his portfolio. Any student who submits a team project should be sure to indicate what her role was in that project, so the contribution is clear to the reader. Similarly, papers written for a political science class, or a small business analysis completed for a statistics class, can also be included in the portfolio.

Portfolio pieces can also be included in LinkedIn profiles, which will be discussed in the next section.

Creating a Resume and LinkedIn Profile

While Career Center staff on the authors' campus remark that many students wait until senior year to think about their resumes, many others spend time earlier in their career on this important document for certain class assignments, summer jobs, internships, scholarship applications, and the like. During their last two years students should be refining and updating the experiences and skills on their resumes, reviewing it with the career center staff and relevant professors, and taking advantage of resume reviews offered by professionals in the field. Many colleges have networks of alumni who have volunteered to review resumes and conduct mock interviews for students and recent graduates. These volunteers are a rich and ready source of job information, and are also valuable additions to a student's professional network. Even an individual not working directly in the field can provide feedback and discover fatal flaws (such as a typo) in a resume.

A resume is sometimes called a 15-second advertisement. This is because the average recruiter spends fewer than 15 seconds reviewing a resume before deciding to pursue it further or sending it to the recycling bin. The purpose of a resume is to get an interview, and that means that it must be a good indicator of what the employer may expect in the interview process.

Resumes can be organized chronologically or functionally, with most recent college graduates choosing the former. A resume should include the following components:

1. A heading. The heading should not say "RESUME" but rather have the name, address, phone number, and email address of the applicant. (It's also important to be sure the email address sounds professional, such as your.name@gmail.com, not something like "krazykitty43" or "tylerthechickmagnet."). Some schools permit students to use their college email address after graduation, and some students set up a separate email just for their job search. In addition to the heading items mentioned above, some students include links to their websites/portfolios or their LinkedIn page at the top. Students who choose to do this should make sure the link is live and working before they submit their resume for a position.

2. Education. For most college seniors, their academic degree can be their most valuable asset. This should be highlighted, along with any double majors, minors or concentrations, and awards and honors received. The grade point average can

also be included if it's over 3.0 out of 4.0. The education section is also a great place to indicate any study abroad experiences that the student may have had.

3. Work experience. The employer is generally not interested in the time a student spent in the produce department of the local supermarket or taking care of a neighbor's child. Rather, the experience section should focus on jobs and experiences that provided the most *transferable skills* that can be applied to the position for which the student is applying, so some students label this section, "Related Experience." This is the hardest part of writing a resume, and care should be taken to include accomplishments and skills used in job descriptions, rather than a list of duties. This section should include internships and positions in co-curricular activities, as well as jobs that relate to the position for which the student is applying. Grouping experiences this way demonstrates that transferable skills can come from more than paid positions in providing students the experiences they can use in future careers.

4. Optional topics, such as volunteer activities, student activities, special skills or training, and honors especially as related to the job. A resume should not include personal information such as religious affiliation or marital status and should rarely include any information from high school.[1] Many students like to include athletics and fraternities/sororities on their resumes. This is acceptable as long as the student can describe skills from these experiences that relate to their ability to do the job they are applying for (e.g., leadership as captain of a sports team; service projects as part of Greek life).

Guidelines for Formatting a Resume

1. A resume should be flawless. A student should proofread it multiple times, get a friend to proof it, get a professor to proof it, and take it to a career counselor. Errors are noise in the communication process and a mistake as minor as a single misspelling will earn a resume a quick trip to the recycling bin. One HR director for an advertising agency that does a lot of media buying reports that even a misplaced comma on a resume would disqualify an applicant, because attention to detail is so important in their client work.

2. Education is important, but in the mass media job hunt it doesn't top experience. Any experience that is tied to the job for which a student is applying should be prominently highlighted. For example, under the title of "Relevant Experience" a student who is applying for a reporting job might include an unpaid internship at the local television station, work as a reporter or editor on the campus newspaper, and freelance reporting done for his hometown newspaper. That student might have done a special project in the community as part of an advanced journalism class, which might also be included. "Experience" does not only have to mean paid positions.

3. It's important to keep the resume simple and professional. Classic fonts such as Times New Roman or Arial should be used, without mixing font types, and it should be printed on white, off-white or light gray heavy-weight paper. Even though most resumes are sent electronically now, it's a good idea to have hard copies for job fairs or in-person interviews. Ideally, an electronic resume should be sent as a .pdf file to minimize any formatting changes that may occur when the recipient opens the file.

4. At all times, a student needs to keep the needs of the reader in mind. While the student wants the internship or the job, the employer wants to fill a position in the company or organization. This is why highlighting skills are such an important piece of a college student's resume. Focusing on the needs of the employer will make it more likely that this resume will lead to an interview.

Many resumes will be sent with cover letters or cover emails. Most college career centers include cover letters in their resume-writing workshops and provide samples on their websites. Or the student can consult *Business Insider, Forbes, Inc.,* and other professional publications. While these samples will provide an idea of what makes a good cover letter, it's important that the language be totally in the individual student's voice to make sure it sounds authentic.

LinkedIn: Social Media with a Professional Slant

Once the resume is in a format that might be called "employer-ready," it can be used as the basis for a LinkedIn profile. If a student has not yet visited LinkedIn.com to create a professional profile, they should set aside an evening or two to get that done. LinkedIn is a social networking site for professional connections....that's PROFESSIONAL connections. LinkedIn profiles are only to help current students or recent graduates to find a job or internship and to network with other professionals. It's not a place to post cute pictures of puppies or dancing TikTok videos or to complain about a media research project or to post political viewpoints. However, LinkedIn is a great place for students to showcase their skills with much more room than they might have on a resume. On LinkedIn there is space to post projects, papers, presentations, videos, and to explain more about experiences and co-curricular and extracurricular activities for prospective employers.

There are many good resources to get a student started on creating a LinkedIn profile. Among the best are on the LinkedIn site itself, as well as *Forbes, Inc.,* and *Business Insider*. It's important to take care to be sure that a profile on LinkedIn accurately reflects the student's professional skill set; many employers are starting to check LinkedIn profiles (and other social media) as soon as a candidate applies for a job, so what is posted there can affect whether a student is called for an interview.

There are many different ways to approach a LinkedIn profile. Some of the most important components are in the prime real estate at the top of the page. Just as an employer might look only at the top third of your resume, a job-seeking student needs to grab the reader's attention with:

1. A professional headshot: There is no anonymity on LinkedIn. A professional headshot that includes the subject facing front and smiling is needed. The subject should be professionally dressed (from the shoulders up) with a neat hairstyle and professional make-up. Cutting a person out of a group shot or taking a selfie in a car is not recommended (it doesn't look professional to have a stray arm around a shoulder or a seatbelt on).
2. A title that says something about the person in the profile: Many students start out by giving themselves the title, "Student at xxxxx College." There are probably between 1,000 and 60,000 other people who have that title, and it doesn't

distinguish an individual. By giving a hint of their professional aspirations, students can make their titles stand out. Some examples from the authors' actual student profiles include:

- "Editorial Intern at Rochester Business Journal."
- "Student Orientation Coordinator, Office of Admissions."
- "Account Executive at Cardinal Courier."
- "Aspiring Advertising Copywriter."

3. A compelling summary that includes a brand statement and what the student has to offer a prospective internship supervisor or employer. The summary needs to grab the reader's attention and make them want to scroll down and read further. There are many ways to write a summary, but here is one example from Alexandra, a rising senior:

I believe in collaboration, energy, and effectiveness. I value the impact I can have on my community and I look forward to a career in the communications field that can allow me to continue to have a positive influence on those around me.
Interested in pursuing a career in Account Services or PR, I continue to grow my organizational and leadership abilities through various activities and involvement throughout the SJFC campus and Rochester community.

LinkedIn doesn't require that a student write in the first person and even incomplete sentences as seen on a resume are acceptable.

4. Experience: Using details from the resume as material for experience and accomplishments is a good plan for LinkedIn, since the resume and the LinkedIn profile should send the same message. On LinkedIn there is more room to be specific and provide information about the work the student did and what they gained from that experience. As with the resume, students should start with the most recent experience.

Other areas to focus on in LinkedIn profiles include asking people for recommendations, posting some projects and work samples, following companies and "influencers," and joining groups. The people and groups a student decides to follow should reflect the professional-related information they receive in their feed (which is kind of like a Facebook news feed, but again with a professional spin). For example, a student interested in sports broadcasting might follow ESPN, CBS Sports, FOX Sports, etc., as well as professional sportscasters they admire.

Once the profile has been established (and has been proofread several times and shared with a friend and/or professor for further proofreading), students can begin connecting with individuals and building their networks. Fellow students, professors, college staff, and people known through work and family connections provide a good starting point. Connections don't all have to be in the mass media field; in fact, it's better to have a variety of contacts to increase the range of opportunities one can be exposed to. Seeking out alumni and asking them to connect is a good strategy, as is asking a professor or career counselor to provide an introduction. While connecting with people, a student may get connection requests from other people. It may be tempting to connect with as many people as possible; however, until they have an established network, it is recommended that students connect primarily with people they already know.

Finally, it is good to remember that, like a resume, a LinkedIn profile is never really "finished." The wise professional keeps LinkedIn updated and constantly makes new contacts to broaden their network of professional opportunities.

The Job Search: Networking

Many students are surprised to learn that the majority of positions are never advertised in the classified ads or on company websites. Some studies report 75-80 percent of professional positions are found through networking. What is networking? Networking is talking to people for information and advice, and using those contacts to meet others who can help in the search for a job or internship. Throughout the process, a student never asks for a job, just for information and advice.

It is easiest to begin with people who are already invested in a student's success: Family, friends, professors, internship supervisors, and academic advisors. From that group alone, most students are able to generate a list of people who would be rich sources of information about careers in the field. The people on this list form the initial network and will be contacted for informational interviews. Students should request no more than 30 minutes of a professional's time when seeking an informational interview.

Contacts can be made in one of two ways:

1. The student can ask someone who knows them to "pave the way" with an introduction. For example, a professor may contact a professional he knows like this: "One of my students, Julie Smith, is very interested in a career in advertising, preferably on the account services side of an agency. I'd like to refer her to you for an informational interview, so she can get some advice on her career path." This makes it easy for Julie to call the contact and request an informational interview.
2. The student can make the contact directly, asking for an informational interview, either in an email or a phone call. "Hello, Mr. Waters, my name is Julie Smith. I'm a senior communications major at St. John Fisher. I got your name from Dr. Rosenberry, who recommended you as someone with a lot of experience in the account services side of advertising. Would you be willing to meet with me for about 20-30 minutes to discuss careers in this area and give me your advice?"

Even school assignments can lead to informational interview contacts. One of the authors, as an undergraduate, interviewed newspaper editors as part of a project for a journalism class. The contact turned into an informational interview, which led to a summer internship at one of the papers.

Once an informational interview is secured, the student should prepare as if this were a real interview, because it just might be! Interview preparation should include:

1. Researching the company.
2. Researching the field.
3. Choosing appropriate attire.
4. Planning an agenda of questions the student would like to ask. A sample agenda of questions is offered in Box 10.2.
5. Securing a quiet place with an appropriate background if this is a remote interview (such as Zoom, Teams, Skype, or Facetime). While students always benefit from going inside organizations and seeing what the work environment is like (and maybe meeting other people), during the COVID pandemic, some students found it easier to do informational interviews over Zoom. Professionals working from home were often more available and willing to give students their time, and students were able to conduct more interviews without the burden of travel and parking.

BOX 10.2

Agenda for an Informational Interview

FIGURE 10.2 Many professionals give freely of their time to help students.
Credit: Christina@wocintechchat.com on Unsplash.

This is a suggested structure with some questions that can be asked, but students should base their questions on the research they conducted on the field before they go to the interview, as well as adapting follow-up questions based on what the interviewee says.

I. Overview of the interview

- Remind the person you're meeting how you got his or her name.
- Emphasize that you are just looking for advice on a career you are considering.

II. Background of the interviewee

- Can you tell me about your career path and how you got to the position you hold today?
- Is this a typical career path for a person in this field?

III. Current job description

- Please describe your current position.
- What is a typical day like for you?
- What do you like best about your job?
- What do you like least about your job?

IV. State of the field

- Some of my research shows that this field is growing/contracting. In your experience is this true?
- What are your predictions for the way the field will change in the next 5-10 years?
- How do you think that will affect the employment picture?

V. Advice

- What would you recommend for a college student considering a career in this field?
- I have my resume with me. Would you mind looking at it and giving me your reaction? Are there any changes you might suggest?
- If this is a field I want to pursue, is there anyone else you might recommend that I should talk to?

VI. Thank you for your time and information.

During an informational interview, the student never asks for a job, just for information. She may ask her contact to review her resume for suggestions, and ask who else she might speak to in the field. And she should always follow up with a thank-you note within 24 hours of the interview. Handwritten thank-you notes often have the biggest impact, because they are so rarely seen, although thank-you emails are also acceptable.

With each informational interview, a student will find her confidence increasing along with her network. She will be more informed about the field and the position and more likely to impress someone enough to get an offer for an actual job interview.

The Job Search: Interviewing

When that job interview does come through, a student should have many of the needed techniques down as a result of doing informational interviews. However, this time the candidate is not the interviewer, but the interviewee. Changing roles will require some practice and training. Students can take advantage of workshops offered by their college career centers and practice mock interviews with career advisors and volunteers (often alumni). In addition to ensuring that the student's resume and appearance are appropriate, these experiences will help the candidate answer questions, which is the key activity in an employment interview.

Everyone is familiar with the common interview questions, such as:

- Tell me about yourself.
- Where do you want to be in five years?
- Why did you choose to go to your university?
- What are your strengths and weaknesses?

However, more and more employers are using a style of interviewing known as behavior-based interviewing or behavioral event interviews. This type of interview is predicated on the belief that past performance predicts future performance. So, rather than asking for a hypothetical answer ("What would you do if..."), the employer is looking for evidence that the student possesses a trait that is required for this position. Behavior-based questions generally ask questions such as, "Tell me about a time when..." followed by a certain situation. It might be something like:

- Tell me about a time when you worked successfully with a team to complete a job under pressure.
- What was the most challenging situation you encountered as president of your school's TV Club last year?
- Tell me about the biggest disappointment you experienced during your internship.

As students prepare for interviews, they should consider significant events from their college years – events related to anything on their resumes (classes, work experiences, extracurricular activities, co-curricular activities) that may be asked about during an interview.

As with the informational interviews, preparation should also include research about the company, preparing the questions to ask about the job and the company, attending to a professional appearance, and being sure to know where to go and how long the interview will take. It is also recommended to take along extra resumes and a pad and pen to take notes. And students should not forget to write thank-you notes to any key people they meet with, ideally sent within 24 hours after they leave the interview. They should request business cards of each person they meet, so they are sure to spell their names correctly and have accurate contact information as well.

BOX 10.3

Job Searches beyond Networking

FIGURE 10.3 Online research can provide job leads and information.
KOBU Agency on Unsplash

While networking has been proven to be the most successful job search strategy, students should not overlook the traditional and newer sources of jobs in mass communication. These include:

- **On-line sources:** The best in the media field include journalismjobs.com, editorandpublisher.com, broadcastingandcable.com, and professional websites such as PRSA.org (Public Relations) and AAF.org (advertising).
- **Classified ads**: While many jobs are never advertised, some actually are, so it pays to keep an eye on the classified ads in the local paper or on the newspaper's website. Students may have to respond to a blind post office box, but it's worth a try. Additionally, if a student wishes to move to a specific location, targeting the classifieds in that particular city may yield some leads.
- **Company websites**: If a student has targeted a particular company or a particular industry, they can check out the postings on the company's web site. For example, at the website of Edelman, one of the largest PR firms in the world (edelman.com/careers), students can search by job type, locations, and divisions of the company. Checking out large employers in a particular area such as medical centers, universities,

and big corporations may also yield openings in communication and media fields.

- **Alma mater**: Students often forget to look in their own backyards. When area employers contact local colleges, those jobs go up on the college's career center website. When professors hear about jobs (often through alumni and social media contacts), they often refer them directly to a student they know who has an interest in that field. It can pay to stay in touch with the career office, professors, and the alumni office after graduation.

- **LinkedIn**: Building and maintaining your LinkedIn network can pay off in more ways than just reading industry updates and setting up informational interviews. More and more employers are using LinkedIn to locate talented candidates for positions and contacting them through the site. It's important for students and new graduates to keep their profiles updated and professional, and be sure to have contact information that they are checking on a regular basis. (Some employers are checking the LinkedIn profiles of applicants before they even make an initial contact, another good reason to keep that profile up-to-date and professional.)

Internships: Transitioning to the Professional World

Students who have done well in their classes, participated in extracurricular activities, and built a portfolio of work are generally rewarded by receiving internships in their chosen field. For many students, it may be their first time going into a professional work environment. Many students have worked their way through college in retail, food service, or child care positions, and it can be a bit intimidating to walk into an office on the first day of an internship. Some internship sites have orientation programs for interns, which will help give the new intern a sense of expectations and appropriate workplace behavior. However, many students just plunge into work on the very first day at a new internship. For those students, the following advice is offered:

Interns should treat the internship like a job, because it very well could be. Many supervisors use internships as a way to try out future employees, and students should consider every day at their internship as a job interview. This includes taking responsibilities seriously, showing up on time, missing a day only when it's an absolute emergency, and keeping the lines of communication open with the internship supervisor as well as between the student and the professor overseeing the internship at their college.

Interns should make sure they are getting professional-level work, similar to what they would get in their first job after graduation. While routine office tasks are part of every job, most of a college student's internship time should be spent using the skills they've acquired during their college experience and getting work samples to add to their portfolio. Many students are still doing unpaid internships only for college credit, so they need to have something to show for their experience. For example, a student interning at a local television station should not only be shadowing reporters and observing in the newsroom or listening to the police scanner. He should be writing scripts and voice-overs and writing stories for the station website. If the intern goes out with a reporter and there is not a need to rush back to the station, the student should ask to record his own stand-up and get to record and edit his own package. If the internship is in a union shop, this won't go on air, but the experience of doing the work and getting feedback from professionals at the station will go a long way toward building an intern's "reel" and his confidence.

Interns should take an interest in everything and everyone. An intern needs to make sure everyone at their internship site knows them and that they are willing to help them out, no matter what the request. Being interested in what every job entails makes a great impression, and, if there is time, interns should ask to meet with people in other departments. One of the author's students who interned at a full-service agency made sure during down time that he visited other departments and lent a hand where he could. Even though he was a PR account services intern, he met the ad copywriters, the producers in the studio, the social media team, even the administrators in HR and accounting. Along the way, he amassed a diverse portfolio just from his three months at the site, and upon graduation he was offered a position. Students sometimes worry about bothering people by asking too many questions, but showing an interest in people and their work is usually welcomed, and most professionals find it flattering to be asked their advice.

An intern should take her cues from the other people around her. This relates to everything from what to wear to policy on personal cell phone use in the office. Every culture is different, and some are more relaxed than others. If an intern is uncertain about a policy, it's okay to ask. For example, a few internship sites have "bring your dog to work" on Fridays. An intern should ask if it's okay if she brings her dog, since there might be policies about which dogs can come and expected behavior for the pooches visiting during the workday.

If things aren't going well, an intern should do something about it. Students in internship programs are generally required to meet with the campus or program internship director before and during the internship to report on how things are going. This is to address any issues before they become real problems. Not all campuses have a formal check-in such as this, but students should discuss any concerns they have with the internship director at their college. Most of the time, it is recommended that students try to work out any problems through their supervisor at the internship site, but sometimes an advocate for the student needs to step in. Many of the issues students encounter at their internships center on not getting enough responsibility and not getting opportunities to create portfolio pieces. Often, a quick conversation with the supervisor can clarify expectations and change the situation. However, if a situation cannot be resolved, the student may need to look for another internship site.

CONSIDERING GRADUATE SCHOOL

Looking for a job as graduation nears can be a frightening prospect for many students. That first professional job represents the official break from the family stability and school routine that students have known for 16 (or more) years. At this challenging juncture in their lives, many graduating seniors consider attending graduate school.

There are some good reasons to attend graduate school directly after an undergraduate program. A student is in the classroom/study frame of mind and knows the routine, although grad school usually requires ratcheting it up a notch or two in terms of both the depth of material that classes cover as well as the intensity of study skills required.

Some graduating seniors are very sure of their career plans, and it may make sense for them to seek an advanced degree in that field right away, to have an advantage in their job search. For example, someone who wants to be a lawyer – maybe even one specializing in media law – must attend law school. Someone who is fully set on working in a large corporate atmosphere might find an MBA beneficial. Many graduate programs also have significant internship and networking opportunities that operate at a higher level than those found in an undergraduate program.

At the same time, there are reasons to put off graduate study at this time. Most students will change jobs several times in the early years after college, before they settle on the career that suits them best. Without specific career goals, choosing graduate school right after undergraduate studies may be putting specialization in the wrong area. Additionally, there is value in having some work experience to apply to the graduate program. Finally, in entry-level jobs in the mass media, there is rarely the requirement for a graduate degree. Indeed, a master's degree will not even earn a higher salary level in most mass media jobs.

As an added factor, finances play a role for many students, who already may be carrying heavy loans from their undergraduate years. While there are some assistantships and other forms of financial aid available for graduate school, paying back undergraduate debt assumes a higher priority for many students. There is also the possibility that a future employer will fully or partially fund a graduate program, which would ensure that the degree program would be part of early career professional development. In conversations with experienced alumni and internship supervisors about their recommendations regarding graduate school, most of them advise students to wait to make the decision and get some work experience first.

CONCLUSION

Many students have a lot of anxiety around the issue of finding a job after graduation, which is natural given the complexity of the media industries and the rapidly evolving nature of the work within them. It should be of some comfort to learn that students who have done their career preparation as advised in this chapter generally have little difficulty finding employment, and most are working in the field within three to six months after graduation.

More and more often, the first job is not with a big advertising or PR firm or with a major television network or large news organization. Students often start their careers with smaller marketing firms or start-ups or with non-profit organizations. Many are doing communications work for businesses, such as Emily, who is in charge of advertising and social media for a large dental chain; or Stephanie, who is in the marketing department of a large insurance company. Some are taking their communication skills outside the traditional fields, such as Brian, who is a recruiter for a technology firm; Theresa, who is working in customer service for a health-care organization; or Qawan, who is coordinating after-school programs for children in the city where he grew up. And still others find their positions at traditional media outlets, such as Cody, who is doing data analysis for a large advertising firm; or Olivia, who is doing a paid internship in social media with the local newspaper. The point is that mass communication is such a versatile field that students have many diverse opportunities for employment and can apply their skills in any number of ways.

However, it is not just the training that students have in writing, designing, photography, video production, and social media skills that provide these myriad opportunities. Communication majors have a grounding in the liberal arts which enables them to be flexible, adapt to new situations, and learn new skills quickly. They have critical thinking skills that apply to a wide range of situations. And they have what some employers think is the most important skill of all: Communication. Communication and media majors know how to plan a presentation, how to analyze an audience, how to work in a team, how to reach out and network, all skills essential to success in any profession.

Mass communication theory and research is no small part of this profile that makes students so successful. Learning the framework for how to explain what happens in the media is essential to understanding how to craft a message ... as well as how to respond and adapt when that message does not have the desired effect. Our students may not say, "that's uses and gratifications," or "I've never seen so much commodification," as part of their workday. One of this book's authors worked in a newsroom for over 20 years and never heard anyone use the word "agenda setting" even though that's what journalists do with every public affairs story they produce. The knowledge students gain of the theories that are explanations stays with them and informs the work that they do. And the ability to do research in a systematic way, whether it's crafting a survey or conducting interviews or doing content analysis, will help to ensure professional success as a media practitioner.

We welcome your questions and comments on this book, the instructor's manual, the companion website, or any of the topics that we have discussed. Please feel free to contact us, and we will respond in a timely manner. We wish you success as you complete your media education and embark on your career as a media practitioner.

Jack Rosenberry and Lauren Vicker, Communications Professors Emeriti
jackrosenberry16@gmail.com   lvicker1@gmail.com

Career Development Activities for Students

1. Ask a professor for two or three contacts from his or her network with whom you could conduct informational interviews. Then do the interviews.
2. Find out whether your college has a database of alumni who are available to do

resume critiques, informational interviews and other career-preparation activities for current students at the school. If it does, spend some time with the database identifying people whom you should try to meet.

3. Visit your college's career center and have your resume critiqued. Find out what other services the center can offer to help you prepare for the job world.

4. If you haven't done an internship yet, make an appointment with your college's or your academic department's internship director and find out what the guidelines are to complete one. If you have done an internship, or are currently in one, identify some people you have met through the internship with whom you could conduct informational interviews.

NOTE

1 An exception might be noting the high school attended if the person interviewing the student for a job also attended that high school.

REFERENCES

Abernathy, P.M. (2020). *News deserts and ghost newspapers: Will local news survive?* Chapel Hill, N.C.: University of North Carolina Press.

Bagdikian, B.H. (2004). *The new media monopoly.* Boston: Beacon Press.

Bartlett, J. (1980). *Familiar quotations* (15th ed.). Boston: Little, Brown and Co.

Batsell, J. (2015). *Engaged journalism: Connecting with digitally empowered news audiences.* New York: Columbia University Press.

Bradt, G. (2016). Wanamaker was wrong. The vast majority of advertising is wasted. *Forbes* online. Retrieved from https://www.forbes.com/sites/georgebradt/2016/09/14/wanamaker-was-wrong-the-vast-majority-of-advertising-is-wasted/?sh=5461f529483b

Bromwich, J.E. (2018, March 7). How the Parkland students got so good at social media. *The New York Times* online. Retrieved from https://www.nytimes.com/2018/03/07/us/parkland-students-social-media.html

Clement, J. (2020, November 19). Percentage of mobile device website traffic worldwide from 1st quarter 2015 to 3rd quarter 2020. *Statista* online. Retrieved from https://www.statista.com/statistics/277125/share-of-website-traffic-coming-from-mobile-devices/

Goldman, J. (2010). Why social experience is the future of online content. *Mashable* online archive. Retrieved from https://mashable.com/2010/06/30/social-experience-content/

Grieco, E. (2020, April 20). U.S. newspapers have shed half of their newsroom employees since 2008. Pew Research Center. Retrieved from https://www.pewresearch.org/fact-tank/2020/04/20/u-s-newsroom-employment-has-dropped-by-a-quarter-since-2008/

Gupta, N. (2021, January 13). COVID-19 and the rise of journalistic product innovation. World Association of News Publishers. Retrieved from https://wan-ifra.org/2021/01/covid-19-and-the-rise-of-journalistic-product-innovation/

Guzman, M. (2016). The best ways to build audience and relevance by listening to and engaging your community. Reston, VA: American Press Institute. Retrieved from -https://www.americanpressinstitute.org/publications/reports/strategy-studies/listening-engaging-community/.

Kitterman, T. (2019, December 31). PR crises that have defined 2019. *PR Daily* online. Retrieved from https://www.prdaily.com/pr-crises-that-have-defined-2019/

McIntyre, D. (2019, July 24). The death of journalism? Here's how many newspapers have shut down in past 15 years. *USA Today* online. Retrieved from https://www.usatoday.com/story/money/2019/07/24/journalism-jobs-2000-american-newspapers-close-15-years/39797141/

Moore, P. (2012). 34 social media truths in a nut shell. Retrieved from https://www.pammarketingnut.com/2012/08/34-social-media-truths-in-a-nut-shell/

Peterson, T. (1956). The social responsibility theory of the press. In Siebert, F. Peterson, T. & Schramm, W. (Eds.). *Four theories of the press*. Freeport, NY: Books for Libraries Press.

Petroff, A. (2018, February 27). KFC apologizes for chicken shortage with a hilarious hidden message. *CNN Money* online. Retrieved from https://money.cnn.com/2018/02/23/news/kfc-apology-ad-shortage-chicken/index.html

PRSA (2012). Public Relations Society of America. Retrieved from https://www.prsa.org/about/all-about-pr

Rooney, J. (2013). Behind the scenes of Oreo's real-time Super Bowl slam dunk. *Forbes* online. Retrieved from https://www.forbes.com/sites/jenniferrooney/2013/02/04/behind-the-scenes-of-oreos-real-time-super-bowl-slam-dunk/?sh=302063a2e66c

Rushkoff, D. (2019, December 29). We've spent the decade letting our tech define us. It's out of control. *The Guardian* online. Retrieved from https://www.theguardian.com/commentisfree/2019/dec/29/decade-technology-privacy-tech-backlash

Schaffer, J. (2016a). DigitalEd: How to teach media entrepreneurship. *MediaShift*. Retrieved from http://mediashift.org/2015/06/digitaled-how-to-teach-media-entrepreneurship/

Schaffer, J. (2016b). Teaching media entrepreneurship: What does that mean? *MediaShift*. Retrieved from http://mediashift.org/2016/06/teaching-media-entrepreneurship-mean/

Schiffrin, A. (2021, January 12). New report explores COVID-era funding efforts around the world. International Journalists' Network. Retrieved from https://ijnet.org/en/story/new-report-explores-covid-era-funding-efforts-around-world

Schumpeter (2020, October 17). Should big tech save newspapers? *The Economist* online. Retrieved from https://www.economist.com/business/2020/10/17/should-big-tech-save-newspapers.

Shirky, C. (2009, May). Newspapers and thinking the unthinkable. *Risk Management* 56 (3), 24–29.

Soto Reyes, M. (2020, December 3). Google, Facebook, and Amazon will account for nearly two-thirds of total U.S. digital ad spending this year. *Business Insider*. Retrieved from https://www.businessinsider.com/google-facebook-amazon-were-biggest-ad-revenue-winners-this-year-2020-12

Stearns, J. (2015). Why journalism needs to build with the community, not for it. *MediaShift*. Retrieved from http://mediashift.org/2015/01/why-journalism-needs-to-build-with-the-community-not-for-it/.

Thompson, D. (2013, February 7). Netflix, 'House of Cards,' and the Golden Age of Television. *The Atlantic* online. Retrieved from https://www.theatlantic.com/business/archive/2013/02/netflix-house-of-cards-and-the-golden-age-of-television/272869/

Appendix

STUDENT PROJECTS IN THEORY-BASED RESEARCH

As described in Chapter 1 and Chapter 7, research grounded in theory has an important role in advancing human knowledge and understanding of the world around us. This type of research is common in academia, where professors are required to complete projects that keep them up-to-date on developments in their discipline so that they can teach more effectively about cutting-edge topics. Graduate students, especially from large institutions with reputations for conducting research, also complete these types of projects as part of their education to become professors themselves someday. The goal for these researchers is to have their work published in academic journals and presented at academic conferences, where their ideas can be examined by colleagues from other universities. The best of these projects create new knowledge that has not been demonstrated before, which advances the state of knowledge in the discipline.

It is helpful for all undergraduate students, not just those who plan to attend graduate school, to acquire some experience doing research on their own. The most basic definition of research is finding the information needed to answer a question, and such questions arise in nearly every aspect of professional and personal life. This makes the skills acquired during a research study transferable to many other settings. Some students who go to work for advertising or PR agencies may do research for their clients. Other communication graduates are employed by firms that use Google analytics and other similar tools. Of course, journalists complete research all the time on the stories they write for broadcast and the web. It's important to mention that research can be helpful in one's personal life as well. Networking with professionals, looking at new places to live, finding medical providers, or buying a new vehicle or a house, all require research to execute properly.

Many undergraduate courses in mass communication do have a requirement that students complete a research project. Instructors frequently limit the assignment to the design of a research proposal, which includes an introduction, review of the literature, and plans for conducting the research (description of the methods). Such projects stop short of actual data collection and analysis that more advanced projects include. However, since some undergraduate projects include original components based on data collection done with tools such as surveys, focus groups, or content analyses, this appendix will describe all of the stages of a project.

CHOOSING A TOPIC

It's helpful when choosing a research project to pick an area of personal interest or passion; with so many mass media choices, it's easy to identify a general focus so that interest or passion can narrow things down. One way is to begin broadly with a particular medium and its sub-areas:

- Media management: corporate communication, marketing, data analysis.
- Broadcasting/video: television, cable, YouTube, podcasts, radio, programming.
- Advertising: traditional print and broadcast messages, social media and online ads, stealth/viral marketing.
- Public relations: agency, non-profit, corporate, government.
- Social media/online: particular platforms (e.g., Twitter, Instagram, TikTok), audio or video streaming services.
- Film: drama, comedy, children, art, documentaries.
- Print/online: newspapers, magazines, newsletters, online publications.

From this list, students can begin to narrow the focus. For example, an interest in television can be further narrowed to a focus on news, sports, advertising, children's programming, reality television, drama, comedy, interview shows, late-night personalities, soap operas – the list is seemingly endless. Within the narrowed category, it is wise to refine the focus further. An interest in sports broadcasting might be narrowed to include news and analysis shows, sports talk radio (national and local), use of social media, sports sponsorship and advertisement, live play-by-play, news magazine shows; this list is also seemingly endless. Sometimes just exposure to the medium will spark an idea – offering a good excuse for watching *Sports Center* or streaming Disney Plus for "my homework."

An alternative strategy for choosing a topic is to pick something very focused that is the subject of great passion or interest: A favorite social media platform, the biggest cable television show, the latest political scandal, to name just a few. From this focused area, reading extensively on the topic will help determine what types of research questions need to be answered – what is deserving of study and explanation? This will be the basis for the research, and the theory that will explain the findings.

Finally, most research articles published in scholarly journals conclude by pointing to a direction for future research, so current articles may be a rich source of topic ideas.

THE RESEARCH QUESTION

The biggest mistake undergraduate students make in trying to complete a research project is defining the topic too broadly, such as "What are student patterns of social media use?" At first, this may seem like an interesting topic, but within the concept of "social media use" many things could be subjects for a research study: Content contribution to TikTok, use of LinkedIn for job searches, targeted ads on Facebook, following celebrities on Instagram, just to name a few. Interest in this topic requires a much narrower focus in order to have a manageable topic that can be completed during a single course, such as, "What social media platforms do college students use to complete group projects?" This is still a little broad since a range of assignments and social media tools might be involved, but it makes a good starting point for a semester-long project. Such a research question will eventually become the hypothesis for the study, but most likely not until the review of the literature is completed.

BACKGROUND RESEARCH

Google Scholar (scholar.google.com), which indexes academic writing, has the motto "stand on the shoulders of giants." What this means is that a researcher always works in the context of other studies in the field. Even the most ground-breaking research is based on the work of others; Jonas Salk developed the polio vaccine using a new process for culturing tissue developed by a Harvard researcher, and those who developed the *oral* polio vaccine built on Salk's work. More recently, the first Covid-19 vaccines used an innovative approach involving cell genetics, but the basic research behind that technique had been done decades earlier (Komaroff, 2020). Similarly in communications, the current view of a theory such as agenda-setting came from multiple studies that can be traced back to McCombs and Shaw's seminal work nearly 50 years ago.

In any field, before beginning any research project, it is important to ascertain what has been done before, what has been found, what works, what doesn't work. This enables the person designing the study to benefit from the errors and successes of those who have researched the topic before. Recall that this is how theory is developed, when research studies build upon one another. Thus, the first step after a topic has been selected is to study the work that has been done before. In the actual research paper, this section is called the "Review of the Literature" and it will be described in more detail later. However, in the initial stage of the project, it is important to acquire a basic understanding of the research designs and findings of the past. Most research studies also end with suggestions for future research, and looking at such suggestions in published articles might provide guidance for selecting or focusing a topic. At this early stage, the researcher also can also take note of what theories might be connected to the chosen topic. Since the theory is the explanation for the findings in the research, this is a valuable tool to guide the researcher.

What is a good starting point for the background research? Students may be tempted to go online and type their topic into Google to see what pops up. While Internet searches have their value, background for the research project should be based on information found in scholarly or refereed journals. These journals contain research done by scholars in a particular field, such as mass media.

The unique feature of a refereed journal is that the articles submitted undergo a peer review process. This means that two or three reviewers, who are also experts in the field, review and comment upon the article, and recommend to the journal editor whether it should be published. These reviews, which are done anonymously, also often include ideas about revising or improving the article that the editor passes along to the author. This vetting process ensures that the journals will publish research that is credible, heuristic (i.e., it will help to generate more research), and valuable for other scholars in the field. Students should always start with refereed journals.

Some research that has been published in these journals will appear in a Google Scholar search. Because of copyright restrictions, many studies cannot be indexed by Google and those that do show up in the search may provide only a title or abstract unless the searcher is willing to pay the publisher for access. A more reliable way to access journals is through databases such as Proquest Central, Academic Search Complete, and Communication Source (specific to communication and media research). Most colleges subscribe to at least a few of these databases, and college reference librarians are experts in helping students search on their topics in these databases. Students also should not overlook open access journals. These include studies that are freely available online. Many follow the same strict peer-review standards of more traditional journals. The timeline for publication is also shorter for open access journals, which means a student may be more likely to find information about a current issue they wish to study. Again the reference librarian at a student's institution will be able to help identify the more relevant sources for a research literature review.

The easiest way to identify a refereed journal is by the presence of a significant number of in-text citations or footnotes in the article. At the end of the article, there usually will be a reference list or a set of numbered end-notes, depending on the journal editor's preference. Not only is this list a good way to tell if an article is peer-reviewed, it's often a good idea to look over titles of the articles in this reference list that an article's author has reviewed for background, and search out the ones that seem relevant and valuable to the student's own project. An instructor or reference librarian can help if the student still cannot tell whether the source of the article is refereed or not.

However, not every topic a student wishes to study will be available in a refereed journal. This is especially true if a very timely topic is chosen, such as the latest video streaming craze, the newest social media app, or the last political campaign. Refereed journals generally work on a schedule that keeps them months, in some cases years, behind public events.

When refereed journals cannot be found, students may use trade publications, such as *Columbia Journalism Review, Editor & Publisher, PR Week, Broadcasting and Cable,* and *Advertising Age.* Media management or other data-driven projects might include media analytics websites such as Hub Spot (www.hubspot.com), Sprout Social (www.sproutsocial.com) Buzz Sumo (www.buzzsumo.com), or Pew Research Center (www.pewresearch.org), to name just a few. These sources are generally more timely in their coverage of events in comparison to refereed journals, and they will provide a starting point for background information, but lack the peer review that is so valuable in the scholarly field.

At the same time, if the topic is so new that it is unavailable even in the trade publications, students may need to use more general news sources such as *The New York Times,* the *Washington Post, Wired, Forbes,* or online sources such as Fast Company, The Huffington Post, or Nieman Reports. Note that trade and general publications will rarely include a theory related to explaining the topic. They also will lack any in-text citations or reference list. Trade and general publications may be included in a review of the literature, but they should not be the *only* sources included in it. This is discussed in more detail later.

Reading about the topic should provide information about what has already been done in the field that the student wishes to investigate. These articles may also suggest avenues for further research, which in turn provide support for the topic the student wishes to study. This information may be valuable in further refining the research question, and for turning it into a hypothesis in which students predict the outcome of their study.

Many professors require that students do an annotated bibliography of their research sources early in the process of working on a project. An annotated bibliography includes a full citation as well as a brief summary and explanation of how the source fits into and supports the overall research project. Detailed guidelines and samples can be found at Purdue's Online Writing Lab at https://owl.english.purdue.edu/owl/resource/614/01/. Purdue's OWL is also a great reference for helping students to format their citations in different formats (e.g., APA, MLA) as well as showing how to cite media examples such as television shows and podcasts that might be included in a student research study.

CHOOSING A THEORY

The theory as an explanation may be chosen at any point in the research process. Often a study is actually built around a theory–for example, a student interested in the use of Instagram by college students may go into the study knowing that uses and gratifications will be the theory applied to this topic. Other times the theory is revealed through the background research on the topic. If many studies of press coverage of an event use the theory of agenda setting, then this could be an appropriate choice for the student's study as well. Some topics will suggest application to more than one theory, which is frequently appropriate for complex topics. The theories discussed throughout this book, especially in Chapters 3 through 6, offer a wide variety of ideas for students to consider in selecting a theoretical basis for their work.

SELECTING A METHOD

Similarly, the research methods discussed in Chapters 7 through 9 provide a range of options for students to use in conducting the research. Which method a student should select depends on other choices in the research design process, beginning with the research question itself. The main purpose of research design is to specify what information needs to be collected and how it must be evaluated to effectively answer the research question. The choice of methodology is closely related to this idea; the appropriate method is one that will generate the data that answer the research question most completely. It's worth recalling that some theories and methodologies align with each other. For example, qualitative methods are often most useful in exploring research questions based in cultural studies or media ecology theories (Chapter 5), while quantitative approaches and hypothesis testing are commonly used in conjunction with media effects theories (Chapters 3 and 4).

WRITING THE RESEARCH REPORT

General Considerations

The research paper in the mass communication theory course can be a new writing experience for many students. Not only is there the need for an original component and the need to tie in a theory as explanation, but the outline and writing style are tightly prescribed. Social science research follows a specific format, which includes:

Writing in the Third Person

Occasionally this rule will be broken in scholarly journals and refereed conference papers, but by and large a research paper is written in the third person. Rather than saying, "My research is about…," it would be phrased, "This research examines…" If the writer needs to refer to himself in the paper, he is "the researcher" or "the author." (Sharp-eyed readers will notice that construction used throughout this book.)

Attention to References and Citations

Some students may believe that they only need to cite direct quotes, but this is not the case. Any information that is not the writer's own idea must be cited. General information that is widely known (e.g., "Texting is popular among college students") does not need to be cited. However, specific facts and information (e.g., "Students don't remember as much course content if they text during a class lecture") must have a citation. In addition, the general rule of thumb is that the citations must be provided in such a way that the reader can easily locate any of the sources.

Citations in the research paper should include in-text citations as well as a reference list or bibliography at the end. There are several different styles for annotating a paper. Three of the most popular are style guides developed by the American Psychological Association (APA), Modern Language Association (MLA), and University of Chicago (Chicago style). Each style guide has its own rules for how to format in-text citations and also for the type of information and how it is presented (order, capitalization, punctuation, dates, etc.) in footnotes, end-notes or a reference list. Some disciplines actually specify a certain style; for example, psychology uses APA exclusively. Journals that publish research about mass media often use APA, but some publications use MLA or Chicago. Some professors specify a certain format for their students and others let them use the style with which they are most familiar. The key is that the writer must use one style throughout the paper, rather than elements of different styles within the same paper. Most college libraries have helpful guidelines on their websites for citing sources. . A thorough description of APA and MLA can be found at Purdue University's On-line Writing Lab or OWL at www.owl.english.purdue.edu. (The references in this book are formatted according to APA, and the reader is invited to look at them, especially at the ends of each chapter, as an example of the type of information needed in an effective reference as well as an example of APA style.)

Avoiding Plagiarism

The use of online resources to complete assignments has increased the incidence of plagiarism. The authors' experience has shown that some plagiarism is the result of misunderstanding by the student as to what constitutes academic dishonesty, which is why it is important for students to understand what constitutes plagiarism in general as well as their institution's policies more specifically.

However, while plagiarism has increased, so has the ability of professors to detect and identify the sources of the plagiarized work. Search engines such as Google as well as software such as Turnitin.com have enabled professors to better ensure that the work students submit will be 100 percent their own. Anything else is plagiarism, which is a serious offense both academically and professionally. Communications professionals who plagiarize the work of others are fired from their jobs; students can expect severe repercussions as well. The authors and many of their colleagues assign a grade of zero on any assignment that the instructor discovers has been plagiarized, with no chance of extra credit or re-doing the assignment. At many institutions, plagiarism also is punishable by further sanctions, up to and including expulsion from school. The lesson is simple: Don't plagiarize and, if in doubt, use a citation in the paper. As a final note, colleges that use Turnitin.com have a feature whereby a student may check his paper before submitting it to the instructor for evidence of plagiarism.

The Writing Process

This section details each part of the research report as it should be written.

Introduction

The introduction seeks to answer the following questions:

- Why is this project being done?
- What interesting/important information will come from it?
- What is the "road map" for the project – the scope of it and means of investigation?

The introduction should then go on to set the stage and clearly lay out the purpose and scope of the project, so the reader knows what to expect. Near the end of the introduction, the hypothesis (testable proposition) or research question (if that is the paper's purpose) should be clearly stated. In terms of length, the introduction will probably be two or three standard, double-spaced pages or 500–700 words.

Theoretical Basis

The theory section seeks to provide:

- The theory (or theories) that underlies the research.
- A brief description of specifics and background of theory, from a properly cited source.
- A description of why this particular theory is appropriate and how the project will use theory to predict/explain real-world phenomena as related to each other in the hypothesis.

The theory may be mentioned in the introduction, but providing its own section will ensure that it is addressed in sufficient detail, usually about one or two standard pages, again, 500–700 words.

Literature Review

The review of the literature is that point in the paper where the writer provides the background research on the topic. In this section, the writer should:

- Describe what other researchers have done on related topics.
- Use prior research to justify why *this* project is being done: In what ways is it similar to but also distinctly unique from what's been done before?

As noted previously, the review of the literature should be drawn mostly from scholarly sources from refereed publications. Trade journals or general literature may also be included but should not be the primary information in the review. Sub-standard material, including most web-based information such as Wikipedia, should *not* be used in the research paper. (Again, students who are having trouble finding material for the research review should put themselves into the hands of a reference librarian.)

In reviewing what others have done before, students do not have to give detailed descriptions of each study. Generally, an overview of the study's purpose, subjects, and findings will suffice. Each study's review can generally be completed in a single paragraph with just three or four sentences. A typical research project published in a scholarly journal will have a deep, thorough review of the literature, usually with several dozen citations drawn from 15, 20 or more previously published research articles. For undergraduate research the bar isn't quite as high, but even for undergrads a good review of the literature will contain a minimum of five to ten studies from refereed publications. For some topics or some theories that have been extensively researched it might be necessary to include even more to provide the proper context for the current study. This material from scholarly publications may be supplemented by trade or general publications where appropriate.

What should students do if there are no research studies in their particular topic area? This is frequently a problem when a student is doing a very current topic, such as a current presidential election or a new social media app. In the event that, after searching databases and enlisting the help of a reference librarian, no research in refereed journals can be found, here are two suggestions:

1. Find research in an allied topic area. For example, when one of the authors was researching the use of role models in teaching public speaking, she found that no research had been done specifically in that field. However, there was research that examined using role models in teaching interviewing. Those studies formed the basis for her review of the literature (and, by the way, they also provided the theoretical foundation, which was Bandura's social learning theory). So, research on a new streaming program might be based on research about a broadcast or cable television show in the same genre (e.g., other sitcoms, crime dramas, reality shows, or news magazines).
2. Locate research studies that use the same theory. A review of the critical research using the theory that will be related to the project can often yield relevant research for a project. Research on agenda setting or the diffusion of innovation will reveal a wide range of studies that may apply to a student's research project.

If even one or two articles that are relevant to the student's research study can be found, the reference lists of those articles may be used to expand the literature review. In other words, by examining some of the same articles that those authors used in compiling their literature reviews, the student researcher can get a more complete perspective on the topic being studied. Any reference list should provide enough information about each source – author's name, date and journal of publication – for it to be found in a database search. Note that this should not turn into plagiarism of the other article or a point-by-point repetition of its literature review. Rather, it should be seen as a way for the researcher to expand the pool of original sources that can be reviewed for information relevant to the new study that the researcher is completing. Looking at sources used by other scholars working on similar topics will provide extra insight into whatever the researcher is investigating. Finally, students can use trade journals and general sources, as well as expert opinions on the topic, to bolster the literature review. But refereed journal studies must be at the heart of the review to ensure the study's credibility.

Methodology

The methodology section (sometimes called Collection of Data) should include:

- The means used to collect/observe data.
- The reason that this method was chosen, and what makes it the most appropriate method.
- A re-statement of the hypothesis, elaborating on how it relates to this method.
- An explanation of the variables studied, and why those were chosen.
- A description of how the variables were operationalized (i.e., turned into measurement).
- A description of the data collection (e.g., number of surveys, dates collected, who they were collected from, how the sample was drawn, etc.) or the method used for a qualitative study.
- If a survey or rating form was used to gather the information, it should be presented in an Appendix at the end of the paper.

Findings

This section, sometimes called Analysis of the Data, should include a description, in the text of the paper, of what was found and (when appropriate) presentation of charts, tables and/or graphs with findings from the study

In this section, the author does not draw any conclusions or make any comments; the findings are presented in an objective and unbiased way. Students may find it particularly challenging to write up the results of a qualitative study, one that used focus groups, interviews, or case study observations. Holliday (2002) suggests that the data collected for a qualitative study should be organized using themes that become the headings when the research paper is written. This may or may not follow the chronology of the study, but the themes become the basis for the arguments/discussion as described in the next section.

Discussion

The discussion is the section where the researcher gets the opportunity to draw the entire project together. It generally includes a summary overview of the findings of the study. This is followed by an analysis or interpretation of the findings: Was the hypothesis supported? If so, what does that mean? If the hypothesis was not supported, what does *that* mean? Were any extraneous variables noted that might have had an impact on the study? For example, if the study analyzed banner ads on social media during a presidential election year, the flood of political advertising that would not be found at other times would have an impact on a content analysis of advertising. Some students have found their research impacted when there is a catastrophic news event, such as a mass shooting or terrorism attack, which might pre-empt regular broadcast programming and clog news sites and social media feeds. Similarly, doing research during a holiday season might be affected by programming and/or advertising in a way that might not be found during other times of the year, and even something like a Twitter gaffe by a prominent athlete can dictate discussion and programming for days on both traditional and social media and skew the results of a content analysis.

The discussion section is also the key area where the researcher uses the theory as an explanation for the findings. Did the study generate evidence that seems to support the theory? If so, what does that mean? If it didn't support the theory, how might that be explained? Is the theory called into question?

Finally, in the discussion the researcher can make some commentary about the issues examined in the research and the implications of the findings, where appropriate.

Conclusion

The conclusion in the research paper is the final statement about the subject, the research, and sometimes the theory. It is generally no more than two or three paragraphs, and usually suggests direction for future research in this area. In some research articles, the conclusion is part of the Discussion section.

References

The final section in the research paper is the references. The goal of the reference list is to provide information that would allow readers to find the cited article if they desired. A complete citation includes:

- Author's name.
- Date of publication.
- Name of the book, book chapter, or article title and name of the publication for articles from a scholarly journal, trade magazine or newspaper. Articles from journals and magazines usually include page numbers as well. Recall that the goal is to be sure that any reader of the paper would be easily able to locate these sources. (Both authors have received student papers with "espn.com" in the reference list. Given the longevity of ESPN as well as the number of sports they cover, it would be almost impossible to find a single story with just a website listed.)

References should follow the particular style, such as APA or MLA, that was used in the text of the paper. (As noted earlier, the references in this book are formatted according to APA and offer an example of the type of information needed in an effective reference as well as an example of APA style.) Many college websites have easy access to online sources to help with formatting, such as NoodleBib, which formats citations automatically. Noodle Tools can also help with some other research functions.

Final Review

When the research paper is completed, it should be proofread and edited carefully, first by the author, then by a friend (or two). Students in the same class can help by proofing each other's work. After working on a paper for an extended period of time, the writer is often unable to catch writing or comprehension errors. Even professors often ask colleagues to proof and edit papers before they submit them to journals or professional conferences (or even proposals sent internally to the dean or provost).

Students who struggle with writing should allow time for an appointment at the college writing center to work with a tutor. Errors in the paper such as misspellings, poor grammar, and incorrect punctuation distract from the message. It is important to make sure the paper has none of these to eliminate such distractions and allow the reader – the professor – to focus on the content that the writer is presenting.

PRESENTING THE RESEARCH PROJECT

Students in mass communication programs generally are used to presenting their ideas in front of their classes. Many programs require classes that include public speaking skills, and even those that don't have such requirements have classes such as advertising, social media management, broadcasting, and public relations where in-class presentations are common. So, it should come as no surprise that presentations are often part of a theory-based course with a research project. Since presentations are generally covered early in the student's academic program, the notes below are meant as a reminder of some of the more salient points for a professional presentation, whether to a class of peers, a panel of professors, or a group of media professionals.

Presentation Tips

The project presentation should summarize the original research project. Regardless of how much time is allotted, it is impossible to discuss everything that is included in the written paper. At the same time, focusing on the most important components should make for a credible presentation. This should include:

- Purpose of the project.
- Short statement of what has been done before.
- Procedures.
- Findings.
- Conclusions – be sure to mention which theory was used.

Whether it's the research project or another topic that is presented, the following guidelines can help to make any presentation more professional:

Organization

A good presentation has an introduction, body, and conclusion.

A good presentation is well-organized and provides transitions linking the ideas.

Delivery

Good delivery is extemporaneous, practiced, and uses notes.

Good delivery means the presenter does not read from notes or slides.

Good delivery means the presenter makes good eye contact with the audience.

Visual Aids

Visuals that accompany a presentation – such as PowerPoint, Google slides, Keynote, among others – should include key words rather than full sentences, a professional design, and appropriate images and graphics to keep the audience's attention.

Speakers should practice beforehand with their visuals so they know how/when to show them and how all the technology works in the presentation room.

Speakers should not turn their backs on the audience and read from their visuals, but should maintain maximum eye and voice contact.

If video clips are shown, they should not be more than two to three minutes total of the presentation time.

Other Considerations

Time. Students should know the time requirements and practice to stay within the limits. Depending on the number of presenters and time available, most undergraduate research presentations in a class will run between five and ten minutes, with a few extra minutes for questions and discussion, but senior project presentations can often run 30 minutes or more. Being prepared for the allotted time will ensure the professionalism of your presentation.

Q&A. Students should be prepared for a question-and-answer session by anticipating questions, listening carefully to the question, and answering in a concise and confident manner. Always answer to the entire audience to keep them involved, rather than only making eye contact with the questioner.

REFERENCES

Holliday, A. (2002). *Doing and writing qualitative research*. London: Sage Publications.

Komaroff, A. (2020, December 20). Why are mRNA vaccines so exciting? *Harvard Health Letter*. Retrieved from https://www.health.harvard.edu/blog/why-are-mrna-vaccines-so-exciting-2020121021599.

Index

Note: Page numbers in *italics* denote figures.